DATE DUE

FE 13 96			

DEMCO 38-296

Pinocchio's Progeny

PAJ Books

Bonnie Marranca and Gautam Dasgupta
Series Editors

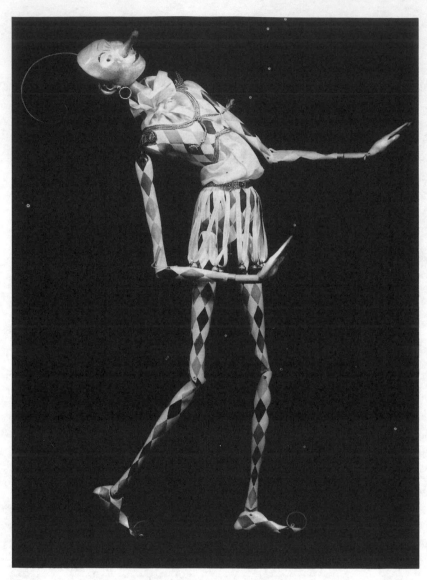

Richard Teschner, Marionette.
(Courtesy Bildarchiv der Österreichischen Nationalbibliothek, Vienna)

Pinocchio's Progeny

Puppets, Marionettes, Automatons, and Robots in Modernist and Avant-Garde Drama

Harold B. Segel

The Johns Hopkins University Press
Baltimore and London

© 1995 The Johns Hopkins University Press
All rights reserved. Published 1995
Printed in the United States of America on acid-free paper
04 03 02 01 00 99 98 97 96 95   5 4 3 2 1

The Johns Hopkins University Press
2715 North Charles Street
Baltimore, Maryland 21218-4319
The Johns Hopkins Press Ltd., London

ISBN 0-8018-5031-2
ISBN 0-8018-5262-5 (pbk.)
LC 95-075204

Design and composition by Wilsted & Taylor

For my son Abbott,
who knows how to pull all the right strings . . .

Contents

Acknowledgments

The author wishes to express his gratitude to the following publishers for permission to quote from the sources below.

University of California Press: Excerpts from Tadeusz Kantor, "The Theater of Death," in Tadeusz Kantor, *A Journey through Other Spaces: Essays and Manifestos, 1944–1990*, trans. and ed. Michal Kobialka. Copyright 1993 by the Regents of the University of California.

Catbird Press: Excerpts from Karel Čapek, *R.U.R.*, trans. Claudia Novack-Jones, in *Toward the Radical Center: A Karel Čapek Reader*, ed. Peter Kussi. Copyright 1990 by Catbird Press.

Marion Boyars: Excerpts from Tadeusz Kantor, *Wielopole/Wielopole: An Exercise in Theatre*, trans. Mariusz Tchorek and G. M. Hyde. Copyright 1990 by Marion Boyars Publishers.

Methuen: Excerpts from *Craig on Theatre*, ed. Michael J. Walton. Copyright 1983 by Methuen. My thanks also to Reed Consumer Books, London.

Unless otherwise indicated in the notes, all translations in the book are by the author. For reasons of space, quotations from the original language are given only to illustrate style or language in certain instances.

Special thanks are due to Bonnie Marranca and Gautam Dasgupta for their enthusiasm for the project from the beginning and their warm encouragement throughout, and to my manuscript editor, Irma Garlick, for her very careful work on the text.

PART ONE

From Cervantes to Symbolism

ONE

Puppets and Their Kin in Fiction and Drama

Shaw loved having the first word. Above all in the form of prefaces to his plays. And so be it here. In 1949 he wrote a puppet play to which he gave the title *Shakes versus Shaw* and which he prophesied would, in all probability, be his last work for the stage. He was prompted to write it by the figures of Shakespeare and himself which were sent him by a major English puppeteer. Maybe it was a knee jerk of vanity. In any case, Shaw's preface to this easily overlooked little play makes an apt preface to my study. In it, Shaw acknowledges the eternal magic and mystery of the puppet and marionette as well as his own debt to them:

> This in all actuarial probability is my last play and the climax of my eminence, such as it is. I thought my career as a playwright was finished when Waldo Lanchester of the Malvere Marionette Theatre, our chief living puppet master, sent me figures of two puppets, Shakespeare and myself, with a request that I should supply one of my famous dramas for them, not to last longer than ten minutes or thereabouts. I accomplished this feat, and was gratified by Mr. Lanchester's immediate approval.
>
> I have learnt part of my craft as conductor of rehearsals (producer, they call it) from puppets. Their unvarying intensity of facial expression, impossible for living actors, keeps the imagination of the spectators continuously stimulated. When one of them is speaking or tumbling and the rest left

3

aside, these, though in full view, are invisible, as they should be. Living actors have to learn that they too must be invisible while the protagonists are conversing, and therefore must not move a muscle nor change their expression, instead of, as beginners mostly do, playing to them and robbing them of the audience's individual attention.

Puppets have also a fascination of their own, because there is nothing wonderful in a living actor moving and speaking, but that wooden headed dolls should do so is a marvel that never palls.

And they can survive treatment that would kill live actors. When I first saw them in my boyhood nothing delighted me more than when all the puppets went up in a balloon and presently dropped from the skies with an appalling crash on the floor.

Nowadays the development of stagecraft into filmcraft may destroy the idiosyncratic puppet charm. Televised puppets could enjoy the scenic backgrounds of the cinema. Sound recording could enable the puppet master to give all his attention to the strings he is manipulating, the dialogue being spoken by a company of first-rate speakers as in the theatre. The old puppet master spoke all the parts himself in accents which he differentiated by Punch-and-Judy squeaks and the like. I can imagine the puppets simulating living performers so perfectly that the spectators will be completely illuded. The result would be the death of puppetry; for it would lose its charm with its magic. So let reformers beware.[1]

The fascination with puppets, to which even George Bernard Shaw was not immune, reaches so far back into human history that it must be regarded as a response to a fundamental need or needs. It is, clearly, a projection of the obsession of human beings with their own image, with their own likeness, the obsession that underlies artistic portraiture, the building of statues, and the extraordinary and enduring popularity of photography. More profoundly, it reveals a yearning to play god, to master life. By constructing replicas of human beings whose movements they can then exert complete power over, artists play at being gods instead of being merely playthings of the gods. Inevitably, the impulse to exert domination over the human experience leads to research into the prolongation of life through advances in medicine and technology—the treatment and eventual cure of infectious diseases and the transplantation of organs, human, animal, or mechanical. And finally, the obsession with becoming godlike expresses itself in the most powerful of all delusions, the belief that one can create real life outside the normal human reproductive cycle.

This book limits its inquiry to a single facet of the fascination with the puppet and such related forms as the marionette, automaton, robot, and projected silhouette. It is not a study of the art of puppetry as such or of the aesthetics and metaphysics of puppetry[2] but a consideration of the impact of the puppet figure—in the broadest sense of the term—on the art primarily of the theater. Its focus is dramatic literature, and its time frame is the late nineteenth and early twentieth centuries, when modernism and the avant-garde discovered a broad range of new relevance in the world of invented man.

By way of an introduction to the modernist and avant-garde interpretations of the puppet figure, I first want to consider the appearance of puppets, marionettes, and the like in earlier literature. My purpose is not to be exhaustive but rather to demonstrate by means of well-chosen examples both the enduring appeal of such figures to the creative artist and the patterns of their assimilation into fiction, poetry, and drama before the advent of the modernist movement.

CERVANTES AND BEN JONSON

Despite the antiquity of puppetry and the appearance of puppet imagery in a number of texts from Plato's *Laws* through the Middle Ages and the Renaissance, the arrival of the puppet and marionette on the literary stage came relatively late. Certainly one of the first memorable appearances occurs in an established classic of world literature, *Don Quixote* (1605, 1615) by Miguel de Cervantes. Two episodes in book 2 (25 and 26) are devoted to Quixote's encounter with a puppet theater. The episodes are entitled, respectively, "Of the adventure of the braying and the entertaining meeting with the puppet-showman, with the memorable prediction of the prophetic ape" and "In which is continued the diverting adventure of the puppet-showman, with other truly entertaining incidents."[3]

In the first episode, Master Pedro, the puppeteer, comes looking for a room at an inn where Don Quixote happens to be staying. He is renowned throughout Spain. Don Pedro entertains people with the tricks of his monkey as well as with his puppets. Afer convincing themselves of the monkey's astonishing intelligence, Quixote and Sancho Panza proceed to watch Don Pedro set up his puppet booth. While the puppeteer works the puppets inside the booth, a boy servant of his stands outside to act as interpreter and explain the mysteries of the show. There then follows, in episode 26, the account of the puppet show. "This true story," the puppeteer's assistant announces, "tells of the release by Señor Don Gaiferos of his wife, Melisendra, who was a captive in Spain, in the power of the Moors in the city of Sansueña, for so they called the city that is now named Saragossa" (712). The boy then narrates the story being acted out on the small stage by the puppets under the direction of Master Pedro. But the performance is disrupted when the appearance onstage of a large force of Moors proves too much for Don Quixote. Again demonstrating his inability to distinguish illusion from reality, Quixote loses sight of the fact that he is watching a puppet show and flings himself on the puppets, sword in hand. The episode closes with a bewildered Quixote having to make restitution for Master Pedro's losses.

The year in which the second part of *Don Quixote* appeared, 1615, also saw the publication of a volume of Cervantes's plays, *Ocho comedias y ocho entremeses* (*Eight Dramas and Eight One-Act Plays*). The short, one-act *entremeses*—light, deft theatrical sketches—are the gems of the collection and Cervantes's primary contribution to Spanish drama. Perhaps the best among them is the *Retablo de las maravillas* (*Puppet Show of Marvels*). Although the date of its composition cannot be established with any certainty, the most informed opinion dates it to 1604, which is about the time Cervantes had already begun working on the first part of *Don Quixote*.

The *Retablo* addresses a social issue—prejudice against converted Jews and illegitimate children—but in a shrewdly comic way. A pair of traveling con men, Chanfalla and Chirinos, come to a town and offer the governor and the rest of the town's elite the opportunity to see their "retablo de las maravillas." When the governor asks what it means, Chanfalla tells him that it is so called because of the marvelous things shown and taught in it. He also mentions that it was "created and composed by the wise man Tontonelo [a 'telling name'; *tonto* in Spanish means a 'fool'] beneath such parallels, bearings, heavenly bodies and stars, with such points, characters, and observations, that no one can see the things shown in it who may be a converted Jew or who may not have been procreated by parents of legitimate matrimony."[4] After demanding, and receiving, money in advance for their performance, Chanfalla and Chirinos present their *retablo* based mostly on stories from the Bible. Of course, the point of Cervantes's *entremes* is that no puppet show is actually presented. Chanfalla and Chirinos describe scenes that do not take place, and hardly anyone in the audience dares admit not seeing anything lest he or she be taken for a converted Jew or a bastard, both objects of scorn and derision in Spanish society at the time.

Around the time Cervantes was completing the second part of *Don Quixote*, the English dramatist Ben Jonson wrote one of his best comedies, *Bartholomew Fair* (1614), in which a puppet performance assumes a much more important role in the design of the play than the one wrecked by Don Quixote in Cervantes's novel. The play deals with the annual fair held in Smithfield, a suburb of London, on Saint Bartholomew's Day (24 August). The fair, noted for its boisterousness, attracted a motley group of people from Puritans to pickpockets and, through the range of human behavior depicted, serves as a microcosm of the world. More complex than it appears on the surface, the comedy exposes the hypocrisy of the Puritan philosophy as well as other human follies and vanities. The resolution is achieved in a concluding puppet show arranged by a hobby-horse seller named Lantern Leatherhead. This entertainment, which takes up virtually the entire fifth act, is written by the law clerk John Littlewit. Scarcely more than a bawdy, vulgarized version of the tales of Hero and Leander and Damon and Pythias, it has been characterized, justifiably, as a "microcosm of a microcosm."[5] If the fair itself is a microcosmic representation of the world, then the puppet show performed in act 5 is the fair in miniature. When Leatherhead tells Bartholomew Cokes, the easily duped esquire of Harrow, that he has "entreated Master Littlewit to take a little pains to reduce it [the puppet play's subject] to a more familiar strain for our people,"[6] he is alluding to the low standards of public taste, which Jonson also addresses in the comedy. The puppet show, in fact a play-within-a-play, outwardly seems aimed above all at the Puritan intolerance toward the stage, about which Jonson obviously had very strong feelings. This is done primarily through the figure of the Puritan rabbi Zeal-of-the-land Busy. While the puppet show is in progress, Busy enters to denounce it as the "profanations" of Dagon, the latter a reference to the Philistine god of whom idols were made. As Busy continues to rail against the show, Leatherhead declares that one of his puppets, Dionysius, will undertake the refutation of the Puritan's attack. When another character in the play, Grace Wellborn, observes, "I know no fitter match than a puppet to commit with an hypocrite!" the point of Jonson's satire is clearly made. So silly are the Puritan's objections that they are most appropriately responded to by a puppet. Here is some of the dialogue:

Busy. I call him idol again. Yet, I say, his calling, his profession, is profane, it is profane, idol.

Puppet Dionysius. It is not profane!

Leatherhead. It is not profane, he says.

Busy. It is profane.

Puppet Dionysius. It is not profane. . . .

Busy. And I say it is profane, as being the page of pride and the waiting-woman of vanity.

Puppet Dionysius. Yea? What say you to your tire-woman [dressmaker], then?

Leatherhead. Good.

Puppet Dionysius. Or feather-makers i' the Friars, that are o' your faction of faith? Are not they with their perukes and their puffs, their fans and their huffs, as much pages of pride and waiters upon vanity? What say you? What say you? What say you?

Busy. I will not answer for them.

Puppet Dionysius. Because you cannot, because you cannot. Is a bugle-maker a lawful calling? or the confect-maker's? such you have there; or your French fashioner? You'd have all the sin within yourselves, would you not? would you not?

Busy. No, Dagon.

Puppet Dionysius. What then, Dagonet? Is a puppet worse than these?

(180–81)

Jonson comes to the crux of the Puritan distaste for the stage when he has Busy declare, "Yes, and my main argument against you is that you are an abomination; for the male among you putteth on the apparel of the female, and the female of the male." But the puppet Dionysius parries this most effectively, in word and gesture: "It is your old stale argument against the players, but it will not hold against the puppets; for we have neither male nor female amongst us. And that thou may'st see, if thou wilt, like a malicious purblind zeal as thou art! (*The puppet takes up his garment*)." Busy is now vanquished, declares that his cause has abandoned him, and from a protestor becomes a spectator for the rest of the show.

Apart from its function as a microcosm of the fair as a whole, the prominence of the puppet show in *Bartholomew Fair* reflects Jonson's desire to ridicule the hypocrisy of the Puritan objection to the stage. But a broader interpretation of the use of the puppet motif is also suggested by Robert E. Knoll's perceptive observation that "one has throughout the play the sense of puppets manipulated by a master puppeteer; and the very arbitrariness of their movement is part of the fun."[7] Observing human behavior at the Bartholomew Fair, Jonson perceived it as a kind of grand puppet show emblematic of the human world. Beneath the broad array of pretensions on display lay a narrow range of motives governing people's actions. When all is said and done, humans are undone by the vanities in which all folly is rooted, and so they most resemble puppets, seemingly able to move on their own yet controlled by the hands and strings of a superior power. Thus the puppet play in *Bartholomew Fair* may be viewed as a microcosm of more than just the fair. It becomes the principal means through which the emblematic status of the fair itself is achieved.

EIGHTEENTH-CENTURY ENGLAND: JONATHAN SWIFT AND JOSEPH ADDISON

Puppet motifs in eighteenth-century English literature offer nothing on the level of interest of Jonson's *Bartholomew Fair*. Nevertheless, a few poems by such major writers as Jonathan Swift and Joseph Addison shed some light on the English Punch and Judy show and have not gone unnoticed by historians of puppet theater in Europe. Swift's "Mad Mullinix and Timothy" was written and published in 1728. Mullinix (or Molyneux) was a Dublin beggar whose madness seemed to manifest itself primarily in his public proclamation of Tory views; in real life, Timothy was a Whig politician named Richard Tighe, who incurred Swift's anger by reporting to the authorities on a sermon by Thomas Sheridan, a young clergyman and schoolmaster with whom Swift had become close friends after resettling in Dublin. Essentially a satire, "Mad Mullinix and Timothy" is cast in the form of a dialogue between the two principals. Taking Timothy (Tighe) to task for his obsession with Jacobite plots and treason, Mullinix compares him to a troublesome puppet-show Punch:

> Why, Tim, you have a taste I know,
> And often see a puppet-show.
> Observe, the audience is in pain,
> While Punch is hid behind the scene
> But when they hear his rusty voice,
> With what impatience they rejoice!
>   . . .
>
> If Punch, to spur their fancy, shows
> In at the door his monstrous nose,
> Then sudden draws it back again,
> O what a pleasure mixed with pain!

. . .

He gets a thousand thumps and kicks
Yet cannot leave his roguish tricks
In every action thrusts his nose,
The reason why no mortal knows.
In doleful scenes, that break our heart,
Punch comes, like you, and lets a fart.
There's not a puppet made of wood,
But what would hang him if they could.
. . .

Thus Tim, philosophers suppose,
The world consists of puppet-shows
Where petulant, conceited fellows
Perform the part of Pulcinellos.[8]

Joseph Addison's "Puppet Show," like "The Battle of the Pygmies and Cranes" and "The Bowling Green," was written originally in Latin hexameters in the style of the popular eighteenth-century mock-heroic poem. Its Latin title was "Machinae gesticulantes, anglice A Puppet Show." The opening lines set the appropriate mock-heroic tone:

Of trivial things I sing, surprising scenes,
Crowds void of thought, and nations in machines.
A race diminutive; whose frames were built
Free from the sacrilege of ancient guilt;
Who from a better new Prometheus came;
Nor boast the plunder of celestial flame.[9]

After establishing the trivial nature of his subject, Addison proceeds—in the traditional manner of the genre—to elevate it to the level of the heroic by acknowledging the puppets' ability to magically transform their miniature stage:

And now the squeaking tribe proceeding roams
O'er painted mansions and illustrious domes.
Within this humble cell, this narrow wall,
Assemblies, battles, conquests, triumphs, all
That human minds can act, or pride survey,
On their low stage, the little nation play.
(580)

A "survey" of typical English puppet show performances follows, concluded by a look behind the scenes at how puppets are constructed:

Now sing we whence the puppet-actors came,
What hidden power supplies the hollow frame;
What cunning agent o'er the scenes presides,
And all the secret operation guides,
The turner shapes the useless log with care,
And forces it a human form to wear:
With the sharp steel he works the wooden race,
And lends the timber an adopted face.
Tenacious wires the legs and feet unite,
And arms connected keep the shoulders right.
Adapted organs to fit organs join,
And joints with joints, and limbs with limbs combine.
Then adds the active wheels and springs unseen,
By which he artful turns the small machine,
That moves at pleasure by the secret wires
And last his voice the senseless trunk inspires.
    From such a union of inventions came,
And to perfection grew, the puppet-frame;
The workman's mark its origins reveal,
And own the traces of the forming steel.
Hence are its dance, its motions, and its tone,
Its squeaking voice, and accents not its own.

  (582–83)

GERMAN STURM UND DRANG TO ROMANTICISM: GOETHE, KLEIST, AND E. T. A. HOFFMANN

The literary and dramatic fascination with puppets, marionettes, automatons, and other animated objects grew considerably in the late eighteenth and early nineteenth centuries. German literature is especially noteworthy in this respect. The interest of Goethe, for example, in puppet theater went back to his childhood and the marionette theater given him one Christmas by his grandmother.[10] As with other dramatists, the miniature stage served him not only as a source of youthful entertainment but also, through the different performances he arranged for it, as an informal school of theatrics. The most enduring monument of Goethe's fascination with puppets and marionettes—apart from the important role assigned them in *Wilhelm Meisters Lehrjahre* (*Wilhelm Meister's Apprenticeship*, 1769–1829)—is the marionette play he wrote in 1769, when he was twenty years old, under the title *Das Jahrmarkts-Fest zu Plundersweilern*. The work has been translated into English as *Junkdump Fair*.[11]

Set in a typical German small-town fair in the eighteenth century and featuring, among others, a typical *Bänkelsänger*, or street balladeer—an old tradition in which German dramatists in the late nineteenth and early twentieth centuries (e.g. Wedekind and Brecht) took a new interest—the little play faintly recalls Jonson's *Bartholomew Fair*. The fairground environment includes a motley cross section of the local populace, whose moral values are the subject of the irony in which the work abounds. When asked what the comedy is to be, the Mountebank—who peddles his "medicines" during the intermissions—replies that it is a tragedy "with sugary and moral speeches; / No swear-word and no smut it teaches, / Since towns have grown so free of vice / That everyone is overnice." [12] But before the "tragedy" proper begins—a humorous takeoff on the biblical story of Esther (who here lacks any enthusiasm for intervening with Ahasuerus to save Mordechai)—the audience is regaled with the rough humor and slapstick of the traditional puppet theater. Esther's abrupt exit at the height of the action brings the "tragedy" to an end, so the Mountebank can use the remaining time before dark to hawk his wares at half price. To close the frame play at this point, another showman appears to present a second play-within-a-play, a shadow show about Adam and Eve in Paradise. Shadow shows, generally referred to by the French term *ombres chinoises* ("Chinese shadows") since France served as the principal European conduit of the original Oriental form, were performances of the silhouettes of cutouts projected by lantern light onto a rudimentary screen in the form usually of a cloth sheet.

As we shall see later, shadow shows enjoyed a stunning revival, and elevation into a truly sophisticated art form, in the European cabarets of the turn of the century. Goethe had apparently seen a shadow show at the Frankfurt fair which served as the model for his *Jahrmarkts-Fest zu Plundersweilern*. A Frankfurt paper reported the visit of a Frenchman exhibiting the "new" Chinese spectacle in 1774, and it is entirely possible that the same entertainer had already visited the city on previous occasions. He could well have been the same Ambroise who exhibited his Théâtre des Récréations de la Chine in Paris in 1775 and in London the following year. However he encountered "Chinese shadows," Goethe was sufficiently impressed by them to introduce the form into his marionette play of 1769. Moreover, it is the concluding shadow show in *Junkdump Fair* which carries the real moral weight of the play as a whole. Recounting, in his own folkish style, the plight of Adam and Eve once ejected from Paradise, the shadow showman rails against the morals of the world for which the Deluge was God's punishment:

> So the world grows on apace
> With lots of godless men.
> Before it was a pious place;
> They prayed and carolled then.
> No belief in any god, you see:
> It's shameful and a mockery!
> Cavaliers and ladies couple up
> In every dell and meadow cup;
> The grass and moss is laid upon
> By pairs that come to carry on;
> Can God permit such things to be?
>   (272)

How seriously Goethe regarded puppet and marionette theater even during his formidable Weimar period is reflected in his most important literary achievement after *Faust* and to which he devoted much of his life, *Wilhelm Meisters Lehrjahre*. Patently autobiographical in nature, much of the work is devoted to Wilhelm's determination to make a career of the stage (which is why the earlier version of the *Apprenticeship* bore the title *Wilhelm Meisters theatralische Sendung* (*Wilhelm Meister's Theatrical Calling*).[13] In it, Goethe credits his hero's enthusiasm for the stage to his early encounters with puppet theater. Book 1 lovingly relates the young Wilhelm's childish delight in the magic world of puppets and his father's ridicule of them as the source of his son's interest in a profession of which he strongly disapproves. The father holds his mother ultimately reponsible for her son's enthusiasm for acting since it was she who first gave him a puppet theater. "How often have I been reproached," the mother declares, "for giving you that accursed puppet theater for Christmas twelve years ago, and for the taste it gave you for the theater!" (12). Wilhelm replies:

> Don't blame the puppet theater; don't regret your love and care for me. Those were my first happy moments in the new and empty house. I can still see the moment before me, I remember how exceptional it seemed, when after we had received the usual Christmas presents, we were told to sit down in front of a door leading to another room. The door opened, but not just to let us in or out. The entrance was decked out for some unexpected

festivity. There stood a high gate that was closed by a mystic curtain. We saw this from a distance, and then, when we were keen to know what was twinkling and rattling behind the half-transparent curtain, we were told to draw up our chairs and to wait patiently. So we all sat quietly until a whistle blew, and the curtain rolled up and revealed a bright red view into a temple. Samuel, the High Priest, appeared with Jonathan, and their strange exchange of voices seemed to me very solemn. . . .

He then asked for the key to where the puppets were kept, rushed off, found them, and for a moment was transported back to the time when they seemed alive to him, when he thought he could animate them by the liveliness of his voice and the movements of his hands. He took them up to his room and guarded them carefully. (12–14)

By far the most intriguing piece of writing on the puppet and marionette to emerge from the entire Romantic movement was the short, elegant, and thought-provoking essay *Über das Marionettentheater* (*On the Puppet Theater*) by the greatest German dramatist of the period, Heinrich Kleist.[14] The essay first appeared in the *Berliner Abendblätter*, of which Kleist himself was the editor, from 12 to 15 December 1810 (227). Reflecting Kleist's mathematical training as well as philosophical interests, the essay is clearly a product of a cohering Romantic *Weltanschauung*. Kleist takes up the matter of the unique art of the puppet theater as a serious dramatist but in so doing is motivated by concerns characteristic of the Romantic movement. By devoting a serious essay to a popular theatrical form largely regarded in Kleist's time as a diversion for children and an unsophisticated populace, the dramatist sought to explore the possible contribution of "low" or "popular" culture to a reanimation of "high" art.

Modern folkloristics began under the aegis of Romanticism. Anxious to break out of the narrow confines of eighteenth-century classicism, the Romantics frequently turned to the culture of the folk—folk speech, folk painting, folk dance, and folk song—as a source of inspiration. The quest was for authenticity in art, an authenticity that came to be identified with the indigenous national culture. The artist had but to seek out that culture, and the path to it led through the folk. In their desire to create new dramatic forms and cut their ties to the formulaic genres of the classicist age, the Romantics rediscovered the theatrical art of past ages with which they felt natural affinities. This translated into a renewed interest in classical Greek tragedy, in Shakespeare—who was now "reauthenticated" after the distortions of eighteenth-century classicism—and in the dramatic art of Baroque Spain, the plays of Calderón in particular. Inspiration was also sought among the entertainments of the folk, hence the serious interest in puppet theater and in the moribund tradition of the Italian commedia dell'arte.

On a higher level, Kleist's essay on the marionette evidences the Romantic belief in the cognitive and creative superiority of the unconscious over the conscious, of spontaneity and intuition over reason. Because the puppet, or marionette, lacks the ability to think, to reason, it can be made capable of an extraordinary fluidity of motion, of movements beyond the reach of the living actor. Precisely because he can think and reason, because he is always conscious of his actions and gestures, the living actor can never achieve the spontaneity of the marionette; thus the grace of the inanimate figure remains ever elusive.

The essay begins in the first-person narrative style that became fashionable among the Romantics.[15] The narrator is Kleist himself. He recalls how he spent the winter of 1801 in M—— and there met a certain gentleman who held the position of first dancer at the opera and was extraordinarily popular. In the course of conversation, Kleist told him how surprised he was to run across him so often at the marionette theater. The dancer replied that he found much pleasure in the pantomime of the marionette figures and that a dancer really could learn much from them. And did not Kleist himself, he asked, find some of the movements of the marionettes, the smaller ones in particular, very graceful? When Kleist wanted to know how it was possible for someone to manipulate the marionettes' individual limbs and their tie points without a myriad of strings on the fingers, he was told that he should not imagine that each member, in the various motions of the dance, had to be regulated individually by the puppeteer. Each movement, the dancer went on to explain, had its own center of gravity, so that as long as that center was controlled, on the inside of the figure, the limbs—actually nothing but pendulums—followed of themselves, in a mechanical way, without further assistance. Moreover, this movement was quite simple, hence even when the center of gravity was directed in a straight line, the limbs began to describe curves, and often, when shaken in a quite random way, the whole puppet assumed a kind of rhythmic motion that was very much like a dance.

Apparently simple when viewed externally, the relation of the puppeteer's fingers to the movements of the figures attached to them was quite precise, the dancer went on, "rather like the relation of numbers to their logarithms or asymptotes to their hyperbola" (6). Reflecting the common attitude toward puppet theater, above all among artists, Kleist expressed his amazement that the dancer would dignify with such attention "this version of a fine art intended for the public at large" (7). But the dancer's exalted understanding of what the marionette might be capable of was embodied in his belief that if a mechanic constructed a marionette according to his (the dancer's) specifications, he could, by means of it, present a dance that neither he nor any other talented dancer of his time, the renowned Vestris included, would ever be likely to achieve.[16]

Everything Kleist relates to this point in *On the Marionette Theater* is merely a preface to the argument he now advances, through his dancer, that the puppet has natural advantages over the living dancer. This is the concept that Gordon Craig was to articulate with respect to the dramatic actor in the late nineteenth century. One distinct advantage of the puppet figure is its lack of affectation. "Affectation appears, as you know," explains the dancer, "when the soul (*vis motrix*) is located at any point other than the center of gravity of movement." Since it is this point, and no other, that the puppeteer controls, all the other limbs of the marionette are, as they should be, dead, pure pendulums, which follow the basic law of gravity. "This," declares the dancer, "is a marvelous quality which we look for in vain in the great majority of our dancers."[17]

Another natural advantage of the marionette over the living dancer is that of *countergravity*. That is because marionettes know nothing of the inertia of matter, which, of all properties, is the most obstructive to dancers. The force that lifts them into the air is greater than that which binds them to earth. The dancer further explains that "puppets, like elves, need the ground only to *alight* on, and through that momentary obstruction to reanimate the swing of their limbs. However, we need it to *rest* upon, and to recover from the exertion of the dance: a moment that is clearly not dance in itself, and with which there is nothing more to be done than to make it disappear in any way possible" (8).

Kleist now assumes the posture of a doubting Thomas who simply cannot believe that there might be more charm in a mechanical doll than in the structure of the human body. The dancer, on the other hand, asserts that the human being could not possibly compete with the puppet: "On this field, only a god could stand up to matter, and this is where both ends of the ring-shaped world interlock" (9). At this point, both Kleist and the dancer recount seemingly disparate personal experiences with a common underlying thread: that the perfection achieved by an unconscious act, gesture, or movement cannot be consciously duplicated. The relevance of this to the alleged superiority of the marionette over the human being is obvious. Because human beings think, reason, act consciously, they can never hope to achieve the perfection of movement of which puppets and marionettes are capable. The point is made in more metaphysical terms by the dancer at the conclusion of Kleist's essay:

> We see how in the organic world, as reflection grows darker and weaker, grace emerges ever more radiant and majestic. But just as the intersection of two lines, on one side of a point, suddenly turns up, after the passage through infinity, on the other side, or the image in a concave mirror, after it vanishes into infinity, suddenly reappears right before our eyes, so will grace, after knowledge similarly undergoes a journey through infinity, return to us. It is just at that moment that it will appear most purely in that bodily form that has either no consciousness at all or an infinite one; that is to say, in the puppet or in the god. (12)

Kleist's graceful essay on the marionette became widely known. Whether it served as the direct inspiration of some of the more prominent literary and dramatic texts built around the puppet theme in German Romanticism must remain speculative. But at least in the case of E. T. A. Hoffmann, who was an admirer of Kleist, the role of the essay, as a stimulus to the creation of one of his best stories, *Der Sandmann* (*The Sandman*), is worth considering. Written within just a few years of Kleist's essay and published in 1816, *The Sandman* has remained perhaps the most durable of Hoffmann's terrifying *Nachtstücke* (literally, "night pieces"). It also acquired, apart from its literary reputation, new fame in the late nineteenth century as the subject of Léo Delibes's very well known ballet *Coppélia ou La Fille aux yeux d'émail* (1870) and as one of the three Hoffmann tales on which Jacques Offenbach drew for his opera *Les Contes d'Hoffmann* (1881).

The Sandman recounts the descent into madness and finally suicide of a young man named Nathanael who falls madly in love with a mechanical woman he believes to be real. She is Olimpia, the "daughter" of Spalanzani, a professor of physics with whom Nathanael has come to study. Equipped with a pair of opera glasses obtained from the barometer seller, Giuseppe Coppola, who is none other than the frightening old lawyer Coppelius of his childhood nightmares, Nathanael is able to observe

Olimpia close up from his lodgings directly opposite Spalanzani's house. The more he uses Coppola's glasses to follow Olimpia's movements, the more ardently does he come to love her. If the opera glasses are truly "rose-colored" in that they distort his vision of reality, his predisposition to see phenomena in romantic terms—that is, in the idealistic, idealized terms of Romanticism—is well established in advance of his first encounter with Spalanzani's "daughter." But once they meet, his fate is sealed, and when enlightenment finally comes, it is too late. Even Olimpia's manner during their dance at a ball fails to alter Nathanael's entranced perception of her:

> And yet, after the dance had started, he found himself to his own surprise standing close by Olimpia, who had not been asked to dance. Barely able to stammer a few words, he seized her hand. It was like ice; a cold shudder passed through him; he gazed into Olimpia's eyes, which beamed back at him full of love and longing; and at the same instant a pulse seemed to start beating in the cold hand and the warm life-blood started flowing. . . .
>
> He imagined that he had been dancing in very good time to the music, but he soon observed from the peculiar, fixed rhythm in which Olimpia danced and which often confused him, that he was badly out of step. Nevertheless, he did not want to dance with any other woman and would have felt like murdering anyone else who asked Olimpia to dance.[18]

So powerful are Nathanael's feelings that he shrugs off Olimpia's reputation for "complete idiocy" because of her relative speechlessness and rigidity of manner. Even his friend Siegmund cannot change his opinion when he asks Nathanael, "How could an intelligent fellow like you have possibly fallen for that waxen-faced wooden doll?" (41). Unpersuaded either by Siegmund's incredulity at his stubbornness and blindness or by the hostility of people in general toward the object of his love, Nathanael decides to ask for Olimpia's hand in marriage. But when he reaches Professor Spalanzani's quarters, the horrible truth of Olimpia's real nature is brought home to him in a gruesome manner. Hearing a commotion within, Nathanael bursts into Spalanzani's study only to find the professor and Coppola quarreling over Olimpia and tugging and twisting her one way and another. After viciously knocking Spalanzani to the floor, Coppola throws the lifeless figure of Olimpia over his shoulder and makes off with her before Nathanael's unbelieving eyes. Standing transfixed, Nathanael can no longer deny the truth: "he had seen all too clearly that Olimpia's deathly pale waxen face had no eyes, but only black cavities: She was a lifeless doll." Spalanzani also drops any further pretense. Urging

Nathanael to pursue Coppola, he speaks with pride of the invention that he has just lost: "Coppelius has stolen my best automaton. I worked on it for twenty years. I put everything into it. The mechanism, the speech, the walk are mine; the eyes he stole from you. The villain, the rogue, after him, bring back my Olimpia. There are your eyes!" (45). Nathanael's end is not far off. Although temporarily restored to health and sanity, he soon goes utterly mad. Confusing his old love, Klara, for Olimpia, he attempts to throw her down from the high tower of the Town Hall but is prevented by her brother, and shortly thereafter he falls to his own death.

Hoffmann's tale of romantic blindness and the resultant confusion of illusion and reality was inspired by more than just Kleist's theoretical advocacy of the superiority of the marionette over the living dancer, though this was probably the immediate stimulus. Long before Hoffmann wrote *The Sandman*, the automaton had become the focus of widespread interest. In 1738, for example, Jacques de Vaucanson attracted considerable attention with a flute player automaton operated by clock mechanisms, which set in motion a system of bellows that in turn produced the musical sounds of the flute (98–100).

Encouraged by the mechanistic-materialistic ideas of a thinker such as the medical doctor Julien Offray de La Mettrie—the author in 1748 of an essay under the title *L'Homme machine (Man the Machine)*—other inventors followed Vaucanson's example and assembled their own automatons. The Swiss father-and-son team of watchmakers Pierre and Henri-Louis Jaquet-Droz constructed a writer-android in 1760 and a draftsman and organ player in 1773. (These figures can still be seen in the Neuchâtel Museum in Switzerland.) One of the most famous automatons of the period was a chess player invented in 1769 by the German nobleman Ritter Wolfgang von Kempelen. Lienhard Wawrzyn reports that in 1809, Napoleon played a game of chess with the figure. In 1836, Edgar Allan Poe wrote an essay entitled *Maelzel's Chess-Player* about the chess player's later owner in which he refuted the idea that the automaton was a pure machine and argued convincingly that it was constructed in such a way as to conceal a man inside it.[19]

THE ROMANTIC PERIOD: GEORG BÜCHNER

Within the German Romantic dramatic tradition, the most famous treatment of the puppet or marionette motif occurs in the play *Leonce und Leona (Leonce and Lena*, written in 1836) by Georg Büchner.[20] An icono-

clast of the first magnitude, Büchner was for long the odd man out of
nineteenth-century German drama. Eventually his genius and uniqueness
came to be recognized, and he is now regarded as one of the foremost
of modern German dramatists. Büchner is known best for his play on
the French Revolution, *Dantons Tod* (*The Death of Danton*, written in
1835), and for the unfinished *Woyzeck* (originally planned for publication in 1837), which Alban Berg made into an opera in 1921. But once the
early disdain for and indifference to *Leonce and Lena* gave way to recognition of its complexity and originality, the ostensible romantic comedy
has come in for its own share of appreciation.[21] The play originated as a
planned entry by Büchner in the comedy writing contest announced by the
book publisher Cotta on 3 February 1836. But Büchner failed to meet the
original deadline for submission as well as the extended one in August,
and so the manuscript was returned to him unopened. It eventually shared
the fate of other manuscripts and papers by him and became lost. When
it was finally printed, in 1838, the text had to be reconstructed from unre-
vised drafts.

This reconstruction posed far fewer problems than that of *Woyzeck*, for
which even something as fundamental as the order of scenes had to be
largely imagined by subsequent editors. But conflicting interpretations of
Büchner's intention with the play have made *Leonce and Lena* not appre-
ciably less controversial than the better-known *Woyzeck*. Once commen-
tators succeeded in overcoming the issue of the play's obvious indebtedness to Shakespeare's *As You Like It* and the fairy tale tradition—which
formed the basis of the play's initial disparagement—their interest came
to assume a largely typological character. Should *Leonce and Lena* be regarded as a romantic comedy, in which case it would be dismissed as a failure; or is it really an attempt to subvert the genre of romantic comedy by
using its constituent features against itself? In light of Büchner's characteristic irreverence and the very structure of the play, it is hard to understand that the issue of intentionality would have generated as much controversy as it did. The sheer banality of the basic plot and the obvious
evidence of romantic irony in the text leave little doubt that in *Leonce and
Lena*, as in his other dramatic writings, Büchner was strongly motivated
by his natural bent toward the subversive.

Now let us see how the puppet/marionette element in *Leonce and Lena*
serves the play's underlying subversive design. Leonce is a prince and the

son of King Peter of the kingdom of Popo. Since the name of the kingdom obviously derives from the colloquial German term for "bottom," "rear end," the tone of the play is established from the very outset. For further proof, there is also the name of the kingdom of which Lena is princess—the kingdom of Peepee. Leonce and Lena are engaged to be married, but it is an arranged marriage of state and the young people have never met. Leonce rebels and flees his kingdom before ever meeting Lena. She does the same thing without the slightest idea of Leonce's actions. Predictability is high and fidelity to reality of no consequence as Leonce and Lena meet on their wanderings, fall in love, and are married before learning each other's true identity. In the end, of course, the truth comes out and all rejoice at the fortuitous turn of events.

What Büchner has done with this banal material is to use it as a peg on which to hang unexpected characterizations and motifs, as if he had planned to draw his audience in by means of plot material so traditional as to seem trite and then thwart its expectations by confronting it with atypical characters and an underlying outlook of extreme pessimism. Surprise begins with Leonce himself. If he is traditional as a fairy tale character in rebelling against his father's plans to marry him to a young woman he has never seen, primarily for reasons of state, he is—uncharacteristically—a serious, and ultimately depressing, thinker. And it is as a thinker that he has come to the conclusion that idleness is the root of all vice, that people do what they do mostly out of boredom. It is in the context of such reflection, rooted in a bleak view of human existence, that Leonce introduces the puppet motif virtually at the beginning of the play. Troubled that it is *his* lot to understand that idleness is the motor of most human action, he despairs: "Why must *I* be the one to know this? Why can't I take myself seriously and dress this poor puppet in tails and put an umbrella in its hand so that it will become very proper and very useful and very moral?"[22]

The puppet-automaton motif is picked up again in act 3, scene 3, when Valerio, Leonce's wily companion, appears before King Peter on the day of the arranged nuptials to introduce Leonce and Lena as a pair of "world-famous automatons." Needless to say, Leonce and Lena, as well as Valerio and Lena's governess, who has accompanied her on her flight, are all masked. In his speech before King Peter, Valerio points out that he too is an automaton:

But I actually wanted to announce to this exalted and honored company that the two world-famous automatons have arrived, and that I'm perhaps the third and most peculiar of them all, if only I really knew who I am, which by the way shouldn't surprise you, since I myself don't know what I'm talking about—in fact, I don't even know that I don't know it, so that it's highly probable that I'm merely being *allowed* to speak, and it's actually nothing but cylinders and air hoses that are saying all this. (*In a strident voice.*) Ladies and gentlemen, here you see two persons of opposite sexes, a little man and a little woman, a gentleman and a lady. Nothing but art and machinery, nothing but cardboard and watchsprings. . . . These persons are so perfectly constructed that one couldn't distinguish them from other people if one didn't know that they're simply cardboard; you could actually make them members of human society.[23]

Intrigued with Valerio's mystifying introduction, King Peter is quick to seize on the idea of proceeding with the wedding of Leonce and Lena by means of the two automatons, in effect marrying Leonce and Lena in absentia through puppets representing them. As if seeking support for the idea he is about to formulate, he asks the President: "President, if you hang a man in effigy, isn't that just as good as hanging him properly?" The President replies: "Begging Your Majesty's pardon, it's very much better, because no harm comes to him, yet he is hanged nevertheless." This is all King Peter needs to convince him: "Now I've got it. We shall celebrate the wedding in effigy" (169).

The notion of the whole of society consisting of nothing but automatons, of puppets, is reinforced at the end of the play when the true identities of Leonce and Lena are revealed and King Peter turns the reins of government over to his son. Once the king and his cabinet leave, Leonce says to Lena, with Valerio and Lena's governess also present:

Well, Lena, now do you see how our pockets are full of dolls and toys? What shall we do with them? Shall we give them beards and hang swords on them? Or shall we dress them up in tails and let them play at protozoan politics and diplomacy and watch them through a microscope? Or would you prefer a barrel organ on which milk-white aesthetic shrews are scurrying about? Shall we build a theater? (171)

But the romantic irony with which the play is informed makes it clear that Büchner intends the audience to laugh at, as well as with, Leonce and Lena. When they pretend to be puppets for the sake of Valerio's deception of King Peter, their masquerade only highlights their true status as puppets. Manipulated by Valerio, who assumes the function of a puppet master, they are no more than dolls in his hands acting out a scenario devised by him. But as a creature of the author's invention, Valerio himself is only a manipulated being, as he himself seems aware in the speech in which he introduces Leonce and Lena to King Peter as "the two world-famous automatons."

Thus by means of the puppet figure Büchner creates in *Leonce and Lena* a type of parable on human existence in which the outward fairy tale aspect and the happy ending mask a dark vision of man. Suffering from the delusion that they are capable of determining their own actions, human beings merely betray their essential puppetlike nature. Life, in Büchner's view, is absurd; nothing one does can alter that fact, and the more one tries, the more one comes to resemble a puppet or marionette whose actions are determined by forces, or elements, beyond its control.

ABSURDITY, RUSSIAN STYLE: GOGOL AND SUKHOVO-KOBYLIN

Two outstanding Russian plays of the nineteenth century owe much to the inspiration of puppet theater without directly employing puppet figures or otherwise overtly introducing the puppet motif. The first is the better known of the two, and universally popular—*Revizor* (*The Inspector General*, 1836) by Nikolai Gogol. The second, the last part of a dramatic trilogy by Aleksandr Sukhovo-Kobylin, is *Smert Tarelkina* (*Tarelkin's Death*, 1869).

The subject of Gogol's *Inspector General* is so well known that it needs only minimal description here. A penniless young adventurer from St. Petersburg named Khlestakov, accompanied by his manservant, Osip, puts up in a small provincial town while traveling about the Russian countryside. Hardly do they arrive when Khlestakov is taken for an inspector general from the capital whose presence is expected any day. Since the town is mired in corruption, from the mayor on down, the arrival of the inspector general is greeted with alarm and fear. In the best Russian tradition, the town's officials, and merchants with grievances against the officials, come to the inn where Khlestakov is staying with the intention of bribing him. The officials want to prevent a bad report about their town from being sent to St. Petersburg, while the merchants would like their grievances against the officials redressed. A natural braggart and con artist, Khlestakov loses little time in sizing up the situation and playing it for all he can. The high point of the deception is Khlestakov's romantic pursuit of the mayor's daughter and his proposal of marriage. The mayor is delirious over the prospect of the "inspector general" becoming his son-in-law. The bubble bursts, however, when the town's postmaster, who is in the habit of occasionally opening incoming and outgoing mail for the sake of gossip, happens upon a letter Khlestakov writes to a Petersburg friend in which he boasts of the good fortune that has befallen him in the town. However, by the time the mayor and others learn of the deception, Khlestakov and Osip have already departed for parts unknown. The comedy ends with a dumb scene in which the mayor and the rest of the group onstage are thunderstruck by the appearance of a gendarme who announces the arrival of the awaited inspector general from St. Petersburg, this time, presumably, the real one.

The great appeal of *The Inspector General* lies in the absurdity of the situation, the caricature-like figures, and the masterful use of verbal as well as physical language. Its originality notwithstanding, the comedy was shaped by antecedents both remote and much closer in time. Parallels between Khlestakov and Don Quixote and between Osip and Sancho Panza—while imperfect—are commonplaces in the secondary literature on *The Inspector General*. Gogol was attracted to Spanish culture (something he shared with other European writers in the Romantic period) and made a point of familiarizing himself with it. The picaresque dimension of his comedy is undeniable.

Gogol had been interested in the theater for some time before he wrote *The Inspector General* and had one farce to his credit. His affinity for the stage also had a noteworthy family aspect. Gogol was of a Ukrainian background, and his father, Vasili Gogol-Yanovsky, was a well-known writer of comedies in the Ukrainian language. Moreover, Gogol knew Ukrainian folklore and must surely have been familiar with the Ukrainian puppet theater tradition known as *vertep*. His grandfather, Vasili Tansky, had in fact written popular sketches inspired by the *vertep*. While not specifically indebted to this tradition as such, *The Inspector General* can easily be regarded as of puppet derivation. What I mean by this is that in its characters, language, and physicality, the play has an undeniable puppet dimension. Although he does not explore the issue, Victor Erlich perceptively remarks on this in his study *Gogol*: "For the world of *The Inspector General* is populated by homunculi rather than by full-blown human beings, by puppets whose precariously contrived mode of existence is pointed up by their blatantly comic names." [24] Not only do Gogol's characters recall puppets and marionettes in their grotesque aspect, but their world is that of puppets manipulated by superior forces. In their feverish and wildly comic attempts to bribe the presumed inspector general, the town officials and merchants behave like puppets. They are incapable of independent action. The forces controlling their movements are corruption and the fear of public exposure. Once he senses what is happening, Khlestakov cannot behave other than he does. His basic naïveté and propensity for boastfulness take over and direct his movements as if he were a figure of wood. The comic pair, Bobchinsky and Dobchinsky, whose purpose in the play is purely farcical, owe as much to the puppet tradition as to their antecedents in ancient Roman comedy.

Apart from the rollicking antics of Bobchinsky and Dobchinsky, who bounce around the stage like a pair of circus clowns, the gesture language of characters in other situations most reflects puppet derivation. This physical dimension of *The Inspector General* is one of the principal sources of its comic appeal. It shows up especially in the bribe scenes between Khlestakov and the town officials and merchants, and then in the courting scene between Khlestakov and the mayor's daughter in the mayor's house. Here, by way of example, from the bribe scenes, is the dialogue between Khlestakov and the local school superintendent, Luka Lukich:

> *Luka Lukich* (*drawing himself up with some trepidation and placing a hand on his sword*). I have the honor of presenting myself, superintendent of schools, titular councilor Khlopov.
> *Khlestakov.* Ah, welcome! Please be seated. Would you like a cigar? (*Offers him a cigar.*)
> *Luka Lukich* (*aside, indecisively*). There you go! Now that's something I didn't expect. Should I take it, or not?
> *Khlestakov.* Take it, go on; it's a fine cigar. Of course, not the the kind you get in Petersburg. Why, there I used to smoke cigars at twenty-five rubles the hundred. They tasted so good, you could kiss your hands afterwards. Here's a light, go on, smoke it. (*Offers him a light.* Luka Lukich *tries to smoke the cigar, but trembles all over.*) No, no, not from that end!
> *Luka Lukich* (*droppping the cigar from fright, spitting, and waving his hand; aside*). Hell with it! That damned timidity of mine ruined everything!

Khlestakov. Well, I see you're no devotee of cigars. But I confess, they're my weakness. Now as regards the female sex, there's no way I can be indifferent. What about you? Which do you like better, brunettes or blondes?[25]

In this representative excerpt, the language of gesture is arguably more important than speech. Attention focuses on the physical activity accompanying the school superintendent's desire to make as good an impression as possible on the "inspector general," and then on the upsetting of his fragile equipoise when Khlestakov offers him a cigar. The humor of the scene derives less from what is said than from the physical actions of the characters, and this gesture language is easily reconciled with and accommodated by puppet and marionette theater. The same is also true for the play's concluding dumb scene, or pantomime, when all the characters onstage, beginning with the mayor, freeze into immobility when the gendarme appears announcing the arrival of the inspector general, who may be authentic or yet another imposter.

In writing *The Inspector General*, Gogol was as concerned about the appearance and gestures of his characters as he was about the dialogue. This is evident throughout, but especially at the very end, where the dumb scene, which is intended to last for a half a minute, is described in precise detail, with each character onstage assuming a different position. Gogol's indebtedness to the puppet tradition even in the conceptualization of *The Inspector General* can be taken for granted despite the absence of figures clearly identified as puppets or marionettes and of any allusions to these as such.

Aleksandr Sukhovo-Kobylin's *Death of Tarelkin* can be viewed in much the same light. In its focus on corrupt government officials, as well as in its grotesqueness, it is also, in part, Gogolian. To better understand *The Death of Tarelkin*, we have to consider briefly the preceding two parts of Sukhovo-Kobylin's *Trilogiya* (*Trilogy*). In the first play, *Svadba Krechinskogo* (*Krechinsky's Wedding*, 1854), a well-bred but impecunious gambler (Krechinsky) wins the heart of the daughter of a wealthy provincial landowner named Muromsky. His interest in her is primarily financial since he is desperate to find a way out of his mounting debts. When the pressure on him becomes unbearable, he borrows a diamond solitaire from her in order to pull off a sleight-of-hand swindle on a local pawnbroker. By the time the swindle is discovered, Krechinsky and his manservant, Rasplyuev, have already left town, like Khlestakov and Osip before them.

The second play of the *Trilogy*, *Delo* (*The Case*, 1861), exposes the corruption and inhumanity of the imperial Russian bureaucracy. After Krechinsky's flight in the first play, Muromsky's daughter is implicated in the plot to deceive the pawnbroker. Anxious to clear her of charges of complicity, her father tries everything in his power but finally has to resort to bribery. But the two corrupt officials he bribes, Varravin and his underling, Tarelkin, are unable to have the case dismissed and wind up stealing his money. Grief-stricken over the injustice suffered by his family and the rampant corruption all around him, Muromsky dies of a heart attack. Varravin and Tarelkin, in the meantime, quarrel over the division of the bribe money. The *Death of Tarelkin* (begun in 1857, completed in 1869, when the entire trilogy was published for the first time in book form) is theatrically the most effective of the three plays. The great Russian stage director Vsevolod Meyerhold was attracted to the modernity of its grotesque and absurd qualities and staged it, with considerable success, on the eve of the Revolution, on 23 October 1917. He mounted it again, five years later, at the experimental GITIS theater in Moscow; but his efforts on this occasion to transform the production into a vehicle for his ideas on constructivism and biomechanics met with a lukewarm reception. Since then, the play has been acknowledged as one of the best Russian comedies of the nineteenth century and is widely performed.

The Death of Tarelkin picks up where *The Case* ends. Muromsky is dead, the case against his daughter is entangled in the cumbersome Russian bureacracy of the time, and Varravin has cheated his henchman, Tarelkin, out of his share of the bribe money. When the play begins, Tarelkin is busy formulating a plan to throw Varravin off his scent. In order to retrieve his share of the bribe money, he has stolen papers incriminating to Varravin with which he hopes to blackmail him. With Varravin now in hot pursuit, Tarelkin hits on the wildly grotesque idea of pretending to have died, and then assuming the identity of a recently deceased neighbor. With the collusion of his maid, he puts a dummy resembling himself in a coffin and, to make sure that nobody gets close enough to inspect the "corpse," he surrounds it with a lot of dead fish. The ruse works only briefly. Varravin soon finds the toupee and false teeth Tarelkin discarded when he assumed the identity of his deceased neighbor, and he has him taken into custody. Tarelkin is accused of being a vampire and of masterminding a conspiracy of vampires against the entire Russian empire. Worn down by torture and the surreal charges brought against him, Tarelkin finally discloses the whereabouts of Varravin's missing papers. He is then released, penniless and broken. At the end of the play, Tarelkin turns directly to the audience and asks for a job, describing his qualifications.

Sukhovo-Kobylin was a wealthy aristocrat and enthusiastic devotee of the theater who spent considerable time in Paris. The genesis of the *Trilogy* was the murder case in which he himself was involved after the body of his French mistress was found with her throat slit. The case was eventually dismissed because of a lack of evidence. Sukhovo-Kobylin did, however, spend a few months in prison after being taken into custody; it was while behind bars that he began writing *Krechinsky's Wedding*. Presumably, his own encounters with the police and the imperial bureaucracy lay behind the nightmarish depiction of both in the *Trilogy*.

One of the stage techniques Sukhovo-Kobylin admired in Parisian boulevard theaters was the lightning-fast transformation of a character in full view of the audience. This was developed to a high degree of perfection by a few comic actors of wide renown such as Marie Bouffé and Pierre Lavassor. The technique involved the use of props but demanded primarily an extraordinary command of the facial muscles. Entranced by the technique, Sukhovo-Kobylin used it as the basis of *The Death of Tarelkin*, in which the major characters, beginning with Tarelkin, undergo such changes in the course of the play.

Though these transformations are not of direct puppet/marionette provenance, they occur in the context of a grotesque and absurd play compatible with the spirit and mechanics of puppet theater. There are, for example, purely comic, puppetlike characters such as the government clerks Chibisov, Ibisov, and Omega, and two policemen named Kachala and Shatala who are manipulated in a boisterous, circus-style interrogation of witnesses in act 3. The scene is one of the high points of the farce and easily reconciled with the puppet tradition in both its physicality and humor.

More immediate evidence of puppet inspiration in *The Death of Tarelkin* is act 1, scene 7, in which Varravin, now in disguise, comes to visit the bier of the "deceased" Tarelkin accompanied by a group of petty clerks. Suspicious of the circumstances of Tarelkin's "passing," Varravin nevertheless agrees that Tarelkin has to be buried, but since he left no money, responsibility devolves on Varravin as his former superior. When it becomes obvious that Varravin intends to collect the money for Tarelkin's burial from the crowd of clerks, they begin making their way out of the apartment one by one. Observing their flight, Varravin halts them. He then grabs Chibisov and Ibisov by the arms and leads them, along with the other clerks, toward the proscenium. From this point to the end of the scene, Varravin plays the role of a puppeteer moving the clerks around like so many puppets for the purpose of having them extract money from each other's billfolds. Here is the remainder of the scene:

> *Varravin.* Gentlemen, listen to me—we're one family after all, aren't we? (*Shakes them by the arms.*) Aren't we one family?
>
> *Chibisov and Ibisov* (*jumping from pain*). Yes! Yes! We're one family.
>
> *Varravin.* Our younger brother is in need. (*Shakes them by the arms.*) Are we not warm people?
>
> *Chibisov and Ibisov* (*jumping and twisting from pain*). Yes, yes, damn it, we're warm people.
>
> *Varravin.* Right you are! We respond sincerely, with open hearts!
>
> *Chibisov and Ibisov* (*tearing free of him*). Yes indeed, sincerely, with open hearts! (*All start running out.*)
>
> *Varravin* (*catching them*). No, no—I'm telling you again, not like that. (*Aside*) What vipers, they just won't give in! (*Aloud*) If you please, gentlemen, we'll arrange it like this. (*Gathers the clerks around him.*) Are you ready now to perform a good deed?
>
> *Clerks.* Ready, ready.
>
> *Varravin.* Then for a good deed you'll willingly take money from another, won't you, that is from another's pocket?
>
> *Clerks.* From another's pocket? Willingly, very willingly.
>
> *Varravin* (*tenderly*). In that case, each of you take another ever so lightly by the collar. That's the way, good. (*Divides them into* pairs.)
>
> *Omega.* Your Excellency! There's nobody to take me by the collar.
>
> *Varravin.* Then you take yourself.
>
> *Omega* (*bowing*). Yes, sir. (*Withdraws and takes himself by the collar.*)
>
> *Varravin* (*reviewing the clerks*). Splendid, gentlemen, splendid! (*Tenderly*) Now each of you take the other's billfold. (*Noise and scrambling; the clerks extract the billfolds from each other's pockets.*)
>
> *Varravin* (*feasting his eyes on the scene*). Lovely! Like brothers! There's true community! Now, count out three rubles apiece, but no more than three rubles! No more, mind!
>
> *Clerks* (*shouting*). Gentlemen, three each . . . But no more, no more! (*They count out the money.* Varravin *accepts it and advances to the proscenium.*)
>
> *Varravin* (*to the audience*). What warmth, what fervor! They even have to be restrained . . . (*Moved*) Such offerings as these move me deeply. (*To*

the clerks) Now, gentlemen, return the billfolds. That's the way. I thank
you. Permit me to extend you my sincere, heartfelt thanks. You have
done a fine deed—a good deed. Your younger brother dies in want—
and you at once . . . I thank you! I am moved—I am weeping—you
weep, too! (*All weep.*) Embrace one another. (*They embrace each
other.*)[26]

GEORGE AND MAURICE SAND AND THE THEATER AT NOHANT

In the period between Gogol's *Inspector General* and the first part of
Sukhovo-Kobylin's trilogy, *Krechinsky's Wedding*, a very different and at
the time far more celebrated writer in France, George Sand, was discovering the pleasures of puppetry. It came about in a casual, actually
rather charming way. Theatrical activity of one sort or another had already become a regular part of life at the Sand country estate in Nohant,
in the department of Indre, in the mid-1840s. It started, presumably, with
character sketches by Chopin during his summers there. Before long the
whole Sand household was caught up in the acting out of improvised play-
lets.[27] As time went on, "productions" became more elaborate—without
losing their improvisatory character—and involved a larger number of
players. But the breakup of the relationship between Sand and Chopin and
the nasty split between Sand and her daughter, Solange, contributed to a
sharp fall-off in the theatrical life of Nohant during the summers of 1846
and 1847. The political disappointments of the revolutionary year 1848
put an even greater damper on the mood at the estate. But then, as if to
lighten it, Sand's son, Maurice, and his friend Eugène Lambert (who later
acquired a reputation as a painter of cats) got the idea of entertaining her
by performing with rudimentary hand puppets from the top of a high-
backed chair. Thus was launched the puppet theater of Nohant in the
summer of 1848. The enthusiasm for this latest entertainment was so
great that Maurice spared no effort in making it a success. He and his
friends carved the puppets' heads, while George Sand herself designed and
sewed their costumes. Although the audience was initially small, consisting of Maurice and his friends, George Sand, and the socialist writer
Victor Borie, who soon became Sand's lover, the puppet theater of Nohant
grew into a more elaborate affair, moved to larger premises, and on the
whole was taken quite seriously. At its peak there were as many as 120
puppets in the company. Fourteen of Maurice's puppet plays were eventually published in book form in 1890.[28]

Although the published collection of his puppet plays bears the title *Le Théâtre des Marionettes*, Maurice Sand's little theater at Nohant was actually one of hand puppets. The figures were manipulated by the thumb, fore- and middle fingers inserted into the puppet's arms and head. Ever bent on refining his puppets and extending the range of his theater, Maurice experimented with different techniques. With one he overcame the problem of the small puppet booth capable of accommodating only two operators, each of whom could handle only two puppets at a time.[29] He set up a line of sticks capable of holding a number of figures. These were then linked by a wire with one or two coils in it which could be slipped into holes on bars across the stage when the puppet had no lines to speak but was required by the action to appear onstage. The nonspeaking puppets could thus be made to move slightly, thereby adding more visual interest. And if the part called for some dialogue, the puppeteer could slip a hand into a puppet's sleeves for the appropriate animation. Maurice also came up with the idea of improving the shape of the puppets by fitting a cardboard chest and shoulders to each one; the puppeteer inserted his fingers only into the figures' forearms, which would then swing from the elbows instead of the shoulders. If the puppet had to sit in a chair, it was kept upright by means of an eyelet concealed in the hair at the back of its head and fastened on a hook. Sand also experimented with perspective. To create the effect of distance, a tiny puppet could be moved across the back of the stage. Once it was offstage, a slightly larger, identical one was entered from the same side and made to recross the stage. In this way the figure kept growing until it reached the usual size downstage. Many of Sand's puppets were equipped with legs. The operator's hand was hidden behind one of the balustrades that formed a part of the stage décor while the puppet's legs hung down in front of it.

Apart from its own near legendary repute, Maurice Sand's puppet theater reinvigorated theatrical life at Nohant in general. Productions resumed in the autumn of 1849 and became notable, above all, for George Sand's experiments with the Italian commedia dell'arte, of which she had by now become a passionate admirer.[30] In 1858 the small acting company at Nohant set itself to the task of putting together an illustrated volume on the commedia and its history. Besides translating some commedia materials, Maurice drew all the stock commedia figures. George Sand translated other commedia texts and took responsibility for editing the final

work. It came out in two volumes, under the title *Masques et bouffons,*
toward the end of 1859.

The seriousness of Sand's interest in both the commedia dell'arte and
puppet theater is attested by more than the theatrical activities at Nohant.
The same year in which *Masques et bouffons* appeared, Sand published a
novel with a Swedish setting called *L'Homme de neige* (*The Snow Man*).
Less well known than other works of fiction by her, its principal interest—
from the point of view of the present study—is the prominence in it of the
puppet motif. This relates primarily to the novel's central character,
Christian (Cristiano) Waldo, a mysterious figure who is rarely seen without a black mask and who is described as an "Italian comic actor, who
goes from town to town entertaining the inhabitants by his pleasant wit
and inexhaustible merriment."[31] In a lengthy account of his strange background to the local town advocate, Mr. Goefle, Christian digresses about
puppets and marionettes. Pursued at a certain point on suspicion of assas-
sinating a cardinal, Christian eludes the police by taking refuge in a show
tent during the performance of a marionette play. He then breaks his narrative by asking Goefle if he knows what a marionette show is. All Goefle
really knows is based on his attendance at a recent show staged by Christian Waldo in Stockholm, without his realizing that the Cristiano who is
sharing his life history with him is none other than the renowned Christian Waldo himself. A marionette show, Christian Waldo begins expatiat-
ing, is a "theater with two *operanti* and four hands, that is to say four
characters on the stage; this makes it possible to have a quite large person-
nel of *burattini*" (263–64). Mr. Goefle's unfamiliarity with the term *burattino* provides Christian the opportunity to launch his digression on
puppets and marionettes. A *burattino,* he explains, is

> the classic, primitive marionette, and it is the best. It is not the *fantoccio*
> that hangs from the ceiling by strings and walks without touching the floor
> or making a ridiculous and impossible noise. That more sophisticated and
> complete invention of the speaking marionette succeeds, by means of great
> improvements in mechanism, in imitating natural gestures and graceful at-
> titudes. There is no doubt that, by means of other improvements, it should
> be able to copy nature perfectly; but, on considering the question, I asked
> myself what would be the object, and what advantage would art derive
> from a theater of automatons? The larger and more like men they are, the
> sadder and more frightening the sight of these fake actors will become. (264)

When Goefle protests that the digression about puppets and marionettes is less interesting to him than the rest of Christian's personal story,
Christian insists on continuing his digression so as to convince Goefle of
the superiority of the *burattino*: "That elementary representation of the
comic artist is, I propose to prove to you, neither a machine, nor a plaything, nor a doll; it is a living being." When Goefle expresses incredulity
at the idea, Christian declares: "Yes, a living being! I insist upon it . . . it
is all the more a being in that its body does not exist. The *burattino* has
neither springs, nor strings, nor pulleys. It is a head, nothing more; an ex-
pressive, intelligent head, in which . . . hold on!" Christian then opens a
box from which he extracts a small wooden figure decked out in pieces of
cloth and proceeds to give Goefle a demonstration of his art from behind
the rail of a wooden staircase:

> Behold the illusion, even without a stage or scenery! This face, just sketched
> out and painted a flat, dull color, gradually assumes in its movement the ap-
> pearance of life. If I showed you a beautiful German marionette, varnished,
> brightly painted, covered with spangles and moved by springs, you could
> not forget that it was a doll, a mechanical piece of work. My *burattino*, on
> the other hand, supple, obedient to all the movements of my fingers, goes
> and comes, bows, turns his head, folds his arms, raises them in the air,
> waves them in every direction, strikes, beats the wall in joy or in despair—
> and you imagine that you see all his emotions depicted in his face, is that
> not so? What is the explanation of this prodigy, that a face so faintly indi-
> cated, so ugly seen up close, suddenly assumes, in the play of the light, a nat-
> uralness of expression that makes you forget its real dimensions? Yes, I
> maintain that when you see the *burattino* in the hands of a genuine artist,
> on a stage where the scenery, the dimensions, the elevations, and the setting
> are properly proportioned to the characters, you forget entirely that you
> yourself are out of proportion to that little stage and those little creatures;
> you forget even that the voice with which they speak is not their own. That
> apparently impossible conjunction of a head as big as my fist and a voice as
> strong as mine is effected by means of a mysterious sort of rapture into
> which I am able to lead you little by little, and the whole of the prodigy
> comes from . . . Do you know what it comes from? It comes from the fact
> that the *burattino* is not an automaton; that it obeys my caprice, my inspi-
> ration, my enthusiasm; that all its movements are the result of ideas that
> come to me and words that I put in its mouth; that it is *I*, in short, that is
> to say, a living being, and not a doll. (266–67)

TWO

The Puppet in Turn-of-the-Century Literature, Drama, and Theater

ETERNAL PINOCCHIO

With the notable exception of Kleist's essay on the marionette theater, the turn of the century far surpassed previous periods in its susceptibility to the allure of the puppet figure. This heightened interest led to new perspectives on invented man and had a decisive impact on the art of the stage. Shaping these perspectives were changes that were then occurring in artistic sensibility and without which the modernist movement would not have developed as it did. In order to appreciate the nature of these changes, we must first consider certain cultural and intellectual currents of the time. I propose to do this now through major texts in fiction, poetry, drama, and theatrical theory reflective of the fresh vision brought to bear on the puppet and marionette.

The first text is by all means the best known, and certainly the best loved. It is *Pinocchio*, or to give its full original Italian title, *Le Avventure di Pinocchio: Storia di un burattino* (*The Adventures of Pinocchio: Story of a Puppet*). Commonly, but not wholly justifiably, regarded as a classic of children's literature—the qualification refers not to its status as a classic, which no one would dispute, but to its universal classification as a story for children—*Pinocchio* was first published in book form in Naples in 1883. It was written by a journalist and author of schoolbooks named Carlo Lorenzini, who used the pseudonym Carlo Collodi. Collodi, as he shall be referred to here, wrote the work for which he is most famous between July 1881 and January 1883.[1] It was published serially, and irregularly, during that period.

Pinocchio is so well known throughout the world and has been so extensively studied that I would like not to cover overly familiar ground in my discussion of it in the context of the scope of this book. When critics and scholars began taking the work seriously and seeing in it a tale for adults as much as for children, virtually every aspect of it was brought under close scrutiny: its "Italianness," its place in the development of society and culture in the newly unified Italy, its pedagogical dimension, its subtleties and ironies, its language and narrative structure, its indebtedness to and subversion of the fairy tale tradition, its reflection of the popular Italian puppet and marionette theater, its use of archetypes, and so on.

What I find important in *Pinocchio*, first of all, is its chronology. Collodi began writing it on the threshold of the turn of the century, the 1880s; at a time, that is, when signs were already appearing of an urgent restlessness among artists to break free of the constraints, as they perceived them, of a bourgeois society they had come to despise. Whether they were justified in their hostility toward it is another matter. The important thing is that they, like many intellectuals, believed that bourgeois society was materialistic, fearful of change, spiritually bankrupt, hypocritical, and self-protective in its attachment to tradition. Without a radical transformation of bourgeois society, or ultimately the overthrow of it, it was felt that new directions in art and culture were impossible.

This contempt for bourgeois society was expressed in different ways. Artists often defied it by flaunting the bohemianism so widespread in the turn of the century. They mocked its values by violating taboos as much as possible, particularly in the area of sexuality. They took refuge from it in exotic travel, in a new romantic escapism. Their loathing was powerful enough to fuel an extraordinary creativity that ushered in the modernist movement and paved the way for the avant-garde of the early twentieth century. Reacting to the narrowness of bourgeois art (read here realism), artists extended themselves as far as they could to open literature and the other arts to the whole range of human experience, both corporeal and metaphysical. European Naturalism was cultivated as a greater and truer realism. And while the Naturalists campaigned in behalf of a more broadly honest depiction of society, the Symbolists explored man's inner life. Since Naturalism, Symbolism, and other aspects of the emerging modernist movement coexisted in the same period, it is important to see these developments as different reactions against the status quo.

One of the ways the modernist artist expressed the desire for freedom from the confines of bourgeois culture was to spurn traditional genres. This manifested itself in a wide range of experimentation involving virtually every aspect of composition. A new preference for smaller forms, for brevity, underlay the "miniaturization" evident in almost all the arts, from the prose sketches of the archetypical turn-of-the-century Viennese bohemian, Peter Altenberg, to the musical pieces of Anton Webern. The efforts of dramatists such as Strindberg and Maeterlinck to create a highly compressed new dramatic form, different from the traditional one-act play, were paralleled by the phenomenal spread of the "little," "intimate," or "chamber" theater of roughly the same period.

The emergence of the dynamic European cabaret culture of the late nineteenth and early twentieth centuries was a related phenomenon. Beginning with the Chat Noir in Paris in 1881 and, in a sense, concluding in Zurich in 1916 with the Cabaret Voltaire, from which issued the Dada movement, the cabaret arose in part as a repudiation by artists of bourgeois society and culture and as a search for alternatives. The early cabarets were elitist in nature. They were generally not open to the public, serving instead as refuges where artists could entertain one another with their own creations while being unconcerned about public acceptance, experiment out of view of "academic" and tradition-oriented critics, mock the bourgeois and their values to their heart's content, and cultivate genres generally regarded at the time as marginal. These "marginal" genres favored by cabaret artists are germane to the subject of this book in that they included puppet and marionette shows together with shadow shows; the chanson, or popular song, which enjoyed a spectacular revival at the time especially in Paris and was widely imitated elsewhere in Europe; small dramatic pieces, or sketches; new forms of dance; monologues; and other types of performance appropriate to the small confines of the typical cabaret.

Another facet of the antitraditionalism of the modernist artist, which determined the entertainments offered in the cabarets, was the desire to seek new forms of creative expression by reaching from the heights of "high" culture to the often scorned lower depths of "popular" culture. Reflected here were not only the search for new sources of inspiration but also changing social attitudes and values. Ordinary people, rural people, the folk, were acknowledged as having a culture of their own which now came to be regarded as often far more representative of what were vaguely perceived at the time as national values than that of higher social strata, particularly the bourgeoisie. Hence seeking out this culture and, more important, incorporating elements of it into more sophisticated art made yet another statement of defiance of traditional bourgeois values.

One form of popular culture of great appeal to the modernist artist, whether involved in the cabarets or not, was puppet and marionette theater. This was regarded no longer as a primitive entertainment for children and the masses but as an area of creativity within the purview of the serious artist. And the fairgrounds where such popular puppet and marionette shows were to be found were no longer looked upon as places of vulgar public merriment. It was from the fairground that the Russian avant-garde director Vsevolod Meyerhold drew inspiration for some of his more revolutionary ideas about the transformation of the contemporary Russian stage. It was also the fairground that similarly inspired a small but important play, *Balaganchik (The Fairground Show,* 1906), which brought together the talents of Meyerhold and one of the greatest modern Russian poets, Aleksander Blok.

Another characteristic enthusiasm of the turn of the century, of far-reaching consequences for virtually every art of the period, and for a work such as *Pinocchio* in particular, was the child. If childhood had had little prior impact on artistic consciousness, except in the most superficial ways, the situation changed radically in the late nineteenth century. This must also be viewed in the broader context of the changes beginning to reshape not just aesthetic ideas but the social and political outlook as well. Put as simply as possible, the world of the child became newly attractive to artists as a source of opposition, and an antidote, to the conservativism and traditionalism of bourgeois culture. In its resistance to change, to new ideas, the old order, which was understood to be the guarantor of bourgeois values, came to be regarded as old in more than just the chronological sense. It was a geriatric case, suffering from crippling arthritis and poor circulation; its joints were numb, its mental capacity diminished, and its vision declining. All that was left for it was a peaceful end, but as its opposition to change became more rigid, that possibility was ruled out.

What was needed, it was felt, was a rejuvenation of outlook, of ideas and attitudes, a rejuvenation in due course of institutions. Culture and society had to be transformed, and this could be accomplished only by fresh vision, boldness, and daring.

The new obsession with rejuvenation, with "youthhood," was reflected in the names of the various modernist movements throughout Europe: Young Germany, Young Vienna, Young Scandinavia, Young Belgium, Young Poland, and so on. Its political correlative could be seen, for example, in the Young Turks organization which arose (though not immediately with that name) in 1889 in opposition to the anachronistic policies of Sultan Abdul Hamid. Journals often had *youth* in the title, and the entire modernist style in the decorative arts especially is known, after all, as *Jugendstil* (literally, "youth style"). The impact on art of the preoccupation with youthhood was formidable. To take merely two examples from German-language literature of the turn of the century: the trailblazing drama of adolescence and awakening sexuality, *Frühlings Erwachen* (*Spring's Awakening*, 1891), by the most provocative German dramatist of his time, Frank Wedekind, and the sensitive, worshipping treatment of children, particularly young girls, in the short impressionistic sketches of the widely admired Viennese bohemian writer Peter Altenberg.

Now, it seems reasonable to assume that the turn-of-the-century enthusiasm for youth would embrace childhood as well. To a considerable extent, of course, it did. But childhood had a fascination for the artist at the time which should be taken on its own terms. Childhood was understood to be a time of innocence, of purity, and was consequently juxtaposed to the corruption of the old order. Spontaneity and intuitiveness in the life of the child were similarly juxtaposed to prevailing patterns of conformist social behavior and thought. Within adult bourgeois society, this conformity was looked upon as a precondition of stability or, in other words, the maintenance and preservation of the status quo. The child's as yet unformed ability to reason, its prerational state, its lack of self-consciousness, if you will, instead of being regarded as a liability in adult terms, now became idealized. The child lived in closer harmony with its own nature. It had not yet developed adult stratagems of disguise and deception. The child was too young for the masks society imposes on adults.

This spontaneity, intuitiveness, and prerationality of the child, together with its capacity for creative imagination, proved immensely appealing to

the modernist artist. Collectively, these qualities became a factor in the rebellion against the norms of "classical" and "academic" art. They inspired
the cultivation of the primitive and the bold experimentation with color,
shape, and line. They encouraged fantasy. And in literature they acted as
a stimulus to the far-flung attempts to revitalize especially poetic language
by shifting the semantic weight from meaning to sound. The common
denominator of experiments—with *zaumny* ("trans-sense") language in
Russia on the part of such poets as Aleksei Kruchonykh and Velimir
Khlebnikov; with syntax, particularly, of the Italian Futurists beginning
with Filippo Tommaso Marinetti; and with sound in the poems of the
Dada poet Hugo Ball at the Cabaret Voltaire in 1916—was the dissatisfaction with prevailing norms of literary language and the urge to "pu-
rify" it of the accretions of bourgeois usage. Wassily Kandinsky's experiments with sound and color in such stage scenarios as *Der gelbe Klang*
(*The Yellow Sound*), *Violett* (*Violet*), *Grüner Klang* (*Green Sound*), and
Schwarz und weiss (*Black and White*)—composed between 1909 and
1914 (only *The Yellow Sound* and *Violet* ever appeared in print)—should
be regarded in a similar light.

The new enthusiasm of artists for such popular entertainments as puppet shows, pantomime, and circus routines can be seen as a convergence
of the rediscovery of both the world of popular culture and that of the
child. The enthusiasms and entertainments of children became in a sense
those of mature artists. The visual arts and literature, especially drama,
offer abundant evidence of the response of the modernist artist to these
new stimuli. One need go no further than a number of works by Kandinsky and Picasso, the latter's famous "Saltimbanques," for example. In the
drama, Frank Wedekind's best-known plays after *Spring's Awakening—
Erdgeist* (*Earth Spirit*, 1895) and *Die Büchse der Pandora* (*Pandora's
Box*, 1904)—both have circus settings (but decidedly adult themes). The
prominent turn-of-the-century Catalan painter and playwright Santiago
Rusiñol is best known as a dramatist for *L'alegria que passa* (*The Joy That
Passes*, 1891), which deals with itinerant entertainers. And the only play
by the once highly popular early-twentieth-century Russian writer Leonid
Andreev to achieve international renown—*Tot, kto poluchaet poshche-
chiny* (*He Who Gets Slapped*, 1915)—has a circus setting.

In light, then, of these various currents in turn-of-the-century European
art and thought, a work such as *Pinocchio* seems very much a product of

its time. It would be convenient to hypothesize that because of its relatively early appearance in book form, in 1883, Collodi's masterpiece proved an impetus to the rediscovery of the the world of the child, the puppet, and popular culture. But there is no evidence that it did. It was more a matter of Collodi's sensitivity to a changing artistic and social climate and his anticipation of what would gain momentum throughout Europe in the years ahead.

If we look at *Pinocchio*, then, from the viewpoint of the transformation of values characteristic of modernism, the work is remarkably compatible with its time. Apart from its elements of purely national concern, such as its language and its reflection of the social and cultural needs of the new Italian political unity,[2] the book is a celebration of puppetry, childhood, and the artistic potential of popular and folk culture. *Pinocchio*'s indebtedness to the Italian puppet and marionette tradition has been amply explored. Of interest here is the novelty of a book—written ostensibly for children but obviously intended for adults as well—entirely about a puppet. That this would not in itself have provided a stimulus to a new interest in the puppet and marionette, not only in Italy, would be difficult to imagine. Moreover, *Pinocchio* not only is about a puppet but also features, in chapter 10, a puppet show of the popular commedia dell'arte–derived Punch and Judy variety. There are a few things worth examining in this particular chapter of Collodi's book relative to the modernist renewal of interest in the puppet and marionette.

The first has already been remarked—the commedia dell'arte–derived puppet show in progress when Pinocchio enters the show tent. By the late nineteenth century, the puppet theater was regarded as the last resting place of the commedia dell'arte, and both together represented a form of entertainment primarily for children and the fairground public. Although it lasts briefly, the disruption of their performance by the puppets onstage as soon as they catch sight of Pinocchio represents a recurrent theme in the modernist interpretation of the puppet tradition, namely the revolt of the wooden figures against the puppeteer, a revolt of slaves against their master, a revolt against authority. Subtextually, what is suggested is the belief in the autonomy of the created entity, which, once brought into the world, has a life of its own. We have already met this theme of the revolt of animated inanimate creatures in Cervantes's *Don Quixote*. We shall encounter it again, in one guise or another, in a number of other texts.

Rebellion against authority—servants against masters, children against parents, one generation against another—would understandably loom large in modernist literature as an expression of the desire to end the hegemony of the bourgeios order. This aspect of *Pinocchio* has not been lost on critics either. The disruption of their own performance by the puppets in chapter 10 is not the only puppet revolt against authority in Collodi's masterpiece. Pinocchio himself is, after all, in a near constant state of rebellion against authority until his final transformation into a real boy. A journalist and a pedagogue, not wholly in the mainstream of a modernism that was only beginning to manifest itself when he began to write *Pinocchio*, Collodi was as if of two minds on the matter of respect for authority. On one hand, the disobedience of Pinocchio carries with it something of the nostalgia of the mature person for the carefree outlook and lack of respect for authority of the young. In rebellion himself against a society whose values he no longer respected and indeed sought to overthrow, the modernist artist could identify with the very young and yearn for a return to that magic time in life when the pressure to conform socially, to settle into one's place in society, to accept hypocrisy and the inauthenticity of masks, did not exist. So, to a certain extent, Pinocchio is a projection of such nostalgia and yearning on Collodi's part. And if this happened to have been of no real significance in Collodi's personal makeup, it was a mood of the time to which he was undoubtedly responsive.

But then there is the other side of the picture to be considered—Pinocchio's own, oft-stated desire to become a real boy and to take his proper place in the world. Unlike the eponymous hero of the extraordinarily popular play of youth everlasting, *Peter Pan* (1904), by Sir James M. Barrie, Pinocchio does not want to remain a puppet forever. His desire to become a real boy certainly can be read as a manifestation of Collodi's social conservatism and his intention in *Pinocchio* to inculcate into the young a sense of responsibility toward society and state. This was a matter of particular relevance in Italy in the wake of the Risorgimento, which finally created a unified nation. The inherent ambivalence in Collodi's story, with its nostalgia for the freedom of childood and the rational adult's understanding of the need to curb such freedom to prepare the child for its future role as an adult in society, elicits these perceptive comments by Nicholas J. Perella in his translation of *Pinocchio*:

Though Collodi seems neither to sentimentalize nor idealize the child, the nostalgia is surely there, albeit masked; and almost surely his need to exorcize it accounts for much of the ambiguity or secret tension felt by adult readers, most of whom are bound to smile indulgently at Pinocchio but not without some concern at his madcap flights and dangerously childish hopes. We are glad to return to the author a knowing wink of relief and complicity at his reassuring if severe curtailments of the puppet's misguided *élan vital*. For Collodi's ambivalence is also our own, an ambivalence that derives from the regressive pull of the child in us even as we enforce the role of responsible adults upon ourselves. Our idea of maturity and a workable social order necessitates the repression of the child whose amoral vitality and primordiality represent a threat to that idea. (48)

Pinocchio's transformation from a puppet into a real boy emblematizes the passage of youth into adulthood and the readiness to accept the responsibility of social integration. If, on a rational plane, Collodi could accept the inevitability of such passage and the need for it in the new Italy of his own time, the writing of *Pinocchio* argues well for an undeniable nostalgia for the carefree, mischevious, rebellious past of childhood. Although it doubtless behooved him to end the work as he did, Pinocchio's disdain for his former puppet self seems, nevertheless, to lack a certain conviction:

> "And the old Pinocchio of wood [Pinocchio asks Geppetto], where could he have gone to hide?"
>
> "There he is over there," answered Geppetto; and he pointed to a large puppet propped against a chair, its head turned to one side, its arms dangling, and its legs crossed and folded in the middle so that it was a wonder that it stood up at all.
>
> Pinocchio turned and looked at it; and after he had looked at it for a while, he said to himself with a great deal of satisfaction:
>
> "How funny I was when I was a puppet! And how glad I am that I've become a proper boy!" (461)

The suggestion in *Pinocchio*, implicit rather than explicit—that the boy Pinocchio becomes at the end of the work is destined to become far more of a puppet once he enters adulthood than he was as a puppet—underlies the metaphoric appeal of the puppet or marionette figure to many modernist artists. Compared to the life of the adult in bourgeois society with its limits and restraints, its conformist pressures, and its role playing, the child's world seems delightfully uninhibited and unfettered. Children are often compared to puppets because they are not yet "real people." But as Collodi and others after him were to suggest, perhaps it is indeed the adults in bourgeois society who are the real puppets, manipulated by a host of powers they think they have control over but in fact do not.

RAINER MARIA RILKE AND THE *DUINO ELEGIES*

This implied natural superiority of the child over the fully formed but so-cially deformed adult, and its metaphoric representation by means of the puppet or marionette figure, serves as the subject of one of the elegies in the Austrian poet Rainer Maria Rilke's *Duineser Elegien* (*Duino Elegies*, begun in 1912, completed in 1922). Widely considered as possibly the most distinguished poetic achievement of the twentieth century, the *Duino Elegies* is an intricate, complex, and profound inquiry into life and death and man's place in the world. The puppet motif, in the context of a differentiation between the world of the child and that of the adult, figures in the fourth of the ten elegies. Although I am jumping ahead over thirty years, there seems to be a logic in following *Pinocchio* with a considera-tion of Rilke's fourth Duino elegy.

The poem was written in Munich on 22 and 23 November 1915. The theme of the elegy—in simplest terms—is man's tragic uniqueness as the sole creature in nature aware of his own finiteness and inevitable death.[3] Because of this, man experiences, and suffers from, an abiding sense of disharmony, of disjointedness, between himself and his world. Whatever man achieves, whatever joy he realizes, whatever the preciousness of at-tachments he forms, the awareness of inescapable separation eats away at him. Man alone perceives the passage of time, the dynamics of change, and the ultimate decay from which no escape, no refuge, is possible. Out of this perception comes the duality characteristic of the human condition and the self-consciousness unknown elsewhere in nature.

Rilke's concern with human self-consciousness and the possibility of overcoming it forms the link with Kleist's essay on the marionette. The in-troduction of the puppet motif is preceded by theatrical imagery. To Rilke the human heart itself is a stage which man sits before, observing the drama of separation and transformation:

> Who has not sat anxiously before the curtain of his heart?
> It rose. The scenery was farewell.

> Easy to understand. The familiar garden,
> all swaying gently. Only then did the dancer come.
> Not *that one*. Enough! No matter how light his movements,
> he is disguised and becomes a bourgeois
> and enters his dwelling through the kitchen.[4]

Through the figure of the dancer, in all likelihood—in this instance—a borrowing from Kleist's essay, Rilke suggests that even when man seems freed from the weight of his own humanness, his self-consciousness inevitably asserts itself and disrupts the harmony temporarily achieved. The dancer may seem graceful as he enters to play his emblematic role in a familiar romantic setting (the parting of lovers, the garden with its gently swaying foliage), but his gracefulness is merely a disguise. He is really a bourgeois and must return to that reality. Thus the aesthetic represented by the image of the dancer onstage gives way to the ordinary citizen entering his everyday environment through his kitchen. The descent from aesthetic heights to the mundaneness of the kitchen underscores the pathos of human duality.

In Kleist's essay, the dancer is an observer who shares with the narrator his perceptions of the inherent superiority of the puppet or marionette over the human dancer. In Rilke's fourth Duino elegy, it is the dancer as emblem of the human condition who is observed onstage by the poem's narrator. And it is this observation that leads Rilke to the same conclusion as Kleist, that of the natural superiority of the puppet over the human which is attributable to the puppet's lack of consciousness. Like Kleist's dancer, Rilke's poet now expresses his own preference for the puppet:

> I do not want these half-filled masks,
> but rather the puppet. It is whole. I want
> to endure the shell and the wire and
> its face looking only outward. I stand before them.
> (275)

Rilke's elegy and Kleist's essay converge shortly thereafter. In the latter work, the dancer tells the narrator, on taking his leave, that on the basis of everything he told him, he, the narrator, has all he needs to understand his point about the superiority of the puppet or marionette over the human dancer. But to make certain that his point has, in fact, been understood he spells it out in a passage previously quoted but worth repeating here since it is germane to the reading of the Rilke elegy:

We see how in the organic world, as reflection grows darker and weaker, grace emerges ever more radiant and majestic. But just as the intersection of two lines, on one side of a point, suddenly turns up, after the passage through infinity, on the other side, or the image in a concave mirror, after it vanishes into infinity, suddenly reappears right before our eyes, so will grace, after knowledge similarly undergoes a journey through infinity, return to us. It is just at that moment that it will appear most purely in that bodily form that has either no consciousness at all or an infinite one; that is to say, in the puppet or in the god. (12)

Kleist's narrator essentially concurs, saying at the end of the essay: "That means that we would have to eat of the tree of knowledge a second time to fall back into the state of innocence." By reaching beyond the self, by freeing oneself of the distractions and dualities of consciousness—indeed, by transcending personal consciousness—one can regain unity. Rilke's view in the fourth elegy is distinctly similar. Once the self is overcome, one stands before the possibility of a heretofore unrealizable interaction of the material world, represented by the puppet figure, and the transcendent world, represented by the figure of an angel. The two polarities, the puppet as unconscious (the opposite of *self-conscious*) unity, and the angel (or god, as in Kleist) as superconscious unity, come together and reveal the path to harmony with the world. In expressing the same sentiments in his elegy, Rilke continues the earlier theatrical image. When the viewer, the poet, sinks completely into the puppet stage, understands it transcendentally—in other words, in the Kleistian sense, by emptying out his own consciousness—he can then behold the angel appearing as puppeteer to direct the real performance of unity regained:

> when I am in the mood
> to wait before the puppet stage, no,
> to watch it so intensely that, in order
> finally to compensate for my watching, as puppeteer
> an angel must come to set the puppets in motion.
> Angel and puppet. Now we will have a play.
> Now will there come together what we always
> Divide because of our presence. Now for the first time
> will the completed cycle of all change emerge
> from our seasons as well. Now will the angel perform over us.
>
> (276)

Meditating on human self-consciousness and its fettering of the spirit, Rilke finds himself inevitably drawn to the world of the child. For the poet, the child's realm is a state preceding the development or formation of self-consciousness. Childhood thus lends itself to easy idealization as a time of innocence, of intuitiveness; the child is one with its world, and the separation, or disjointedness, attributable to self-consciousness has not yet set in. The objects that fill the child's imaginative realm are an integral part of its existence; the adult's duality, rooted in the awareness of inevitable separation, has not yet entered to disrupt the essential unity. Hence the note of nostalgia and yearning struck in the following lines:

> O hours of childhood,
> when behind the figures was more than only
> the past and before us not the future.
> We were indeed growing and we pressed sometimes
> to grow up soon, half for the sake of those
> who had nothing else but grownupness.
> And were nevertheless satisfied in our being alone
> with duration and stood there
> in the space between world and toy,
> in a place which from the beginning
> had been destined for a pure event.
>
> (277)

Unlike the adult, the child inhabits, and is content with inhabiting, a place of duration. Progression, in any temporal sense, means little or nothing. Thus the discomfort that comes with the perception of advancing time remains unfelt, and the child, like the angel encountered previously in the elegy, enjoys a certain timelessness.

As he advances toward the finale of his poem, Rilke tries to come to grips with the matter of the inevitable death of the child. For whatever the timelessness of the child's world, its unity, the child continues to move through life to death. How, Rilke asks, can one depict the child, timeless and yet corporeal, unaware of mortality and yet destined to die? He poses this question at the beginning of the elegy's concluding section, acknowledging the transcendent dimension of childhood (the child is placed among the stars) and the child's superiority over the adult in that the child has placed in its hand the "measure of distance, or space," signifying the distance between the still whole, or unified, world of the child and the disjointed one of the adult who is now trying to depict the child.

Who portrays a child as he really is? Who places
him among the stars and puts the measuring rod
of distance in his hand?

(277)

From here, the poet passes to a juxtaposition of the child's privileged
position among the stars and its inescapable physical reality. Notwithstanding the superiority of the child's consciousness over that of the
adult's self-consciousness, the child is mortal and hence must share the
fate of all living things. But the poet ultimately is forced to acknowledge
the difficulty in trying to depict the child, and the child's realm, transcen-
dental and physical at the same time, timeless yet containing within itself
the death that awaits all mortals. The complexity of the task is suggested
above all in the striking reference to the ease with which murderers can
be understood:

Who makes the child's death
of gray bread that hardens—or leaves
it inside the rounded mouth like the core
of a beautiful apple? . . . Murderers
are easy to understand.

(277)

The importance of the puppet figure for Rilke is manifest not only in
the fourth Duino elegy, though this is by all means the occurrence with the
broadest ramifications for the development of his thought. In early 1914,
thus within a year before the composition of his elegy, Rilke wrote a short
(ten-and-a-half-page) essay on dolls (or puppets, since *Puppe* in German
can mean one or the other). The essay is titled simply *Puppen* and is dedicated to the wax figures created by Lotte Pritzel, a puppeteer whom Rilke
had met in Munich in October 1913 on the occasion of an exhibition of
her work. He entered into a correspondence with her in late 1913 and
early 1914 and met her once again in spring 1914. The essay first appeared
in the Leipzig monthly *Die Weissen Blätter* in March 1914 (no. 7). Wolfgang Leppman comments on it in his biography of the poet: "Like much
of what he wrote at the time, these few pages also represent a kind of finger
exercise for the *Elegies*, in the fourth of which the doll would be given an
important function."[5]

Although Pritzel's life-size wax figures were mostly of grown-up fe-
males of little or no particular interest to children, they stimulated Rilke's

recollection of his own childhood affection for toys and his belief in their eventual harmful effect on the child's psyche and its later relationship toward the world.[6] At one point in the essay, the poet draws a curious contrast between the affective power of the marionette (*Marionette*) and that of the doll or puppet (*Puppe*):

> A poet can fall under the spell of a marionette, since the marionette is nothing but fantasy. The doll has none and is just that much less than a thing than the marionette is more. But this being-less-than-a-thing, in its utter incurableness, holds the secret of its predominance. The child must accustom itself to things, it has to accept them; each thing has its pride.

Rilke then goes on to examine the lowly status of the doll in relation to other objects, and the nature of the child's relationship with it:

> Things tolerate the doll, nothing loves it. One can imagine the table knocking it off; hardly does one wish it away than it appears again on the floor. Beginners in the world, as we were, we could not be superior to anything, except to such a half object, which was set down next to us the way one puts bits and pieces of things next to the fish in aquariums so that they might find in them a measure and sign of their environment. We oriented ourselves on the doll. . . . But we soon perceived that we could not make it into a thing or a person, and at such moments it became something unknown to us, and everything familiar that we had filled it with and heaped on it became unknown to us in it.
>
> That we did not make you then into an idol, you puppet, and did not succumb to you in fear, was, I want to tell you, because it was not *you* we had in mind. We had in mind something quite different, invisible, that we held over and above ourselves and you, secretly and full of presentiment, and for which we both were only pretexts, so to speak. We had in mind a soul—the puppet soul. . . . Only one could not rightly say *where* you, puppet soul, really were.[7]

Because of its passivity, its lifelessness, the doll (or puppet) is unable to respond to or return the affection lavished on it by the child. Unable to animate it, the child assumes the role of the figure represented by the doll. Thus the conversations between the child and the doll are conversations between the child and itself. For Rilke, this indicates the child's first loss of unity with the world, which is replaced by an attitude, or relationship, of skepticism or even hostility.

A comparison of the short essay *Puppen* and the fourth Duino elegy reveals the complexity of Rilke's thought. In the essay, which actually ante-dates the elegy, the focus is on the pernicious role played by the doll in the child's life. The discovery that the doll is incapable of responding, despite efforts to make it respond as well as the love lavished on it, becomes the source of the child's first disappointment. At least, this is how Rilke chooses to view it. The unity of the child and its world is thus compromised. But the puppet motif of the fourth elegy is introduced primarily for the purpose of contrasting the unity represented by the puppet as an entity lacking consciousness and the disunity of the dancer as a symbol of personal self-consciousness.

MAURICE MAETERLINCK, PUPPETS, AND SYMBOLIST DRAMA

The human-being-as-puppet metaphor assumes a metaphysical deterministic basis for the first time significantly at the turn of the century in the plays of the once internationally celebrated and now largely ignored Belgian writer and thinker Maurice Maeterlinck. Although remembered as the author primarily of *Pelléas et Mélisande* (*Pelleas and Melisande*, first performed in 1893), on which Debussy based his equally famous opera, and *L'Oiseau bleu* (*The Blue Bird*, first performed, in Moscow, in 1907), Maeterlinck first attracted attention as a dramatist with several plays of a shadowy otherworldliness, vague medieval settings, and a preoccupation with death. The Symbolist orientation of the plays was immediately apparent. Their style—rhythmical, incantatory dialogue, poetic and musical structure, strange, mysterious characters, the subordination of action to mood, a portentous atmosphere—was different, new, and totally at odds with the prevailing patterns of realistic and naturalistic drama. It is evident above all in such early short plays as *L'Intruse* (*The Intruder*) and *Les Aveugles* (*The Blind*), both first performed in 1891 at the Théâtre d'Art of the Symbolist director Aurélien-Marie Lugné-Poe, and in the trilogy of "little plays for marionettes" published in 1894 and comprising *Alladine et Palomides* (*Alladine and Pallomides*, never performed), *L'Intérieur* (*On the Inside*), and *La Mort de Tintagiles* (*The Death of Tintagiles*).

Although Maeterlinck might conceivably have intended his early trilogy of plays "for marionettes" to be performed by marionettes, the greater likelihood is that they were written for living actors performing in the manner of marionettes. Now mostly forgotten as a dramatist, Maeterlinck was an early and major force in the development of Symbolist theater; and it was principally his short plays of the 1890s which were in-tended as exemplary in this respect. The metaphysical and supernatural proclivities of Symbolism obviously demanded a new kind of drama, one capable of drawing an audience into the mysteries of the human soul. Maeterlinck's achievement lay in demonstrating the feasibility of such a drama. In the best, and most representative, of his early plays, the center of gravity has shifted from external action—which Maeterlinck derided as diversionary—to the real drama of man, which in his opinion was spiri-tual. The preoccupation of realism and naturalism with man's corporeal and social existence was abandoned in favor of an emphasis on the spiri-tual and eternal. The body was doomed to death and decay, but the spirit lived on and therefore deserved to be man's proper concern.

Now, how did Maeterlinck realize the metaphysical outlook of Symbol-ism in dramatic form? In reducing external action to a negligible quantity, he also minimized movement, thereby making it easier to stylize in the measured, otherworldly rhythms of the play. The proximity of death cre-ated the dominant mood, which was ominous, grim, full of foreboding. Only in the presence of death, the gateway to the mysterious beyond, does one become acutely aware of one's spiritual nature. Thus it was in the ap-proach of death and the individual reaction to it that the dramatic conflict came to be located.

Appropriate to the new contents of Symbolist drama were the new dia-logue and the new stylization of acting. The metaphysicality of the play necessitated dialogue as far removed as possible from the accents and rhythms of everyday speech, from the speech, in other words, of realism and naturalism. Maeterlinck's solution to the problem of how to create such dialogue was, as I suggested earlier, to bring the speech of his charac-ters as close as possible to the texture of music and poetry. Hence its delib-erateness, its repetitions, and its pauses. Words matter less in the arche-typical Maeterlinckian Symbolist play than their evocative power, the mood they create, the sense of uneasiness they induce in the viewer. Since Maeterlinck believed that what was unsaid was often more important than what was said, silence or longer-than-average pauses in the dialogue are as aesthetically important as unpainted spaces in traditional Japanese painting. The movements of the actors also had to fall in line with the other elements in the play; that is to say, the physical—or gestural—lan-guage onstage had to replicate the rhythms of the dialogue, the emphasis on internal as opposed to external action, and the mood of solemnity and portentousness. This was accomplished by stylizing the movements of the actors in such a way that they no longer resembled everyday reality. The tempo was slowed, and gestures became more studied, "artificial," if you will.

The relative absence of external action in Maeterlinck's programmatic Symbolist plays, together with the stylization of speech, gesture, and movement, made for an undeniably static quality. But this was precisely what Maeterlinck sought in his "new" drama, as he himself set forth his views on the matter in a famous essay, "Le Tragique quotidien" ("The Tragedy of the Everyday"), included in his book *Le Trésor des humbles* (*The Treasure of the Humble*, 1896). The impact of these views and Maeterlinck's playwriting on contemporary dramatists desperate to end the hegemony of realism and naturalism and thereby resolve the perceived "crisis" of the stage is splendidly exemplified in the plays of Chekhov. Like Maeterlinck, and patently under the Belgian's influence, Chekhov wrote a type of play which, while different in important respects from those of Maeterlinck, was long on mood and short on external action in any conventional sense. Again, as in Maeterlinck, but lacking his grimness and fixation on death, Chekhov concentrated on atmospherics and the diminution of the importance of speech as well as external action. Pauses are also an important ingredient in the Chekhovian play, as is the language of gesture and the emotional subtext.

Although less immediately obvious in Chekhov than in Maeterlinck, the plays of both turn-of-the-century dramatists illuminate the particular appeal of the puppet and marionette in the period. Maeterlinck designated his 1894 trilogy as plays "for marionettes" because of his desire to use the plays not just as vehicles for his ideas on static and stylized drama but also as metaphysical stage metaphors. That is to say, the plays embody a metaphysical viewpoint for which Maeterlinck devised what he regarded as an appropriate dramatic style. Man, believed Maeterlinck (and, as we shall see in due course, the belief was shared by other modernist artists), was dominated by supernatural forces over which he had no control. He was, in other words, a plaything in the hands of fate, death, his fear of the unknown. As such, he could be likened to a marionette compelled by his own helplessness to follow the direction of the strings or wires held by these powers. Probably the best of Maeterlinck's short plays "for marionettes," *L'Intérieur* can serve as a good introduction to his dramatic style and the metaphysical outlook his early plays especially were meant to embody.

The subject of the play, outwardly, is death, specifically the death of a young girl by drowning and, in all likelihood, suicide. As usual in Maeterlinck, the death itself is unseen. More important is its impact on the living, who because of the death are reminded of their own mortality. Maeterlinck has created a highly effective dramatic tension through space, both temporal and physical. The dead girl's family—her father, mother, two sisters, and a child—who are inside their house (hence the play's title, literally "Interior" but better rendered as "On the Inside") are unaware of what has happened to her. They remain silent throughout the play. They are always seen from outside, through the windows of the house. The setting, as one might expect, is night. The only illumination comes from lamps on the inside. Another set of characters, who speak—an old man, his granddaughters, a stranger, a peasant, and a crowd of people—occupy the external area, that is, the garden outside the house. Just as they are separated spatially from the family inside the house, they are also separated from it in a temporal way—they already know that the young girl has drowned and are bringing the news of her tragic death to the family. Thus, in a symbolic collective sense, the people outside the house represent Death, and more important, since they are bringing news of the girl's death to her family, they represent the *approach* of Death, which is usually the most dynamic element in the early Maeterlinck play.

Since the family members in the house never speak and barely move, their silence not only establishes the importance of this element of the Maeterlinck play but also creates an ominous and suspenseful mood for the inevitable visitation of Death. In symbolic terms, the implication is that the family, not only by being inside the house but also by having virtually barricaded itself in, is doing its utmost to keep Death at bay. All the doors are closed, the windows are barred with iron, the walls of the old house themselves have been strengthened, and the three oaken doors have been bolted. The symbolic inference, of course, is that the family inside the house is everyman, who attempts to do his utmost to deny his own mortality in the delusion that somehow Death can be thwarted. But, as the play demonstrates, no matter what defenses one erects against Death, its coming is inevitable.

The silence on the inside and the paucity of movement also facilitate the stylization Maeterlinck sought to achieve. Movements are few and deliberate. Toward the end, when the famly becomes aware of their daughter's drowning, they act out a silent tragedy, a pantomime, in essence, of the impact of death. The people on the outside fulfil other functions. They are the bearers of sad tidings and, as they deliberate among themselves on when to break the news to the family, they acquaint the audience with the dead girl's background. At the same time they describe the appearance and activity, such as it is, of the family on the inside. Thus, in the space of a very short play, Maeterlinck has succeeded in delineating three perspectives: the family members on the inside, looking out, saying nothing, unaware of the drama being played out around them; the people outside observing them, describing them, and speculating on their reactions to the news soon to be delivered to them; and the audience, able to see both groups, as well as the family on the inside through the observations of the people in the garden.

When the time comes for those inside to learn of the girl's death, it is as if they intuit the approach of misfortune. The two sisters at one point go to different windows and peer, expectantly, into the darkness. The elder smiles, but the eyes of the younger one are "full of fear." Outside, the Old Man, referring to the crowd slowly making its way toward the house with the body of the drowned girl, universalizes the nature of the experience: "Although they turn their backs to it, misfortune is approaching one step at a time and has grown larger for more than two hours past. They cannot prevent it from growing larger; and those who are bringing it are powerless to stop it . . . It is also their master and they must serve it . . . It knows its goal, and it takes its course. It is untiring and has but one idea."[8] The meaning is plain. When it is time for Death to come, no one and nothing can bar its way, and the efforts of the family inside the house to do so are futile. The Old Man speaks directly of this futility when he tells one of his granddaughters: "They have too much confidence in this world . . . There they are, separated from the enemy by some poor panes of glass . . . They think that nothing will happen because they have closed the doors and they do not know that it is in the soul that things happen and that the world does not end at the doors to their house" (190–91).

At the end of the play, the Old Man finally takes it upon himself to go in and tell the family what has happened to the missing daughter. The scene on the inside is described from without by the Stranger. The crowd that has by now gathered around him presses close to the windows to see

better. All the action inside, when the family comes forward to greet the
Old Man, is mimed, the gestures speaking far more eloquently than any
words of the tragedy that now strikes. The only voices heard are those of
the Stranger, as a reporter of the events inside, and those of the crowd, acting to all intents and purposes like a Greek chorus. Death, having broken
down their pitiful defenses, has come to the family members, who at last
go outside to claim their dead daughter.

The concept of man as self-deluded into believing he controls his own
destiny underlies most of Maeterlinck's dramatic writing and especially
the early programmatic Symbolist plays represented by *On the Inside*.
Not only does man not control his own destiny, Maeterlinck suggests; he
does not know who does—some omnipotent being, fate, death, chance.
Hence the appropriateness of the puppet or marionette metaphor and the
dramatic style that embodies it. Given the brevity of a play such as *On the
Inside*, the primacy in it of gesture, and its rhythm, it is not hard to imagine
it being performed by marionettes. But if that never was Maeterlinck's
purpose, the movements of the characters onstage and especially the
mimed action of the family inside the house are clearly intended to convey
to the audience a viewpoint of man as marionette. Only at one point is direct reference made to the idea of man as a doll-like figure. This is when
the Old Man tells the Stranger, speaking about the drowned girl:

> Perhaps she was one of those who have nothing to say, and every one bears
> within himself more than one reason not to live . . . You cannot see into the
> soul the way you can into that room. They are all like that . . . They say
> nothing but trivial things, and no one suspects a thing. . . . They have the
> look of lifeless dolls [or puppets, *poupées immobiles*], and yet so many
> things are passing in their souls (181).

GOING THE MARIONETTE ONE BETTER:
EDWARD GORDON CRAIG AND THE SUPERMARIONETTE

The influence of Maeterlinck's new Symbolist drama was enormous, as
evidenced in the case of Chekhov. But Maeterlinck's antirealistic, highly
stylized writing, as well as his furtherance of the man-as-marionette metaphor, resonated also in contemporary theatrical theory, as the career of the
outstanding English director Edward Gordon Craig bears out.[9] Maeterlinck's influence on Craig need not, however, be exaggerated, despite
Craig's interest in the Belgian and his desire to stage his works. In some

sense it may be more important to view Maeterlinck's dramatic writing and Craig's theatrical innovations as basically similar responses to the same stimuli. From this perspective, Craig's work in the theater paralleled that of Maeterlinck in the drama without the issue of influence having to be excessively argued or demonstrated. Like Maeterlinck, Craig was an ardent exponent of an antirealistic and antinaturalistic stylized theater. His models were classical Greek theater and the theatrical conventions of the Far East, Japan in particular, which were attracting considerable attention among artists at the turn of the century. Like Maeterlinck, Craig also played down the primacy and importance of spoken language onstage, shifting the emphasis to the language of the body as a more felicitous vehicle of stylization.

Although he actually wrote plays for marionettes, which curiously lack real literary or theatrical merit,[10] Craig's enthusiasm for puppet and marionette related mostly to his desire to transform the human actor into a totally submissive instrument by means of which the director, who now stood at the center of the production, could realize his personal vision of the theatrical work. Reminiscent of Anatole France's remarks on the marionette mystery plays of Maurice Bouchor and especially Kleist's essay *On the Marionette Theater*, which he undoubtedly knew, Craig regarded the human actor's very humanness, his self-consciousness and emotions, as his greatest flaw. Since this was an insurmountable obstacle, Craig fantasized about substituting puppets and marionettes for the living actor. But his pronouncements on the subect did not have as their goal the elimination of the theater of human actors. He makes this point unequivocally in his well-known essay, *The Actor and the Über-marionette* (1907):

In the beginning the human body was not used as material in the Art of the Theatre. In the beginning the emotions of men and women were not considered as a fit exhibition for the multitude. An elephant and a tiger in an arena suited the taste better, when the desire was to excite. . . .

As I have written elsewhere, the theatre will continue its growth and actors will continue for some years to hinder its development. But I see a loophole by which in time the actors can escape from the bondage they are in. They must create for themselves a new form of acting, consisting for the main part of symbolical gesture. Today they *impersonate* and interpret; tomorrow they must *represent* and interpret; and the third day they must create.[11]

Nevertheless, Craig's idealization and mythicization of the puppet and marionette, expressed with his characteristic flair for exaggeration and self-dramatization, could easily have been regarded as a call for a new theater of inanimate beings. Elsewhere in *The Actor and the Über-marionette* he writes:

> The actor must go, and in his place comes the inanimate figure—the Über-marionette [supermarionette] we may call him, until he has won for himself a better name. Much has been written about the puppet, or marionette. There are some excellent volumes on him, and he has also inspired several works of art. To-day in his least happy period many people come to regard him as rather a superior doll—and to think he has developed from the doll. He is a descendant of the stone images of the old temples—he is to-day a rather degenerate form of a god. . . . (85–86)
>
> To speak of a puppet with most men and women is to cause them to giggle. They think at once of the wires; they think of the stiff hands and the jerky movements; they tell me it is "a funny little doll." But let me tell them a few things about these puppets. Let me again repeat that they are the descendants of a great and noble family of Images, images which were indeed made "in the likeness of god"; and that many centuries ago these figures had a rhythmical movement and not a jerky one; had no need for wires to support them, nor did they speak through the nose of a hidden manipulator. . . .
>
> I pray earnestly for the return of the image—the Über-marionette to the Theatre; and when he comes again and is but seen, he will be loved so well that once more will it be possible for the people to return to their ancient joy in ceremonies—once more will Creation be celebrated—homage rendered to existence—and divine and happy intercession made to Death. (87)

Craig's term *Über-marionette* was obviously inspired by Nietzsche's concept of the *Übermensch*, the superman who achieves the strength of will to overcome his own weaknesses and rise above the limitations of Judeo-Christian morality. In Craig's thinking, the *Über-marionette* was to be the actor who overcomes his own human limitations, psychological, emotional, and even physical, by modeling himself instead on the puppet and marionette—emotionless, obedient, the perfect servant of his master's will. The master, of course, was to be the theatrical director; by making himself utterly submissive to the director, to be operated by him like a puppet or marionette, the actor could achieve the status of an *Über-marionette*. The point comes through clearly, notwithstanding Craig's usual flamboyance, in the essay *Gentlemen, The Marionette* (1912):

> There is only one actor—nay, one man—who has the soul of the dramatic poet, and who has ever served as true and loyal interpreter of the poet. This is the marionette. So let me introduce you to him. . . .
>
> The marionette, through his true virtues of obedience and silence, leaves to his sons a vast inheritance. He leaves to them the promise of a new art.
>
> The marionette is a little figure, but he has given birth to great ones who, if they preserve the two essentials, obedience and silence, shall preseve their race. The day that they hunger for further power they shall surely fall.
>
> These children of his I have called Über-marionettes, and have written of them at some length.
>
> What the wires of the Über-marionette shall be, what shall guide him, who can say? I do not believe in the mechanical, nor in the material. The wires which stretch from divinity to the soul of the poet are wires which might command him. Has God no more such threads to spare—for one more figure? I cannot doubt it. I will never believe anything else.
>
> And did you think when I wrote five years ago of this new figure who should stand as the symbol of man—and when I christened him the Über-marionette—to see real metal or silken threads?
>
> I hope that another five years will be long enough for you to draw those tangleable wires out of your thoughts. (26)

THE CABARET: PUPPETS, MARIONETTES, SHADOW SHOWS, AND LIVING DOLLS

Craig's enthusiasm for puppet and marionette was echoed in the contemporary cabaret. As a refuge for scrious artists, and as an alternate performance environment, the cabaret—or what the French refer to as *cabaret artistique* ("artistic cabaret")—dates only from the late nineteenth century.[12] It was by and large a product of those same impulses that gave rise to modernism. Although cabarets as tavernlike drinking places with often rudish impromptu entertainment had existed for centuries, the new cabaret of the turn of the century emerged as an expression of a changing sensibility. It was antibourgeois, antitraditional, antiacademic, and oriented toward the symbiosis of "high" and "low" cultures. Since the early cabarets, unlike those that dotted the map of Europe in the post–World War I era, were primarily elitist rather than commercial in nature, their premises were generally, though not always, on the small side. By elitist, I mean that the cabarets were established by artists mostly for artists and their fellow travelers. Some permitted free access to the general public; others did so on a limited basis only; some did not do so at all.

The small dimensions of the early cabarets meant that the area set aside for performance also tended to be limited in size. These spatial limitations favored the "small art" (*Kleinkunst*, in German) so typical of the cabaret, which, relative to other arts of the period, should itself be regarded as a type of small art. The entertainments usually subsumed under the rubric of small art include chanson and ballad singing (above all in Paris and Munich); poetic recitations, often of an experimental character (as in the Zurich cabaret, the home of Dada); monologues (as in the Parisian Chat Noir); dancers, solo or group (especially in Berlin, Vienna, and Zurich); puppet and marionette theater (in virtually all the early cabarets, but of particular interest in Barcelona, Munich, Vienna, and Cracow); shadow shows—which originated in the Chat Noir and were widely imitated in other European cabarets; "living doll" routines (human actors imitating puppets or marionettes), as in the Letuchaya mysh (Bat) cabaret in Moscow; short dramatic works, mostly one-act sketches, written for cabaret performance (particularly in Berlin, Munich, Vienna, and St. Petersburg); and pantomime (in Munich, Moscow, and St. Petersburg).

Although puppet and marionette shows were offered in the Chat Noir, they soon yielded in importance to the two entertainments for which this most celebrated of all pre–World War I cabarets became famous, chansons and shadow shows. Puppetry fared considerably better in the Barcelona Quatre Gats (Four Cats), in which the young Picasso participated. Established in 1897 primarily by a small group of Catalan painters, the Quatre Gats achieved distinction as a showcase for Catalan artistic creativity at a time when a vigorous Catalan cultural revival coincided with the emergence of the modernist movement. The emphasis was heavily on the Catalan (as opposed to Castilian) creative genius. This favored a new cultivation of Catalan native arts, one of the most prominent of which was puppet theater. Called *putxinel-lis* in Catalan, the puppet shows of the Quatre Gats won an immediate following after their introduction in late 1898 and were presented on an elaborately tiled miniature theater that was the highlight of the cabaret's interior. If the lack of original source material and documentation makes it difficult to reconstruct the puppet shows staged there, contemporary accounts by visitors to the cabaret provide at least a tantalizing glimpse. This is the case, for example, with the section dealing with his visit to Barcelona, and the Quatre Gats, in the travel book, *España contemporanea* (1901), by the celebrated Nicaraguan poet Rubén Dario:

> Since it was the day for the marionettes, I stayed to watch the performance. . . . The puppets are somewhat like those which once upon a time attracted the curiosity of Paris with the mysteries of Bouchor, little pieces by Richepin, and others. For similar actors of wood Maeterlinck composed his most beautiful dramas of profundity and dream. There in the Quatre Gats they were not all badly manipulated. I arrived there after the performance had begun. . . . Mugs of bock beer circulated to the accompaniment of the screeching of the puppets. Naturally, the puppets of the Quatre Gats speak Catalan, and I could barely make out what was happening onstage. It was a work of local character, which must have been very witty since everyone was laughing so much. About all I was able to understand was that blows with a club rained down on one of the characters, as in Molière, and the police came off badly. The stage settings are real little paintings and one can see that whoever organized this diminutive theater did it with love and care.[13]

Puppet shows also became a regular early feature of the most important pre–World War I German cabaret, the Elf Scharfrichter (Eleven Executioners) in Munich. In existence from 1901 to 1903, the cabaret presented not only puppet performances, which followed the pattern of cabarets elsewhere, but also drew on the talents of an active community of puppeteers in Munich's bohemian Schwabing district at the time. The most renowned of these was the sculptor Waldemar Heckler, who was affiliated, like Kandinsky's friend Alexander von Salzmann, with the famous Marionetten Theater Münchener Künstler (Munich Artists' Marionette Theater), which Paul Brann had founded in 1905 and which won justifiable acclaim through the 1930s for its productions of operas as well as plays by Goethe, Molière, Maeterlinck, and others. Munich, in fact, had an interesting antecedent tradition of puppet theater.[14] In 1858, Joseph Leonhard ("Papa") Schmid established the first permanent puppet theater in the city. One of the principal writers of plays for it was Count Franz Pocci, director of the court musicians and later lord high chamberlain. In 1900, at the beginning of the German modernist interest in puppets and marionettes, the Munich municipal authorities honored Schmid by building a special theater for him.

Of the puppet shows staged at the Elf Scharfrichter, the best known were Willi Rath's *Die feine Familie* (*The Fine Family*), subtitled *Ein europaisches Drama in 3 Sensationen und einem Prologo* (*A European Drama in Three Sensations and One Prologue*), and Otto Falckenberg and Paul Larsen's *Prinzessin Pim und Laridah, Ihr Sänger* (*Princess Pim and Laridah, Her Singer*), subtitled *Grosse Kartoffel-, Rettig-, Rüben- und Apfeltragödie, Insceniert und mit eigenem Obst und Gemüse aufgeführt von Paul Larsen* (*A Great Potato-, Radish-, Beet-, and Apple-Tragedy. Staged and Performed with His Own Fruit and Vegetables by Paul Larsen*). Performed on the opening program of the cabaret on 12 April 1901, Rath's *Fine Family* is a sharp satire against Germany's growing imperialist ambitions set in the time of the Boer War in South Africa and the Boxer Rebellion in China. *Princess Pim and Laridah, Her Singer* is a more traditional puppet theater fairy tale; it made its debut at the Elf Scharfrichter on the March-April program of 1902.

Puppet theater was a more marginal feature of the programs of Vienna's Fledermaus (Bat), the most brilliant of the former Habsburg capital's cabarets. The visiting Munich Artists' Marionette Theater presented the naïve puppet shows of Count Pocci featuring the German folk figure Kasperl and also staged, as a puppet show, Arthur Schnitzler's *Der tapfere Kassian* (*The Gallant Cassian*), one of a trilogy of small plays by Schnitzler in which the puppet/marionette motif operates primarily metaphorically. By far the most arresting Austrian theatrical work inspired by the puppet and marionette mania of the turn of the century was the painter-playwright Oskar Kokoschka's short play *Sphinx und Strohmann* (*Sphinx and Strawman*). In the form in which it was staged at the Fledermaus on 12 March 1909, the work was designated a "comedy for automatons." Dealing with the then modish theme of sexual conflict, the work delineates its principals as living marionettes totally submissive to and manipulated by the power of sensuality. Together with Schnitzler's marionette plays of 1903, *Sphinx and Strawman* is discussed in a separate section elsewhere in this book.

One fairly original contribution of the Vienna Fledermaus to the theatrical culture of the early-twentieth-century cabaret was a combination of puppetry and pantomime in the form of animated illustrations in the tradition of *tableaux vivants*. The best example of the style was a social satire entitled *Die Wohltäter* (*The Do-Gooders*), which the cabaret staged in March 1908. Based on a text by the Norwegian writer and caricaturist

Olaf Gulbransson, who was a frequent contributor to the famous Munich satire magazine *Simplicissimus* (where *The Do-Gooders* first appeared), the work assumed the form of an illustration come to life in a series of short scenes. Although the success of the *Do Gooders* was not repeated at the Fledermaus, similar animated illustrations became the most successful and "transportable" entertainment offered by the most famous of all Russian cabarets, the Letuchaya mysh in Moscow. It came into existence in 1908, and its "living doll" routines surpassed in brilliance their Viennese forebears.

Supporting the interest in puppetry of the Fledermaus in Vienna was the distinguished applied arts collective known as the Wiener Werkstätte (Vienna Workshops). The Viennese equivalent of similar turn-of-the-century collectives elsewhere in Europe, the Wiener Werkstätte turned out everything from postcards to furniture and also became closely affiliated with the Fledermaus. At one time, the Werkstätte had planned to establish its own marionette theater and invite as its director the great Czech-German puppeteer Richard Teschner, creator of the unique form of puppet theater known as *Figurenspiegel*. Unfortunately, for reasons still unclear, the plan never materialized. All that remained of it was the enthusiasm for puppet and marionette theater brought to the Fledermaus by Werkstätte artists who collaborated with it.

One of the most striking examples of the embrace of puppet theater by the pre–World War I cabaret was Cracow's Zielony Balonik (Green Balloon). The first cabaret in Poland's history, the Green Balloon opened on 7 October 1905. Elitist in nature, its performers and clienetele were recruited mostly from Cracow's community of artists and intellectuals. Its moving spirit was a medical doctor named Tadeusz Żeleński, who wrote under the pen name Boy. As time went on, Boy's medical practice took a back seat to his literary activity. He had a superb command of French and French culture and became an extraordinarily prolific translator of French literature. His knowledge of cabaret was acquired in Paris, where, he confessed, he developed a lifelong love affair with the Parisian chanson. It was Boy who imported the chanson to Cracow and who became the principal contributor of chansons, mostly satirical in nature, to the Green Balloon. Boy also took a leading part in the preparation of the cabaret's annual *szopka*, or puppet show, once that entertainment came to be presented at Green Balloon evenings.

The *szopka* was an indigenous Cracovian Nativity puppet show in

Richard Teschner, Marionette.
(Courtesy Bildarchiv der Österreichischen Nationalbibliothek,
Vienna)

which wooden rod puppets depicting biblical and local characters and
made to speak in naïve, folkish style were intermixed on a two-level miniature stage modeled on the architecture of the Renaissance royal castle on
Wawel Hill or the late medieval Church of Mary in Cracow's main square.
Prompted, in part, by the popularity of puppet and marionette shows in
cabarets in Western Europe, but to a greater extent by the spellbinding adaptation of the *szopka* form to a play about contemporary Poland by the
outstanding Polish modernist dramatist Stanisław Wyspiański, Boy and

Rod puppets representing real personages used in
Cracow Green Balloon szopka.
(Courtesy Jagiellonian University Library, Cracow)

his fellow Green Ballooners set about adapting the *szopka* to cabaret performance. They devised a full evening's entertainment consisting of satirical songs and skits addressed to a variety of topical issues. The puppets were lovingly created by the artists who participated in Green Balloon evenings; for the most part, they represented caricatures of well-known Cracow personages.

The first Green Balloon *szopka*, of February 1906, proved such a great success that others were mounted, and they continued through 1912, when the cabaret began fading into oblivion. But the demise of the Green Balloon did not end the career of the *szopka* as premier Polish cabaret entertainment. In the interwar period, when Poland was again an independent state, cabaret life flourished in Warsaw. As elsewere in Europe during the same period, cabarets now catered mostly to paying customers and employed mostly professional entertainers. The transformation of the Polish cabaret from elitist to commercial had no profound effect on the genre of the *szopka*. The puppet show, which had long since lost any connections to its religious origins, proved extraordinarily viable despite the

Fragment of a wall painting in the Cracow Green Balloon
depicting participants in the cabaret carrying a szopka.
(Courtesy Jagiellonian University Library, Cracow)

changes in Polish social and cultural life in the transition from partition
to independence. Moving with the times, the *szopka* itself underwent a
slight transformation. Since political satire was virtually impossible in the
pre–World War I Cracow cabaret because of Austrian censorship, the emphasis was on social satire. But in independent Poland censorship functioned differently and political satire again became possible. Adjusting to
the change, the new interwar cabaret became a major vehicle of so-called
szopka polityczna (political satire), most of it curiously directed against
the foes of the authoritarian Piłsudski regime. The genre was a highlight of
the Warsaw cabaret virtually down to the German invasion in September 1939.

The popularity of puppet and marionette shows in the turn-of-the-century cabarets was challenged and possibly surpassed by another form of entertainment for which the cabaret functioned as a natural venue. That was the shadow show, a miniature theater of projected silhouettes commonly known by the French name, *ombres chinoises* ("Chinese shadows"). Shadow shows of different types were immensely popular in Asia and the Near East centuries before they appeared in Europe. One of the richest traditions was that of the Turkish *karagöz* ("black eye"), named for the principal figure, who was probably intended to represent a gypsy and was distinguished in appearance by a round face, a pug nose, thick curly black hair, and above all a very prominent large black eye (hence his name)—*eye* in the singular because *karagöz* is seen from only one side.[15]

European interest in "Chinese shadows" began to develop in the seventeenth century but attracted real interest only in the eighteenth, when so-called magic lanterns were employed for the projection of both human silhouettes and those of figures cut from cardboard and other materials.[16] The Swiss Johann Kaspar Lavater invented a machine for the projection of silhouettes that might also have been black and white drawings; in 1772 the Frenchman François-Dominique Séraphim established at the Hôtel Lannion in Versailles what was to become an immensely popular theater combining marionettes and silhouettes. The form was cultivated well into the nineteenth century, especially in France, where in the hands of one of its most talented practitioners, Louis Lemercier de Neuville, it became a sophisticated art form, technically and pictorially.[17] A professional journalist, Lemercier de Neuville became so fascinated by shadow shows he abandoned journalism in order to devote himself entirely to the design and projection of silhouette figures. He gave performances at literary and fashionable salons and was even invited to perform at the Tuileries.

The spectacular popularity of the shadow show at the turn of the century, above all among serious artists, cannot be explained merely by reference to the longstanding European interest in the form. Consideration has to be given, for example, to the stimulus represented by the new, more serious phase of Occidental interest in Oriental culture, especially painting and theater. Craig's enthusiasm for Japanese theater was anything but an isolated phenomenon. Participation by Oriental artists and performers in international expositions, exhibitions of Chinese and Japanese painting, and tours by Japanese and other theatrical and dance troupes attracted immense curiosity. The impact of this "rediscovered" or, in some cases, newly discovered world of Oriental art on an emerging European modernism was formidable. Symbolist metaphysicality also responded felicitously to the incorporeality, suggestiveness, and mysteriousness of projected shadow figures. Spatially, the shadow play seemed to acquire the dimension of a strange, almost mystic or psychic area lying beyond the boundaries of conventional perspective. More important, however, than the stimulus given by symbolism to the cultivation of "Chinese shadows" was the symbiosis of shadow play and mystery drama, which sank deep roots, as we shall see, in turn-of-the-century French theater. But modernist dramatists elsewhere—Valle-Inclán in Spain, Hjalmar Bergman in Sweden, and Massimo Bontempelli in Italy, for example—explored the metaphoric potential of shadows in plays at a greater remove from the fashionable Symbolist neomystery.

Arguably the greatest single stimulus to the popularity of shadow shows in turn-of-the-century Europe was the extraordinary level of production achieved at the Chat Noir cabaret in Paris.[18] Although virtually every form of cabaret entertainment was offered at the Chat Noir in its long history, chansons by popular singers and shadow shows soon became the greatest draw. The idea of introducing *ombres chinoises* at the cabaret originated with the artist Henri Rivière, to whom the founder and proprietor, Rodolphe Salis, had entrusted the production of the first puppet show. While working with puppets, Rivière thought of adding shadow shows to the cabaret's program as well. One night, as the chansonnier Jules Jouy was singing one of his most popular songs, "Sergots" ("Cops"), Rivière extginguished the lights in the auditorium and then, from behind a napkin suspended across the opening of the small stage used for the puppet shows, mimed Jouy's chanson with silhouettes cut out from cardboard.

It was from these modest beginnings that shadow shows went on to become one of the Chat Noir's leading attractions. By far the most ambitious, and certainly one of the most spectacular shadow shows produced at the Chat Noir was a vast Napoleonic epic in two acts and fifty tableaux. In its final version, the work was appropriately titled *L'Epopee* (*The Epic*); in its earlier, more modest form, it was known as *1808!* Its author was another well-known Parisian caricaturist and cabaret denizen, Caran d'Ache (real name Emmanuel Poiré). The scope of the shadow show and the audience's reaction to it at its inaugural performance were described by the writer Maurice Donnay, himself a contributor to Chat Noir shadow shows:

> The epopée consisted of the Italian, Egyptian, and Prussian campaigns; it was Marengo, Austerlitz, Wagram, and Jena; it was the reckless charges, the magnificent marches which, in the darkness of the auditorium, the gentle poet and pianist Albert Tinchant accompanied with appropriate music, stirring marches, patriotic songs, and bravura airs. Carried away by all these tableaux dedicated to French valor, stirred by the martial music, and electrified by the banter of Rodolphe Salis, the audience applauded and stamped its feet. When the silhouette of the Emperor appeared surrounded by his generals and the gentleman cabaretier [Salis] shouted "The Emperor!" the audience, impassioned, roared back "Long live the Emperor!" The windows of the room trembled. The shouts could be heard outside on the street. One could imagine that a Bonapartiste movement was ushering forth from the Chat Noir.[19]

As spectacular as Caran d'Ache's *L'Épopee* must surely have been, the adaptation of the "Chinese shadows" to the then highly fashionable mystery play was an even more striking development. Besides the Symbolists' efforts to revive the medieval mystery and adapt it to their own times and outlook, the writer Maurice Bouchor was assembling an impressive repertoire of his own mystery plays primarily for marionette theater performance. When the Chat Noir enhanced the reputation of its already popular *ombres chinoises* by presenting several mystery shadow plays of considerable technical sophistication, the genre entered the domain of the cabaret. The most famous were *La Tentation de Saint Antoine* (*The Temptation of Saint Anthony*), doubtless based on Flaubert's work of the same name but with a contemporary Parisian setting, and *La Marche à l'étoile* (*The Procession to the Star*), whose brilliance almost obscured its brevity—it ran for only ten minutes. In both instances, the production was designed by the very gifted Henri Rivière.

The important technical innovation of the Chat Noir mystery shadow shows was Rivière's abandonment of both cardboard and zinc cutouts in favor of colored glass panels on which not only individual figures but entire scenes were painted, with paints designed specifically for use on glass. When projected, these color scenes created the visual effect of motion pictures. Rivière also experimented with the mechanics of lighting and animation. As productions became more ambitious and the cast of characters in the shadow show grew in number, Rivière discovered that he could achieve more dynamic effects, especially with crowd scenes, by attaching the figures to one another so that a large number of them could be paraded across the screen in a broad band. The traditional practice had been to move each figure independently. Rivière was similarly innovative in the area of lighting. Set against the screen, in the traditional shadow show, the back-lit figures would project as true silhouettes, that is, uniformly black. In order to achieve a broader range of shades from solid black to a variety of grays, Rivière began placing his figures in grooves at different distances from the screen.

Writing his impressions of the Chat Noir's shadow plays, the prominent French critic Jules Lemaître observed that

> they have made of the 'Chinese shadows' the generalizing and philosophical art par excellence, an art that affords pleasure to children by its simplicity and supreme clarity, and to thoughtful mature minds by its power of synthesis, by everything that its black or colored blots convey. The shadows of Rivière and Caran d'Ache are truly the shadows of Plato's cave. That is because the outlines and appearance of things are the things themselves. All reality is nothing but a reflection.[20]

The great popularity of the shadow shows, some forty of which were produced at the Chat Noir, survived its closing in 1897. Even before the end of the greatest of all Parisian cabarets, shadow shows of one sort or another began springing up elsewhere. The chanson singer and cabaretier Vincent Hyspa, who in 1892 was one of the organizers of a Chat-Noiresque cabaret named Chien Noir (Black Dog) located on the faubourg Saint-Honoré, presented a *Noël* shadow play with music by Eric Satie and the shadows and stage décor designed by the Catalan artist Miquel Utrillo. (Utrillo was the father of the painter Maurice Utrillo and a member of a small cirlce of Catalan artists who had come to Paris, mostly from Barcelona, to assimilate the new trends in art.)[21] In 1892 the Théâtre des Ombres Lyriques du Lyon d'Or, which was devoted exclusively to shadow theater, was established. Between 1898 and 1900, shadow shows were regularly presented at the Théâtre d'Application (later the Théâtre de la Bodinière), located at 18 rue Saint-Lazare. Another *théâtre d'ombres*, La Boîte à Musique, opened on the boulevard Clichy in Pigalle in 1898. As if in acknowledgment of the contemporary enthusiasm over shadow shows, established Parisian theaters also began mounting their own productions. The famous Antoine, of the Théâtre Libre, staged *Le Juif errant* (*The Wandering Jew*) by Henri Rivière and Georges Fragerolle shortly after the turn of the century. The Théâtre des Mathurins followed suit with a program of shadow shows, among them the popular *Aladin* in fifteen tableaux by Lucien Métivier.

Several of the Chat Noir's epigones also tried to keep alive the tradition of cabaret shadow theater, but none more so than the Cabaret des Quat'z' Arts (Cabaret of the Four Arts). It was here in 1900 that Dominique Bonnaud mounted some of the most famous of the Chat Noir shadow shows as well as a few of his own. After leaving the Quat'z' Arts, Bonnaud installed himself in 1904 in the Cabaret de la Lune Rousse (April Moon Cabaret), which was first located on the boulevard de Clichy and later on the rue Pigalle. Under Bonnaud's direction virtually all the programs of the Lune Rousse consisted of shadow shows, and when the cabaret changed locations, its premises on Clichy were taken over by the Cabaret de la Chaumière (Thatched-Roof Cottage Cabaret), which continued featuring shadow shows.

The spectacular success of Parisian cabaret shadow theater inspired imitations throughout Europe as the cabaret phenomenon itself spread from Barcelona to Petersburg. The most impressive experiments with the form, after Paris, were in Barcelona, Munich, and Vienna. At the Quatre Gats (1897–1903) in Barcelona, the prime mover behind the cabaret's shadow shows was Miquel Utrillo, whom we met before as a participant in programs of the Parisian Chien Noir. Once back in his native Barcelona and armed with his extensive Parisian experience, Utrillo threw himself with a passion into the organization of the cabaret's shadow theater. He was assisted by the painter Pere Romeu, another founding father of the Quatre Gats and, like Utrillo, a Catalan denizen of Parisian cabaret life who had also participated in Léon-Charles Marot's Ombres Parisiennes on its tour of the Chicago World's Columbian Exposition in 1893.

Objectively speaking, the shadow shows presented at the Quatre Gats from 29 December 1897 until early April 1898 lacked the narrative and visual sweep of those for which the Chat Noir won justifiable renown. Despite Miquel Utrillo's enthusiasm and skill and the general high quality of the artwork, what the Quatre Gats lacked most was the elaboration of a specific shadow theater repertoire such as that of the Chat Noir's. In other words, there were too few artists with a strong commitment to shadow theater, apart from Utrillo himself. When this showed signs of changing, interest in the genre had already begun to wane. Another factor in the relatively early decline of shadow theater in the Barcelona cabaret was the overriding loyalty of the participating artists to the Catalan cultural renascence. Since shadow theater lacked any tradition in Catalonia and had been imported from Paris largely by Utrillo, the support for it was considerably narrower than for puppet theater, for example, which had a substantial indigenous history.

While similarly inspired by the popularity of the Parisian shadow theater, the interest in the genre among German artists in turn-of-the-century Munich eventually went deeper than that of their Catalan counterparts. Shadow shows began to be presented by the Elf Scharfrichter cabaret not long after its establishment. The May 1901 program reflected, however, the initial reliance on French sources, an acknowledgment of the absence of an authentic German shadow play tradition. It featured, as the cabaret's first shadow show, the well-known Parisian shadow epic *The Sphinx*. With background and figures designed by the artist Vignola, and with original music by Fragerolle, the work portrayed the dreams of the Sphinx from ancient Assyrian times to Napoleon's Egyptian campaign. It was a shadow play conceived along the panoramic lines of Caran d'Ache's *L'Epopee*. The writer Willi Rath, one of the Elf Scharfrichter's original "executioners," wrote the German text. The shadow show presented on the program of November 1901 was, however, an original German piece by the prolific cabaret dramatist Hanns von Gumppenberg (pseudonym Jodok). Titled *Truppen-Einzug in Berlin* (*Troop Entry into Berlin*), it was based on a work by the German Romantic writer Theodor Fontane. The shadow figures were created by the graphic artist Ernst Neumann, who, as "executioner" Kaspar Beil (the "eleven executioners" all took assumed names), bore responsibility for the sets and silhouettes of the cabaret's shadow theater. Otto Falckenberg, who later became director of the renowned Munich Chamber Theater (Kammerspiel) and was known at the Elf Scharfrichter as Peter Luft, conducted the performance. Shadow shows continued to be presented at the Munich cabaret until its demise in 1903. One of the more outstanding was another French import—the nine-scene show *Moissons* (*Harvests*; *Ernte*, in the German version) which Clément-Georges (Abel Georges Clément Moulin), who had performed at the Chat Noir, presented in October 1903. But, as in the case of the Quatre Gats in Barcelona, the emergence of a form evidently more felicitous to the genius of the cabaret eventually diminished the appeal of shadow shows. At the Quatre Gats, the revival of the native Catalan puppet tradition thrust the shadow show into obscurity. At the Elf Scharfrichter, dramatic productions came to dominate the programs. The development was logical, for two reasons. The cabaret, though small, had the most technically advanced stage of any European cabaret of its time and so was well equipped for compact but serious theater. Then, in the dramatist Hanns von Gumppenberg, who, as we have seen, also wrote at least one shadow show for it, the Elf Scharfrichter had a prolific dramatist who wrote a series of so-called *Überdramen* (*Superdramas*) specifically for cabaret performance. When Frank Wedekind also began performing his ballads at the Elf Scharfrichter and permitted a few of his early theater pieces to be staged there, the die was cast: Gumppenberg's and Wedekind's plays would establish the primacy of drama at the Elf Scharfrichter, followed by Wedekind's cabaret songs, sung either by him to his own guitar accompaniment or by the celebrated German cabaret singer Marya Delvard.

If shadow plays were displaced by regular dramatic productions at the Elf Scharfrichter, they sank roots elsewhere in Munich's vibrant turn-of-the-century artistic community. Of crucial importance to this development was the renowned circle of writers grouped around the figure of the poet Stefan George, above all the poet and dramatist Karl Wolfskehl.[22] Wolfskehl became a leading exponent of the mystery play as the drama of the future and took a keen interest in shadow theater. This interest found a major outlet in the Schwabinger Schattenspiele (Schwabing Shadow Plays, or Shadow Theater), which the prolific writer Alexander von Bernus, himself an enthusiast of the mystery play, established in 1907 on Ainmillerstrasse, in Munich's Schwabing district.[23] The small theater, devoted exclusively to shadow show performances, was immensely popular with the Stefan George circle, to which Bernus himself was close, as well as with other members of Munich's artistic community, including former leading lights of the Elf Scharfrichter cabaret. The Schwabing Shadow Theater lasted until 1912, which to all intents and purposes marked the end of Munich's "Schwabing era." In the five years of its existence, the theater gave nearly five hundred performances, more than four hundred alone during the "Munich 1908" exhibition, where the architect Fritz Klee designed a special stage for it alongside that of Paul Brann's Marionetten Theater.[24] The repertoire consisted to a great extent of adapted works by German Romantic writers (Joseph von Eichendorff, Friedrich de la Motte Fouqué, Heinrich Heine, Justinus Kerner, Ludwig Tieck, Eduard Mörike, and others), for whom Bernus felt a particular affinity; but it also included original shadow shows by Bernus and Wolfskehl. The silhouette figures themselves were the work of local artists such as Rolf von Hoerschelmann (who designed the theater's poster for the "Munich 1908" exhibition), Emil Preetorius, Dora Polster, Greta von Hoerner, Doris Wimmer, Karl Thylmann, and Marie Schnür. Wolfskehl's three contributions to the theater were *Wolfdietrich und die Rauhe Els* (*Wolf-dietrich and Rude Els*), which actually introduced the Schwabing Shadow Theater's public programs in 1907; *Die Ruhe des Kalifen* (*The Caliph's Silence*, 1908); and *Thors Hammer* (*Thor's Hammer*, 1908). Bernus's shadow plays, which ranged from the folkish to the spiritual, were admired for their light verse and vivid interplay of color and movement. They enjoyed a wide following in Munich and were occasionally incorporated into the programs of the Elf Scharfrichter.[25]

Although shadow theater played a generally insignificant role at the Fledermaus in Vienna, there was, nevertheless, one exceptional performance by a major artist worth recalling. Listed in the first program book among the numbers to be presented at the cabaret's opening in the late fall of 1907 was the shadow play *Das getupfte Ei* (*The Spotted Egg*) by the Expressionist painter and dramatist Oskar Kokoschka. The work was performed, in fact, a week after the opening. Based on an Indian folk tale and indicative of Kokoschka's interest in Oriental art during this period, the shadow play was notable for its brilliant colors reminiscent of Oriental miniatures. Noteworthy also was the play's technical construction, of which Kokoschka himself took charge. After designing and painting the figures on paper, he glued them to copper sheet cut accordingly. The figures, which were movable at the joints rather like marionettes, were placed within a box lighted from the inside and were manipulated by a spring mechanism. Their silhouettes were then projected by means of a large mirror.

Puppet and shadow shows were also introduced at the first Russian cabaret, the Letuchaya mysh, which opened its doors in Moscow the end of February 1908. But the paucity of information concerning them suggests that they were probably of no enduring significance over the life of the cabaret. Again, as in Barcelona and Munich, a type of performance emerged which rapidly overshadowed other entertainments and remained the basis of the cabaret's fame even when it resettled in Paris after the Russian Revolution and toured both Western Europe and the United States in the 1920s. I am speaking of the Letuchaya mysh's "living doll" productions. To be sure, these were outgrowths of the cabaret's puppet and shadow shows, which originally served as vehicles of theatrical parody. But under the inspiration of the Moscow cabaret's founder and leading spirit, Nikita Baliev, puppet and shadow shows soon yielded to more visually striking performances in which live actors, pretending to be puppets, marionettes, or dolls, composed an inanimate picture or tableau and, at a certain point, came to life, danced, sang, recited dialogue in verse or prose, and at the end of the production resumed their original "lifeless" state.[26] Such scenes were either silent or accompanied by music.

Since the "living doll" numbers owed their success as much to their visual appeal as to the skill of the performers in effecting the transition from dolls to living actors and back again, more emphasis came to be placed on colorful settings and brilliant costuming.[27] The outfits of the traditional masks of the Italian commedia dell'arte—Harlequin, Pierrot, and Columbine—were especially appealing in this regard and provided the inspiration for several numbers. So, too, did the rococo style of late-eighteenth-century France. As the visual became paramount in Letuchaya mysh performances, the cabaret came to rely more heavily on the cooperation of painters, who designed costumes, sets, and even programs and whose sketches preserved a stunning visual record of productions. Thanks both to the great popularity of the Moscow cabaret and Nikita Baliev's personal powers of persuasion, such prominent figures in early-twentieth-century Russian painting as Aleksandr and Nikolai Benois, Nikolai Remizov, Sergei Sudeikin, and Vasili Sukhaev actively participated in Letuchaya mysh productions. The great visual appeal of the "living doll" numbers spared the Moscow cabaret from becoming another casualty of the Revolution. Language played virtually no role in the productions. The emphasis was on virtuosity and stunning displays of set and costume, in both the cosmopolitan numbers and those characterized by a stylized Russian folkishness. The "living doll" productions could be enjoyed by Russians and foreigners alike, so that when the Letuchaya mysh was reestablished a few years after the Revolution in Paris as the Chauve-Souris (Bat, in French), the universal appeal of the Russian cabaret's staple assured its success in its new incarnation.

Program cover from American visit of Nikita Baliev's Chauve-Souris
Moscow Bat cabaret showing "living dolls."
(Author's collection)

Against a broad background of the literary and theatrical interest in the puppet, marionette, automaton, and related human likenesses from Cervantes's *Don Quixote* through the turn-of-the-century European cabaret, we are now ready to examine the uses of such figures in European drama in the period approximately 1890–1935. No period or movement in the history of the European stage ever found as much creative relevance in the puppet figure as modernism and the avant-garde. This can best be appreciated by a closer view of the varieties of puppet experience across a broad spectrum of Continental drama. For the sake of a more felicitous management of a substantial body of texts in several European languages, the rest of this book has been organized as a series of largely autonomous essays, in loose chronological order. Some are devoted to developments within different national literatures—French, Spanish, Italian, Russian—where the weight of the material argued for the preservation of the integrity of the discrete tradition; others are built around certain major plays, or groups of plays, by individual dramatists—Austrian, Polish, German, Swedish, Czech—whose interpretations of the puppet figure are the most noteworthy in their respective cultures in the modernist period.

PART TWO

Modernist and Avant-Garde Readings

THREE

Après Maeterlinck

From Bouchor's Mysteries to Ghelderode's, with Visits en Route with Jarry, Apollinaire, Cocteau, Rostand, and Claudel

MAURICE BOUCHOR: OF MYSTERIES AND MARIONETTES

Arguably the most characteristic turn-of-the-century manifestation of the French interest in puppets and marionettes after Maeterlinck was their adaptation to the neomystery play genre cultivated by the Symbolists. The greatest practitioner of this type of drama written for marionette performance was Maurice Bouchor, and if there are few who remember him any more, his reputation in his own time was formidable. Indeed, Bouchor's fame rested principally on the full-length mystery plays (*mystères*) he wrote for production by Henri Signoret's marionette theater, the Petit-Théâtre.[1] Bouchor mentions in the preface to his major collection, *Mystères bibliques et chrétiens* (*Biblical and Christian Mysteries*) that Signoret was a friend of his.[2] He further informs us (5–6) that, although some of the plays included in the two volumes of his *Mystères* were not performed by the marionettes of Signoret, and although some that were performed are not included in that edition, in all probability none of his *Mystères* would have been written had the Petit-Théâtre not been in existence. It was, therefore, the existence of the marionette theater that inspired him to attempt to transfer the popular turn-of-the-century neomystery play to the diminutive arena of the puppet stage.

Located in a little hall (seating capacity about 250) in the Galerie Vivienne, just behind the Palais Royale and the Bibliothèque Nationale, the

Petit-Théâtre was founded for the purpose of presenting marionette productions of the dramatic masterpieces of the world, especially those rarely seen on the stage. It opened in June 1888 with a production of Aristophanes' *Birds*. Shakespeare's *Tempest,* an *entremés* by Cervantes, and the German writer Hrotswitha's *Panuphtius* and *Abraham* followed soon after. The success of the Petit-Théâtre especially among literary people was considerable. Anatole France, who wrote a few essays on Signoret's marionette productions, was one of its most steadfast admirers. His piece "Hrotswitha aux Marionettes" ("Hrotswitha at the Marionettes"), which first appeared in the journal *Temps* on 7 April 1889, served both to acquaint readers with the tenth-century Saxon nun who wrote comedies and to express France's genuine delight in marionette theater. "I have already acknowledged it," he begins,

> I love marionettes, and those of M. Signoret please me particularly. They are shaped by artists; they are displayed by poets. They have a simple grace, a divine awkwardness, as of statues which condescend to behave as dolls; and it is delightful to watch these little figures acting in comedy. Consider further that they were made for what they do, that their nature conforms to their destiny, and that they are perfect without effort.[3]

In trying to capture the essence of the marionette performance, Anatole France found it impossible to avoid the idiom of the newly fashionable Symbolist movement:

> Now, what I am going to say is almost unintelligible, but I shall say it all the same, because it responds to a true sensation. These marionettes are like Egyptian hieroglyphics, that is, they have a certain pure and mysterious quality, and when they perform a drama of Shakespeare or Aristophanes I seem to watch the poet's thought unfold in sacred characters along the temple's wall. In short, I venerate their divine innocence, and I am very sure that if old Aeschylus, who was highly mystical, had returned to earth and visited France on the occasion of our Universal Exhibition, he would have had his tragedies played by M. Signoret's company. (24; 12)

For all the exaggerated sense of the uniqueness of his ideas, France did touch on a fundamental aspect of the eternal appeal of the puppet and marionette in the essay on Hrotswitha:

> I wanted to say these things, because, without flattering myself, I do not believe that anyone else would say them, and I strongly suspect my folly to be

unique. The marionettes respond exactly to my idea of the theater, and I confess that this idea is singular. I should like a dramatic representation to recall, in some degree, so that it may truly remain a game, a box of Nuremberg toys, a Noah's ark, or a set of clockwork figures. But I should further desire these artless images to be symbols; I should like these simple forms to be animated by magic; I want them to be enchanted toys. This may seem a curious taste; still, it must be remembered that Shakespeare and Sophocles satisfy it well enough. (24; 12)

In his first piece on the Petit-Théâtre, "Les Marionettes de M. Signoret" ("M. Signoret's Marionettes"), written less than two weeks after the theater opened and published in *Temps* on 10 June 1888, France echoed the growing dissatisfaction of contemporary theater artists with living actors and their desire to replace them with puppets, marionettes, and other non-human surrogates:

> In the meantime I have seen the marionettes of the rue Vivienne twice, and I have enjoyed them very much. I am infinitely thankful to them for having replaced living actors. If I must speak my whole mind, actors spoil comedy for me. I mean good actors. I might perhaps come to terms with the other sort! But decidedly I cannot endure excellent actors such as are to be seen at the Comédie-Française. Their talent is too great; it overwhelms everything. There is nothing but them. Their personality effaces the work they represent. They are important. I would like an actor only to be important when he has genius. I dream of masterpieces played in a slap-dash style in barns by strolling players. But perhaps I have no idea of what the theater is. It is much better for me to leave to M. Sarcey the task of speaking of it. I only want to speak of marionettes. It is a subject which suits me, and on which M. Sarcey would not be much good. He would treat it rationally.[4]

Yet the enthusiasm of writers such as Anatole France and others was not paralleled among the public at large. Their response was lukewarm at best, and attendence at Petit-Théâtre productions declined rapidly. In order to keep the enterprise from going under, Signoret decided on a change of strategy. Instead of concentrating on adaptations of major pieces of world drama, he would shift the emphasis to plays written primarily for the puppet or marionette theater. It was in that spirit that Maurice Bouchor, who had translated Shakespeare's *Tempest* for the Petit-Théâtre, wrote *Tobie* (*Tobias*), based on the story in the Old Testament. It was first performed in 1889.[5] In his essay "M. Maurice Bouchor et l'histoire de Tobie" ("Maurice Bouchor and the Story of Tobias"), which first appeared in the journal *Temps* on 8 December 1889, Anatole France observed:

> M. Maurice Bouchor has versified this venerable and childlike tale for the marionettes and has put it into dialogue. He has attacked the task with a happy simplicity, wholly unaffected, and has produced a unique mixture of drollery and enthusiasm. His poem has delighted us all; one hardly knows what to call it, but it is delicious. . . . The other night, on leaving the little theater in the Passage Vivienne, with my soul intoxicated by this poetry of a mystical wine-bibber, my eyes full of the little marionettes, as charming as Tanagra statuettes, beholding once more the dream landscapes drawn for these distinguished puppets by Georges Rochegross, Henri Lerolle, and Lucien Doucet, my ears delighted by listening to verse spoken by poets—for they are real poets who speak for M. Signoret's puppets. (220–21; 223)

Bouchor followed *Tobias* with a play about the birth of Christ, *Noël ou le mystère de la Nativité* (*Noël, or The Mystery of the Nativity*). It opened in the fall of 1890 and was an overnight sensation. Bouchor went on to become the leading purveyor of plays to the Petit-Théâtre. Most are contained in two volumes. *Mystères bibliques et chrétiens*, published by Ernest Flammarion, contains *Tobias* and two mysteries based on Christian subjects, *Noël ou le mystère de la Nativité* and *Conte de Noël* (*The Story of Christmas*). *Conte de Noël* had been written originally with the Petit-Théâtre in mind, but upon its completion, Bouchor decided that it was too difficult for performance as a marionette show. It went instead to the Théâtre-Français, where it was mounted in 1895. An earlier volume by Bouchor also contained a play on another Christian subject, *La Légende de Sainte Cécile* (*The Legend of Saint Cecile*). Two one-act pieces, one on a Christian subject (*La Dévotion à Saint André* [*Devotion to Saint André*]), the other Eastern in nature (*Le Songe de Khèyam* [*The Dream of Kheyam*, subtitled *A Caprice*]), were performed by Signoret's marionette theater in 1892 and published separately by Lecène, Oudin et Cie of Paris in 1894. The Petit-Théâtre lasted until 1893. The final work Bouchor gave it was *Les Mystères d'Eleusis en quatre tableaux, en vers* (*The Mysteries of Eleusis in Four Acts in Verse*), which was based on classical Greek mythology. It, too, was published in 1894 by Lecène, Oudin et Cie. After its closing performance, the theater's marionettes were divided among its collaborators.

In response to the question posed him once as to why he wrote plays of a religious content for marionette theater performance, Bouchor acknowledged his preference for what he called "comédiens en bois" ("actors made of wood") over "les marionettes de chair et d'os" ("marionettes of flesh and bone"). He amplified his remarks in the introduction to his *Mystères païens* (*Pagan Mysteries*):

> I had to admit that if the marionettes are, in principle, superior to ordinary actors, this is not the case in all spheres. I was not at all thinking, of course, of modern drama or the bourgeois comedy. I abandoned the merry satire and the coarse farce to our friend Guignol, to the pupazzi moved by three fingers, and where a marvelous agility is precisely the opposite of our sluggish marionettes who are well-formed, above all, and, except by chance, very noble in their movements. The drama in verse, à la Shakespeare, à la Hugo, even when interspersed with the comic, was quite ill-suited to my argument. Nothing rough or violent was appropriate to the marionettes; neither horror nor terror were within their province; they had no need of anything too dramatic, too passionate, or too real, at least externally. Marionettes—I have had the opportunity of observing—are above all lyrical, and the ideal place of their action cannot be other than poetry; all the gates of dream open before them; the highest speculations are naturally familiar to them, and these strange figures move comfortably within the systems, beliefs, and symbols of all times and all peoples; everything that is distant, fairylike, mysterious, is particularly suited to them. Moreover, emotion, even the most profound, the most human, is not inaccessible to them; they can excel in tenderness and grace, freely mixing delicate irony, humor, fantasy, and comic lyricism.[6]

And a few pages later, Bouchor again stressed the limitations of the physical presence and personality of the living actor for the type of drama he was writing:

> I persist in believing that the appearance of Saint Michael, of celestial voices, of miraculous flowerings of lilies and roses, and the transfiguration of a martyr are more appropriate to our small stage than to conventional theaters where the personality of the actor, too real and too familiar, destroys all impression of the supernatural. (9)

With respect to *Tobie*, for example, he mentions in his preface to *Mystères païens* that he could not find a subject more appropriate to the "genius of marionettes"(11). The version of the play that was performed by the Petit-Théâtre and was subsequently published in 1889 had five acts and contained elements of buffoonery which Bouchor later thought had best be omitted. Bouchor also mentions in the *avertissement* accompanying the text of the play in *Mystères bibliques et chrétiens* that the original play was written for the small stage of a marionette theater and was produced before a public limited for the most part to literary people and artists. "I recall these details which explain—if indeed they do not justify—the original liberty of a work written in the tradition of our ancient mysteries and where the author was unafraid to mix the profane and sacred, the burlesque and serious, the contemporary and the ancient"(11). The version of the play published in *Mystères bibliques et chrétiens* was reduced to three acts and underwent other changes as well.[7] The original version written for the marionette theater can be found in Bouchor's *Trois Mystères*.

Although Bouchor may have had second thoughts about the degree of buffoonery in a mystery play such as *Tobie* and softened this element when he published an abbreviated and revised version, it was indeed his ability to blend the "profane and sacred, the burlesque and serious, the contemporary and the ancient" that made his mystery plays for marionettes so successful. Here, by way of example, are passages from his Nativity play *Noël*, where in his typical light, colloquial verse, Bouchor accommodates conventional racial attitudes of the time while introducing the appropriate exotic note into the scene where the Three Magi pay homage to the infant Jesus; the speaker is the African king:

Le Roi Nègre.

                Je vous rends
Mille grâces; merci; vous êtes bons et grands;
Moi, fils de Cham, je suis l'esclave de mes frères.
Mes paroles seront peut-être téméraires.
Tandis que vous doutez, moi, sans effort, je crois
D'un coeur inébranlable; et portant, nobles rois,
Je porte, comme un signe affreux que rien n'efface,
La malédiction de Noé sur ma face.
   . . .

Dans cette monstrueuse Afrique d'où je sors,
J'ai vu l'homme écraser l'homme sans un remords,
   Toute multitude asservie,
D'horribles dieux, ouvrage informe de nos mains,

De rouges lacs de sang, des mers de pleurs humains,
  La mort plus douce que la vie.
Mais quelquefois, après le dur labeur du jour,
Mes pauvres frères noirs dansaient, ivres d'amour,
  Devant leurs misérables huttes.
Ils dansaient innocents, pleins de grâce, enfantins;
Leurs beaux yeux rayonnaient; des rires argentins
  Se mêlaient aux sanglots des flûtes.[8]

African King.
I am deeply in your debt. Thank you, you are good and great. I, the son of
Cham, am my brothers' slave. My words may perhaps be reckless. While
you doubt, I have no difficulty in believing with unshakable faith; and bearing as I do, noble kings, the malediction of Noah on my face, like a frightful sign that nothing can efface. . . . In that monstrous Africa whence I
come, I have seen man kill man with no remorse, multitudes enslaved by
horrible gods, the shapeless work of our hands, of lakes red with blood, of
oceans of human tears, death sweeter than life. But sometimes, after the
hard labor of the day, my poor black brethren would dance, drunk with
love, before their miserable huts. Their dances were innocent, full of grace,
childlike; their beautiful eyes shone; tinkling laughter mixed with the sobs
of flutes.

In the following scene (act 3, scene 3), Bouchor adds a slightly comic,
and balancing, touch to the apearance of the African king by means of a
"profane" character named Farigoul:

C'est moi, Farigoul, le vieux drôle.
Je suis presque au bout de mon rôle;
Et j'aurai bientôt le chagrin
De m'en aller sans un refrain,
Car on dit que ma voix est aigre
Comme un verjus. Mais le roi nègre!
Ah! c'est lui qui doit en savoir,
De fins couplets! Je viens le voir.
Il est, dit-on, fait comme un masque.
Il a surtout un certain casque.
  . . .
Enfin, suffit. Drôles de rois! (204)

It's me, Holly,[9] the funny old guy. I'm almost finished with my part; and
I'd be real sorry to leave without a final word, since they say my voice is

sharp as gooseberries. But that black king! Oh! He's the one that ought
to know some nice ditties! I'm going to see him. They say he's decked out
like a mask. Especially the headpiece he has on. . . . Well, enough of that.
Strange kings!

ALFRED JARRY: KING UBU

During the period when Henri Signoret and Maurice Bouchor were most
creatively engaged in marionette theater in Paris, the seeds of a revolution
in French drama were being planted in provincial Rennes. The penchant
of Alfred (Henri) Jarry for lampooning his teachers and fellow pupils had
manifested itself before he entered the Rennes *lycée* in October 1888. But
it was in Rennes that his friendship with two other school scamps, Henri
Morin and his brother Charles, laid the groundwork for his future play
Ubu roi (*Ubu the King*), which would scandalize the Parisian stage in December 1896.[10]

When Jarry entered the Rennes lycée at the age of fifteen, Henri and
Charles Morin had already written a satire on a certain Monsieur Hébert,
their physics teacher. The work was called "Les Polonais" ("The Poles").
A Poland that had disappeared from the map of Europe in the Third Partition of 1795 and was not to be reconstituted as an independent state until
1918 made a splendid choice of a never-never land where all sorts of wild
and grotesque things might occur. And so it was that Monsieur Hébert,
transmogrified in the Morins' satire as "le Père Ebé" ("Papa Ebé"), experi-
enced horrendous adventures as the king of Poland. Once the Morins discovered in Jarry a kindred spirit, the newcomer became a welcome literary
collaborator. The first fruit of this prankish schoolboy collaboration was
a play version of the Morins' satire which Jarry conceived for marionette
performance. It was in this form that the original primitive version of *Ubu
roi* was presented by Jarry's self-styled "Théâtre des Phynances" in the
Morins' home in 1888. Subsequently, Jarry performed the marionette
play in his parents' home in Rennes. Before leaving Rennes in October
1891 for Paris and the Lycée Henri IV, Jarry, probably with the collaboration of Charles Morin, wrote a follow-up to his play version of "The Poles"
under the title *Onésime ou les tribulations de Priou* (*Onesime or The Tribulations of Priou*). Subtitled a *Pièce alquemique* (*An Alchemical Play*), the
work eventually became the second of Jarry's three-play Ubu cycle, *Ubu
cocu* (*Ubu Cuckolded*).

Jarry's enthusiasm for live performance increased if anything during his stay at the Lycée Henri IV from 1891 to 1893. Both early versions of *Ubu roi* and *Ubu cocu* were put on by Jarry and friends at a miniscule hideaway he rented not far from the apartment on the boulevard de Port Royal where he lived with his mother (until her death in 1893), and in the grander apartment on the boulevard Saint-Germain he inhabited next. With Henri Morin, who had also come to Paris, and with Léon-Paul Fargue, who became his closest friend in this period, Jarry set up a makeshift puppet theater where the two future "Ubu" plays were performed before delighted audiences consisting mainly of his fellow students from the lycée. It was during this early Paris period, and his further refinement of the plays, that Jarry dropped the original names for Monsieur Hébert— "le P. H.," "Père Heb," "Ebé"—in favor of the definitive "le Père Ubu"; and "la Mère E. B." of *Onésime ou les Tribulations de Priou* finally became "la Mère Ubu."

By 1896, when *Ubu roi* reached the stage under that title, Jarry had already published two books as well as a few smaller prose pieces and had established important contacts in the world of French publishing. When he was introduced in January of that year to the young actor-director of the innovative new Théâtre de l'Oeuvre, Aurélien Lugné-Poe, Jarry lost little time before trying to persuade him to mount a production of either a further revision of *Ubu roi* or *Les Polyèdres* (the original title of the first version of *Ubu cocu*). While Lugné-Poe was taking his time considering the proposal, he offered Jarry the job of *secrétaire-régisseur* of his theater. That same month, June 1896, Editions du Mercure de France, which was owned by Jarry's close friend Alfred Vallette, published *Ubu roi* in a single volume under Jarry's full title: *Ubu roi. Drame en cinq actes en prose. Restitué en son intégrité tel qu'il a été représenté par les marionettes du Théâtre des Phynances en 1888* (*Ubu the King. Play in Five Acts in Prose. Restored in its Entirety As Performed by the Marionettes of the Théâtre des Phynances in 1888*). The publication of the play, as well as Jarry's abandonment of the idea of productions of both *Ubu roi* and *Les Polyèdres*, finally persuaded Lugné-Poe that a production of *Ubu roi* might be worth the gamble.

Since Lugné-Poe never really quite knew what to make of the play, Jarry was left pretty much in charge of the production. The original conception of the play as a puppet show, as a *guignol*, was preserved in the version mounted at the Théâtre de l'Oeuvre on 10 December 1896, except that instead of real puppets or marionettes, living actors performed as marionettes. This was very much in accord with Jarry's wishes. Besides imitating the typical jerkiness of marionettes' movements, the actors also wore masks; Firmin Gémie, who played the part of Ubu roi, wore a heavy, pear-shaped or triangular mask, designed for him by Jarry, as well as a huge cardboard belly. The whole idea was to distance setting and costuming as much as possible from anything even suggestive of historical accuracy. Hence, besides their masks and their movements imitative of puppets and marionettes, the actors were permitted to wear everyday street dress beneath their costumes and were also encouraged to develop special voices appropriate to their roles. The plain blackdrop that was originally called for was abandoned in favor of a composite setting depicting the indoors and outdoors, and all the climate zones together, as a child might imagine them. Apple trees in bloom, beneath a blue sky, appeared at the back of the stage, and against the sky a small, closed window and a fireplace were visible. On the left was painted a bed, at the foot of which stood a bare tree with snow falling all around. To the right were palm trees, a boa constrictor coiled around one of them, a door opening against the sky, and a skeleton hanging from a gallows alongside the door. In a touch foreshadowing future Expressionist theater, an old man in a long white beard, in evening dress, tiptoed across the boards and hung placards on a nail at the side of the stage to indicate the scene.[11]

The clamor that erupted at the premiere of Ubu roi, the tumultuous reception by public and critics alike, and the heated debate that followed over the play's meaning have been described many times and need no repeating here. The work became the talk of Paris; if Jarry had planned from the very beginning to turn the contemporary French stage on its head, he succeeded handsomely.

Maeterlinck and Jarry were contemporaries; only two years separate the publication of the Belgian's early collection of plays "for marionettes" (1894) and the premiere of Jarry's Ubu roi at the Théâtre de l'Oeuvre. Despite the enormous differences between their plays, they were intended to achieve a revolution in French theater by ending the hegemony of realistic drama and the so-called well-made play—both the mainstays of French bourgeois audiences and the commercial stage. If Maeterlinck sought to effect his revolution in a quieter way through a highly stylized and static drama of supernatural portentousness and death fixation, Jarry went straight for the jugular with a play calculated to shock, offend, disturb, and mystify. Their differences notwithstanding, a common link connects Maeterlinck and Jarry—the centrality of the puppet or marionette figure in the design of their plays, overt in Jarry, whose *Ubu roi* was conceived as a grand *guignol*, or Punch and Judy show; oblique in Maeterlinck, for whom the marionette served as both metaphor of the human condition and model of the new stylized movement of actors regarded as appropriate to the new static drama of the spirit.

Jarry's intention to shock and offend his audience is apparent from Père Ubu's first word (repeated often throughout the play)—*merdre*—a distortion of the French *merde* ("shit"). If the audience wondered if it was hearing correctly, the subsequent few lines of dialogue, between Père Ubu and Mère Ubu, left no doubt as to the nature and style of the play:

> *Mère Ubu.* Oh! Voilà du joli, Père Ubu, vous estes un fort grand voyou.
> *Père Ubu.* Que ne vous assom'je, Mère Ubu!
> *Mère Ubu.* Ce n'est pas moi, Père Ubu, c'est un autre qu'il faudrait assassiner.
> *Père Ubu.* De par ma chandelle verte, je ne comprends pas.
> *Mère Ubu.* Comment, Père Ubu, vous estes content de votre sort?
> *Père Ubu.* De par ma chandelle vert, merdre, madame, certes oui, je suis content.[12]

> *Ma Ubu.* Oh! There y'go now! Pa Ubu, you're nothin' but a real hooligan.
> *Pa Ubu.* Mind I don't bash your head in, Ma Ubu!
> *Ma Ubu.* Not me, Pa Ubu, but somebody else you'd better have it in for.
> *Pa Ubu.* By my green candle, I don't get you.
> *Ma Ubu.* How so, Pa Ubu, you're content with your lot, are ye?
> *Pa Ubu.* By my green candle, shitr, madame, you're damn right I am.

Coarse, riotous, bawdy, absurd—the play was bound to fascinate as much as repel; nothing like it had been seen before on the French stage. Père Ubu, former king of Aragon, is now captain of the dragoons and aide de camp to King Wenceslaus of Poland. If he is content with his status, Mère Ubu is not, and she urges him to finish off the king and his family and replace him on the throne. Or, in the language of the play, she urges him to set his *cul* ("butt") on a throne if he really wants to live in the grand manner. Père Ubu enlists the aid of Captain Bordure who, though willing to serve him, cannot refrain from asking him

> Eh! vous empestez, Père Ubu. Vous ne vous lavez donc jamais?
> *Père Ubu.* Rarement.
> *Mère Ubu.* Jamais!
> *Père Ubu.* Je vais te marcher sur les pieds.
> *Mère Ubu.* Grosse merdre! (42)

Man, how you stink, Pa Ubu. Don't you ever wash?
Pa Ubu. Occasionally.
Ma Ubu. Never!
Pa Ubu. I'm goin' to tread on your toes.
Ma Ubu. Fat piece of shitr!

Bathed or unbathed, Père Ubu succeeds in unseating the king of Poland and taking his place. Only the queen and her son Bougrelas survive the massacre of the royal family. Ubu's reign is one of monstruous tyranny as he has his opponents killed en masse while he himself runs around squeezing as many taxes as he can out of the populace. Meanwhile, Captain Bordure and Czar Alexis of Russia conspire to depose Ubu and restore Bougrelas to the Polish throne. When war erupts and Père Ubu's attention is diverted, Mère Ubu plots to assassinate Bougrelas and get her hands on the Polish royal treasury. But her plot is foiled by the sudden arrival of Bougrelas and his men. The great battle scene between the Russians and the Poles under Père Ubu's command provides Jarry the perfect occasion to uneash a childlike torrent of mayhem in the best tradition of puppet theater. Amid much clamor, soldiers are slain in droves and Ubu kills anyone who gets in his way by tearing him to pieces, as with Captain Bordure ("Il se rue sur lui et le déchire," 99). Driven off by the czar and his forces, Père Ubu and some of his followers take refuge in a cave in Lithuania. Snow is falling all around. Pursued across Poland by Bougrelas, Mère Ubu finds her way to the same cave. Once aware of each other, Père and Mère Ubu exchange insults and recriminations until Père Ubu starts tearing her to pieces. But before he can finish, Bougrelas and his men arrive and launch an assault on the cave. Ubu and company are driven off and flee across the snows to Livonia, whence they board a ship and sail west on the Baltic. The play ends on an appropriately absurd note:

> *Père Ubu*. Mer farouche et inhospitalière qui baigne le pays appelé Germanie, ainsi nommé parce que les habitants de ce pays sont tous cousins germains.
> *Mère Ubu*. Voilà ce que j'appele de l'érudition. On dit ce pays fort beau.
> *Père Ubu*. Ah! messieurs! si beau qu'il soit il ne vaut pas la Pologne. S'il n'y avait pas de Pologne il n'y aurait pas de Polonais! (130)

> *Pa Ubu*. Wild and inhospitable ocean which washes the land called Germany, so named because the inhabitants of this country are all first cousins (*cousins germains*).

Ma Ubu. Now that's what I call erudition. They say it's a quite beautiful country.

Pa Ubu. Ah, m'dears, beautiful as it may be, it can't hold a candle to Poland. If there weren't a Poland, there wouldn't be any Poles!

Like Maeterlinck and the Symbolists, Jarry was out to transform the French stage. The method he chose was shock and deliberate offense. Apart from the ludicrousness of the Polish setting, which remotely recalls the seventeenth-century Spanish dramatist Calderón's use of a kind of mythic Poland as the setting for his renowned *La vide es sueño* (*Life Is a Dream*), *Ubu roi* has obvious parallels with Shakespeare's *Macbeth*. Since these would, in all probability, have been rather easily perceived by the audience, the obscenity, rowdiness, and grotesqueness of Jarry's play would obviously have been taken for provocative irreverence. A mockery of Shakespearean tragedy would have been regarded as an assault by an outlandish bohemian writer on the whole classic tradition of the stage; indeed, it is difficult to imagine that that was not, in fact, Jarry's intention. Reducing a classic tragedy such as *Macbeth* to the level of an outrageous infantile puppet show was truly an act of subversion.

Jarry's subsequent career (he died at the age of thirty-four) and the fate of the other plays in the Ubu cycle are of less interest here; our concern is with *Ubu roi* and its place in the history of the stage. Although Jarry wrote a second version of *Ubu cocu*, neither the first nor the second was published or performed in his lifetime. It was only in 1944 that an edition of the second version was printed from a manuscript that had come into the possession of Paul Eluard. Jarry worked on the third play in the cycle, *Ubu enchaîné* (*Ubu Enchained*), during 1899. Although it was published the following year, it remained unperformed until 1937.

The inherent puppet character of *Ubu roi* led to a performance of the play on 20 January 1898 by the Théâtre des Pantins, a marionette theater established in December 1897 by Jarry himself, Claude Terrasse, who had written the musical accompaniment for the first production of *Ubu roi*, the artist Charles Bonnard, and others. The marionettes were supplied by Bonnard; Jarry was the voice of Père Ubu, and Louise France, who played Mère Ubu in the original 1896 production, reprised her role on this occasion. Consisting mostly of writers and artists, the audience greeted this first production of *Ubu roi* as a marionette show with great enthusiasm. Jarry's last involvement with the Ubu cycle was a further reworking of *Ubu roi* as a two-act guignolesque musical. Eventually known by the title

Ubu sur la Butte (*Ubu on Montmartre*), the newest incarnation of Ubu was performed in November 1901 at the Cabaret des Quat'z' Arts by the marionettes of the Théâtre Guignol des Gueules de Bois (*gueules de bois* means literally "wooden faces" or "wooden jaws," referring here to the marionettes; the expression *avoir la gueule de bois* means "to have a hangover"). André Antoine, of Théâtre Libre fame, directed the production. The text of the play was published for the first time only in 1906, a year before Jarry's death.

In light of the conservatism of French bourgeois theatrical taste at the time, it is easy to appreciate the storm that erupted over the production of *Ubu roi* in 1896. The combination of obscene language, grotesque characters, slapstick action, wildly exaggerated cruelty, absurdity, and fast changes of scene was too much for the audience to handle. As the meaning of the play—if indeed it had any—was debated back and forth, Jarry was accused of everything from deliberately provoking a scandal to perpetrating a hoax. But *Ubu roi* made his literary reputation and itself came to be regarded as a turning point in the history of the modern French stage.

APOLLINAIRE, COCTEAU, AND THE BEGINNINGS OF SURREALIST THEATER

Jarry's most notable immediate followers, Guillaume Apollinaire and Jean Cocteau, openly acknowledged their indebtedness to him in their efforts to create an antirealistic drama. In his later preface to the play for which he is best known, *Les Mamelles de Tirésias* (*The Breasts of Tirésias*), which was begun in 1903 (the year Apollinaire and Jarry first met) and finished in 1917, Apollinaire characterizes the work as a "drame surréaliste," aware that *surréaliste* and *surréalisme* (which he also uses in the preface) were neologisms. He further expounds his views on the new type of drama he is attempting to fashion in the programmatic prologue, where he mentions the "right of the dramatist to use / All the illusions he has at his disposal," among them the "right for him to make crowds and inanimate things speak / If he wishes."[13] Widely regarded as a spoof on the realistic "problem play" (the issue here being the decline in the population of France, which Apollinaire attributes to the fact that the French no longer make love often enough) as well as turn-of-the-century feminism, *The Breasts of Tiresias* recounts the rebellion of Thérèse of Zanzibar, who refuses to be a breeder of children and demands the same rights and privileges as men. In short order the other women on the island join her rebellion. Faced with such a challenge, Thérèse's husband resolves to have children without her and in proper Surrealist fashion manages to do so effortlessly and abundantly, giving birth to 40,049 children in a single day. So pleased is he with his success that he vows to continue having them. At the end of the short, two-act play, Thérèse and her husband reunite amid mounting fear that his phenomenal success in having children on his own now threatens their homeland with overpopulation.

Thérès's transformation into Tiresias, the woman who renounces childbearing in the name of liberation, is heralded when, with superb Surrealist ease, she announces that she is growing a moustache and beard and that her bosom, the most obvious outward sign of her femininity, is falling off. Hardly are these words uttered when her blouse opens and her breasts, one red and the other blue, fly away like toy balloons. After playing with them for a while by the strings still attached to them, she explodes them with a cigarette lighter. Then, mocking the audience, she throws balls at them which she has in her bodice. These actions are repeated at the end of the play. When Tiresias's husband tries to persuade her to restore her bosom by means of new balloons, she refuses to do so and releases them into the air, at the same time taking more balls and hurling them at the audience.

Although Apollinaire announced his intention in the prologue to make crowds and inanimate things speak, the only inanimate thing that acquires human characteristics is the newspaper kiosk containing a picture of a newspaper woman with a movable arm. The kiosk comes to life and joins other characters in the singing and dancing that bring the first act to an end just after Thérèse's husband vows to bear his own progeny. The figure appears nowhere else in the play and serves primarily to enhance its overall surreal aspect. Just as the people of Zanzibar are represented by a single character, following Jarry's example in *Ubu roi*, the "news"—so important in informing the world of the remarkable developments on Zanzibar—is also anthropomorphized and represented by a single figure, the animated kiosk. Indeed, much of the dialogue of the play is made up of newspaper headlines barked out—sometimes through megaphones— in the manner of a typical newsboy. Despite Jarry's considerable impact on the shaping of Apollinaire's ideas about antirealistic drama, the puppet element underlying the very conception of the *Ubu* plays left Apollinaire largely unaffected. In *The Breasts of Tiresias*, the puppet-inspired grotesqueness of *Ubu* gives way to that surreal alogicality with which

Apollinaire aimed at a further detonation of the drama of photographic realism. In this light the animated kiosk relates less to the puppet tradition than to Apollinaire's sense of the elements from which he hoped to construct his surreality. It may indeed be possible to imagine *The Breasts of Tiresias* produced as a puppet play in the manner of Jarry's *Ubu*, but there is no evidence that this was ever Apollinaire's intention or that anyone else ever saw his play in this way.

Although closer in spirit to Jarry, Jean Cocteau hewed more to the path of Apollinaire's surrealism in his earliest theater pieces, which also owed much of their inspiration to the influence of Diaghilev and the Ballets Russes. It began with *Parade*, which Cocteau ironically designated a "ballet réaliste" when it was first performed on 18 May 1917 by Diaghilev's troupe at the Théâtre du Châtelet. Although built around a slim scenario—some circus performers go through a few of their routines outside the tent in order to lure the public to the main show on the inside—Cocteau succeeded in assembling such stellar artists from different fields that he took the contemporary ballet world by storm. Besides being danced by the Ballets Russes, *Parade* was choreographed by Léonide Massine, who also performed in the role of the Chinese Conjuror. Erik Satie composed the score, and sets and costumes were designed by Pablo Picasso, who was among Cocteau's closest friends at the time and with whom he collaborated on *Parade* at a very early stage. And finally, as if to lend his imprimatur to the event, Apollinaire himself prepared the program notes, crediting the ballet with giving rise to a kind of "sur-réalisme." This may have been the first use of the term *surrealism* which, in its adjectival form, Apollinaire applied to his own play *The Breasts of Tiresias* in the preface to it. The combination of Massine's vigorous choreography, Picasso's Cubist costumes for the characters of the Managers, and the unabashed incorporation of variety theater and circus routines into the ballet stunned the audience, outraged the defenders of traditional ballet, and provoked the protests and scandals that made *Parade* the legendary sensation that it became.[14]

Parade actually makes no more use of the puppet or marionette figure, or of animated inanimate things, than *The Breasts of Tirésias*. But the Cubist costumes of the Managers, relatable as they seem to be to the Futurist puppet figures in Fortunato Depero's "plastic ballet," *I balli plastici* (*Plastic Dances*, 1918), or to Alexandra Exter's famous marionettes of 1926, originated in a similar aesthetic.[15] The difference is that Italian Futurists such as Marinetti and Depero, and the Russian painter and stage designer Exter, who was close to the Cubists, consciously experimented with puppets and marionettes; there is no indication that either Picasso or Cocteau shared that specific interest beyond their general enthusiasm for popular culture. The point of departure for the costumes of the Managers in *Parade* was Picasso's own attraction at the time to Cubism. However, unlike the figures in Depero's *Plastic Dances*, the Cubist costumes of the Managers are just that, costumes worn by actors whose legs are visible beneath them. They are not meant to represent marionettes or robots; if anything, they more closely resemble animated billboards, as Picasso's studies for the figures clearly suggest,[16] and in this respect recall Apollinaire's anthropomorphized kiosk. Yet, as Roland Penrose points out in his biography of Picasso, the huge size of the actors playing the Managers in their tall Cubist costumes "reduced the dancers, whom they introduced, to the unreal proportion of puppets."[17] This may well have been Picasso's intention.

Cocteau's fascination with ballet, so evident in *Parade*, is reflected as well in his next experiment in surreal theater, *Les Mariés de la Tour Eiffel* (*The Wedding on the Eiffel Tower*). It was produced for the first time in 1921 at the Théâtre des Champs-Elysées. Choreographed by Cocteau himself together with Jean Borlin, with set by Irène Lagut and costumes and masks by Jean Hugo, it was danced by the new Ballet suédois, founded by Rolfe de Maré in 1920. A brashly comic exercise in Surrealist nonsense about a wedding that takes place on the first platform of the Eiffel Tower, the work is particularly interesting for its separation of dialogue and action. Two actors dressed as phonographs, stationed to the right and left downstage and partly hidden by the proscenium arch, narrate the play and recite all the dialogue of the characters. The bodies of the two actors represent the cabinets of the phonographs, while horns replace their mouths (recalling the megaphones in Apollinaire's play *The Breasts of Tiresias*). As the living phonographs speak, the other actors playing the parts of the characters simultaneously mime the appropriate actions. Thus the actors who are dressed as phonographs are transformed into machines and speak accordingly: very loudly, very rapidly, and pronouncing each syllable distinctly. In his play *Methusalem, or The Eternal Bourgeois* (1922), the Franco-German Expressionist poet and dramatist Yvan Goll, of whom more later in this book, employs a similar technique to satirize Methusalem's son, Felix, as the epitome of the bourgeois businessman. With a copper megaphone in place of a mouth and a telephone receiver for a nose, Felix's speech is made up principally of stock quotations and business communiqués. But Goll's purpose is wholly satirical, whereas for Cocteau his human phonographs serve primarily a narrative function in part derived from the conventions of popular theatrics. Cocteau speaks of this in his preface to *The Wedding on the Eiffel Tower*, which has the same programmatic character as Apollinaire's preface and prologue to *The Breasts of Tiresias*:

> The human phonographs, at the right and left of the stage, like the chorus in ancient drama, like the compère and commère [the masters of ceremonies in music halls], describe, without the least literature, the absurd action that is unfolded, danced, and mimed between them. I say absurd because, instead of trying to stay on this side of the absurdity of life, to lessen it, to arrange it the way we arrange, when telling a story, an incident in which we play an unfavorable part, I accentuate it, I thrust it to the fore, I try to paint *more truly than the truth*.[18]

Like Apollinaire, Cocteau does not seek inspiration for his early stage pieces in puppet theater, nor does he make specific use in them of puppets, marionettes, and related figures. But the Cubistic, mechanical-looking Managers in *Parade* and the human phonographs in *The Wedding on the Eiffel Tower*, like Apollinaire's dancing kiosk in *The Breasts of Tiresias*, do reflect the early-twentieth-century artist's new awareness of the world of ordinary objects. For Cocteau the key to a revitalized art was the willingness to see the ordinary—commonplaces of speech as well as objects—from a fresh perspective. As he writes in the preface to *The Wedding on the Eiffel Tower*:

> The poets ought to bring objects and emotions out from under their veils and their mists, to display them suddenly, so naked and so quickly that they are barely recognizable. It is then that they astonish us with their youthfulness, as if they had never become official old fogies.
>
> This is the case with commonplaces, old, powerful, and universally esteemed the way masterpieces are whose beauty and originality no longer surprise us because of overuse.
>
> In my play I rejuvenate the commonplace. My task is to present it from such an angle that it will become twenty all over again. (43)

In common, then, with a precursor of the avant-garde such as Jarry, who found inspiration in the world of the puppet and marionette for much the same reason, Cocteau was driven by the desire to shake art free of its tired conventions and restore its lost youth. In *Parade* he undermined traditional ballet by tossing elements of variety theater, circus, and ballet into the same subversive mix. With *The Wedding on the Eiffel Tower*, the Jarry-esque irreverence of *Parade* extends the boundaries of the new surrealism by using the animated artifacts and clichés of a bourgeois wedding to project that mundane event onto the level of the dreamlike. Dissociation, employed to differentiate speaker from actor, in a radical departure from traditional dramatic practice, underlies the structure of the work as a whole. By becoming animated, objects, like commonplaces, take on a life of their own and demand to be seen apart from their conventional contexts. Moving beyond the animation of puppets and marionettes, Cocteau, even more than Apollinaire, looked ahead to the preoccupation of the avant-garde with man and machine.

EDMOND ROSTAND: DON JUAN AS PUPPET

Internationally renowned for *Cyrano de Bergerac* (1896–97), the only play for which he is really remembered any more, Edmond Rostand wrote one play with a puppet theme very late in his career. It was, in fact, his last and doubtless remained in an unfinished state at his death. The play is *La Dernière Nuit de Don Juan, Poème dramatique en deux partes et un prologue* (*The Last Night of Don Juan, A Dramatic Poem in Two Parts and a Prologue*). Rostand had apparently completed the work before the outbreak of World War I in 1914. Published only posthumously, however, it was first performed on the stage of the Porte Saint-Martin on 10 March 1922, hence when the bold avant-gardist experiments of Apollinaire and Cocteau were still fresh in people's minds. The play proved an utter failure. Written near the end of his life when Rostand might have felt that death was not far off, the play is marked by a sadness unfelt previously in Rostand's work. Behind this sadness is a loss of the enjoyment of life, a loss of the enthusiasm and zest for life which Ronsard once had in abundance, and an unmistakable disillusionment brought about by his treatment at the hands of critics and public alike. Lacking the verve and romanticism of *Cyrano*, *The Last Night of Don Juan* is interesting primarily for its philosophical somberness and its puppet element, for which Rostand had never previously demonstrated any attraction.

In the prologue the Statue of the Commander is leading Don Juan down a spiral staircase into Hell. With every step he takes, Don Juan recites the name of another of his many mistresses. Impressed by his courage, the

Statue decides to allow Don Juan to return to earth for ten more years of life. When part 1 opens, those ten years have come to an end. The scene is a palace in Venice, and Don Juan is still reciting the names of his mistresses. As he rhapsodizes on Venice as the appropriate city for him to die in, a puppeteer's voice is heard in the distance announcing his theater. Invited in to perform for Don Juan, he sets up his little booth and stages what at first appears to be a typical Punch and Judy show but soon becomes a boisterous puppet version of Don Juan's own adventurous life. The show culminates in the appearance of the Devil, against whom Punch—Don Juan's alter ego in the play-within-a-play—valiantly but vainly fights. As the Devil is about to carry off Punch, slung over his shoulder, Don Juan boasts that he has no fear of the Devil and accepts his offer of a bet that the Devil will yet vanquish him. But when the show ends, the puppeteer emerges from his booth to reveal that he himself is the Devil and that he has come to claim his victim now that the ten-year reprieve is over. Before they depart, Don Juan tears up the list containing the names of his 1,003 lovers, all of which he knows by heart anyway. The Devil then produces a fiddle on which he begins playing. As he does so, the scraps of paper from Don Juan's list begin dancing and whirling about until they come to rest on the water of the lagoon outside. There, each one turns into a black gondola bearing the soul of one of Don Juan's conquests. At the Devil's command, they disembark from their gondolas, masked, cloaked, each carrying a fan. Don Juan is then instructed to guess each ghost's name, but he errs badly. The point of the "test" is that in his long history of romantic affairs, Don Juan came to know only the flesh but never the spirit. As the curtain descends on part 1, Don Juan is still trying, in vain, to identify the female souls who keep on arriving by gondola.

Part 2 opens at the break of dawn the same day with a greatly disillusioned Don Juan utterly failing to identify a single former lover and now being mocked by all of them. It is at this point especially that the play's puppet motif is fully realized. If indeed he came to know women only carnally, Don Juan can still boast that he possessed them by dominating them. But this last vanity is stripped away when the ghosts reveal that his "domination" was but the gratification of their own wishes and desires. So the great romantic "hero"—Don Juan—was nothing more than a puppet of love in the hands of the many women he boasted of conquering. As the Devil approaches to take him to Hell, Don Juan puts him off another time by saying that there remains to him at least one source of pride, namely that he gave pleasure. This illusion, too, is stripped away, whereupon the Devil humbles his opponent completely by telling him that Don Juan's life was no more than a flight from real love and that as a lover he cannot compare to Romeo and Tristram. Don Juan counters by boasting:

> What matters it?
> As Attila the Hun laid landscapes waste,
> I ravaged faces that I scorned to fathom.
> I am the scourge of the most potent god!
> That's more than Romeo, eh? More than Tristram?
> Love means but this—one weeps, and one looks on;
> I always was the one—so much is left—
> To gaze with frigid eye while woman wept![19]

But after Don Juan collects in a goblet the tears of the women he made weep, the Devil reveals that all are false save one belonging to a woman representing the only blank space in Don Juan's list of lovers. She is, in symbolic terms, the love Don Juan might have found in each of the women had he but tried. But Don Juan attempts yet another parry:

> For, had I found, I would have died of boredom.
> Don Juan has sought nothing but the search
> And his own self! Woman was after all
> A pretext, nothing more! No, triumph not!
> I took you but to leap above myself
> To something higher, as one takes a weapon,
> A thyrsis, or a goblet, or a torch!
> (105)

Once again he is humbled. The ghosts taunt him by pointing out that, if they indeed were no more than the pretexts by which he could leap above himself, toward what goal was it? Stripped of all his vainglory, Don Juan begs the Devil to take him to Hell. But the Devil has a more cruel fate in store for him. Don Juan shall hereafter be a puppet, "Eternally enacting gallantries / Before a bluish backdrop"(121). Don Juan cries for mercy and refuses to play the role now assigned him: "Not that foul box!—Give me the circle of flame / My pride deserves! . . . I long to suffer! / I've never suffered! I've a right to hell! / I've earned my hell!"(122). Hell, however, is wherever the Devil decrees, and he tells Don Juan that, while some celebrated men are damned within their statues, he, Don Juan, is damned within his puppet. As he is shoved into the puppet booth at the end, Don Juan appears as a travesty of himself, a puppet proclaiming that he is the "famous burlador," referring to the original Spanish Don Juan, who appeared for the first time in 1630, in the playwright Tirso de Molina's well-known *El Burlador de Sevilla* (*The Seducer of Seville*). Though "fit to wield a mighty sword," he is now reduced to playing the role eternally of a puppet beating other puppets with a stick.

PAUL CLAUDEL: FROM *BUNRAKU* TO A BEAR ON THE MOON

Paul Claudel was one of the best traveled French writers of his generation, with a particular fascination with the Orient. He had three lengthy so-journs in China (1895–99, 1900–1905, 1906–9) and served as French ambassador in Tokyo from 1921 to 1927. His literary career primarily as a dramatist made his discovery of Japanese theater a foregone conclusion. Claudel's interest, however, was anything but superficial. He wrote several prose pieces on various aspects of Japanese society and culture, including a few devoted to Japanese theater: "Nô" (1925–26), "Kabouki" (1926), and "Bounrakou" (1924). It was in the last essay, about the Japanese *bunraku* puppet tradition, that Claudel revealed the depth of his appreciation for puppetry in general:

> A puppet is the complete animated likeness, not only of the face, but of the limbs and the whole body. A living doll, a tiny man in our hands, a concentration of movement. A puppet is not, like a human actor, held captive by its own weight. It has no contact with earth, and moves with equal ease in all dimensions. It floats in an intangible element like a drawing in an empty space. Its life is in its center, and its four limbs and head, spread out like rays around it, are merely its elements of expression. It is a talking star, untouchable. The Japanese have not tried to make it walk; that is impossible, for it does not belong to the earth but stands on an invisible stalk and turns its mocking face to every side. Legs and feet are not simply means of progress or support, but the instrument of every attitude, walk, and witty contortion, expressing anxiety, eagerness, resistance, defiance, weariness, awakening, and the wish to go or stay. Look—we'll lift him up so that you can see him! Look at that funny little man—he can do anything! Look at this lady and gentleman in the air—a whole slice of life at the end of a stick! And behind—it's so amusing to keep well hidden and make someone come to life; to create that little doll that goes in at the eyes of every spectator to strut and posture in his mind!

In all those rows of motionless people only this little goblin moves, like the wild elfish soul of all of them. They gaze at him like children, and he sparkles like a little firecracker![20]

This (relatively late) interest in puppet theater notwithstanding, Claudel experimented only minimally with the puppet motif in his own playwriting. In 1919, about two years before he set sail for Japan, Claudel published his first play with a puppet or marionette element. *L'Ours et la lune* (*The Bear and the Moon*), a one-act "farce pour un théâtre de marionettes" ("farce for a marionette theater"), was written during Claudel's diplomatic assignment in Rio de Janeiro in 1917–18. Darius Milhaud, who accompanied Claudel to Brazil as his secretary, composed the rhythm for the three voices chanting to the accompaniment of a drum at the end of the second scene. The little play was printed together with the two-act "drame satyrique" ("satyr play") *Protée* in a volume entitled *Deux Farces lyriques* (*Two Lyrical Farces*).

Although Claudel has become the subject of a voluminous critical literature since his death in 1955, very little has been written about *The Bear and the Moon*.[21] Despite this neglect, the play was performed in the United States at a meeting of the Modern Language Association in Chicago on 28 December 1973.[22] In light of Claudel's weightier contributions to the drama, the critical neglect may be understandable. But his "lyrical farce" is no less representative of both his outlook and his style and deserves a little more attention. In essence a dramatized dream, the play is set in a prison camp in northern Germany during World War I. As a French prisoner falls asleep at a table, he calls out to his wife and children. There may be a reflection here of Claudel's own separation from his family during his stay in Rio de Janeiro, where the play was written, and his deep feelings of nostalgia at the time. As if in delirium, the Prisoner has a vision of his son's room with its toys, among them a bear in a bed with dolls. The Moon—like Dawn and the Prisoner one of the "Acteurs" (actors) of the play—then appears as a shaft of light and engages him in conversation. After recounting the Prisoner's previous life with its joys and sorrows, in the familiar poetic prose of Claudel's plays, the Moon encourages him to feel free, telling him that he can take flight if he but has the will:

Forget your existence for a second and you will again find yourself on the other side of all the walls.

You can fly with no wings other than your will. It is I who has made this possible. . . .

The body is neither the instrument of your servitude, nor the jailer, but the agile servant of your spirit, the form externally most suitable to it and its realization of all the points of space you wish, successive or simultaneous.[23]

The Prisoner then asks the Moon to unite him with the beam shining on his children. The Moon assents, assuring him that as a father he has the right to be a child, to be with them as one. "Now the magic lantern begins," she declares. The "realm of dreams"—heralded by the banging of a drum—is about to be entered. As the Moon exhorts the Prisoner to sleep, a marionette theater appears onstage behind him. The scene is that of the children's room of which he had an earlier vision. Besides the Moon, who now appears dressed as an old woman in an outfit "similar to pictures of Queen Victoria" (149), the characters ("Marionettes") appearing in the marionette show include the Bear; the Choir, who leads the Moon around and ignites her, or extinguishes her, at appropriate moments; the Legless Aviator; Rhodo, whom the Aviator loves; the Bone-Setter, Rhodo's father; and the Black Dwarf.

Most of the humor of *The Bear and the Moon* is concentrated in the scenes performed by the marionettes. Reflecting the early-twentieth-century artistic interest in the world of the child, the dream sequence was conceived by Claudel as a marionette show because of its association with childhood and the specific recollection of a children's room with its toys and dolls.

Of all the characters in the marionette show, the most entertaining by far is the Bear. He is portrayed as an ursine financier gone bad, a down-to-earth, practical, money-loving "man of the world," who dominates the intrigue and manipulates the other characters (except for the Moon) as if he were controlling their strings. In the surreal-absurdist stye of the playlet, the Bear at one point boasts that all Paris knew him and that he once owned a yacht called *Apache*, where he promenaded with "members of the French Academy and with a lady from a Subsidized Theater" (202). Assuming the role of a frail woman easily given to weeping to whom no one gives a thought any more, the Moon asks the Bear's help. Before she tells him what she has on her mind, the Choir, acting as her spokesman, tells the Bear that the Moon is in love with a young man named Paul, an aviator who has lost both his legs and has been in a hospital bed for several months. He and the Moon have been observing each other nights through an open window. Beneath his pillow he keeps a letter from his fiancée, Rhodo, who writes that she has heard that he has lost his legs, that she loves only him, but that she is going to marry his cousin, who is an engineer in a chemical factory.

At a dinner attended by the Bear and the Bone-Setter, as well as the Moon and the Aviator, the Bear attempts to further turn the Aviator against his fiancée by demonstrating his knowledge of her letter and telling him that she doesn't love him. Callously, he adds that the Aviator's legless condition is an impediment to love. "Love," he says, "is desire, and one desires only that which is whole." Would he be anything other than "a husband whom one would be obliged to carry in one's arms like a mannequin?" (180). He then tells him that there is a well-to-do lady "of a certain age" who has fallen in love with him and who expects of him no more than his feelings. When Rhodo appears and takes her place at the dinner table between the Bear and the Moon, the Bear immediately begins professing his affection for her. Undaunted by her rejection, the Bear says now that he is in love with Rhodo, that she loves him, and that he will marry her, thus enabling the Aviator to marry the person who is interested in him and whom he identifies as the "owner of a very large lighting company, rural as well as urban" (190). When the Choir illuminates the Moon so that he can see into her soul, the Bear is struck by her "pure love, her chivalrous fidelity undemanding of reciprocity, in life or death, and even beyond life and death." He renounces further pursuit of Rhodo and will henceforth devote himself solely to the Aviator and his happiness. When Rhodo tells the Bear that she might take him on in her postwar business as a cashier because of his financial experience, but with a monetary contribution from him, he denies having any money. She replies that he does have "something that shines beneath his skin like a star" (202). He tells her that it is just a fake diamond, but she replies that it is made up of the tears of all those he has cheated and that he must give it to her. With the help of the Aviator and the Choir, Rhodo succeeds in seizing it from the Bear. However, the Choir takes it, proceeds to the front of the stage, and ceremoniously returns it to the Prisoner, who wants it given back to his child, from whom the Bear originally took it. Alluding to the diamond as a symbol of the things of this earth and of no value compared to the brilliance of the stars in the sky—in other words the spiritual realm—the Choir causes the diamond to dissolve in a burst of dazzling light. When the Prisoner laments that his child's property has disappeared, the Choir assures him, in Claudelian terms, that it has simply been reconstituted in him: "You did not give him life, but instead sowed the light in him. This particle of eternal light in us that gives us no rest until it is freed from our blind body. The spirit of flight and bounding and shouting and joy and giving and vision and desire!" (210). Shortly thereafter, a servant brings the Moon a card announcing the arrival of Le Bourguinon (The Burgundian), meaning the Sun. They all rush to flee with the breaking of day. The Aviator declares that it is time for him to go back to his hospital; Rhodo will return to the munitions factory where she is employed. In the half-hour the Choir says they have left, the Bear invites them to board his ship, the celestial Great Bear, for a trip to Heaven.

In the fifth and last scene of the play, the setting is again the prison camp in northern Germany. The "sad light of day" is coming up. Dawn makes his appearance. The Prisoner regards him as "homely, old, and sad," and prefers to be asleep than to be awakened. Awake, he is back again in "this eternal captivity"; again he has to "reopen his eyes and recover his soul and his body and all the horrible and boring things." But if he must get up, he asks that "at least the memory of those things seen a second before awakening not be effaced" (221). The Prisoner's last monologue, spoken just before Dawn removes the veils in which he is enveloped, is typically Claudelian. If what he has seen in dream is to be effaced after all, the Prisoner can take consolation in the fact that it represented a mysterious sign, which he interprets as follows:

> The limit of the earth in the middle of an abyss of light as slight as the edge of a cup, as thin as the taut wire of a harp,
>   An island lashed by the foam of the sea, a beach at the feet of somber mountains all littered with huge withered palms. (222)

The Bear and the Moon may easily be overlooked in the company of Claudel's grandiose dramatic works. Though rarely performed, it was staged in Paris in 1968, the centennial year of Claudel's birth, by Dominique Houdart, but with real actors playing the parts of the marionettes and in a circus clown style.[24] While reiterating familiar Claudelian themes—the symbolism of captivity and liberation and of light and moon, the deprecation of the material world, the yearning for transcendence—the play is a refreshing change of pace in its tongue-in-cheek humor and surrealism. The scenes set in the prison camp merely frame the marionette show, which is the heart of the play; and there is reason to believe that Claudel originally had in mind that the work would be performed by marionettes. The writer's interest in puppets and marionettes deepened considerably during his years of diplomatic service in the Far East. But *The Bear and the Moon* suggests that before these experiences Claudel was aware of the contemporary artistic interest in puppets and marionettes as well as in the fantasy realm of the child. The Prisoner's dream in the play is the pretext for the conception of a marionette show, which owes little to traditional puppet or marionette theater. It serves as the license, as it were, for a rare display of the wit and humor of which Claudel was capable, but here offered up in an atmosphere of unrestrained surreal alogicality.

MICHEL DE GHELDERODE: A LIFE WITH DOLLS

Although "discovered" by French audiences only in the 1950s and still too infrequently performed on foreign stages, Michel de Ghelderode has a legion of admirers and must surely be judged one of the most original, if controversial, dramatists of the twentieth century.[25] A Belgian of Flemish origin, Ghelderode was steeped in the history and folklore of his native region and often sought inspiration for his plays in these sources. Most of his works are set in Flanders, especially in the medieval to Baroque periods. For Ghelderode it was in these older centuries that popular and religious rituals and practices formed a more integral part of the everyday culture of the Flemish people. This was particularly true for the old Flemish puppet and marionette theater, to which he was strongly attracted both personally and as a man of the theater. A practitioner of "theatricalized" theater, Ghelderode spurned realism-naturalism in favor of a drama of striking visual images, of mask, mime, dance, song, and puppetry. Carnival, vaudeville, musical hall, circus, and marionette theater were his principal performance models. His fondness for the bizarre and grotesque, often for the scatological, shows up in most of his dramatic writing. Impelled by his keen but unorthodox interest in religion, biblical and popular, Ghelderode continued to cultivate the mystery play long after it had outworn its fervent welcome by the Symbolists. Typecasting Ghelderode is a futile exercise; he is a dramatist of surprise, unpredictable, outrageous, engrossing. He could with equal facility write on medieval Flanders, Saint Francis of Assisi, the biblical Barabbas, or the Faust legend, or he could concoct a dramatic fairy tale based on the life of Christopher Columbus.

Ghelderode's lifelong love affair with puppets and marionettes is widely appreciated and is sometimes pointed to as the key to his dramatic out-

look. In August 1951, at the height of the excitement surrounding his
"discovery," he gave a series of interviews that were recorded at Ostend,
Belgium, and broadcast by Radiodiffusion et Télévision françaises in
1951–52. In one of the interviews, he spoke of the role of marionettes,
puppets, dolls, and objects in his life and in the shaping of his ideas on
theater:

> Yes, marionettes were the great concern of the whole of my childhood; I'd
> even say of the whole of my career.
>
> Even today I collect marionettes, dolls, puppets, little rag creatures of
> yesterday that the children of today scorn; also dummies with lovely mortal
> faces of wax, models of hands, adorable heads of young martyrs, severed
> by what executioner?
>
> I welcome to my home all these human shapes and reminders of human
> shapes; I collect these image-beings as if they were precious objects. They
> are silent presences; I say they are presences, presumptions.
>
> All these effigies thrill me by virtue of their somewhat magical nature,
> and even though flesh and blood actors can weary me and often disappoint
> me, marionettes, because of their natural reserve and perfect silence, man-
> age to console me for the cacaphony of the play and the crazy glibness of the
> impudent creatures that theater people most often are.
>
> Furthermore, I owe them the revelation of the theater, the theater in its
> pure state, the theater in its savage state, the original theater.
>
> Naturally, I wasn't able to understand all this from my first games. The
> marionette was then a toy, my favorite toy, even my passion—other toys
> gave me no pleasure. But even then I believed, and this strange belief is not
> yet dead in me, that objects were sensitive, living.[26]

Appropriately—in light of these sentiments—several of Ghelderode's
plays are designated as having been written for marionette performance,
whether or not the dramatist actually had real marionettes in mind. The
earliest was *Le Mystère de la Passion de Notre Seigneur* (*The Mystery of
the Passion of Our Lord*), the first of a series of five plays for marionettes
allegedly "reconstructed according to the Brussels marionette show" but
actually written by Ghelderode himself in 1924–25 for the marionette
theater of the Renaissance d'Occident, a Belgian literary society which
also published a journal of the same name (Ghelderode was elected president of the society on 17 October 1924). The other plays in the series were
La Tentation de Saint Antoine (*The Temptation of Saint Anthony*), *Le*

Massacre des Innocents (*The Massacre of the Innocents*), *Duvelor ou la farce du diable vieux* (*Duvelor, or The Farce of the Old Devil*), and *La Farce de la mort qui faillit trépasser* (*The Farce of the Dead Man Who Refused to Die*). The series for the marionette theater of the Renaissance d'Occident was followed by *Les Femmes au tombeau* (*The Women at the Tomb*, 1928), which originally bore the subtitle *Drame pour marionettes* (*A Drama for Marionettes*). Ghelderode subsequently deleted this lest it be assumed that the play was reserved "just for actors made of wood, although it contains certain expressions appropriate to them as well as specific gestures as painted by artists of the Flemish 'primitives' school")[27]; *Le Siège d'Ostende* (*The Siege of Ostend*, 1933), subtitled *Epopée militaire pour marionettes* (*A Military Epic for Marionettes*); and *D'un diable qui prêcha merveilles* (*About a Devil Who Preached Miracles*, 1934), subtitled a *Mystère pour marionettes* (*A Mystery for Marionettes*). Other plays of Ghelderode, while not specifically written for marionettes, contain puppet, marionette, or related figures or imagery. These include *Le Cavalier bizarre* (*The Bizarre Horseman*, 1920), a *pochade* (rough sketch) in one act; the three-act *Don Juan ou les amants chimériques* (*Don Juan, or The Wistful Lovers*, 1928); *Le Ménage de Caroline* (*Caroline's Household*, 1930), another *pochade*, consisting of eleven scenes; *Mademoiselle Jaïre* (1934), a four-part "mystery"; the one-act *Hop, Signor!* (1935); the "drame" *L'Ecole des buffons* (*The School for Clowns*, 1937); and the "action dramatique" ("dramatic action") *Le Soleil se couche* (*The Sun Is Setting*, 1943).

In this latter group of plays—those not written specifically for marionette performance but containing puppets, marionettes, and the like—puppet and marionette motifs, whether discrete images or subtextually metaphoric, are invested with greater significance than may appear to be the case at first glance. *The Bizarre Horseman*—to consider the earliest first—seems outwardly Maeterlinckian, reminiscent specifically of *L'Intruse* (*The Intruder*); but so different is it in spirit and tone that it may best be regarded as a take-off on Maeterlinck. The "rough sketch," as the play is subtitled, dramatizes the reactions of the inmates of a Flemish home for the aged when they believe that Death is heading their way. Instead of the ominous and portentous atmosphere of Maeterlinck, the reigning silence, Ghelderode imbues his play with the grotesqueness, boisterousness, and plasticity of a Breughel canvas. When they are convinced that the horse-

man riding toward them is Death coming to claim them, the old men decide to greet it with a dance accompanied by accordion playing and ca-
cophonous singing:

> Fourth Old Man (*breaking out an accordion*). I'll lead the dance, the
>   macabre ball!
> Fifth Old Man. Let's dance to Death! Let's dance the macabre! It's the
>   festival of the old, it's the quadrille of the moribund!
> The Old Woman. I'll dance till I drop! (19)

Following the dance, they all hurry to confess their sins. But when it appears that the rider is not only not coming for them but is in fact bearing
a newborn child in his arms, the old people rejoice and resume their dancing. The final stage direction, calling for mimed action, introduces the
marionette motif:

> (*He [the watchman] smiles softly and turns away from the window. The old
> woman crosses herself. The accordion resounds. The racket is ear-splitting.
> Shouts. Spasmodic dance of the old people, their mouths open, their fists
> shut tight like stiff marionettes.*) (25)

Besides resembling marionettes in their spasmodic closing dance, now a
celebration of life instead of a greeting of death, as in their previous *danse
macabre*, the old people also suggest puppets or marionettes in their reactions to the news of approaching Death. Disbelief yields to fear, fear to a
grotesque dance welcoming Death, followed by relief that Death has this
time passed them by, and then a new dance celebrating life. Sensing the
approach of Death, humans are marionette-like in their "programmed"
response. In his early plays "for marionettes," Maeterlinck drew on the
image of the wooden figure to convey the ominous aura of approaching
Death and the terror that grips the human spirit. Ghelderode employs the
suggestive power of the marionette figure to go beyond Maeterlinck's spiritual dread to the down-to-earth physical acceptance of Death and the release of primal energy in the celebration of life reclaimed, at least for a little longer.

   Caroline's Household, which was first staged in Brussels on 26 October
1935 at the Théâtre de l'Exposition, is Ghelderode at his lightest. Little
more than an entertaining confection with dolls, *Caroline's Household*
brings together a trio of mannequins and the classic masks of the Italian
commedia dell'arte—Pierrot, Columbine, and Harlequin. The manne-

quins—two males (Suskanel and Spiridon, the latter being black) and a female (Paméla)—belong to a fair entertainer named Borax who uses them in a ball-throwing game. But Borax is having trouble with his mannequins, whom he inherited from a certain Caroline in return for his favors. Even when struck right in the heart, they refuse to budge and, in other ways as well, behave recalcitrantly. Borax is so upset with them that he talks about destroying them since they are hurting his business. Overhearing Borax's threats, the mannequins believe they owe him no more allegiance and march out of the fair tent. Besides exulting in their newfound freedom, the mannequins seethe with the desire for vengeance on Borax for all the time he has mistreated them. But before they decide on how best to punish him, a romantic rivalry threatens their unity. Both Suskanel and Spiridon confess their love for Paméla. She decides to resolve the conflict by giving herself to the one who performs the most sensational exploit or crime that night.

When the mannequins quit the scene, in come the aging, dilapidated stars of the old commedia dell'arte—Pierrot, Columbine, and Harlequin. Their entrance is accompanied by Chopin's funeral march. Pierrot and Columbine are now sixty, while Harlequin, who carries a beggar's sack slung over his shoulder, is in his eighties. They complain bitterly of their wretched existence; they are unemployed, broke, and homeless and even contemplate death. When they come upon Borax's tent, they decide to use it as a temporary shelter. His sign seeking new mannequins fills them with hope of employment at last. They will pretend to be mannequins and will apply for the jobs. In the meantime, Suskanel and Spiridon return and whisper into Paméla's ear their sensational exploits of the previous night. Paméla's continued indecision incites them to fight each other until Columbine's shout for help takes them by surprise. Surmising that the commedia dell'arte figures are their replacements, the three mannequins decide to test their endurance by hurling balls at them. The commedia masks are quickly vanquished, but the game is interrupted by the arrival of a very drunk Borax. Catching sight of the mannequins, he vents his anger by using them for target practice, first with a rifle and then with a pair of pistols. But the mannequins weave and bob and duck his bullets. Thinking he has "killed" them, Borax announces his intention to destroy the tent. Alarmed, Pierrot, Columbine, and Harlequin show themselves; Borax takes them for the mannequins' ghosts and begins hurling balls at them while the three mannequins, hiding behind the commedia figures, are hilarious. When all six disappear from view, Borax gloats over his triumph and then begins to look for the "corpses." However, the mannequins suddenly appear and start tossing balls at Borax, to the applause of the commedia figures.

With Borax subdued for the time being, the mannequins strip off their outer garb and appear in resplendent costumes. But the quarrel resumes between Suskanel and Spiridon, and Paméla proposes that they use Borax's pistols to fight a duel over her. At this point, Harlequin steps forward to suggest that the quarrel be settled amicably by all three staying together in a loving trinity, just like Harlequin, Pierrot, and Columbine. As soon as the mannequins leave, Borax reappears, boasts that the "suffering of others fills him with a sense of well-being," and threatens to strangle the commedia figures, whom he now takes to be the mannequins in disguise. When Columbine screams for the police, Borax orders them into the tent, where all four of them will stand rigid, like mannequins. Using his sword to determine if all four figures are real mannequins, the gendarme who arrives on the scene quickly ferrets out Borax and arrests him. He also tells him that he will be condemned to death for the terrible crimes committed the previous night by Suskanel and Spiridon and now attributed to Borax. One of the crimes he will be charged with is sneaking into a worker's home in the guise of a funeral attendant and cutting the throat of a newborn baby while its parents were asleep. When he tries to escape, Borax is seized by the gendarme, who begins carrying him off by force. Accidentally striking the tent as they go, Borax causes it to collapse, burying the three mannequins. In the last scene of the play, Pierrot, Columbine, and Harlequin crawl out from under the debris and bemoan their lot anew. Their final words capture the spirit of play of *Caroline's Household* as a whole:

> *Harlequin.* Come on . . . our fortunes will hardly ever change . . . We are
> without a country, without a roof over our heads. One has to go on . . .
> there's nothing else.
> *Columbine.* Unless some old-fashioned author . . . some Belgian, maybe
> . . . agrees to put us in a play. (5:206)

Cast in a more familiarly grotesque and sinister aspect, *Hop, Signor!* carries the viewer back into the realm of old Flemish folk customs with which Ghelderode was always comfortable. As often in his plays, death is again prominent; but in this work it claims victims. Marguerite is the dissatisfied wife of Juréal, the town sculptor. Both are impotent, but in different ways, and the play in general pivots on the theme of impotence. Juréal is no longer able to sculp artistically and is derided by the townspeople as a pathetic, ludicrous figure. Marguerite has never known a man's love and also despises her husband. A fanatic monk named Pilar wants to bring Marguerite to her ruin because of her pride in her purity, which the monk regards as an affront to the Virgin Mary. Only the Mother of Jesus, he declares, can be without sin. He seizes on the arrival in town of two handsome young foreign noblemen, Helgar and Adorno, to plant the seed in Juréal's mind that Marguerite is unfaithful to him with one or both of them.

During a town festival, Juréal is killed when a red sheet in which he is tossed up and down in the air like a doll—a carnival practice at the time—is allowed to drop to the ground. Each time Juréal is tossed in the air, the crowd cries out, mockingly, "Hop, Signor" (the derisive name applied to Juréal). It later appears that Helgar and Adorno, both strongly attracted to Marguerite, were responsible for Juréal's death. The two noblemen accompany the townspeople bearing Juréal's body to Marguerite. Exhibiting no remorse, Marguerite bids the procession continue; she has no desire to view the corpse. Shortly thereafter she decides to take both Helgar and Adorno as lovers, to experience what she has so long lived without. The two men quarrel over which shall be the first to enter Marguerite's room, and Adorno stabs Helgar to death, then flees. Pilar enters and accuses Marguerite of being responsible for the deaths of Juréal and Helgar. He paints her as a demonic temptress, a sorceress, and calls for her to be executed, but not before she exposes his own suppressed lust for her in a wild scene. When Pilar rushes away to fetch the authorities, Marguerite, now deranged from grief, ignores the danger to her and has only the fulfilment of the sex act in mind. When the two grotesque dwarfs, Mèche (Wick) and Suif (Tallow), who worked for Juréal, come in to tell Marguerite to flee a menacing crowd gathering outside her house, she urges them to come into her room, where she offers to undress them "like two puppets" ("Venez dans ma chambre. Je vous déshabillerai comme deux fantoches," 1:62).

After Marguerite is led off to certain execution, Mèche and Suif remain alone onstage at play's end. At Suif's insistence, the two of them play a macabre game, at the center of which is a marionette. Echoing Ghelderode's own outlook, Suif says, "What makes you shudder contains what you must laugh at." He then proposes to Mèche: "Let us immortalize the am-

bitious fellow who rose up to the clouds. Hop! To the firmament!" What
follows is a reenactment of the death of Juréal with a marionette inside
the sheet:

> *(He [Suif] unfolds the sheet. Mèche takes out of the sheet a small disjointed*
> *marionette, dressed as a lord, with plume and sword. He kisses it and*
> *pushes it in Suif's face, who also kisses it. Then the sheet is pulled tight. And*
> *the marionette is flung into the air, collected again in the sheet which is*
> *pulled tight again, and made to rebound.)* (65)

As the macabre little game progresses, Suif and Mèche keep shouting:
"Hop, little Signor! You were noble!" "Higher. Hop, Signor . . ." "Hop,
Signor." (65). The marionette going up and down in the air is the play's
concluding—and haunting—image. Suif and Mèche go out, playing. The
stage stays empty. Outside, bursts of laughter and applause from the
crowd greet the two dwarfs. Soon all are shouting "Hop, Signor!" In the
window of the room from which the dwarfs have just exited "the little
marionette can be seen rising and falling like a wounded bird hesitating
between sky and earth" (65). By now, of course, the marionette rising and
falling in the air has become more than just the symbol of Juréal; it is that
of human beings in general, playthings of irrational forces, forced to vac-
illate between heaven and earth.

Marionette imagery as subtext also informs one of Ghelderode's most
striking, and disturbing, plays, *The School for Clowns*. Ghelderode regarded it as his favorite. Set in Flanders during the second half of the six-
teenth century, it tells the story of a group of thirteen grotesque, wretched
buffoons on their last night in a school for buffoons presided over by Sir
Folial (Le Chevalier Folial), knight and "master of buffoons" ("Maître des
bouffons"), with the assistance of his beadle, Galgut. Before they are set
loose in search of employment to uplift them from their dreadfully low status as social outcasts, freaks, and men of uncertain origin, the secrets of
their profession will be revealed to them by their master. From their first
appearance, the buffoons recall puppets or marionettes. As Galgut beats
on a tambourine, they enter in single file, executing a pilgrims' march. It
is, as the stage direction indicates, a "*grotesque procession*." The buffoons
sing in muffled tones; their strolling is accompanied by "*bows and little*
ridiculous gestures." The description of them creates the impression of so
many absurd puppets:

(Not all of them are misshapen or deformed; but not a single one of them is without obvious defects: limps, gibbosities, various hydrocephali, to say nothing of facial ugliness, which is accentuated all the more by their makeup. . . . They are uniformly attired in short frocks of coarse sackcloth and vair mantlets, but they wear colorful stockings and wooden sandals, which make their footsteps resound. In contrast, they display eccentric headdress: one, a steel helmet; another, a little wreath of roses; the next, a crown of peacock feathers; the fourth, a felt hood; or a hennin; or a cap made of vine branches; a miter; copper spokes borrowed from a saint's head; a Beguine's cornet; an upside-down nest; and the rest wear a ram's horns, a small beehive, and a turban.) (3:291–92)

The puppet aspect of the buffoons is reinforced in their choral chanting, the shuffling, bearlike dance they perform in place, and their uniform responses to Galgut's words and orders. Actions of this type recur throughout the play. At one point, for example, in act 1, scene 5, Galgut orders the buffoons to perform the Night Dance. As soon as he starts beating on his drum, eleven of the buffoons onstage leap in place without gesturing. The rest of the stage direction makes the nature of the dance explicit:

(It is a ballet of automatons, reminiscent of an Inca dance, in which only the feet and shoulders move. The drum ceases and the dance continues silently. Then the drum resumes its beat, in a frantic crescendo. The dance becomes wild, a kind of forced stamping. When the roar reaches its maximum, Galgut whistles and everything comes to a stop. In unison, the dancers fall to their haunches and place their candles in such a way as to form a luminous band at the front of the stage.) (306–7)

When the time comes for Folial to disclose the secret of their art, of great art, in fact the secret of genius, he falters and suggests that because of his age and frail health, he no longer remembers it! The buffoons become indignant and restive. To calm them and to reawaken Folial, who has fallen into a faint, Galgut orders the buffoons to take up their instruments and perform for Folial. The lengthy stage direction at the beginning of act 1, scene 7, calls for mimed action in which the principal performer is none other than a Folial who increasingly comes to resemble a puppet. As the buffoons play, Folial revives, stirred by the music, and begins executing a dance. In ecstasy, transfigured, he again becomes the actor he used to be, and he *"improvises the strange figures of a tipsy puppet (poupée chavi-*

rante)." When the music ends, the dancer *"remains as though suspended on wires,"* moribund.

As the play draws to an end, Galgut, at Folial's urging, stages a play-within-a-play called *A Night in Escorial* calculated to astonish the Master. The play is a merciless recounting of the wedding night of Folial's daughter, Vénéranda, and a clown identified in the play as Folial II and played by the buffoon Bifrons. When he moves to possess his young wife, she rebuffs him. Insult is added to injury when she tells him that the only reason she married him was to excite the jealousy of the prince, Don Carlos, whom she loves but who scorned her. When her clown-husband menaces Vénéranda with a dagger, Folial goes beserk, accuses Bifrons of trying to kill "your Master's daughter," and hurls him from the little stage. When Folial collapses from exertion, Galgut and the buffoons believe him dead and begin celebrating the demise of their tyrannical master. But hardly do they begin their merrymaking, when Folial comes to, seizes a whip, and commences to crack it over their heads like an animal trainer in a circus. Cowed and whimpering, the buffoons are whipped into a merry-go-round encircling a catafalque containing two buffoons forced by Folial to act out the remainder of the play-within-a-play as two cadavers. As Galgut chants the *Dies Irae* from the requiem mass, Folial exhorts the buffoons to move faster and faster. When Galgut is unable to continue his chanting, Folial takes over himself, chanting and whipping in a mad frenzy. The action reaches a crescendo and pandemonium erupts, with the buffoons bumping into one another, falling down, then scrambling for the exit. When everyone has managed to flee, including the buffoons still in the catafalque, Folial, alone onstage, finally blurts out the long-withheld secret:

> Listen to your old Master, listen . . . I say unto you, in all truth . . . The secret of our art, of art in general, of great art, of all art that seeks to endure . . . (*A moment of silence. In a low, but distinct voice.*) It is CRU-EL-TY! (331)

As Folial resumes whipping empty space, since no one else is in the room, his eyes fill with tears and his face turns radiant from inner joy. Taking ever wider swings, he ends up flagellating himself, without pity, feeling nothing. Again, Ghelderode closes a play with the haunting image of man as a nonhuman figure mechanically repeating gestures beyond his command, "like an automaton, tragically" ("comme un automate, tragique-ment," 332). Not without relevance for the time when it was written, *The School for Clowns* employs the full arsenal of Ghelderode's grotesqueness and horrific scenic effects to explore the nature of social intolerance and humiliation and of authoritarian absolutism as a duality of terror and clownishness.

Folial's revelation of the secret of art as cruelty naturally brings to mind Antonin Artaud's blueprint for a new theater which he laid out in two manifestoes entitled "The Theater of Cruelty" and "The Theater and Cruelty" and incorporated into his most famous book, *Le Théâtre et son Double* (*The Theater and Its Double*, 1938). Cruelty, as Artaud used the term, did not mean physical violence or bloodletting in any conventional sense, though that was certainly possible in his theater. Instead,

> I employ the word "cruelty" in the sense of an appetite for life, a cosmic rigor, an implacable necessity, in the gnostic sense of a living whirlwind that devours the darkness, in the sense of that pain apart from whose in-eluctable necessity life could not continue; good is desired, it is the conse-quence of an act; evil is permanent.[28]

The new theater based on Artaud's concept of cruelty was to

> seek by every possible means to call into question not only the objective and descriptive external world but the internal world, that is, man from a meta-physical point of view. It is only thus, we believe, that we may once again be able to speak in connection with the theater about the rights of the imagi-nation. Neither Humor, nor Poetry, nor Imagination means anything un-less by an anarchic destruction generating a fantastic flight of forms, which will constitute the whole spectacle, they succeed in organically calling into question man, his ideas about reality, and his poetic place in reality.[29]

Much of what Artaud has to say about the need to overcome the subju-gation of the theater by the text, about the creation of a metaphysics of speech, gesture, and expression, in order to rescue the theater from its psychological and human stagnation, and about spectacle, dance song and music, lighting, masks, puppets, and the actor, was echoed in Ghelderode's dramatic practice. This has of course raised questions concerning Ghelderode's possible indebtedness to Artaud, despite their differences as dramatists. But in trying to determine the extent of the Belgian's knowledge of Artaud's writings on the "theater of cruelty," scholars have generally come to the conclusion that he conceived *The School for Clowns* independently of Artaud. There is, moreover, no indication that Ghelderode was any more aware of Artaud's ideas in 1942 and 1943, when *The School for Clowns* was edited and then published, than he was in 1936, when he wrote the play. Epistolary evidence, in fact, suggests that Ghelderode had already begun considering the value of cruelty to the dramatic artist before the publication of Artaud's essays and that Goya rather than Artaud was his principal inspiration at the time.[30] In any case, a comparison of Artaud and Ghelderode from the viewpoint of their ideas on and practice of cruelty in the theater makes for an intriguing exercise, one that may ultimately tell us more about the intellectual and artistic currents of the period the two men lived in than about influences.

The play-within-a-play in *The School for Clowns* becomes, as we have seen, the pretext for Folial's revelation of his "secret" about cruelty and art. This really should be regarded as the core of the play as a whole since Ghelderode obviously intended it as a vehicle for his own quasi-Artaudian ideas. In *The Sun Is Setting*, another play-within-a-play assumes a similar centrality, but in this instance it is cast wholly in terms of marionette theater. The subject of the play, in brief, is the last days of the old and infirm emperor Charles V (Charles Quint) in Spain and, inferentially, the last days of Flanders under the rule of his son, Philip II, as Holy Roman Emperor. It used to be said of Charles V that the sun never set on his vast empire. The meaning of the title of Ghelderode's play is that, with the transfer of power from Charles to Philip, the sun has begun to set and night is descending above all on the Flanders so dear to Charles. It was in the reign of Philip that the Inquisition was visited on the northern Protestant provinces of Flanders and the Duke of Alba dispatched at the head of an army that sowed death and destruction wherever it went.

In the immediate background of the play, Charles has abdicated in favor of his son. As profoundly Spanish as his father is Flemish, Philip has all but imprisoned Charles in the monastery of Yuste in Estremadura, Spain, there to live out his remaining days surrounded by zealous Spanish prelates. The time is the last day of August 1558. Philip hopes that in his new somber surroundings, far from the earthly delights of his native Ghent, Charles will prepare himself for death in a manner befitting his imperial status. However, the former emperor has no intention of allowing his

Flemishness to be completely compromised by the austerity of a Spanish monastery. He decorates his quarters with typical Flemish sumptuousness and taunts the monks, especially the most unyielding of them, Fray Ramón, for their disdain for everything secular and for their macabre Spanish Catholicism.

For entertainment, and to take his mind off his "imprisonment," Charles asks to see "les mécaniques," in this instance an automaton in the form of a black devil, horned, with quivering tail and an unbelievably long tongue. In his brief appearance, which Fray Ramón vehemently condemns, the devil-automaton alternatingly thrusts forward and withdraws a trident. The automaton is followed by a marionette show, a favorite entertainment of Charles's still permitted him at Yuste. This becomes the play-within-a-play of *The Sun Is Setting*.

Set in Brussels, the marionette show begins innocently enough with droll banter between figures representing Saint Michael and Ulenspiegel. But with the appearance of two other marionettes, the sniveling, hunchbacked, and potbellied clown, Paep-Theun, and a burgher of Ghent, the dialogue—despite the outwardly primitive syle of a typical marionette performance—assumes the unexpected character of a critique of Charles's reign as emperor. With Ulenspiegel playing the role of a kind of devil's advocate and inciting the burgher of Ghent to air his grievances, Charles soon finds himself on the defensive. Sriking back at the criticism ushering forth from the marionettes' mouths, he defends his reign as being that of a "good father to a bad son."[31] Since his people were, he says, incapable of governing themselves and were just "devouring one another," he wielded a firm hand and made them the "subjects of a prestigious empire." He also "raised them up, glorified them, opened up to them the ports of the world and the oceans." And instead of being any help to him in his grand designs for them, "hatred and treachery were [their] rule," "haggling [their] politics" (39). Offended by the performance, Charles ends it abruptly when he picks up a sword and moves menacingly in the direction of the tiny stage. The marionettes disperse amid much pushing and howling. Alone and angry, Charles demands that the manipulator of the marionettes present himself, if he dares.

The play now turns eery. In answer to Charles's call, a strange, otherworldly figure who introduces himself as Ignotus ("unknown," "strange," "ignoble," in Latin) appears. Ghelderode describes him in these terms:

(This being who could come from the other world only appears to be a man since a coarse grayish sackcloth covers him from head to foot, and a knotted cord hangs at his waist. His head is hidden beneath a close-fitting hood in which the two eyeholes reveal the flame of an unbearable look. A reversed cross painted black is suspended on the chest of this odd penitent. On his cuffs—a symbol perhaps—hang the fragments of broken chains.) (41)

A demonic alter ego of Charles Quint, born the same day, month, year, and even hour, Ignotus reveals to Charles that he has utterly lost his faith in man and declares that all one can expect from humankind is the "irrefutable bestiality of our species." Moreover, he says, "I have learned that the oppressed are just as odious as their oppressors; I have come to understand that the eternal condition of man consists in never becoming humanized" (46). In his loathing and profound disenchantment, Ignotus has turned from "this flock of wild beasts who devour themselves . . . toward the sublime outcast, the bearer of light." "Lucifer," exclaims Charles.

The symbolism of Ignotus seems evident. As the dark side of Charles, his grim alter ego, it was Ignotus who arranged the marionette show, not to entertain the once proud and mighty emperor but to confront him with verities to which his own pride and arrogance had blinded him. But there is one final illusion, his "last love," as Ignotus calls it, of which Charles must be stripped before he can be ready to embrace death willingly, and that is his love of country. Going into a trancelike state, teeth clattering and hands trembling, Ignotus causes the room to darken, as during an eclipse of the moon, and an unreal aura to envelop everything. He then conjures up a phantasmagoric tableau of Flanders suffering under the rule of Charles's son, Philip of Spain. Charles screams that it is all too much for him and begs Ignotus to cease his incantations. But yet another image remains to be conjured—Death, as pictured by Holbein, Dürer, or Urs Graff. Death then sweeps Charles into the *Todentanz*, or dance of death, of the Middle Ages. The spell is broken only when Ignotus declares that "the game is over!" (51).

With his illusions dispelled, having confronted the dark side of his own rule and the fate of his legacy, Charles can now turn his thoughts wholly to his demise. So that his funeral will accord with the grandeur of his reign, he orders something tantamount to a dress rehearsal. The monks of Yuste will conduct the solemn rites in the monastery church, Charles himself will assist in the proceedings, and at the end the bier containing his mortal remains will be borne away to the singing of hymns. He then tells Dom

Martin de Angulo, the prelate who will be in charge of fulfiling his wishes, that when everything is under way he should approach the former emperor and announce: "Sire, come!" But in a sinister surprise twist, no sooner does Charles finish speaking than the prelate immediately orders him to come. Charles is puzzled, but Dom Martin imperiously directs him to follow him and then opens up the large doors to the church. Inside, Charles is met with an astonishing sight: a dark pit of burning, bubbling wax surrounding a huge catafalque. A line of monks with cowls pulled over their eyes and bent over moves slowly toward the choir. Unsteady on his feet before this spectacle—which is, in fact, the auto-da-fé he and Ignotus had already talked about—Charles asks Dom Martin who ordered it: God, the Devil? The prelate replies unemotionally, "the king," meaning Philip II. Charles seems vanquished. He crushes and throws away the letter in which Philip had written that "when a monarch of divine right believes that he has accomplished the last acts of his reign, a final deed of accomplishment remains to him. Such a monarch must know how to die" (56). But Charles immediately retrieves the letter when he sees a large coffin being carried across the threshold of the church by eight officers. Its cover is askew and the tail of a coat can be seen sticking out of it. We can assume that the coffin contains the body of Ignotus. Becoming impassive, his legs bent and his chest sunken, Charles advances toward the church, where Dom Martin gestures him inside. As bells toll once, then stop, the church organs initiate the office for the dead. The officers continue carrying the bier toward the choir. Charles follows them while the voices of the choir intone the appropriate Gregorian chant. The final stage direction of the play announces: "*The funeral rites of Charles-Quint have commenced*" (58).

With the exception of *The Women at the Tomb*, which takes place in Jerusalem on Good Friday evening after the crucifixion of Jesus, Ghelderode's plays written for marionettes are set in old Flanders. *Le Siège d'Ostende* is a colossal farce, its tone of play and nonsense set by the announcement at the beginning of the printed text that the work was

> composed by Don Adhémaro-Adolpho-Luiz de Ghelderode, captain of the royal Frankish lancers in the service of Spain, a former combatant in the Siege and decorated with various illustrious orders. The manuscript was discovered in the Archives of his Catholic Majesty, Alphonso XIII, brought to the stage and purged of historical errors and its racy elements by his descendant, Don Miguel de Ghelderode, the last of his name and a member

of the Free Academy of Belgium, the year 1933, and presented before an assembly of gentlemen in the Théâtre de la Sainte Boutique [Theater of the Holy Workshop] with the marionettes of Messire Toone de Locrel, known as Toone IV, Amsterdam.[32]

A "celebration" of the Flemish resistance to the Spanish siege of Ostend (1601–4), the work originated on 1 March 1933 as a homage to the prominent Anglo-Flemish painter, James Ensor (1860–1949), whom Ghelderode greatly admired and whose paintings inspired a few of his plays. But hardly had Ghelderode begun his "Eloge de James L'Ostendais" than he decided to add to it an "épopée militaire pour marionettes." This was intended to recall the siege of Ostend and the heroic resistance of the Ostenders under the leadership of none other than James Ensor. Once the new addition was well under way, by early May 1933, Ghelderode abandoned the original eulogy and concentrated his efforts entirely on the dramatic work; he finished it on 31 May.

In conceiving *The Siege of Ostend* as a boisterous and farcical marionette play, Ghelderode pulled out all the stops. Consisting of nineteen episodes, more than fifty named characters and dozens of anonymous ones, and a prankish language all its own, the work splendidly exemplifies Ghelderode's love of play which sought expression through the medium of puppet and marionette theater. It would be hard to imagine that Ghelderode did not enjoy himself thoroughly in writing *The Siege of Ostend*. But the reception of the play must surely have been an unexpected disappointment. Critics took objection to its scatological elements, while James Ensor—who appears in it as "Sir Jaime, baron of Sydney, marquis of Polders, artist-painter and head of the resistance" and to whom Ghelderode sent it on 1 February 1934—disliked it, presumably for its absurdity, and regarded the whole thing as an embarrassment. Ghelderode himself believed that what Ensor was really upset about was the play's antimilitaristic tone and its mockery of valor.[33] Although *The Siege of Ostend* had its admirers, negative criticism was sufficient to keep it even from being printed until 1980, eighteen years after Ghelderode's death and forty-seven years after it was written.

Apart from its farcically irreverent treatment of the historical episode itself, to which no summary can do justice, *The Siege of Ostend* is particularly striking for its language, a Ghelderodian concoction of French, Spanish, Hispanicized French, Flemish and Brussels dialect, and sheer nonsense speech doubtless inspired by the puppet and marionette theater tradition. Here, by way of example, is some of the dialogue from the first meeting between a Polish engineer named Klabotsky and Captain Don Pacheco:

Klabotsky. Zâzêzuza pour vous servir . . . [*Zâzêzuza* is Klabotsky's corruption of *azûzâze*, a Brussels idiom for "so she says."]
Don Pacheco. Quelle douce langue, le castillan! Assistez-vous . . .
Klabotsky. Y a pas de quoi s'assister, messire . . .
Don Pacheco. Sur vot' pouce . . . Z'êtes noble?
Klabotsky. . . . turellement, mais en Pologne . . . noblynsky in Polscky!
Don Pacheco. C'est tofsky! . . . Parlissez, mais pas de postillonsky . . .
Klabotsky. Messire don Pachéco, étincelant capitaine à la flamberge valeureuse, vous dont les exploits chroniques emplissent les échos de l'univers, inspiré par mon génie et désirant augmenter votre prestige . . .
Don Pacheco. Crénomdidios! . . . Mon prestige qu'il dit? Ce qui doit augmenter, c'est le grados, foutu pékinos, le grados, scrognognos, je veux dire, les sardinos sur mes manchos.[34]

Klabotsky. Zâzêzuza, at your service . . .
Don Pacheco. What a sweet language, Castillian! Come help . . .
Klabotsky. What is there to help with, messire . . .
Don Pacheco. . . . You noble?
Klabotsky. . . . 'fcourse, but in Poland . . . noblynsky in Polscky!
Don Pacheco. That's great! . . . Talk, but no more about your rank . . . [*Tofsky* derives from *tof*, meaning "good," "fine," in Brussels speech, while *postillonsky* is a combination of the Spanish *postillón* ("rank") and a Slavic adjectival ending.]
Klabotsky. Messire don Pachéco, brilliant captain of valorous sword, you whose historic exploits fill the echoes of the universe, inspired by my genius and desirous of augmenting your prestige . . .
Don Pacheco. In God's name! [*Crénomdidios* is a combination of French and Spanish.] . . . My prestige, you say? What has to be augmented is the rank, hopeless pekinese [*pékinos*, a term used apparently for "stranger" in the play], the rank, scrognognos [similar in meaning to *pékinos*], I tell you, the stripes on my sleeves.

Reminiscent in its language and boisterousness of Alfred Jarry's *Ubu roi*, untranslatable, unplayable—the work has never been performed, as far as I know—*The Siege of Ostend* displays Ghelderode's unrestrained Flemishness perhaps more than any of his other plays. In designating it a

work for marionettes, he had in mind, as elsewhere, not so much a marionette theater production in the strict sense as a spirit of exuberance and a
style at once grotesque and absurd.

We see this as well in another of his plays "for marionettes" with a Flemish setting, *About a Devil Who Preaches Miracles* (1934). In this instance,
Ghelderode's designation of the work as a "mystery for marionettes" also
seems motivated by the desire to maintain a certain distance from himself
and the play's anticlericalist irreverence. To put it in somewhat different
terms, Ghelderode uses puppet and marionette motifs and figures in a variety of ways. In *About a Devil Who Preaches Miracles*, the marionette
designation signals more than just a spirit of play. The work's patent anti-
clericalism—which crops up in other works by Ghelderode—is mitigated,
at least to an extent, by its marionette aspect. It is as if Ghelderode were
saying, "It's all just for fun; no need to take it seriously."

Set in the city of Brugelmonde (obviously a telling name: read here
Breughel-world) in olden Flanders, the play deals with the imminent visit
of a nasty monk-preacher named Bashuiljus (from Dutch *bassen*, "bark,
bray," and *huilen*, "howling"), who has been sent by the Holy Father himself to investigate the city's moral standing, or lack of it. No one is more
upset over his impending arrival than the local clerics, whom Ghelderode
portrays as mired in licentiousness. Dom Vispoel, for example, Bishop
Breedmag's chaplain, complains that he never feels at ease any more since
his thinness is not a sign of holy frugality, as he believed, but of cupidity.
Then there is the pretty abbess Didyme whose relations with a young Italian monk are not confined to pieties. She confesses, in fact, that a little
figure is beginning to move in her stomach who will speak Flemish with
an Italian accent. Lady Cloque Uttekas, a prominent member of local society, also has reason to be anxious. Besides giving the abbess Didyme a
remedy for her "swelling," she sleeps with many men and even gets into
bed with her own son. Her husband, the town treasurer, suffers violent
colics. He has exhausted a fair part of the municipal treasury and falsified
his records all because of his wife's insatiability. Has he not had, after all—
he asks himself rhetorically—the "platonic and heartrending pleasure of
contemplating her erotic gambols, unbeknown to her, of course, through
a hole in the ceiling?"[35] The Jew Abraham Goldenox acknowledges that
conversion to Christianity has brought him the lucrative position of
banker of the Catholic church. His plan to take flight with all the clerical
gold of Flanders is nipped in the bud by a judge, a lawyer, and a notary

who are themselves anything but models of integrity. The roster of shady and disreputable types grows longer and more sordid.

After this parade of sinners, in comes the devil Capricant, the lover of the beggar Fergerite, who appeared at the very beginning of the play lamenting Capricant's apparent loss of interest in her. In order to win back her lover's affection, she promises Capricant that in return for a night of love, she will tell him how he can satisfy his "superiors'" demands that he show proof of greater zeal. When he agrees, Fergerite suggests that he take the place of Bashuiljus, whose arrival is expected any moment. Capricant then leaves. Before long, Bashuiljus arrives along the road and asks Fergerite for directions. The beggar sends him in the wrong direction and thus buys time for Capricant.

The second act consists mainly of a lengthy sermon Capricant preaches as Bashuiljus. He declares at the outset that he has been sent by the pope to rid Brugelmonde of sin. When the sermon is over, Capricant throws flowers to the members of the congregation and pokes fun at the Devil. But his identity is almost revealed in a wildly hilarious scene when Fergerite, who has been hidden during the sermon under the steps of the pulpit, succumbs to the temptation to bite the part of Capricant's tail that sticks out from his frock. Beside himself, the false monk throws himself at her and the two tussle. The crowd, believing that the "preacher" is struggling with the Evil One, cheers wildly. Thanking heaven for helping him, Capricant exits carrying Fergerite by a leg "like a doll." In the third and final act, Capricant tries desperately to rid himself of Fergerite, who insists on being paid for her service to him, and without delay. Capricant reluctantly agrees and the two make love in the street where Fergerite originally appeared at the beginning of the play. They are observed by the watchman Lamprido, who takes Capricant for a cleric and declares, resigned, that "there is nothing new under the moon except that now monks will do openly what they've been doing secretly" (207). Then Lamprido sees another monk—Bashuiljus—coming toward him and shows him what is happening in the street. But a tired Bashuiljus pushes him aside, lowers himself onto the road, and falls asleep on his haunches. Eventually awakened by Capricant's prayers (that he is at last free of Fergerite), Bashuiljus rejoices that he has found at least one pious man in the foul city of Brugelmonde. As he and Capricant are about to depart for Rome to be jointly canonized, Fergerite appears. But before she can reveal Capricant's identity, he denounces her as a sorceress and Bashuiljus knocks her down with the jawbone of an ass. The watchman Lamprido carries her off to marry her, and Capricant and Bashuiljus continue on their way to Rome singing the Te Deum.

The mystery play for marionettes, inaugurated by Bouchor in the late 1880s, had indeed come a very long way.

FOUR

Puppets, Marionettes, and the Debunking of Traditionalism and National Myths in Spanish Modernist Drama

Some of the most imaginative applications of puppet and marionette figures to the drama have come from twentieth-century Spanish playwrights who were quick to grasp their potential for the debunking of the traditionalism and national myths that have weighed so heavily on Spanish art, politics, and society.

Perhaps the first Spanish dramatist to incorporate puppet figures in his plays in the twentieth century was Jacinto Benavente, who was long regarded as Spain's foremost modern dramatist. Esteem for him still remains high despite the retrospective upward reevaluation of other Spanish dramatists whose careers were developed in the first half of the century. Benavente's reputation also rests on the fact that he was the second Spanish writer to win the Nobel prize for literature (in 1922). It is generally acknowledged that the prize was awarded to him principally for two of his best-known plays, the farcical *Los intereses creados* (*The Bonds of Interest*, 1907), a modern adaptation of the commedia dell'arte, which had its premiere in Madrid's Teatro Lara on 9 December 1907, and *La malquerida* (*The Passion Flower*, 1913).

A native of Madrid, Benavente was studying law at the University of Madrid when he decided to abandon further work on his degree in order to devote himself entirely to literature. His first published drama was included in his collection *Teatro fantástico* (*Fantastic Theater*), which originally appeared in 1892 but was reissued in an expanded edition in 1905. Of the eight short, romantic sketches in the later edition—which antedates *The Bonds of Love* by two years—five of the works attest to Benavente's early interest in the Italian commedia dell'arte, puppets, and animated inanimate beings. Of obvious commedia inspiration are *Comedia italiana* (*Italian Comedy*); *La blancura de Pierrot* (*The Whiteness of Pierrot*), subtitled *An Argument for a Pantomime*; and the more substantial *Cuento de primavera* (*Tale of Spring*), a *Comedy in Two Acts and a Prologue*. *La senda del amor* (*The Path of Love*) is the only sketch in the *Teatro fantástico* collection specifically designated a *Comedy for Marionettes*. It is very slight but contains an amusing point at the end. The Poet stages a puppet show for the Marchioness, whom he loves, in which Leandro, although he swears eternal love to Celia, is haunted by his past— people he has killed and women he has abandoned. Celia refuses to go away with him, telling him that they cannot be happy together, that their way is blocked by "so much blood, so many dead people, so many tears!" Leandro replies, in the closing words of the interior puppet show, "Do you know of any joy that costs less?" [1] But Leandro's words return to haunt the Poet himself when, after the performance, he asks the Marchioness how she liked the play. Her praise expresses particular interest in the sixteen-year-old boy who manipulated the puppets. His agility and feeling, she says, assure his future success with women. When the Poet tells her that he is returning the boy to his native village the next morning, the Marchioness informs him that he cannot do that since she is immediately taking him into her own service. Before the Poet knows how to respond, the Marchioness cuts him off: "Isn't that the morality of your comedy? On the path of love a woman shouldn't be detained by the dead"(59).

In *El encanto de una hora* (*The Magic of an Hour*), the first sketch in *Teatro fantástico*, Benavente stakes his own claim to the widely fashionable turn-of-the-century interest in the animation of inanimate figures. The play is something of a parable on life and love. Set in an elegant study, two Sèvres porcelain figures—Merveilleuse (Wondrous, a female) and Incroyable (Unbelievable, a male)—appear atop two columns. When the curtain rises, two clocks sound the hour of midnight and the figures come to life. Merveilleuse declares that some supernatural power has invested her not only with life but also with a soul, which enables her "to reason with luminous intuition"(10). What is truly luminous in the play is Benavente's humor and charm. When Incroyable begins speculating on which supernatural powers infused him with life, Merveilleuse petulantly shuts him up in no uncertain terms, urging him not to waste the time alive remaining to them on idle philosophizing. Offended, Incroyable tells her to go easy on the epithets and then complains about how hard it is to descend from their columns.

The juxtaposition of shifting male and female attitudes, evident here, becomes a leitmotif of Benavente's sketch. Where Merveilleuse is initially all boldness and action, taking the initiative at every turn, Incroyable is ponderous and cautious. When Merveilleuse exclaims her delight at being able to move about, run, and jump, Incroyable reminds her that they are made of porcelain and easily broken. Uninterested in books, which fascinate Incroyable, Merveilleuse just wants to sing and dance. But then her restless nature quickly tires and she begins complaining of boredom. Incroyable, on the other hand, proclaims the beauty of life and expresses the desire to go beyond the confines of their narrow existence where there is surely much more to life. It is now Merveilleuse who waxes philosophical. Declining to leave their study, she tells her partner that life everywhere is the same and no matter where one goes people are bored and always yearning for something else, which, for sure, they never find. She prefers to stay where they are, the world in them and the beloved nearby. At the mention of love, Incroyable agrees that in all the human wretchedness he has beheld there is one moment of life, one hour of magic—that of love, the only thing that makes life worth living—when people seem as "radiant as good spirits." Merveilleuse, too, begins to yield to the magic of passion and tells Incroyable: "Feeling you near me, I understand what you are saying better than through your words. The two of us, separated, did nothing or thought nothing other than nonsense and the only thing we achieved was to bore ourselves like two fools. But now, together, we seem the most understanding people in the world, and who would have thought it! Two boredoms united . . . are one amusement" (19).

Observing love around her in humans, Merveilleuse thought it no more than pleasant time-passing. But now that she has discovered her own capacity for love, she declares that her whole life depends on it; no more will she laugh at two lovers just gazing at each other without exchanging words. Incroyable exults in their common understanding: "What more could my words tell you than what my eyes say, avid as they are to behold you? Not as before, when they wandered uncertain and yearning for new sensations. My glances are limited now just to you; you are their entire world" (21).

As Incroyable becomes carried away with passion and draws closer to Merveilleuse, it is her turn to remind him that they are made of porcelain and hence fragile. But abandoning caution in his desire, Incroyable grabs her and kisses her, thereby damaging her. Merveilleuse laments that now nobody will want to look at her anymore with her broken face and that she will probably be thrown out with the garbage. But professing even greater love for her, Incroyable wants only to kiss her. When she fears that he will finish her off completely with more kisses, he draws her close and tells her that as long as they remain together that way her imperfection will be hidden. The play closes on a tender note. Embracing her, Incroyable comforts Merveilleuse by telling her that the mysterious power that gave them life will respect what love has united. And perhaps, he concludes, "this love that has been in our lives the magic of an hour will be the eternal magic in another eternal life" (23).

Arguably Benavente's best-liked play, *The Bonds of Interest* brings together different strands of the contemporary fascination with Italian commedia dell'arte and puppets, marionettes, and related figures already manifest in the earlier *Teatro fantástico* collection. Employing such traditional masks of the Italian commedia as Colombina, El Doctor (Dottore), Polichinela (Pulcinella), Arlequín (Arlecchino), El Capitán (Capitano), and Pantalón (Pantalone), *The Bonds of Interest* is a comedy in two acts, three sets (*quadros*), and a prologue that tells the story of what ensues when Leandro and Crispín, two characters straight out of the picaresque tradition, arrive penniless in a certain city after escaping their creditors. The two are a study in contrasts. Crispín is a manipulative rogue, wily servant, and satirical observer of life all in one. Leandro, on the other hand, is a dreamy idealist. Pretending that Leandro is a nobleman on some secret mission, Crispín secures them lodgings in an inn—free of charge, of course. With great bravado he secures similar arrangements for the impecunious poet Arlequín and the blustering Captain, whose lineage goes back all the way to Plautus's *miles gloriosus* ("braggart soldier").

The scene shifts to the intrigues of the matchmaker, Doña Sirena. She is upset with her adopted niece and confidante, the beautiful Colombina, for being in love with Arlequín instead of getting herself a wealthy suitor to whom Doña Sirena could marry her. In the meantime, Doña Sirena must content herself with trying to arrange an appropriate match for Silvia, the daughter of the prosperous Polichinela. Silvia has attracted the attention of Crispín, who persuades Colombina to obtain an invitation for Leandro to the party being planned by Doña Sirena for Polichinela. Since Doña Sirena has run out of credit with the servants, musicians, and tradespeople on whom she depends for her party, she is receptive to Crispín's suggestion that his master Leandro, whom he portrays as a wealthy man, will provide everything necessary to assure the success of the affair. He also promises her a handsome "fee" for bringing Leandro and Silvia together.

The party takes place as planned. Previously recalcitrant tradespeople have resumed cooperation, and Arlequín and the Captain have brought musicians and their own men to help out. During the affair, Crispín, who has obviously prepared himself well, introduces himself to Polichinela and recalls a past acquaintanceship that Polichinela would sooner forget. Crispín has to operate on two fronts: he must intimidate Polichinela by insinuating the possible revelation of past misdeeds, and he must keep the idealistic Leandro in check. Leandro is now madly in love with Silvia but would rather flee than have her discover that he is a pauper and a fugitive from creditors. In order to consolidate Silvia's romantic feelings for Leandro and her mother's support for their marriage, the wily Crispín convinces Polichinela that in no circumstances should he allow his daughter to wed Leandro. He reasons that the more the father opposes her wishes, the more both daughter and mother will want Leandro, just to thwart the intentions of the stern Polichinela.

Crispín also conspires to have Leandro "attacked" by a band of ruffians ostensibly hired by Polichinela on the way back from Sirena's party. News of the "attack" only intensifies Silvia's longing for Leandro and resentment against her father. Sirena soon appears in the sumptuous house the innkeeper made available to Leandro and Crispín and demands half the sum promised her for her part in bringing Leandro and Silvia together. She also informs Crispín that Polichinela is wise to him and has informed the police about him. Before long, Polichinela and the authorities, including Pantalón, a pedantic process server from Bologna, arrive to take Crispín and Leandro into custody. They are joined by the innkeeper and other tradespeople, who have their own claims to press against the picaresque pair. Wily and manipulative as ever, Crispín uses Pantalón's long-windedness to convince them that their chances of recouping their money would be much enhanced if they played along with his scheme instead of having him and Leandro carted off to jail. In the play's final scene a much beleaguered Polichinela, confronted with the bonds of love between Leandro and his daughter, as well as by his wife's support of the union, is persuaded to allow Leandro and Silvia to wed. Leandro, in the meantime, has confessed the truth of his circumstances to Silvia, who loves him despite his lack of money. Polichinela is so upset at the prospect of his daughter marrying a pauper that, while permitting their marriage, he vows to withhold her dowry. But he finally yields to the pressure of all present (as well as to Crispín's threats to make public certain information about his past) and relents.

More important in *The Bonds of Interest* than Benavente's revamping of the Italian commedia dell'arte—with which he had already tentatively experimented in the *Teatro fantástico* collection—is the conception of the play as a primitive puppet show. The prologue, spoken by Crispín, who is the motor of the action, adheres to an old theatrical convention but is used here principally to explain the form of the farce. Crispín first establishes that the work is a revival of the old commedia dell'arte:

> Here you have the scaffolding of the ancient farce, that which relieved in country inns the fatigue of carters, which amused the simple rustics in the squares of humble towns, which in populous cities brought together the most varied crowds, as in Paris on the Pont Neuf when from his wooden carnival platform Tabarin solicited the attention of every passerby, from the surprised doctor who stops his mount for a moment in order to briefly smooth the wrinkles on his brow, always burdened with grave thoughts, as he listens to some quip of the merry farce, to the roguish bully who spends his idle hours there, cheating his hunger with a smile, to the prelate, noble lady, and illustrious grandee in their carriages, as well as to the cheerful maid and soldier and merchant and student. People of every rank, who would never have been brought together anywhere else, shared their joy. Often, more than at the farce itself, the serious person laughed upon beholding the laughter of the cheerful, the wise man at the simpleton, the poor at seeing the laughter of the grandees, who ordinarily have a scowl on their faces, and the grandees at the sight of the laughter of the poor, their consciences eased by the thought: Even the poor can smile![2]

Once having established the ancient popular origins of the Italian commedia and its eventual elevation by such distinguished forebears as the

Spanish dramatist Lope de Rueda, Shakespeare, and Molière to "the highest throne of Poetry and Art," Crispín goes on to declare that the farce about to be presented cannot claim "such glorious lineage." It is instead

> a farce of puppets (farsa guiñolesca), of nonsensical content, without any reality. You will soon see how whatever happens in it could never happen, how its characters are not, nor do they resemble, real men and women, but are mere dolls and puppets of paste and cardboard, with crude wires which are visible even in poor light and to the most nearsighted of spectators. They are the same grotesque masks of that Italian commedia dell'arte, no longer as merry as they once were, because they have aged much over such a long period of time. (53)

Crispín's closing words, in their tone of mock apologia, underscore the broader implications of Benavente's use of the commedia as puppet show:

> The author is well aware that so primitive a spectacle is not the most appropriate for the sophisticated audience of the present time. Therefore, he begs the protection of your refinement and good will. He asks only that you become as young as possible in spirit. The world is already old and in its dotage. But Art is not resigned to growing old, and in order to seem a child feigns nonsense . . . And that is why these old puppets presume to amuse you today with their trifles. (53)

The meaning is clear enough. The nonsensical play, its childlike quality further accentuated by its puppet form, was conceived by its author in the turn-of-the-century spirit of rejuvenation which art alone could accomplish. The key word occurs when Crispín declares that the author of the play "asks only that you become as young as possible in spirit." In the original, the line reads: "El autor sólo pide que *aniñéis* cuanto sea posible vuestro espíritu" (italics mine). The verb *aniñarse* means literally not just "to become young," but "to become a child." This, then, is at the heart of Benavente's intention—through his farcical commedia-type play, presented as an unsophisticated puppet entertainment unworthy of a sophisticated audience, to enable that audience, through art, to rejuvenate its collective spirit and hence overcome the age of the world. Only such rejuvenation could eventually accomplish the necessary abandonment of antiquated and ossified forms, not just in the drama but in culture and society as a whole.

The linkage of puppet, marionette, and commedia dell'arte in Benavente's *Bonds of Interest* recurs in the one-act play *Hechizo del amor* (*Love's Enchantment*), written in 1908, a year after *The Bonds of Interest,* by Benavente's younger contemporary Gregorio Martínez Sierra.[3] This *Comedy of Puppets [fantoches] in One Act and Four Scenes,* as the play is subtitled, was staged for the first time on 14 November 1908 in Madrid's Salón Nacional. Featuring only commedia dell'arte figures, and again devoted to the triumph of romantic love, the play's puppet character is established at the outset by the Prologue, who happens to be a puppet. Apologizing for not being a poet and thus being unable to present a play about love as it should be, he affects the same self-deprecating posture as did Crispín in Benavente's play, but without the latter's allusion to childhood wonderment:

> I should like, ladies and gentlemen, to be a poet at this moment so that I might present to you in a bouquet of the most fragrant words the panegyric of that dear misfortune, that delightful pain, that fatal passion, that enchantment, that stellar influence, that consuming of the soul, that microbe—or whatever it is that you may decide this delicious inquietude to be—which, through the centuries, men and women have agreed to call love. . . . You would lick your fingers with delight, ladies and gentlemen, listening to my discourse, if I were a poet; but I have already told you that I am not one; I am only a puppet and the Prologue. You smile? Smile on, then, but don't disdain me. . . . Puppet! This single word has ignited a spark of joy in all your eyes. Do you suppose that it is a small glory to possess a name which is perennially a source of amusement? And do you suppose it is nothing, once you have it, to be able to bear it throughout the ages with all the dignity of folly? And we have indeed borne it splendidly, majestically, ladies and gentlemen. Our little bodies are our witnesses. For the sake of applause they disjoint themselves, twist, turn, toss their arms and heads into the air, or lose a leg in a leap only to recover it in a pirouette. Look at us, palpitating from head to foot as if our bodies were all hearts. And yet, ladies and gentlemen, we have no hearts. What need would we have of them when we can vibrate so continuously and prodigiously without them?[4]

There follows a slight but diverting comedy in which Columbine, here married to Pierrot, bitterly complains to the wise Polichinela that Pierrot seems no longer to love her. A poet, he is in love with the colors and scents of nature, with Beauty, but fails to appreciate the beauty of his own wife. As a remedy, Polichinela gives her a potion, of which she must let one drop fall whenever Pierrot appears wrapped in poetic ecstasy. The potion has the power to change his mood immediately. Thus, when Pierrot enters carrying a bunch of purple roses over which he rhapsodizes, the magic potion causes his hand to be pricked by thorns. But the more Columbine uses the potion, the more counterproductive it becomes. Turning away in disillusionment from Nature and Beauty, Pierrot also turns away from the natural beauty of his wife. It is at this point that Columbine's maid, Pierrette, comes to the rescue. She encourages her mistress to receive her long-admiring Harlequin, who at once pleads his love for her. Pierrette then makes Pierrot jealous by telling him that Columbine is not indifferent to the handsome and amorous Harlequin's attentions. That does the trick. Pierrot rushes out to exchange angry words with Harlequin and Columbine, and when he and Columbine reappear, they are locked in an embrace, their eyes full of happiness. Disappointed in the romance that fails to materialize with Columbine, Harlequin then turns to the wily Pierrette for consolation. The dialogue between the two is some of the best in the play:

> Harlequin (with sudden resolution). Could you love me, Pierrette?
> Pierrette. Ha, ha, ha! I have no desire to conquer by force of spite.
> Harlequin. Don't be cruel!
> Pierrette. My lady is much more beautiful than me.
> Harlequin. Illusion! The beauty of woman is all one great, perfect body, of which every beautiful woman is an individual part. Your lady is beautiful; you are as beautiful as she—both different parts of the same beauty.
> Pierrette. But where, pray tell, do I belong in this univeral body of which you speak?
> Harlequin. From what my own tells me, you must be very near the heart! (They embrace.) (276)

When Polichinela appears bearing yet another vial of magic potion, he is ridiculed, especially by Pierrette, who now lectures him on how best to cure love and disdain. As a scandalized Polichinela rushes from the scene, the two pairs of lovers begin a slow and stately dance that brings the merry comedy to an end.

That the turn-of-the-century Catalan dramatist shared his Castilian counterparts' enthusiasm for puppet and marionette theater is exemplified in the case of Santiago Rusiñol, a leading painter and writer of the period who also played an important role in Barcelona cabaret life. Known as a dramatist primarily for his archetypically modernist one-act play L'alegría que passa (The Joy that Passes, written 1898, first staged

1901), Rusiñol also wrote an entertaining one-act comedy for the puppet theater, *El titella pròdig* (*The Prodigal Puppet*, or *The Prodigal Doll*), subtitled *Comedia de putxinel-lis en un acte i quatre quadros* (*A Puppet Comedy in One Act and Four Scenes*). The work had its premiere in the Teatre Català (Romea) in Barcelona on 29 January 1911.

Owing more to the indigenous Catalan puppet tradition than to the modernist revival of commedia dell'arte, Rusiñol's play recounts the alliance between the twenty-year-old Robin and the Devil. Thrown out of his home because of his love for Cristeta, whom he is considered too young to marry, Robin tries to kill himself by beating his head against a door but succeeds instead in summoning the Devil. In order to assist Robin in making good on his threat just to enjoy himself from now on, to "raise the devil," the Devil takes him to the estate of a marchioness, to whom he will make love on the Devil's command. Once in the marchioness's house, where four other marchionesses are also present, Robin and the Devil, introduced as his tutor, have a merry time dancing and flirting. While Robin is arduously persuading the marchioness to run away with him, in comes her husband, Christopher. Claiming that he is the biggest devil outside of his own house, Robin provokes Christopher into playing cards with him. But when Robin loses, he accuses Christopher of cheating, at which point they begin beating each other in the best tradition of the Catalan puppet theater. In the last scene, Cristeta laments the disappearance of Robin, who thereupon appears, swathed in bandages, in the company of the Devil. When Robin vows to commit suicide with a revolver given him by the Devil, Cristeta fetches his mother and father and convinces them that Robin has been put up to everything by the Devil, whose true identity she reveals by making the sign of the cross over him. Robin included, all fall on the Devil and begin beating him. During the melee, a firecracker goes off in his back, fizzing and sputtering. The others beat it out and leave the Devil for dead hanging over a balustrade. The play ends shortly thereafter as Robin asks his parents' permission to marry Cristeta. They grant it, and Robin and Cristeta join hands and retire slowly toward the rear, where, the stage direction indicates, "*a large fan opens in an extravagant apotheosis, after the manner of puppet shows at country fairs.*"[5] Both couples then embrace to the grand chorus of the traditional Catalan *tururut*, which was also danced on previous occasions in the play.

Rusiñol's play for puppets has less in common with the Benavente and Martínez Sierra works than with the Spanish poet Federico García

Lorca's later plays in the folk puppet tradition. Anticipating Lorca, Rusiñol sought to breathe new life into the long-dormant Catalan drama by drawing on the techniques of the indigenous puppet tradition, with which he already had ample experience in the Quatre Gats cabaret. The "prodigal son" Robin, Cristeta, and the mischievous Devil are all stock characters in the Catalan puppet tradition. Equally indebted to the folk tradition is the play's physicality—the beatings given a recalcitrant Robin by the Devil, the pummeling of the Devil by everyone else later on, and the *tururut*. If Benavente and Martínez Sierra sought to reinvigorate the stultified Spanish drama of their own time through the infusion of fresh blood from old traditions such as the Italian commedia dell'arte and the puppet and marionette theater, Rusiñol hewed to the Catalan modernist path of exploring the resources of the native Catalan folk culture.

PYGMALION THE MASTER PUPPETEER:
JACINTO GRAU'S *EL SEÑOR DE PIGMALIÓN* (*MISTER PYGMALION*)

Together with Jacinto Benavente, Gregorio Martínez Sierra, Eduardo Marquina, Manuel Linares Rivas, Ramón del Valle-Inclán, and Federico García Lorca, Jacinto Grau is rightly regarded as one of the luminaries of twentieth-century Castilian Spanish drama. His reputation has grown steadily since the Spanish Civil War of 1936–38 and his death in 1958; and there are those who do not hesitate now to rank Grau as the foremost Spanish dramatist of the century. Of Catalan and Andalusian origin, Grau was born in Barcelona and educated at the universities of Barcelona and Valencia. Although he studied law briefly, he abandoned it in favor of a literary career and published his first work, a collection of short stories under the title *Trasuntos* (*Likenesses*), in 1898. Four years later, his first play, the one-act *Horas de vida* (*Hours of Life*) came out. From then on, Grau devoted himself almost exclusively to playwriting. He wrote some criticism, as well as a novelette—*El dominio del mundo* (*Mastery of the World*, 1927)—but these were mere pauses in a literary life overwhelmingly dedicated to the stage.

Grau was the author of over two dozen plays. Some of these derive from biblical, classical, and legendary subjects such as *La redención de Judas* (*The Redemption of Judas*, 1903), an original reinterpretation of the New Testament account; *El cuento de Barba Azul* (*The Story of Bluebeard*, 1915), a *zarzuela* prized for its creative interweaving of music, song, and dance with the dramatic action; *El hijo pródigo* (*The Prodigal Son*,

1917); *El Rey Candaules* (*King Candaules*, 1917), inspired by a story in Herodotus; and *El Señor de Pigmalión* (*Mr. Pygmalion*, 1921), based, of course, on the Greek myth of Pygmalion and Galatea. Two plays deal with the Don Juan theme: *Don Juan de Carillana* (*Don Juan of Carillana*, 1927), in which a middle-aged Don Juan unwittingly pursues his own daughter, and *El burlador que se no burla* (*The Unrepentant Seducer*, 1927), about a Don Juan who never regrets any of his romantic episodes in view of the joy he believes he has brought into the otherwise drab lives of so many women. Like other twentieth-century Spanish dramatists from Benavente to Lorca, Grau also sought inspiration in classical Spanish literature. His one-act *zarzuela, Las bodas de Camacho* (*Camacho's Wedding*, 1903)—which he wrote together with the important Catalan dramatist and theatrical entrepreneur Adrián Gual—is based on *Don Quixote*, while *El Conde Alarcos* (*Count Alarcos*, 1907) was suggested by the well-known sixteenth-century Spanish ballad "El romance del conde Alarcos y de la Infanta Solisa" ("The Ballad of Count Alarcos and the Infanta Solisa"). Other plays such as *Entre llamas* (*Amid the Flames of Passion*, 1907), *El Caballero Varona* (*The Gentleman of Varona*, 1925), *La Señora guapa* (*The Pretty Lady*, 1932), and *Destino* (*Destiny*, 1945) explore the fatalastic attraction between a man and a woman in modern settings. *En Ildaria* (*In Ildaria*, 1913) is one of Grau's very few plays with an overt political content. Elements of the fantastic and supernatural, visions, and greater abstraction—the influence, in large measure, of German Expressionism and French Surrealism—characterize such plays as *Los tres locos del mundo* (*The Three Madmen of the World*, 1925) and *La casa del diablo* (*The Devil's House*, 1933).

Grau's creative originality and sure sense of stagecraft set him apart from most Spanish dramatists of his time, whose sights were trained primarily on commercial success and whose reluctance to transgress the boundaries of the conventional mired them in banality. Like the few other innovative and individualistic dramatists with whom his name is usually linked, Grau decried the commercialization of the contemporary Spanish stage and opposed its stagnation on all levels from the literary to the administrative. His boldness as a dramatic writer had already won him a large following before the outbreak of the Civil War in 1936, and he had begun to acquire an international reputation. After the war and the assumption of power by Generalissimo Francisco Franco, Grau chose to leave Spain. He settled in Argentina and remained there until his death in

1958. Emigration proved no obstacle to the growth of his reputation. Productions of his plays were mounted in several South American countries, and the esteem in which he is held now in post-Franco Spain is so great that for some he has displaced Benavente as the country's foremost twentieth-century dramatist.

Of Grau's many plays, most of which are notable for their author's avoidance of the mundane and conventional, the best known by far is *Mr. Pygmalion*. Its immediate appeal owes much to its individual interpretation of the myth of Pygmalion and Galatea. But its theme of the creation of life from inanimate matter also relates it to two other, much better-known European dramatic works written the same year, 1921—Karel Čapek's *R.U.R.* and Luigi Pirandello's *Sei personaggi in cerca d'autore* (*Six Characters in Search of an Author*). Although the important twentieth-century Spanish philosopher Miguel de Unamuno had also dealt with the independence of created characters in his play *Niebla* (*Mist*, 1914), Grau's more theatrically engrossing treatment of the theme drew far greater attention than Unamuno's play. Once Čapek and Pirandello became aware of a play by a Spanish writer of Grau's reputation dealing with themes similar to theirs, they lost little time in arranging for productions in their own countries. But the distinction of staging the world premiere of *Mr. Pygmalion* belongs to one of the greatest figures of the twentieth-century French stage, Charles Dullin, the director of the Atelier Company. Dullin's successful production of Grau's play at the Vieux Colombier theater in Paris, where some of his most important productions were mounted, took place on 16 February 1923 under the title *Monsieur de Pygmalion*. The translation was by Francis de Miomandre. When Čapek's *R.U.R.* was produced in Paris not long afterward, the Czech writer was told that it would have attracted greater attention had Grau's *Mr. Pygmalion* not preceded it. This seems to have been how Čapek became aware of the Grau work. Once he had permission from Grau for a Czech production, Čapek mounted his own version in Prague on 25 September 1925. Pirandello also directed a performance of the play in the Teatro d'Arte in Rome the following year. *Mr. Pygmalion* finally had its Spanish premiere on 18 May 1928, five years after Dullin's production in Paris. It was performed by the Meliá-Cibrián company at the Teatro Cómico in Madrid.

Grau's *Mr. Pygmalion* tells the story of an extraordinary and near legendary puppet master named Pygmalion (Pigmalión) who is widely presumed to be English but is in reality a Spaniard who left Spain at an early age to make his fortune and knows English well, even speaking Spanish with an English accent. Pygmalion's fame rests on his invention of such technically perfect marionette figures that they are virtually indistinguishable from human beings. They have arteries, nerves, veins, real hearts taken from animals, and a juice that takes the place of blood. Much time and research went into the formulation of the material from which the bodies would be made. They consist of radium and magnetized sheets of special steel, all blended and finished by Pygmalion himself. They are in some ways superior to human beings. Not only can they speak and reason, but they also run on a perpetual mechanism. Should the marionettes ever experience a breakdown, Pygmalion can repair them; but if extensive repair is called for, he destroys the figures and builds new ones.

The marionettes, all seventeen of them, consist of Pomponina (the name possibly derived from the Colombina of the Italian commedia dell'arte) and her four maids, and the remaining twelve male marionette figures, all of whose names are rooted in the Spanish folklore tradition: Juan El Tonto (Juan the Fool); Don Lindo (Handsome), who is in love with Pomponina and jealous of Pygmalion's interest in her; Pedro Urdemalas ("Schemer"); El Capitán Araña ("Spider"); El viejo ("The Old Guy") Mingo Revulgo (the name derived from a character in the fifteenth-century Spanish satire *Coplas de Mingo Revulgo*); El Tío Paco (Uncle Paco, who deflates exaggerators); Perogrullo (someone who constantly repeats obvious truths); Bernardo El de La Espada (Bernardo of the Sword, in the sense here of a person who is not good for anything); Ambrosio El de La Carabina (Ambrosio of the Carbine); El Enano de La Venta (Dwarf of the Inn, here meaning someone who pretends to be more than he is); Periquito entre Ellas (a young man who enjoys being around women); and Lucas Gómez (someone vulgar). The only marionette who is unable to speak is, appropriately, Juan el Tonto, the "fool," the least complicated of any of them. Dressed like a classical comic actor, he can utter only the sounds "cu, cu." But for all his outward simplicity, Juan el Tonto is a sinister figure. As a fool he lacks the ability to conceal the resentment the marionettes feel toward Pygmalion's authoritarian ways. He is the first to manifest outward signs of disobedience toward his creator, sticking out his tongue and mocking him whenever his back is turned. Pygmalion disciplines him by boxing his ears, but Juan el Tonto remains unfazed.

A millionaire many times over because of his worldwide success, Pygmalion declares that his marionettes mean more to him than anything else in life. In fact, he has become their slave and is even hopelessly in love with Pomponina, the most beautiful and fragile of all of them. Ironically, he observes that he, like so many men, loves a puppet, but the difference between his own situation and theirs is that he knows that it is a puppet he loves. However, to Pygmalion's creations, he is far more master than slave. They resent what they regard as his autocratic ways and eventually rebel against his authority, killing him and going their own way into the world.

It is in fact the revolt of Pygmalion's marionettes that constitutes the play's principal action. After he opens the large boxes in which his figures are kept when not onstage, in order to display them to the still dubious theater managers, Pygmalion discovers that they have found a way to open their own locks and leave their boxes at will. He vows to change the entire set of locks the following morning. Shortly after Pygmalion leaves, Juan el Tonto is the first of the marionettes to emerge from his box in the shadowy quiet of the deserted theater. Soon other male marionettes leave their boxes, and, demonstrating their all too human characteristics, attempt to persuade the female marionettes to come back into their boxes with them, or to permit them to enter their own boxes. The beautiful Pomponina willingly joins Mingo Rivulgo in his box, which drives Don Lindo, who also fancies her, into a rage of envy. His jealous antics, as well as the feuding and fussing of other marionettes, faintly recall the slapstick aspect of the commedia dell'arte. But the humor of the scene turns ominous when the marionettes scheme to free themselves from Pygmalion's rule. Before further light is shed on their plans, the scene is brought to an end by the appearance of the Duke, who has come to open Pomponina's box so that he can lure her into running away with him.

The scenes of the Duke and Pomponina in flight from Pygmalion also have a humor of their own. Pomponina is a study in feminine vanity, ever anxious to show herself nude so that all can admire the perfection of her form and indignant that the Duke will not allow her to do so. She also rebuffs his attempts to make love to her and frequently diverts his attention to ask for water, which she needs to lubricate her mechanism. At one point, Pomponina succeeds in locking the Duke in a room, but before she can flee the small hovel thay have taken refuge in after the Duke's car broke down, she is seized by Julia, another woman in the Duke's life, who has been looking all over for him. In the meantime, the marionettes, who have made good their rebellion, have come to the same small town and arrive in time to save Pomponina from harm. They lock Julia in with the Duke and plan to move on, until Urdemalas cautions them that Pygmalion is in hot pursuit and that they cannot risk moving by daylight. It is also Urdemalas, the "schemer," who is the first to suggest doing away with Pygmalion before he succeeds in subjugating them again and making them perform for him.

At the end of the play, when Pygmalion's marionettes are about to set off into the world, he does indeed catch up with them and again attempts to impose his will on them. Brandishing a whip, he lashes out and strikes several blows at Juan el Tonto's legs. As the other marionettes cower in fear, Urdemalas, who has been functioning as their ringleader, fires point blank at their tormentor with a shotgun that he had managed to remove earlier from a wall and conceal in his clothing. With Urdemalas shouting "Freedom, freedom!" and exhorting them to flee as fast as they can in pursuit of adventure and their destiny, the marionettes exit one after the other, repeating their leader's cry of "Freedom, freedom!" Only Juan el Tonto remains behind, hovering over the body of Pygmalion, who is still alive but losing blood rapidly. Lamenting his plight, Pygmalion regards it as the "eternal triumph of the gods over him who wishes to steal their secrets." Wanting to surpass the human being, he was destroyed, ironically, by the treachery of the very first marionettes he made—"The sad fate," he despairs, "of the heroic man, constantly humiliated up to now in his pride by the creatures of his own imagination!"[6] His dying thoughts are interrupted by the "cu, cu" of Juan el Tonto. Believing that despite everything he can call on his puppet simpleton to save him, Pygmalion urges Juan to help him, reasoning that "it would be a shame . . . Nobody will ever again be able to make puppets as perfect and alive as I can" (134). Still "cu, cu"-ing, Juan el Tonto merely approaches Pygmalion and smashes his head with the butt of the shotgun left behind by Urdemalas. The play ends with the expiration of Pygmalion and the rapid departure of Juan el Tonto as he casts a final glance at Pygmalion's body and thrice utters his "cu, cu." The ending is a chilling moment of theater, in its own way as haunting and memorable as the murder of the young intellectual Artur by the boor Edek and the play's closing tango in the post–World War II Polish dramatist Sławomir Mrożek's widely performed play *Tango*.

Apart from Grau's interest in the theme of the creation of life from inanimate matter and the hubris of the artist who belives he can improve upon nature, *Mr. Pygmalion* also reflects its author's concern with the plight of the contemporary Spanish stage. Grau's scorn of its traditionalism, conservatism, and low artistic standards is concentrated primarily in the prologue, in which the business agent Don Augustín and the impresarios Don Lucio, Don Javier, and Don Olegario are satirical portraits epitomizing the rank commercialism and disdain for art and artists endemic (in Grau's view) to the entire managerial stratum of the Spanish theater. Grau is only slightly less contemptuous of actors and actresses, whose professional envy and vanity are also satirized in the prologue in the figures of Ponzano, Doña Hortensia, and Teresita.

The prologue—more particularly the tenth and last scene—also serves Grau as a vehicle through which not only to satirize the state of the contemporary Spanish theater but also to express an avant-gardist attitude toward the puppet as the supreme actor. Through a long narration of Pygmalion about the background of his interest in the world of puppets, marionettes, and masks, Grau conveys his own fascination with and knowledge of puppets and their various traditions. He also allies himself with such great directors of the early twentieth century as Gordon Craig and Vsevolod Meyerhold, who sought to transform the theater by overcoming the limitations of the human actor. Pygmalion's narration, which is really the highlight of the prologue, reads as follows:

When I was a child, here in Madrid, I happened to see, by chance, in the collection of a very wealthy Englishman, some ancient puppets made of wood. They were marvelous and were the creations of the renowned Juanelo, the watchmaker of Charles V, and of Vaucanson. These automatons moved and walked perfectly. They made a tremendous impression on me. Then, as if it had been my destiny that thrust them toward me, I had the opportunity to see Japanese and Chinese puppets, gigantic masks, and two figures made by Lafitte Daussat which were a consummate imitation of a woman. I left Spain, and in Nuremberg, that children's paradise, where so many toys are created, I became interested in the manufacture of marionettes. But one day, in a museum, I came across masks by Debureau, faded countenances of Pierrot, with dilated nostrils. There were also masks from Japan made of bronze and laquered wood; masks of the Italian comedy, some of painted wax, others of silk, and some of gauze spread across thin wire; Venetian masks, of enigmatic expression; a veritable compendium, in sum, of cutting and heterogeneous histrionics, a world of grimaces, of inspired plastic deformations. Seeing all this, the idea arose in me of artifi-

cially creating the ideal actor, a mechanical one, without vanity, without
defiance, submissive to the poet-creator, like mass in the hands of sculp-
tors. (49)

THE PUPPET WORLD OF DON RAMÓN DE VALLE-INCLÁN

Beyond any doubt, the most extraordinary body of twentieth-century
Spanish drama inspired by the puppet and marionette tradition belongs
to one of Spain's most innovative and individualistic playrights, Ramón
de Valle-Inclán. Born Ramón José Simón, he changed his name to Ramón
Valle Peña, and eventually to Ramón del Valle-Inclán.[7] A leading representative of Spanish modernism and a man of broad literary and philosophical culture, Valle-Inclán was as outspoken as he was idiosyncratic. A
native Galician, steeped in that region's lore, he came naturally by an anar-
chism that is reflected in many of his works. His contempt for Spanish
traditionalism and formalism, in all spheres of life, fueled much of his
writing. For Valle-Inclán there really were no sacred cows. The exaggerated Spanish code of honor, the traditions of the Spanish military, the shallow ritualism of Spansh politics, literary classics such as *Don Quixote*,
Spanish settlers in the Americas, the state of the Spanish theater in his own
time, the pretensions of academics—everything was fair game. And his
mockery could be devastating. Valle-Inclán had an extraordinary command of language. He was a true virtuoso in whose hands language could
be made to perform astonishing acrobatics and feats of musicality. His
playfulness and inventiveness showed up not only in his satire and characters but also in his facility at coining new words. Yet, as important as language was to him, he never subordinated the physical to it. His plays are
alive with movement, both in the physical sense and in the kinetic energy
of his imagery. Even if many of his stage directions seem to defy scenic realization, they must be read for their cleverness, color, and dynamism.
Dance was an important inspiration to him, and the rhythms of his dialogue often approximate those of dance.

Strongly attracted to farce, which he used on occasion for social satire,
Valle-Inclán also became a master of the grotesque, which became another superbly effective weapon of social criticism in his arsenal. Indeed,
he invented a type of grotesque parodic drama that he called *esperpento*,
a Spanish term denoting something nonsensical and absurd and derived
from the distorting mirrors of the fun house.

In light of the richness of the Spanish puppet theater, Valle-Inclán's extensive use of puppet and marionette material in his plays comes as no surprise. A restless experimenter and innovator, eager to explore new means of theatrical expression, Valle-Inclán discovered the potential of the puppet figure early in his career. This is evident, for example, in his play *Farsa infantil de la cabeza del dragón* (*Children's Farce about the Dragon's Head*), which was written in 1910 and performed for the first time in 1914. The sprightly play outwardly resembles a children's fairy tale in its imaginary castle setting and puppetlike characters. But the resemblance is deceptive. Valle-Inclán had nothing but contempt for the Spanish monarchy, which he regarded as having long outlived its usefulness, and he sought to ridicule it in several of his works. *The Dragon's Head* was the first of such plays conceived in this spirit.

The anachronistic and ridiculous nature of the Spanish monarchy was nowhere more in evidence, from Valle-Inclán's point of view, than in the artificiality and elaborate protocol of the court. This, together with the absurdity of the Spanish code of honor and fondness for boasting, are the principal objects of his satire. *The Dragon's Head* recalls the fairy tale tradition of the dragon slayer. This time, the hero who slays the terrible monster is Prince Verdemar, one of the sons of King Mongucián. At the beginning of the play, Verdemar and his two brothers are playing ball in the castle courtyard. At one point the ball is hit into the window of a turret where a mischievous forest sprite is being held captive. The sprite agrees to return the ball in exchange for his freedom. The princes, however, renege on their promise. When the ball is lost a third time to the sprite, Verdemar takes it on himself to get the key to the turret which his mother, the queen, wears attached to a belt. After freeing the sprite, Verdemar must leave home because of what he has done. Along his travels, he puts up at an inn in the realm of King Micomicón, where he is soon embroiled in a fight with a local bullying braggart named Espandián, the embodiment of Spanish swagger. After besting Espandián, Verdemar makes friends with him. While at the inn, Verdemar hears about the dragon in the area which has vanquished all the knights sent out to fight it; it is now demanding the sacrifice of King Micomicón's lovely daughter, the princess. The king promises his daughter's hand in marriage plus half the wealth of his kingdom to anyone who kills the dragon and spares his daughter. Prince Verdemar, who in the meantime has become known to the princess in the guise of a jester and is captivated by her beauty, decides to fight the dragon. He kills the monster but is loath to reveal himself because of the circumstances in which he left his father's kingdom. Espandián then comes forward to present himself as the heroic dragon slayer, and he has his men haul in the dragon's head as proof. But when King Micomicón is about to give his daughter to the braggart, Verdemar announces that it is he who really killed the dragon and that he has the beast's tongue as proof. He then reveals who he is and why he pretended to be a jester. Espandián is taken away for a whipping, and Verdemar and the princess are now free to wed. At play's end, Verdemar is reconciled with his parents and happiness reigns over both kingdoms.

The play is alive with humor and the wit of Valle-Inclán's mockery of the institution of the monarchy and the empty pomp and ceremony of the royal court. There are too many amusing lines to quote here, but a few will suffice to convey the dramatist's style. When the princes playing ball hear the forest sprite singing from the turret early in the play, Valle-Inclán mentions in one of his typical stage directions (which can often be read with as much pleasure as the play itself) that the song is also being listened to by storks with one leg in the air. He then goes on to point out that the posture of the storks *"forebodes the admirers of Richard Wagner."*[8] When Prince Verdemar's mother discovers the theft of the key, she exclaims: "There are traitors in the palace! It's just like Russia here!" The king replies: "Worse than in Russia, because we have no police!" (287). In a swipe at the royal court, Valle-Inclán puts the following words in the mouth of the forest sprite after Prince Verdemar has slain the dragon and cut out its tongue: "I'll extract the venom from the tongue and sell it in King Micomicón's court to the poets and ladies who grumble about everything" (317). Typical of Valle-Inclán's frequent jibes at academics and intellectuals is Espandián's comparison, when he proudly displays the head of the dragon before King Micomicón and his court, that "it is as heavy as a doctoral thesis" (324). In a typical put-down of the Spanish code of honor and the chivalric tradition, Valle-Inclán has one of Prince Verdemar's brothers, Prince Ajonjolí, berate the wood sprite for asking him to give him his word, as a "man of honor" ("hombre de bien"), that he will free him : "You lack the respect due me as a prince of the blood. 'Man of honor' is said of a peasant, of a wine grower, of a workman. But nobody is so insolent as to say it of a prince. 'Man of honor' is said of a captain, of a nobleman, of a duelist, and of some rogues who fight with cardboard swords." The forest sprite replies: "I know indeed that cardboard swords and sabers are the best piece of equipment for fancying oneself a knight" (284).

Although *The Dragon's Head* is not actually designated a play for puppets or marionettes, its fairy tale character, broad humor, slapstick, and lively dialogue easily lend themselves to puppet treatment. That Valle-Inclán had the puppet tradition in mind, at least to some extent, when he wrote the play in 1910 seems evident from the stage direction at the beginning of the fourth act. The scene is a *"thousand-year-old forest"* in the kingdom of King Micomicón. The princess appears amidst a large entourage of ladies, pages, and chamberlains. The master of ceremonies walks among them striking the ground with a silver stick. In moments of silence. the members of the entourage gesticulate *"with the childlike air of puppets whose movements are directed by a decoy. They exchange courtesies and smile with their eyes motionless, wide open, and bright, like the beads of a necklace"* (309).

Valle-Inclán's interest in farce and the grotesque, which grew as time went on, is evident, to varying degrees, in the next two plays he wrote after *The Dragon's Head*. The first was *La marquesa Rosalinda* (*The Marchioness Rosalinda*, 1912), subtitled *A Sentimental and Grotesque Farce*. The "sentimental" dimension of the play is represented by the elegance of its eighteenth-century court setting and the figure of the Marchioness Rosalinda herself. There is a distinctly Mozartian aura to be felt here. The "grotesque," on the other hand, is epitomized in the classic figures of the Italian commedia dell'arte. The originality of *The Marchioness Rosalinda* lies in the ironic contrast between the mannered poise and sophistication of the marchioness and her court and the slapstick and improvised buffoonery of the Italian commedia. It is from this contrast, as visual as it is stylistic, that the play develops its grotesque character. Long interested in music and dance, Valle-Inclán also used *The Marchioness Rosalinda* as a type of theatrical laboratory in which to experiment with the fusion of theater and dance. The play as a whole seems conceived in terms of balletic movement, with musical accompaniment. Dialogue replicates the rhythms of sounds and physical movements, a feature also of later plays by Valle-Inclán.

Following *The Marchioness Rosalinda*, Valle-Inclán wrote *El embrujado* (*The Bewitched*, 1913), *A Tragedy of the Salnés Region*. Although rejected by the artistic director of Madrid's Teatro Español, Benito Pérez

Galdós—a force to be reckoned with then in Spanish literature—the
rather short three-act work is important in tracing the evolution of Valle-
Inclán's concepts of tragedy and farce. An outgrowth of the dramatist's
keen interest in the rural world of his native Galicia, it explores the inter-
connections between lust, murder, and greed. The play has no discernible
puppet elements, yet Valle-Inclán included it in his 1927 collection in
book form of five plays, *Retablo de la avaricia, la lujuria y la muerte* (*Puppet Theater of Avarice, Lust, and Death*). The other plays comprising
what is in essence a puppet quintet are *Ligazón* (*The Bond, An Auto for
Silhouettes*); *La rosa de papél* (*The Paper Rose, A Melodrama for Marionettes*); *La cabeza del Bautista* (*The Head of the Baptist, A Melodrama
for Marionettes*); and *Sacrilegio* (*Sacrilege*, another *Auto for Silhouettes*).

By the time Valle-Inclán came to assemble his *Puppet Theater of Avarice, Lust, and Death* in 1927, his earlier belief in man's tragic destiny had
given way to an outlook for which the puppet figure seemed the most perfect metaphor. Abandoning the heroic dimension of tragedy, Valle-Inclán
adopted a diametrically opposite viewpoint according to which man was
no more than a helpless puppet or marionette manipulated by the strings
of uncontrollable passions or collective social myths, not the least among
them the "national spirit." Looked at from sufficient distance to permit a
dispassionate critical perspective—which he would eventually advocate
as an aesthetic principle—the human world and its pretensions seemed
small, ridiculous, and even absurd. For the dramatist intent on capturing
this absurdity, the proper stance was that of the puppeteer beholding his
puppet creations from above. There was also a theatrical dimension to
this "puppetized" worldview. By cultivating a type of theater as remote by
its very nature as possible from traditional forms, Valle-Inclán was im-
plying both a defiance of those forms and their subversion.

Once confirmed in this change of attitude toward the human condition,
Valle-Inclán went on to create a spectacular and original drama of the farcical, absurd, and grotesque. It was also a drama rich in parody. The turning point for Valle-Inclán's dramatic writing seems to have been the year
1920; after that the overwhelming majority of his plays were written
either as puppet plays or with the clear intention that they be performed
by human actors emulating the movements of puppets or marionettes.
Furthermore, the inclusion of an earlier play such as *The Bewitched* in the
puppet collection of 1927 suggests a reinterpretation of its dynamics in
accordance with his new outlook on man.

The years 1920–26 were especially fruitful for Valle-Inclán's new puppet-inspired dramaturgy. The first play in this spirit was a verse satire of the monarchy entitled *Farsa italiana de la enamorada del rey* (*Italian Farce of the Young Woman in Love with the King*, 1920). It was followed the same year by another verse satire, this time directed specifically at the court of Isabel II: *Farsa y licencia de la reina castiza* (*Farce and License of the Purebred Queen*). Both, together with *The Dragon's Head*, were published in 1926 in a single volume entitled *Tablado de marionetas para educación de príncipes* (*Tableau of Marionettes for the Education of Princes*), the point being, mockingly, that since all three plays reflected Valle-Inclán's jaundiced view of the monarchy, they were eminently suitable as pedagogical material for princes. As in the case of the inclusion of *The Bewitched* in the puppet collection of 1927, this would seem to attest to Valle-Inclán's belief now that the earlier play was suitable for performance in the puppet style.

Valle-Inclán wrote three other plays for puppets or marionettes in the 1920s, the most important being *Esperpento de los cuernos de Don Friolera* (*The Horns of Don Friolera*, 1921). It first appeared in the review *La Pluma* and was subsequently published in book form in 1925. Because of its ridicule of the Spanish code of honor among the military, it was long banned in Spain and was performed only by clandestine student groups. Two "melodramas for marionettes" followed in 1924: *The Head of the Baptist* and *The Paper Rose*, which originally had been subtitled *A Novela Macabra* (*Macabre Tale*). As he had done before, Valle-Inclán later combined certain plays into collections largely along thematic lines. Thus *The Horns of Don Friolera* became the centerpiece of the trilogy of *esperpentos* to which he gave the title *Martes de carnaval* (*Shrove Tuesday*). Published in 1930, the new collection also contained *Las galas de difunto* (*The Well-Dressed Corpse*) and *La hija del capitán* (*The Captain's Daughter*). The unifying thread in the trilogy is Valle-Inclán's view of the Spanish military from the disaster of the Spanish-American War of 1898 to General Miguel Primo de Rivera's coup d'état in 1923. *The Well-Dressed Corpse* originally appeared as a *novela* under the title *El terno de difunto* (*The Corpse in a Three-Piece Suit*). It was subsequently designated an *esperpento* and its title changed slightly to *The Well-Dressed Corpse*. The play is about an ex-soldier's theft of a dead man's clothes and his relations with a prostitute; it serves as a vehicle for Valle-Inclán's skewed attitude toward patriotism. *The Captain's Daughter*, which has never been performed in Spain, deals with a series of military and political scandals involving prostitution, gambling, murder, and blackmail which lead to an absurd but real coup d'état by the army. Also designated an *esperpento*, the play originally appeared in a monthly issue of sensational stories and was immediately removed and censored, supposedly for its implicit attack on the government of Primo de Rivera.

Let us now look more closely at those plays of Valle-Inclán from the 1920s specifically intended for puppet or marionette performance. The first are *Italian Farce of the Young Woman in Love with the King* and *Farce and License of the Purebred Queen*, published with *The Dragon's Head* as a collection under the title *Tableau of Marionettes for the Education of Princes*.

Of the three plays, *The Young Woman in Love with the King* is alone in bringing onstage the figure of a puppeteer. His name is Maese Lotario and he is an itinerant Italian. The farce is called Italian both for this reason and for its borrowings from the commedia dell'arte. Underlying the more obvious satire of monarchy is Valle-Inclán's treatment of the theme of illusion and reality. The *enamorada* is the young woman, Mari-Justina, who works in an inn. In the tongue-in-cheek humor of the farce's literary and artistic allusions, the patio of the inn is described in the stage directions as "*humanist and picaresque, with the flavor of halls of learning and the popular flavor of the roads. It has the whiff of the writings of Quixote.*"[9] Similarly, in the second act, the gardens of the duke of Nebreda are characterized as "architechtonic gardens, as painted by Rusiñol," a reference to the prominent Catalan artist, Santiago Rusiñol.

Mari-Justina is in deep sorrow. Having glimpsed the king (Carlos III) once from afar, she is madly in love with him and does not know what to do about it. Apprised of the cause of her unhappiness, Maese Lotario tells her that "her dreams saw the sad blue of the ideal," and that it was a "shadow and she imagined a king." The puppeteer has a chance to come face to face with the object of Mari-Justina's love when an emissary of the duke of Nebreda named Don Facundo comes to fetch him. The duke, it happens, is playing host to the king and would like to hire as entertainer the talented Italian puppeteer-poet staying at the local inn. Regarding himself as learned and a connoisseur of the arts, Don Facundo professes his own disdain for Lotario's puppet theater, dismissing it as consisting of *farsas chabacanas* —crude, primitive farces—the term, in fact, often applied pejoratively to Valle-Inclán's own farces for marionettes. They are, however, to the taste of the king, whom Don Facundo also makes light of as *bendito* ("simpleminded"). Before departing with Don Facundo, Maese Lotario promises Mari-Justina that he will tell the king of her love.

Maese Lotario's reputation has preceded him at the duke's court in more than one sense. Altisidora, a member of the court, has heard that he was a poor student (*sopón*) in Salamanca who conceals his true name and boasts of being a poet. Moreover, he had to flee to Spain from his native Italy because he is a villain. The Caballero de Seingalt (Casanova), who is sojourning in Spain, also knows Maese Lotario by virtue of a less-than-savory reputation in Italy.

When the king finally makes his appearance, he is a grotesque figure: old, hunchbacked, bandy-legged, and big-nosed. Told of a girl who has fallen madly in love with him when she saw him one afternoon while he was out hunting, he responds incredulously: "Is it possible that there exists so crazy a girl? Is she sick in the head, or sick in sight?"(235). In a very funny scene between the king and Altisidora, he asks if she believes what Lotario has told him, and if girls such as the one from the inn fall in love that way. Not wishing to offend him, Altisidora describes her own ardent feelings for him. To every one of the ailments or shortcomings the king enumerates, she responds with ecstatic approval:

> *King*. Even if I wear three bodices?
> *Altisidora*. It drives me mad.
> *King*. In winter seven.
> *Altisidora*. One can never have enough clothing!
> *King*. I don't sleep at night.
> *Altisidora*. I, too, am sleepless.
> *King*. If I cough?
> *Altisidora*. I'll give you a caramel for the cough.
> *King*. It's an old person's cough.
> *Altisidora*. I'll give you a marshmallow.
> *King*. If I'm more jealous than a Berber?
> *Altisidora*. Because love inflames you!
> *King*. Because I'm maniacal and besides, I have rheumatism!
> *Altisidora*. I will love you rheumatically.

When he learns where Mari-Justina can be found, the king, accompanied by Don Facundo, sets out for the inn to talk her out of her romantic obsession. Both men are disguised as workers. At the inn, the king reveals himself to Mari-Justina. She is frightened by his appearance, which she is really seeing for the first time. When she thought she saw him before, she lowered her eyes when she was aware it was the king. But she still does not know for sure that it is with the king she is now speaking. Her doubts are removed by Maese Lotario when he returns to the inn and confirms the king's identity. "The sad light of reason" has at last come to Mari-Justina. As if by way of compensation for the loss of her dream, the king will marry her to Don Facundo. In a mockery of Spanish traditions typical of Valle-Inclán, Mari-Justina accepts the king's offer with less than wholehearted enthusiasm:

> *Mari-Justina.*
>   This gentleman is always grousing.
> *King.*
>   But he is a glory of Spain.
> *Mari-Justina.*
>   Such an old one!
> *King.*
>   All the glories of Spain
>   are old, my dear. (270)

Interest now shifts to Maese Lotario's past, which has finally caught up with him. In flowing veils and black cape, a woman identified as La Dama del Manto (The Lady of the Cloak; her real name is Violante) bursts into the king's court demanding justice for her dishonor.[10] When she had spurned Maese Lotario's romantic advances, he mocked her in a scandalous sonnet. Then, when her brother sought to avenge her honor by challenging him to a duel, Maese Lotario killed him. As retribution, the king demands that Maese Lotario marry the woman, but then he also orders him incarcerated. Although Violante manages to secure his release, he returns to the inn at the first opportunity. Violante soon catches up with him and demands that he fulfil his obligations. He is unwilling to do so and is obviously romantically attached to Mari-Justina, who now pleads his cause before the king. She also offers to renounce her marriage to Don Facundo. The king agrees and in turn orders Don Facundo to marry Violante for the sake of her honor. Once they are married, he wants them far from his court. The king then appoints Maese Lotario his personal adviser. Converted to and enlightened by poetry, the king moves closer to the common people as the play draws to an end:

I want to change the crude rites of shysters by means of the standards of
poetry. Only imagination is fit to reign, and my kingdom is in the hands
of plebeians. (276)

Valle-Inclán's most pungent satire in *The Young Woman in Love with
the King* is reserved for Castilian pomposity and pretensiousness. These
are embodied primarily in the figures of Don Facundo, the king's minister,
and Don Bártolo, an academician and queen's confessor. In their exchanges with Maese Lotario over literature, Valle-Inclán contrasts the
Castilians' humorless pedantry and formalism with the Italian puppeteer-
poet's celebration of poetic fantasy. It is, after all, Lotario who is described as "*enamored of the face of the moon.*" Defending his verses
against the ridicule of the two courtiers, Maese Lotario declares at one
point that they belong to the "true, Spanish, Minerva, " adding: "I do not
blaspheme when I say that / they are verses in the manner of El Cid" (241).
Pompous as ever, Don Facundo replies: "Neither Boscán nor Garcilaso
nor Góngora ever used such means, / and a clown certainly can't use
them." Lotario's riposte contains the essence of Valle-Inclán's deflation of
Castilian tradition:

Since I am a clown,
I prefer the style of the common people
to the rhetorical one,
And I compose my poems like
Mingo Revulgo.

It is thus through the poetic imagination and its popular roots, here represented by Maese Lotario, whose own poetry is animated by the spirit
of Mingo Revulgo, that the Spanish court and the Spanish people can be
reconciled. By assimilating the poetic view of reality of the Italian puppeteer and Mari-Justina—the view, that is, of Quixote—the king can break
free of the inauthenticity and grotesqueness of his court and reach out to
his people. Only in this way can the malaise of contemporary Spain at long
last be overcome. Although a puppeteer, it is as a lyric poet and defender
of poetic fantasy that Maese Lotario ends the unreal isolation of the king.

Valle-Inclán's next play, *Farce and License of the Purebred Queen*, identified in a short verse preface as a "farce for puppets, malicious echoes of
the revolutionary weeklies *La Gorda*, *La Flaca*, and *Gil Blas*," first ap-

peared in the literary review *La Pluma* (nos. 3–5) in 1920. It was published in book form in 1922. In it, the dramatist's sharper satire takes aim squarely at Queen Isabel II (the grandmother of King Alfonso XIII) and her court. A coquette whose consort, Don Francisco, was insignifcant and weak, Isabel was deposed in the revolution of 1868. A gem of wit, color, and movement, the play is one of Valle-Inclán's best-conceived and most diverting puppet works.

As depicted in the play, the royal court is little more than a viperous nest of gossips, sycophants, and intriguers. The hope represented by the poetic conversion of the king in *The Young Woman in Love with the King* is totally absent here. The all-pervasive corruption and cynicism of the queen's inner circle create an atmosphere in which poetry cannot breathe. The play turns on the queen's uncontrollable passion for writing indiscreet romantic letters. One of them, arranging a tryst, is in the possession of a poor student who appears very early in the play with a plan to trade it for favors with the Grand Provost (Gran Preboste), the power behind the throne and the archvillain of the piece. What the student has in mind specifically is the archbishopric of Manila. The Provost balks at the excessive demand but is willing to consider another, lesser church position. More concerned about the dances she enjoys, against the Grand Provost's advice, the queen is rather casual about the matter. While news of the epistolary indiscretion causes a furor among her favorites at court, chief among them Don Gargarabete, she empowers the Provost to bargain with her would-be blackmailer as he sees fit. In a play crackling with clever dialogue, the conversation in act 1 between the Grand Provost and the queen about her letters is some of the best, especially when the two discuss her literary style. The student, meanwhile, disguised as a Franciscan friar, is also using the queen's letter to blackmail her jealous and suspicious consort into paying him an exorbitant sum. Before long, the existence of other incriminating letters by the queen and schemes of blackmail by different parties becomes the gossip of the court. When the consort's favorite, a hunchbacked guitarist named Torroba, whispers excerpts from one of the queen's letters into his ear, he recognizes it as something he himself had written and for which he too is trying to exact money from the Grand Provost. His threat to divorce the queen notwithstanding, the consort still insists on exercising his rights as consort. When he tries to enter her bedroom, he is turned away by the queen's ladies-in-waiting on the grounds that he has come on a Thursday, a day of abstinence. In the absurd style in which the puppet play was conceived, the queen's ladies and the consort's men argue about which day of the week it is. Arriving at the scene, the Grand Provost orders all present to leave and then threatens to declare publicly that the consort is insane if he doesn't desist from his efforts to force his way into the queen's bedroom. A puppet theater slapstick scene ensues as the consort's supporters (Tragatundas and Lucero del Alba) menace the Grand Provost and the hunchbacked guitarist, who takes his side. Although the consort urges them not to fight because he can't stand the sight of blood, Torroba (the hunchback) and Lucero del Alba presumably kill each other off. The sound of the fracas awakens the queen, who now enters "with a bonnet over her ear and winking. The flabby lard quivers pinkishly beneath the muslin of her white nightgown" (429). When she sees the two bodies, she orders her lady-in-waiting, Mari-Morena, to kick them into an upright position so they can be carted away. Since the play is, after all, a puppet farce, the two "corpses" spring to life under the blows of Mari-Morena's clogs. The queen then expresses her pleasure at seeing the consort and welcomes him to her bedroom. Lucero del Alba, newly "resuscitated," closes the farce by declaring his intention to extinguish the light with his blunderbuss and "disentangle with this trick all the threads of the farce" (431). The last words of the play are those of a blind man in the square hawking an extra edition of *La Gaceta* announcing the naming of the new archbishop of Manila.

Apart from its satirical conception of the court of Isabel II as an absurd and grotesque puppet show, *Farce and License of the Purebred Queen* is alive with movement. This is signaled by Valle-Inclán in his verse preface, in which he compares his muse to dance:

My modern muse
arches her leg,
sways, undulates,
bends, and prances
with the rhythmic fanciness
of the tango,
and gathers her skirt back.
(339)

In *Farce and License of the Purebred Queen*, not just people, but nature and even objects come alive with movement. In the description of the opening set, for example, "*the moon soaks through the foliage and illumi-*

nates the royal palace, which, acrobatic in the reflections of the lake, does a somersault" (341). When Mari-Morena leaves the chamber of the Grand Provost on the entrance of the consort's crony Lucero del Alba in act 1, her waist moves *"with the undulations of a female cat, and the saucy rhythm of her heels"*(345). As the first act ends, *"the orchestra of crickets strikes up and the moon makes an acrobatic leap on the top of the little blacks that serve it as a springboard"*(368). When the curtain rises on the third act, *"the portraits of the dynasty are dancing a dance upon the walls"* (411).

The Horns of Don Friolera, which followed *Farce and License of the Purebred Queen* in 1921, is noteworthy among Valle-Inclán's puppet plays for its literary theoretical implications. In writing it the dramatist's primary goal was to expose what he regarded as the absurdity of the Spanish code of honor as embodied, above all, in the Spanish military. Don Friolera is an army lieutenant who, because of an anonymous note, suspects that his wife, Loreta, is being unfaithful to him with the local barber, the crippled and long-nosed Pachequín. Loreta and Pachequín are friends, and Pachequín is enamored of her, but she remains loyal to her husband. Don Friolera believes that the note was written by a baldheaded neighbor named Doña Tadea. Although she denies authorship, she goads Don Friolera by planting deeper suspicions about the relationship between Loreta and Pachequín. Don Friolera loves his wife, with whom he has a daughter, but by responding to suspicion as if it were fact, he is reduced to a marionette, a figure of no independent judgment here being manipulated by the strings of the social code. As an army officer he—and his family—must be above reproach. If he discovers his wife to be adulterous, he has no choice but to kill her. Assuming her guilt on the basis of mere gossip, Don Friolera has an ugly confrontation with Loreta at home and then pursues her through the streets, pistol in hand. When Pachequín tries to assure him that Loreta is faithful to him, Don Friolera refuses to believe him and now threatens to kill both of them. Transformed into an automaton by a grotesque code of behavior, he is beyond reasoning. It is only the appearance of Manolita, the daughter he loves, which stays his hand for the time being. Overcome by fear, Loreta, in the meantime, allows Pachequín to take her home with him for safety's sake. But when he continues to press her romantically, she asks him to demonstrate his love by allowing her to leave, which he does.

Don Friolera's fate is sealed not only by his own suspicions but by the assumption of his fellow officers that Loreta has indeed cuckolded him. In order to punish "dishonor" and uphold the prestige of the military, they agree to recommend that Don Friolera be discharged from the army. In its satirical use of absurdity, scene 8, in which his fellow lieutenants Rovirosa, Cardona, and Campero discuss the matter, is one of the most entertaining in the play. Taunted mercilessly by Doña Tadea and condemned by his fellow officers, Don Friolera resolves to redeem his honor, above all in the eyes of the military, by delivering the heads of his wife and her presumed lover. When he comes across Loreta and Pachequín, his wife has finally yielded to the barber's entreaties that they flee Don Friolera's wrath under cover of darkness and that they take Manolita with them. Just as Pachequín is scaling a wall with Manolita in his arms, Don Friolera bursts into the garden and fires his pistol at them, believing them to be his wife and Pachequín. He then races off to his commanding officer, Colonel Don Pancho Lamela, to declare that he has avenged his honor and that the blood of adultery "has flowed in torrents." Assuming at first that Don Friolera is just drunk, the colonel assures him that if his statement is true, he has helped save the honor of the corps. As he is about to offer him a congratulatory cigar, the colonel's wife bursts into the room to inform him that the woman Don Friolera killed was his daughter, not his wife. Convinced that Don Friolera has lost his mind, the colonel allows the distraught man to take himself to the hospital. The play proper ends at that point.

Valle-Inclán has reinforced the puppet aspect of *The Horns of Don Friolera* in two ways, primarily—with a prologue and an epilogue. The prologue takes the form principally of a fairground performance by a *bululú* (puppeteer) of a rudimentary puppet show about a cuckolded Lieutenant Don Friolera. The high point of the show comes in the bloody stabbing to death by the lieutenant of his supposedly unfaithful girlfriend. The folk character of the play's frame has been carried over as well into the epilogue. Here, however, the primitive puppet show of the prologue is replaced by a blind man's ballad (*romance de ciego*) about the Don Friolera of the play proper. But the balladeer's perspective lacks the ironic detachment of the puppeteer. Taking aim at the mythic-heroic propensities of Spanish tradition, Valle-Inclán now transforms Don Friolera into a hero in the balladeer's version. After accidentally shooting his own daughter, Lieutenant Friolera chops off the heads of his wife and her admirer and presents them to his garrison commander. He is appropriately rewarded for his deeds and then goes off to continue his heroic exploits in North Africa, where, the balladeer informs us at the end of his song, the good lieutenant has singlehandedly killed one hundred Moors!

The puppet show of the prologue serves more than a single purpose. Besides setting the stage for the drama of Don Friolera, which will then assume the character of a puppet show of real people, or of real people whose actions transform them into puppets, it also reflects Valle-Inclán's literary outlook at the time he was writing some of his best works under the inspiration of puppet theater. Before the *bululú* begins his performance, two elderly and faintly comic Basque intellectuals appear discussing painting and literature. They are Don Manolito, a painter, and a former clerical heretic known just as Don Estrafalario (Oddball). The conversation between the two is another in a long series of jibes by Valle-Inclán at the pretensiousness of intellectuals. But Don Estrafalario's observations on art express the desirability of artistic distance, to which Valle-Inclán himself was persuaded by the time he came to write *The Horns of Don Friolera*. Using the example of the bullfight, Don Estrafalario argues that

> the sentimental people who feel the agony of the horses . . . are incapable of experiencing the aesthetic emotion of the fight itself. Their sensitivity turns out to be similar to equine sensitivity, and through unconscious cerebration they come to suppose their own luck to be the same as that of those disembowled nags. If they didn't know that they keep thirty yards of blood sausage in their own bellies, believe me they wouldn't be so touched. By chance, have you ever seen them shed any tears watching a drill gut a rock quarry?[11]

In another, more striking example, Don Estrafalario declares that his aesthetic "is overcoming pain and laughter, the way conversations among the dead must be when they tell each other stories about the living . . . I would like to see this world as it is seen from the other shore"(1125). The great appeal of the puppet show to Valle-Inclán, here expresed through Don Estrafalario, is thus twofold. The puppet master always achieves the desirable aesthetic distance by holding himself superior to the dolls he makes perform. This is in contrast to Shakespeare, for example, who, in Don Estrafalario's words, "rhymes the beat of his heart with the heart of Othello. The Moor's jealous fits become his own. Creator and creature are made of the same human clay"(1130). The puppet show thus becomes the model for the view of the world Valle-Inclán sought to achieve in his own dramatic writing. Don Estrafalario also addresses the matter of the natural superiority of the puppet show to the Spanish (Castilian) theatrical tradition: "This puppet show on the shoulders of an old chatterbox is, for me, more appealing than all of the rhetorical Spanish drama"(1128). This is a familiar refrain in Valle-Inclán's writing and the basis of his experimentation with the more fun-loving and earthy puppet tradition. What he objects to especially in Spanish drama is, to quote Don Estrafalario, its "cruelty and dogmatism," which can only be found in the Bible. "Shakespearean cruelty is magnificent," Don Estrafalario, clearly Valle-Inclán's spokesman, opines, "because it is blind, with the greatness of natural forces. Shakespeare is violent, but not dogmatic. Spanish cruelty has all the barbarous liturgy of the autos-da-fé. It is cold and repugnant"(1129).

La cabeza del Bautista (*The Head of the Baptist*), originally subtitled *Novela macabra* (*A Macabre Tale*) but later changed to *A Melodrama for Marionettes*, was Valle-Inclán's next dramatic work in the puppet mode. It is a one-act play of about eleven pages in print in the original and typical of Valle-Inclán's inclination toward more compressed forms in the 1920s. Its premiere took place at the Teatro El Centro in Madrid on 17 October 1924. In its melodramatic aspect a play about the murder of a son seeking vengeance on a father he believes guilty of the murder of his mother, the play is notable for its treatment of the theme of Eros and Thanatos, lust and death. El Jándolo, his son from his first marriage, has come to Spain in search of his father, Don Igi, a *gachupín* (a Spaniard who went off to the Americas in search of his fortune and eventually returned to Spain). Don Igi's status as a *gachupín* in the play was no whim on Valle-Inclán's part. In 1921 he made a trip to Mexico on the invitation of the government of President Álvaro Obregón and the Universidad Nacional to participate in Independence Day celebrations. While there, he developed a keen dislike for the *gachupínes* which shows up in his subsequent writing.

Described in the stage directions as having the "*sad and twisted sneer of a puppet*"—one of several references to the character as a *fantoche*— Don Igi is a boastful hypocrite by nature, a common attribute, Valle-Inclán now believed, of the *gachupín*. Not long after El Jándolo's arrival, the purpose of his return to Spain becomes clear. He demands a sum of money of his father in cash as the price of his silence in Spain concerning Don Igi's role in the death of his mother, Don Igi's first wife. El Jándolo claims that his father killed her and then implicated him in the crime. Don

Igi had been tried while in the Americas on suspicion of murder, but despite the prejudice against such *gachupínes* in the New World, the case was dismissed because of a lack of evidence. Don Igi tries to convince his son that in any case he is in no position to pay him the blackmail he demands. He bemoans the money he has lost opening cafés and billiard rooms in the town in which he now lives. Moreover, he declares that his former wife's money and property went to pay off her mortgage. But El Jándalo, as greedy in his own way as Don Igi himself, refuses to believe him and demands money. Attention at this point shifts to Don Igi's mistress, La Pepona. Hardly anxious to share anything she and Don Igi have with his son, she and her lover concoct a scheme to get rid of him. La Pepona, with whom El Jándolo has already flirted on his first visit to Don Igi's inn, will entice the young man when he returns, and the moment he comes into her arms, Don Igi will stab him from behind with a dagger.

When El Jándalo returns to the inn at a time when it is normally closed to the public in order to collect the money, he is greeted cordially and invited to drink. But he insists that he will drink only with La Pepona, after which he starts talking to her in a suggestive way. Demanding that his father count out three thousand pesos for him, El Jándolo continues flirting with La Pepona, at one point threatening to take her away with him. He taunts Don Igi further by claiming that La Pepona is not suitable for an old man. Don Igi at last agrees to give his son a check, but for a smaller amount. La Pepona keeps telling them to put off the business until the following day, but El Jándolo is adamant and sends Don Igi for his checkbook. While his father is gone for the moment, El Jándolo draws a willing La Pepona to him for a kiss. Don Igi, who has reentered the room, sneaks up from behind and plunges a dagger into his son's back. As El Jándolo expires, La Pepona feels his mouth turning cold against her own. Her ecstasy is explosive: "Flower of youth! I killed you just when you were giving me life!" (903). Don Igi cannot understand her: "Girl, what are you doing? You're kissing his mouth after finishing him off?" Caught in the grip of her grotesque ecstasy, La Pepona turns on her lover with contempt: "I bite him and I kiss him! He was worth more than you, you villainous old man!" She orders Don Igi to take the body of El Jándolo and bury it beneath the lemon trees in the garden outside, and her delirious passion now reaches a crescendo. Addressing the corpse, she screams: "I want to descend into the ground in the embrace of this body! Kiss me again, my lovely flower!

Return me the kisses I am giving you, stiff head! Embraced by you, I want to descend into the ground! I didn't know you at all! To come to die in my arms from so far away!" She screams for El Jándolo to kiss her again, to return the kisses she is giving him. Unable to distinguish reality and fantasy, she asks if he is a delusion. In the same breath, she ecstatically declares that she will bite his mouth and appeals to life to pull her out of the dream she is in. All of this is more than Don Igi can bear. As the play ends, understanding at last that he has lost everything, he forlornly expresses regret at not having given El Jándolo the money he had asked for in the first place.

Eros and Thanatos intertwine in a more macabre way in another short play by Valle-Inclán from 1924, *The Paper Rose*. Like *The Head of the Baptist*, it was originaly subtitled *A Macabre Tale* and subsequently changed to *A Melodrama for Marionettes*. Even more powerfully than in his previous play, Valle-Inclán uses the twin motifs of greed and death to dramatize the ironic contrast between spontaneous, instinctive behavior and socially conditioned attitudes. The latter motivate the marionette-like behavior of a character whose descent to the level of the puppet keeps pace with his responses to external stimuli.

The two principals in the play are the village blacksmith, Simeón Julepe, and his dying wife, Floriana. Simeón's treatment of his wife is coarse and unfeeling, even as she lies on her deathbed. The plot is set in motion by Floriana's revelation to her husband that she has hoarded a tidy sum of money (7,000 *reales*) in a bundle of rags. She has been fearful of telling him its whereabouts while she is still alive lest he squander the money on drink and not look after their children. However, just before Simeón accedes to her wish that he go fetch neighbors who will prepare her body for death, she reveals the hiding place of the money. Yet as soon as he leaves their house, she summons her last drop of energy and changes the hiding place of the bundle. When Simeón returns, drunk, two neighbors (La Musa and La Disa) are already with Floriana, comforting her. Simeón's thoughts now are only on money. But not finding it where Floriana told him she had concealed it, he immediately suspects the two neighbors of having stolen it. When they berate him for his drunken behavior and for not respecting the memory of his now deceased wife, he locks the door to the house and threatens to cut them to pieces. His threats to no avail, Simeón, now desperate, his children beholding the scene in terror, brandishes an old revolver in front of the two women, who continue pleading their innocence. At that moment, one of the children tells Simeón that she saw her mother hide the bundle of rags in a scarf. He makes a mad dash up the stairs, bowling his children over in the process, and soon retrieves the scarf and the bundle. By this time other neighbors have come to the house to pay their respects to the deceased. The final preparation of Floriana's body for burial proceeds without interruption, and, when all is ready, a neighbor places a paper rose in her hands. Candles are placed about the bier and lit, and all gather around it. As they exchange comments on the splendid looks of Floriana in death, Simeón stumbles in bearing a tasteless floral crown made of brass, which he places at the feet of the deceased and which Valle-Inclán characterizes in the stage direction as of "*German sentimentality.*" Responding now, like a puppet, to social expectations with behavior deemed appropriate to the occasion, he launches a bombastic oration in praise of his dead wife in the demagogic style he had previously demonstrated. Carried away by the sight of his wife's cadaver with the paper rose in her hands and her legs sheathed in striped stockings, Simeón scandalizes his neighbors by his behavior. As he tries to draw still closer to the corpse, he stumbles and knocks a candle into the bier, setting the paper rose ablaze. In no time, all the raiments in the bier are on fire. At the end, with the fire burning all around him, Simeón sweeps the corpse into an ecstatic embrace, shouting hysterically. The group of women falls back, gesticulating wildly. The entire forge appears to be on fire.

The Head of the Baptist and *The Paper Rose* were the last of Valle-Inclán's plays inspired by and in all likelihood intended for the puppet and marionette theater. Together with his previously published farces, *The Young Woman in Love with the King* and *The Purebred Queen*, *The Head of the Baptist* was included in a trilogy published in 1926 under the title *Tablado de marionetas para educación de príncipes* (*Tableau of Marionettes for the Education of Princes*). Both *The Head of the Baptist* and *The Paper Rose* were performed at the experimental theater La Mama in New York in 1970, which was unusual in view of the rarity of productions of Valle-Inclán's plays in England and America.

Valle-Inclán wrote two other short plays in 1926 and 1927 which, while not directly related to the puppet tradition, have elements in common with it. They are *Ligazón* (*The Bond*, 1926) and *Sacrilegio* (*Sacrilege*, 1927), both one-act plays subtitled *Autos para siluetas* (*Mystery*

Plays for Silhouettes). In the puppet plays, Valle-Inclán conceived of his characters as puppets responding like automatons either to external stimuli—social customs and traditions, for example—or to basic human drives, especially the erotic, by which they are dominated. In *The Bond* and *Sacrilege* the grotesqueness of ironic transformations of character, of startling reversals of roles, is achieved not by puppet imagery but through a suggestive interplay of light and dark. Everything is reduced to shadows, to half-light, obscuring identities and motives, creating a sense of mystery and deception, of dark, even satanic forces at work.

The bond alluded to by the title of the first of these plays is the blood bond between the two principal characters—an itinerant knife grinder and the virginal daughter of an innkeeper who is anxious to marry her off to a wealthy Jew. Spurning material gain, represented by the Jew, the girl follows the instinct that draws her to the knife grinder. Lust, as elsewhere in Valle-Inclán, overrides greed and leads to death, in this case that of the Jew; Eros and Thanatos again merge. Now sexually awakened, and the dominant partner in the relationship with the knife grinder, the girl becomes the embodiment of satanic evil as she lures her lover into the reenactment of a ritualistic sacrifice. A scene in which the lovers drink from the same glass foreshadows the macabre scene in which they suck each other's blood, sealing the evil bond between them. The murder of the Jew, which is the culmination of the blood lust of the erotically possessed girl, occurs when her mother, still anxious to promote marriage between them, admits the Jew into the girl's bedroom one night. The transformation of the girl (La Mozuela, "virgin") into the embodiment of lust, into a temptress, brings about that ironic reversal of character which is often at the heart of Valle-Inclán's grotesque art. Once overcome by the erotic drive, the girl is no more the master of her destiny than the puppetized humans of Valle-Inclán's other plays. Grasped by demonic forces, she is then swept into the execution of a ritualistic sacrifice. The knife grinder is similarly transformed. From the seducer he becomes the seduced, helpless, as a slave of love, in the hands of the virgin now become evil temptress. Both are thus manipulated by forces over which they exert no control, actors in a puppet mystery play of lust and death.

Valle-Inclán could easily have cast *The Bond* in the puppet idiom of his other plays of the 1920s. Instead, as experimental as ever, he conceived it as predominantly visual, one in in which the churning of dark forces and the pervasive sense of mystery would be conveyed, above all, by silhouettes. The silhouettes are not only of human figures but of objects as well, creating visually striking but often enigmatic or vaguely suggestive and associative images.

Sacrilege is an even more provocative and intriguing play of silhouettes than *The Bond*. Ironic reversal of character again culminates in death. Owing much to Julián de Zugasti's ten-volume history of banditry published in Madrid between 1876 and 1880,[12] the work explores the transformative power of the confessional. The scene is a cave of bandits. One of their number (El Sordo de Triana) is accused of betraying the group by selling information about them to the authorities. He is sentenced to death and asks for confession. Seizing on the confession as a possible means of extracting information, the bandits agree and appoint one of their number (El Padre Veritas) to play the priest hearing the confession. Just as the confession is about to begin, the bandits are warned of approaching horsemen and leave. The striking reversal of character on the part of the two men participating in the ritual of confession now occurs. As he begins to confess, El Sordo de Triana is so carried away by the experience that what originally might have been an excuse to buy time becomes a moving outpouring of genuine emotion. El Padre Veritas is also transformed: playing the role of priest, he too succumbs to the power of the ritual and feels the full weight of the sacrilege he is committing. When the other bandits return, they come upon a profoundly penitent El Sordo de Triana in the thick of his confession. Incredulous at first, they try to dispel the genuine solemnity of the occasion by laughter and mockery. But the intensity of the accused's confession and the authenticity of El Padre Veritas's conduct of the ritual alter their mood. Before their own transformation runs full course, however, El Sordo is shot dead at the height of his confessional ecstasy by the captain of the band (El Capitán), who declares: "If I don't shut his mouth, that crook will steal our hearts!"[13] How far the rest of the bandits had been overcome by the spectacle of their two fellows yielding to the power of the ritual is conveyed by the stage direction almost immediately preceding the shooting of El Sordo de Triana: "*The troop of horsemen, with astonishment, press together above the mirror of the pool and advance with the inadvertent movement of sleepwalkers*" (917).

Again, as in *The Bond*, Valle-Inclán's fascination with the ironic transformation of character and role reversal could also have been realized through the puppet analogy. Succumbing to the power of ritual, the two bandits undergo an ironic transformation. Approaching the confessional at first with an apparent lack of conviction, his thoughts primarily on escape, El Sordo de Triana becomes wholly identified with the role he is playing. Once he ceases acting, his behavior is compelled by the force of the ritual. The same is true of El Padre Veritas. From acting out the part of a priest-confessor, he becomes a genuine confessor; the player has become dominated and consumed by his role. Once the process of transformation is initiated by the reflection El Padre Veritas sees of himself as priest-confessor in the pool of water, it is irreversible. His subsequent behavior is conditioned no less than that of the now penitent El Sordo de Triana, desperate to atone before God for his sins. But instead of the puppet imagery of his previous plays, Valle-Inclán experiments with the reflections from a pool of water in the bandits' cave and from the "crystalline arcades" of the cave illuminated by a flaming torch. Additionally, a lantern is carried from one part of the set to another, depending on the action, creating a theater of shadows in the cave. Compared to *The Bond*, *Sacrilege* is a play of greater depth and resonance. If Valle-Inclán sought in these two plays to dramatize the mystical transformative power of ritual, he succeeded more handsomely in *Sacrilege*. Although intriguing in its interplay of light and dark, *The Bond* is less provocative a use of the silhouette motif than *Sacrilege*. Here, shadows created by flickering, mobile light alternate with a play of reflections, especially from the pool of water, conducive in turn to reflections and perceptions of a mystical character.

Valle-Inclán's last play, dating from 1927, was the *Esperpento de la hija del capitán* (*Esperpento of the Captain's Daughter*). When it appeared originally in *La Novela Mundial*, a monthly magazine devoted to stories of a sensational nature, it was immediately censored. Since it depicts a series of military and political scandals involving prostitution, gambling, murder, and blackmail and culminates in an absurd but real coup d'état by the army, it was interpreted as an attack on the government of the dictator Primo de Rivera, who had assumed power in September 1923 by means of a coup d'état. The same year that *The Captain's Daughter* appeared, Valle-Inclán published a new collection of *The Bond*, *The Paper Rose*, *El embrujado* (*The Bewitched*), *The Head of the Baptist*, and *Sacrilege* under the title *Retablo de la avaricia, la lujuría y la muerte* (*Puppet Theater of Avarice, Lust, and Death*). It was followed three years later by another collection bearing the title *Martes de Carnaval* (*Mardi Gras*) and consisting of the *esperpentos The Well-Dressed Corpse, The Horns of Don Friolera,* and *The Captain's Daughter.*

LORCA AND THE SPANISH PUPPET TRADITION

Valle-Inclán's immediate succesor as a dramatic innovator and enthusiast of puppet theater was the great poet Federico García Lorca. The first manifestation of his serious interest in puppets was the theatrical program he and his friend the composer Manuel de Falla organized for the younger children of the family in the Lorca home in Granada to celebrate the Feast of the Epiphany on 6 January 1923. The program began with an *entremés* by Cervantes entitled *Los dos habladores* (*The Two Chatterboxes*). It was performed by hand puppets to the accompaniment of Stravinsky's *Histoire du soldat*, arranged for clarinet, violin, and piano, and played by a three-piece orchestra with Manuel de Falla at the piano. The Cervantes *entremés* was followed by a puppet play written by Lorca himself under the title *La niña que riega la albahaca* (*The Girl Who Waters the Basil Plant*), subtitled *An Andalusian Tale in Three Engravings and One Color Print* and derived from a popular tale, *La mata de albahaca* (*The Basil Plant*). Obviously intended for his younger audience, the play is about a prince who falls in love with, and eventually marries, a shoemaker's daughter who waters a basil plant outside her window right across from the prince's palace. It was staged by the Teatro de la Ciudad de Buenos Aires in 1962 on the basis of the text supplied the director, Roberto Aurlés, by Manuel de Falla, and it was first printed in Madrid in 1982.[14] The centerpiece of the Feast of the Epiphany program was an early-thirteenth-century Spanish mystery play, *Los reyes magos* (*The Three Magi*). The scenery was based on illuminations in a medieval manuscript in the possession of the University of Granada. The puppet figures this time were cut out of heavy cardboard, then painted and gilded, and moved along wooden tracks placed at different levels. They were controlled from the sides by Lorca, his sister Concha, his brother Francisco, and other members of the Lorca household, who also recited the dialogue. Music was selected by Falla from the *Cantigas* of the medieval king Alfonso X. During set changes for the three plays, the figure of Don Cristóbal of Spanish puppet tradition appeared on the small puppet stage that had been set up in the wide doorway between the front parlor and the main living room of the Lorca home. Don Cristóbal—played by Lorca himself—carried on a dialogue with the delighted children in the audience.

Lorca's interest in the puppet theater was neither ephemeral nor limited to the celebration of the Feast of the Epiphany on 6 January 1923 After *The Girl Who Waters the Basil Plant,* he wrote three other puppet plays, all built around the traditional puppet figure of Don Cristóbal. The first, possibly a warm-up for the later two, is just called *Cristobical* and is quite short (four pages in print). It introduces such familiar figures from the Don Cristóbal tradition as the romantic girl Doña Rosita, her lover Currito, and the old billy-club bully himself, Don Cristóbal. The play consists of two scenes and an intermezzo. The setting is an Andalusian town on the morning of the fiesta of Saint John. A group of girls await the stroke of midnight to wash their faces in bewitched water. When midnight comes, twelve women, representing the hours, appear. They are dressed in the style of the mid-nineteenth century—bustle, long train with ruffles, and a traditional Andalusian hat with turned-up brim and chin strap. They also carry enormous brown hats. The women dance the twelve hours of midnight. Only two figures appear in the intermezzo, Don Woodsman-Heart, a little stooped man all dressed in red and wearing a crown of red poppies, and Don Cristóbal. Burdened by age and infirmity, Don Cristóbal is on his way to get married but can barely walk farther. He says that he has been sent by his Director so that Woodsman-Heart can wind up his wheel. Woodsman-Heart obliges and Don Cristóbal is on his way again. Appealing primarily for its music and dancing, the tiny play seems little more than a preface to the two puppet plays for which Lorca is best known— *Los títeres de cachiporra: Tragicomedia de don Cristóbal y la seña Rosita* (*The Billy-Club Puppets: Tragicomedy of Don Cristóbal and Mistress Rosita*), subtitled *Farse guiñolesca en seis cuadros y una advertencia* (*A Puppet Farce in Six Scenes and a Preface*), and the much shorter, if more ribald, *Retablillo de Don Cristóbal* (*The Little Puppet Show of Don Cristóbal;* also translated as *In the Frame of Don Cristóbal*), subtitled *Farsa para guiñol* (*A Puppet Farce*). The first play probably dates from 1922 and would seem to have been begun before Lorca's Feast of the Epiphany program; however, it was printed for the first time only in 1948. The *Little Puppet Show of Don Cristóbal* dates from 1931.

The Billy-Club Puppets, the most important of Lorca's "Don Cristóbal" plays, is a rollicking puppet farce about the marriage of Rosita and

Don Cristóbal. When she agrees to marry, Rosita's impecunious father is elated, seeing a way out of his financial misery. But Rosita is in love with the penniless Cocoliche. The spirit of absurdity with which the play is informed manifests itself early when Rosita tells Cocoliche that she wants to marry him. His immediate reply is that he is going to write away to Paris to ask for a baby boy ("En seguida voy a escribir una carta a Paris pidiendo un niño").[15] Rosita answers: "Paris? Not on your life! I don't want him imitating the French with their chau, chau, chau" (112). As they exchange kisses from a distance, a carriage approaches drawn by little cardboard horses with panaches of feathers. Cristobita (as Cristóbal is familiarly called) alights and begins expressing his delight at Rosita's beauty. He is potbellied and hunchbacked and carries a billy club, which he uses as a walking stick. When her father enters shortly thereafter, Rosita is shocked to learn that he intends marrying her to Cristobita, not Cocoliche. While Cristobita gloats that his bride to be is a "juicy little dish" ("Es una hembrita suculenta" [116]), Rosita, in despair, threatens to commit suicide by swallowing matches or some "corrosive sublimate" ("sublimado corrosivo"). The first scene closes when, in a borrowing from his earlier *Cristobical*, Lorca has an Hour appear from a wall clock dressed in yellow and wearing a bustle. Signaling one o'clock, the Hour tells Rosita to bide her time and be patient.

In the second scene, Rosita tells Cocoliche that because of her father she cannot marry him. In the meantime, a blustering Cristobita shows up to pay his future father-in-law money he promised him and to demand that the wedding ceremony be held the next day. Set in a tavern, where Cocoliche and some friends first appear, followed soon by Cristobita, the third scene is full of the boisterous humor and slapstick of the puppet tradition. At the sight of Cristobita coming toward the tavern, Cocoliche and the youths scatter, some exiting, others hiding behind wine casks. As Cristobita boasts of the wine he will consume at his wedding, the youths behind the casks taunt him. Believing that it is the tavern keeper who is mocking him, Cristobita chases him about, flailing with his billy club. Currito, a former sweetheart of Rosita's, whom Lorca had introduced earlier in *Cristobical*, reappears in scene 4 anxious to see his old flame again. He and a youth from the village persuade the shoemaker, Cansa-Almas, who is going to try on Rosita's bridal shoes the next day, to let Currito take his place. More bluster and beatings from Cristobita dominate the next scene when the bully comes to Fígaro the barber for a prenuptial haircut. For the first time in the play, Cristobita is mocked for being a puppet. When he falls asleep in the barber chair, Fígaro points out that the bully's head is made of wood: "This is splendid! Pretty much as I thought! But how stupendous! Don Cristobita has a wooden head. Poplar wood! Ha, ha, ha! . . . And look, look, all the paint on it! Ha, ha, ha! . . . He's got two knots in his forehead. That's where he sweats the rosin" (142). The sixth and last scene is the longest and most farcical. As Rosita is preparing for the wedding, Currito enters, but Rosita is unhappy to see him because he had left her before. When her father comes into her room, Currito pretends to be the shoemaker trying on Rosita's shoes and asking her to raise her skirt higher and higher. No sooner does the father leave than Cristobita approaches. Rosita hurriedly hides Currito in her wardrobe. Impatient to get married, Cristobita is at once lustful and swaggering. Admiring Rosita's figure, he declares: "Ay, what a tasty morsel you are! What a pair of buns you've got!" When she starts to protest, he boasts of his prowess with his club: "Let's get married right away . . . Hey, listen, you never saw me kill anyone with my club, did you? No? Well now you will. I go: pow, pow, pow! And smack into the gully" (148). Cristobita's exit is followed by Cocoliche's entrance. The stage is now set for the anticipated flurry of fast action with which the play culminates. Cocoliche discovers Currito hidden in the wardrobe and exhanges angry words with him and Rosita. Cristobita's return sends Cocoliche racing to hide in the same wardrobe as Currito. While the wedding of Rosita and Cristobita proceeds on schedule, Cocoliche and Currito continue trading insults in the wardrobe. In Rosita's room after the ceremony, Cristobita wants to make love to his bride, but whenever he kisses her, Cocoliche and Currito cry out from the wardrobe. Rosita deflects Cristobita's suspicion by telling him the noise is coming from outside. When Cristobita falls asleep from drink, Currito leaves his hiding place to bid Rosita farewell forever. But just at that moment, the character Mosquito—part spirit, part goblin, part insect, the representative of the "joy of the free life, and of the grace and poetry of the Andalusian people" (105)—blasts his toy trumpet in Cristobita's ear, waking him up with a start. From this point until nearly the end of the play, the action proceeds at a furious pace. Cristobita, club in hand, chases wildly after Currito, who manages to stab him, but the dagger gets stuck in Cristobita's back in an odd way. While this is going on, Rosita shrieks or laughs hysterically and then releases Cocoliche, with whom she plays out an incongrous romantic scene in the style, García Lorca informs us, of an idyllic operatic duet. Flutes and whistles from a small orchestra are also recommended for musical background. The play reaches its peak of puppet theater nonsensicality when Cristobita discovers Rosita and Cocoliche together; when he lunges toward them, he explodes amid a great popping of springs and then falls backward over the footlights. Inspecting the "corpse," Cocoliche is amazed that no blood flows from Cristobita, and he announces that the great bully was not a person after all. The farce ends with a funeral cortege of puppets led by Mosquito which enters the stage with torches and wearing red capes and black hats. Mosquito carries a banner and plays his toy trumpet. An enormous coffin is brought in, but when Cristobita's body is lifted up, a comical sound like that of a bassoon emerges from him. The sound eventually abates, Cristobita is thrown into the coffin, and the cortege circles the stage to the accompaniment of a funeral march. As Mosquito joyfully assures the assembly that the drunkard Cristobita and his club will never ever return again, Cocoliche and Rosita embrace to the strains of a symphony.

The Little Puppet Show of Don Cristóbal is a shorter, cruder version of *The Billy-Club Puppets*. Both in its prologue and in the Director's closing address to the audience, Lorca emphasizes the popular origins of the puppet farce and its primitive vitality. He suggests, moreover, that it is just such native ingenuity and freshness that hold out the best hope of driving tedium and vulgarity from the Spanish stage. In the prologue, for example, he declares, by way of an introduction to the Poet, who will also address the audience before the play begins:

> The poet who has interpreted and adapted this puppet farce from the lips of the people has evidence of the fact that the disinguished audience this afternoon will be able to appreciate, with intelligence and good heart, the delicious and crude language of the puppets.
>
> Every popular puppet show has the same rhythm, the same fantasy, and the same enchanting freedom which the poet has sought to preserve in the dialogue.
>
> The puppet show is the expression of the people's imagination and offers the temperature of its grace and innocence.
>
> The poet thus knows that the audience will hear with joy and simplicity the expressions and words born of the earth and that they will serve as examples of purity in an age when vulgarities, falsehoods, and troubled feelings reach deepest into the home. (675)

The "delicious and crude language" of *The Little Puppet Show of Don Cristóbal* to which Lorca refers in the prologue pours from the mouths of Cristóbal, Rosita, and her mother. Since they have been reincarnated as grotesque exaggerations of themselves in this later play, their language perfectly accords with their temperaments. In his wilder violence, Cristóbal easily brings Jarry's Père Ubu to mind; Rosita is lustful and yearns to bed down with as many men as she can; her foul-mouthed mother, a chip off Mère Ubu's block, is as anxious as her daughter to see her wed and promotes her this way:

> I'm the mother of Doña Rosita
> and I want her to get married,
> because she's got a pair of breasts
> like two tangerines,
> and a little ass
> like a round of cheese,
> and a little birdie
> that sings and screams.
> And like I tell you:
> she needs a husband bad,
> and if possible, two.
> Ha! Ha! Ha! Ha!
> (684)

When Rosita first appears, she rhapsodizes:

> Ay! A night so crystal clear
> breathes over the tiles.
> This is the hour when boys
> count the stars,
> and old men snooze
> beneath their horses.
> But I want to be:
> on the divan with Juan,
> on the mattress with Ramón,
> on the settee
> with José,
> on the seat
> with Medinilla,
> on the floor
> with the one I care for,
> stuck to the door,

with handsome Arturo,
and in the big chaise-longue
with Juan, José, Medinilla,
with Arturo and Ramón.
  (687)

Apart from its boisterousness and earthy lustfulness, *The Little Puppet Show of Don Cristóbal* is distinctly theatricalist. In this respect it brings to mind other plays in the puppet style by major writers, such as the Russian Aleksandr Blok's *Balaganchik* (*The Fairground Booth*) of 1906 and the German Gerhart Hauptmann's monumental *Festspiel in deutschen Reimen* (*Festival Play in German Verse*) of 1913. Lorca's theatricalism employs the familiar device of the periodic intervention in the play's action by the Director for the purpose of complaining about something, in this instance, to the Poet. Near the beginning, for example, the Director interrupts the poet's address to the audience to inform him that his prologue was supposed to end earlier. When, at a certain point, the Poet expresses his belief that Cristóbal "at heart is good, and perhaps could be so," the Director lashes out at him in the manner of Cristóbal himself: "Nuisance. If you don't shut up, I'll crack open that cornbread mug of yours. Who are you to determine the law of evil?" (676). Following this exchange, again in typical theatricalist style, the Director calls the other characters onstage. When Cristóbal is slow to appear, the Director asks: "What's that? Cristóbal snoring again, is he?" Cristóbal answers, in the true spirit of the play: "I'm coming, Mr. Director. I'm just pissing, that's all" (678). Exchanges like this continue throughout the play until the end, when, in an absurdist touch, Rosita begins having one child after another and Cristóbal begins slapping and beating her and her mother until they confess that they are not his. After the mother is beaten dead and Cristóbal resumes his beating of Rosita, the Director enters, grabs the puppets, and, holding them up to the audience, delivers the play's final words, which essentially repeat the theme struck in the prologue:

> The Andalusian folk often hear such comedies beneath the gray branches of the olive trees and in the dark air of abandoned stables . . . where, with merriment and enchanting innocence, there burst forth those words and expressions which we do not resist in the surroundings of cities, muddled by alcohol and cards. These naughty words acquire ingenuity and freshness when spoken by puppets acting out the charm of this ancient rural farce. Let us fill the theater with fresh ears of grain, from beneath which coarse

words will emerge to do battle with the tedium and vulgarity to which we have been condemned, and let us today greet the rough-and-ready Cristóbal, the Andalusian, cousin of the Galician *Bululú* and brother-in-law of Aunt Norica of Cádiz, brother of the Parisian Monsieur Guiñol, of Paris, and uncle of Harlequin, of Bergamo, as one of the characters from whom trails, pure, the old smell of the theater. (697)

Lorca never seemed to tire of repeating the "message" of his puppet farces—the belief that the path to the "purification" of the Spanish theater led through the indigenous popular tradition. Considering the importance of the farces, collectively, for his own sense of theater, it is doubtful that without this experience he could have written the plays on which his reputation as a dramatist is based: *Amor de don Perlimplín con Belisa en su jardín* (*Love of Don Perlimplín with Belisa in His Garden*, 1924); *La zapatera prodigiosa* (*The Shoemaker's Prodigious Wife*, 1930, 1933); *Así que pasan cinco años* (*So Pass Five Years*, 1931); *Bodas de sangre* (*Blood Wedding*, 1933); *Yerma* (1933–34); and *La casa de Bernarda Alba* (*The House of Bernarda Alba*, 1935). For a production of *The Billy-Club Puppets* in Buenos Aires on 26 March 1934, Lorca wrote a prologue to the main prologue in the form of a dialogue between Cristóbal and the Poet, with Lorca himself stepping before the public in the role of Cristóbal, and Manuel Fontanals playing the part of Lorca. Referring to himself as the "drunken puppet who marries Doña Rosita" and recalling the first time that he left the hand of García Lorca in spring 1923, in the Lorca family drawing room in Granada, Cristóbal confesses to a certain discomfort at appearing onstage in Buenos Aires. Alluding to his popular origins, he has always performed, he says, "among the water reeds at night, during the Andalusian summer, surrounded by simple girls, given easily to blushing, and by shepherd boys with prickly beards like pine needles." But now, uneasy because he speaks poorly, he is being brought out by the Poet "in these theaters where the painted drops and the moon of the sensible theater triumph." Even before a friendly audience, Lorca still could not resist the temptation to take yet another swipe at the conventional stage. And if any doubt still lingered as to the significance he attached to the popular tradition represented by the puppet farces, he has his Poet declare by way of a reply to Cristóbal: "You are a pillar of the theater, Don Cristóbal. All theater emerges from you. There was once a poet in England, who was called Shakespeare, who created a character known as Falstaff, who is your son."[16] When modernist writers sought to breathe new life into the drama by opening it up to the world of the puppet, the inspiration of an indigenous puppet theater tradition greatly energized their efforts. This was especially true of both Castilian and Catalan dramatists in Spain and of their counterparts in Belgium, Poland, and Russia. García Lorca's uniqueness, however, lay less in pumping fresh blood from the robust Spanish puppet tradition into the tired arteries of the drama of high culture than in revitalizing that very tradition through the force of his own creative genius.

FIVE

Puppetry and Cabaret in Fin-de-Siècle Vienna

Schnitzler and Kokoschka

Arthur Schnitzler's range of dramatic writing and willingness to experiment made it likely that the turn-of-the-century enthusiasm for puppets and marionettes would not go unnoticed by him. Between 1903 and 1905 he wrote three one-act plays involving puppet and marionette figures in both the literal and figurative aspect. They were originally published in different Vienna newspapers and journals. The first to appear was *Der Puppenspieler* (*The Puppet Master*), which was published in the *Neue Freie Presse* on 31 May 1903. It was followed by *Der tapfere Cassian* (*The Gallant Cassian*), which appeared in the journal *Die Neue Rundschau* in February 1904. The third and last play, *Zum Grossen Wurstel* (perhaps best translated as *The Great Prater Puppet Theater*), was published in *Die Zeit* on 23 April 1905. All three made their theatrical debuts soon after their appearance, *The Puppet Master* in Berlin's Deutsches Theater on 12 September 1903, *The Gallant Cassian* in Berlin's Kleines Theater on 22 November 1904, and *The Great Prater Puppet Theater* in Vienna's Lustspieltheater on 16 March 1906. The plays were also published as a cycle, in 1906, under the title *Marionetten* (*Marionettes*).

Schnitzler's great sensitivity to the impulses of his own time might have led him to explore the puppet theme in his writing anyway; but the original impetus to the interest could well have been the emergence of cabaret in Germany in 1901. Although the last of the three *Marionettes* to appear in print, *The Great Prater Puppet Theater* was in fact the first to be written. In its original, unprinted form it was staged by the first cabaret to appear on German soil, the Buntes Theater (Motley Theater; also known as Überbrettl, Super Stage), which Baron Ernst von Wolzogen founded in Berlin in 1901. Cabaret was not to appear in Vienna for another five years, so it is quite possible that, given the great interest in Wolzogen's new enterprise, Schnitzler could not resist the temptation to contribute to it. His choice of play can be viewed in the same light. The variety theater nature of cabaret performance accommodated primarily short forms and so favored theatrical sketches or at the most one-act plays. Since puppet and marionette shows—mostly because of the ease with which they could be performed on small stages—had already established themselves in the repertoire of the early cabarets, Schnitzler might well have been guided by such considerations.

Other aspects of *The Great Prater Puppet Theater* can also be related to the cabaret environment of the time. One is its amusement park setting. The turn-of-the-century rediscovery of folk and popular culture as a source of artistic rejuvenation directed attention again to the fairground as a popular performance environment. A great amusement park such as Vienna's Prater was simply the urban equivalent of the rural fairground. Since puppet and marionette shows were a staple of the kinds of fare regularly offered at the Prater, Schnitzler had readily available models. *The Great Prater Puppet Theater* is also a play-within-a-play, or more precisely in this case, theater-within-theater. The central importance of the illusion-versus-reality dichotomy to the turn-of-the-century neoromantic outlook prompted the theatrical cultivation of the play-within-a-play motif. Schnitzler's *Great Prater Puppet Theater* certainly merits consideration within this frame. And finally, the cabarets that began springing up like mushrooms throughout Europe in the turn of the century proved a remarkably felicitous venue for parody. Since the so-called artistic cabaret of the late nineteenth and early twentieth centuries arose in part as a reaction to prevailing bourgeois norms of art and social behavior, parody as well as satire would obviously come to play an important role in cabaret programs. Viewed in this respect, Schnitzler's play, as parody, accords with both the mood and tenor of the cabaret of his own time.

There is a further possible link between Schnitzler and cabaret which ought to be considered for the sake of an appropriate context in which to situate the origins of his first marionette play, and indeed the cycle as a whole. Although *The Great Prater Puppet Theater* seems originally to have been written for Wolzogen's Buntes Theater, it is worth noting that the first printed play in the cycle, *The Puppet Master*, had its premiere in the Deutsches Theater in Berlin, with which Schnitzler's fellow Viennese, the future world-famous director Max Reinhardt, was affiliated at the beginning of his career. Together with the actor Friedrich Kayssler, the director Martin Zickel, and others, Reinhardt established a literary cabaret called Schall und Rauch (Sound and Smoke). The group began performing on 1 January 1901 in different locales, including the Deutsches Theater, before settling into the quarters in the Hotel Arnim which it would occupy until Reinhardt's growing fame as a director took him in 1906 to the directorship of the Deutsches Theater. Reinhardt's personal contributions to the programs of Schall und Rauch were literary parodies, which could easily have come to Schnitzler's attention. Then, soon after Schall und Rauch was installed in the Hotel Arnim, Reinhardt, as his tastes and interests evolved, began presiding over its transformation into an intimate "chamber" theater, now called Kleines Theater (Small Theater), in which regular dramatic productions, initially for the most part one-act plays, would take precedence over cabaret numbers.

Reinhardt's involvement in the premiere of Schnitzler's *Puppet Master* at the Deutsches Theater in Berlin is yet to be established, but it is conceivable that his affiliation with that theater determined it as the venue for the premiere of Schnitzler's first published puppet play. It is also more than likely that as a budding cabaretist himself, Reinhardt would have known of a performance of *The Great Prater Puppet Theater* at Wolzogen's Buntes Theater. Significantly, Schnitzler's second puppet play, *The Gallant Cassian*, was staged for the first time in Reinhardt's Kleines Theater in 1904. The evidence may be largely circumstantial, but it is convincing enough to argue for the new cabaret phenomenon of the turn of the century, beginning in Germany with Wolzogen's Buntes Theater of 1901, as the immediate source of inspiration for Schnitzler's *Marionettes*, beginning with *The Great Prater Puppet Theater*.

The best of Schnitzler's marionette plays, and the one most obviously linked to the German cabaret environment of the beginning of the twentieth century, *The Great Prater Puppet Theater* is the first we shall look at here despite its publication after *The Puppet Master* and *The Gallant Cassian*. Subtitled *A Burlesque in One Act*, *The Great Prater Puppet Theater* is the most intriguing of Schnitzler's marionette plays. It is set in that part of Vienna's Prater amusement park known as the Wurstelprater where the great city's ordinary folk found the amusements of greatest appeal to them.[1]

When the curtain rises, the theater-within-theater structure is immediately apparent. Dominating the stage is a big, new marionette theater named Zum Grossen Wurstel. Other traditional and older entertainments such as a Wursteltheater, or puppet show, and a carousel, are all overshadowed by the newcomer. As people desert other performances then under way in order to see the new theater, a side-show-barker-type director mounts a podium to acquaint the gathering audience with the marionette play to be presented. However, no sooner is the performance about to begin than the author of the piece, identified just as Dichter (Author), complains to the Director (also just generically identified in the dramatis personae) that people are eating and that this shouldn't be permitted during a performance of his work. The Director ignores his complaint, and the show gets under way. But the exchange between Author and Director sets up a pattern that runs throughout. At different points in the performance, in response mostly to the reactions of the audience, the Author and Director will feud about what should or should not have been cut from the play to make it more palatable to the audience. This stepping forth on the part of Author or Director to discuss, or argue about, the merits of the work being presented alludes in part to the anti-illusionary program of turn-of-the-century theatricalism. We have already observed it in one of Lorca's Cristóbal farces. By baring the technical aspects of the production, or interrupting the performance by means of direct addresses to the audience by the players or discussions about the play by various members of the company as well as the author, the theatricalists sought to drive home to the audience that a play was theatrical artifice and not a faithful "slice of life" or "fourth wall" representation of any given reality.

The play-within-a-play—which is in verse, unlike the frame play—of *The Great Prater Puppet Theater* deals with the complications in the lives of a romantic young couple identified as Hero and Liesl. That the play is a burlesque on the kinds of theatrics served up regularly in the Wurstelprater's puppet theaters soon becomes obvious. Hero complains that he is obliged to fight a duel the following morning because of his seduction of some girl. Of greater concern to him, however, is that he has become the target of the Prince von Lawin's wrath because of the prince's unfounded belief that he is the princess's secret lover. A parody of the turn-of-the-century demonic female whose passions are aroused by the proximity of Death, the Princess von Lawin describes herself as "der Sensationen Sucherin" ("the seeker of sensations").[2] Hero had never even laid eyes on her before, but now that the princess has heard that her husband is expected to kill him in a duel, her passion is aroused. She rushes to Hero, invites him to do with her as he will, and flings herself into his arms. Although men are mad for her, she is now interested only in Hero since his anticipated death makes him beautiful in her eyes.

The arrival of the prince and his retinue produces one of the play-within-a-play's funniest scenes, a combination of slapstick and the broad farce of the puppet tradition. Boasting of his physical prowess, the prince challenges the strongest boxer to fight him, and when one steps forward, the prince quickly disposes of him, knocking a piano player off his stool in the process. When the prince boasts next that any woman would die for him, a shot is heard and the body of a dead girl is brought through a window and deposited on a couch. A note in one of her hands reads: "I loved the Prince von Lawin, / But he loved me not, and so I die for him!" (133).

When Liesl arrives on the scene, she is shocked to see the prince there, for it seems that she, too, has been one of his female adorers. Now it is Hero's turn to challenge the prince to a duel, but the prince declines since fighting a duel over the likes of a simple girl like Liesl would be beneath his dignity. On emerging from her hiding place, the princess acts as though she no longer recognizes Hero. Feeling betrayed by Liesl, Hero is all set to plunge into a torrid affair with the princess, but she begs off, saying that the only man she wants is the one who's supposed to die the next morning. Since the prince is no longer willing to fight Hero in a duel, he has lost his attraction for the princess. Stripped of the aura of death, he is just an ordinary male and of no possible romantic interest to her. After the princess leaves, Hero expresses his disenchantment to Liesl in terms that make clear Schnitzler's intention to mock turn-of-the-century symbolism: "And that you once belonged to the prince / I willingly accept, too, as symbol— but tell me, of what?" (136). Liesl refuses to die for Hero in order to show her love for him and rushes off to marry a young man who has been waiting for some time to wed her and who appears near the end of the play-within-a-play together with her father. Abandoned by both Liesl and the princess, Hero bemoans his fate and expresses his wish to die. When

Death now enters as if in answer to Hero's wish, the audience erupts in anger at the morbid turn of events, and the play-within-a-play concludes in disarray.

For all the fun Schnitzler derived from spoofing certain aspects of turn-of-the-century art and the typical theatrics of the amusement park puppet tradition, the parodic weight of *The Great Prater Puppet Theater* comes down heaviest on the bourgeois public presented onstage as the audience witnessing the play-within-a-play puppet show. But the ingenuity of *The Great Prater Puppet Theater* lies in Schnitzler's use of the audience beholding the puppet show as a mirror held up to the real audience in the theater. What Schnitzler is in fact parodying is the common responses to his own plays on the part of the theater-going bourgeois Viennese public. Two of the onstage members of the audience are identified generically as the Cutting One (Der Bissige) and the Well-Disposed One (Der Wohlwollende). Hardly does the play-within-a-play begin than the Cutting One dismisses it as "An old story!" When the Well-Disposed One asks him what he means, he responds: "Y'know, the sweet young thing (das süsse Mädl) and all that, it's comin' out of my throat already!" (125). The "sweet young thing," more precisely the young girl of working-class background from Vienna's poorer outer districts, who worked in the inner city and was an easy prey for men about town interested in unentangling affairs, is a familiar type in turn-of-the-century Austrian literature and nowhere more so than in Schnitzler's fiction and plays. The allusion, therefore, to common reactions to Schnitzler's own writing is unmistakable. So, too, is the parody of the disagreement among the public as to the meaning of his works. When the threat of a duel between Hero and Prince von Lawin looms, the Well-Disposed One remarks: "It's a biting satire on the duel." The Cutting One replies in his usual caustic way: "For the time bein', nothin's bitin' me" (129).

Other members of the onstage audience also meant to typify the average bourgeois Viennese theatergoer are: the Naïve One (Der Naive); a bourgeois couple identified just as First Bourgeois (Erster Bürger) and his wife (Die Frau); the Second Bourgeois (Zweiter Bürger) and his two daughters (Seine beiden Töchter); and First Scandalmaker (Erster Skandalmacher) and Second Scandalmaker (Zweiter Skandalmacher). The Naïve One represents the uncultured theatergoer who barely understands what he sees and passes all sorts of inane remarks. When the play-within-a-play opens, the marionettes are all displayed in the background with their wires visible. To this, the Naïve One remarks: "They're all attached up above! That's somethin', ain't it? (*To his friends*) Take a look!" (123). At the mere mention of a duel between Hero and the prince, the wife of the First Bourgeois tells her husband that if there's going to be any shooting, she won't stay. "But, honey," her husband tries to reassure her, "don't get yourself all worked up" (129). The behavior of the Second Bourgeois and his daughters is meant to parody the frequent expression of hypocritical outrage over Schnitzler's frank treatment of sex. At the mere hint of anything erotic in the play-within-a-play, the Second Bourgeois threatens to take his daughters away at once. When, for example, the Princess von Lawin declares when she first appears that "one man is too few" for her and that "I am, as they say, demonic," the Second Bourgeois gets up and tells his daughers that this show isn't for them. But when one of them replies, "But father, we don't understand what it means," he relents, saying, "In that case, if you don't understand anything, we'll stay put" (123). This occurs a few times, and what Schnitzler is mocking is the feigned moral indignation on the part of the parent and the no less feigned innocence on the part of the daughters.

Schnitzler is also in his element when representing the generally low taste of the average bourgeois theatergoer of his time. The part of the play that excites the onstage audience most is when the Prince von Lawin appears, boasts of his great strength, and challenges the strongest boxer to fight him. The immediate response of the Cutting One is a typical, "That beats everythin'!" The Naïve One is all excited: "I really like this! Bravo, bravissimo! Now they'll really go at it! (*Applauds*.)" The Author is appalled that this is the sort of thing the audience likes best: "This is just what they like! Brutes!" When the prince knocks the prizefighter off the stage and into the piano player, the Author shouts in panic, "My God, what's happening?" The Director, however, couldn't be happier: "Be glad! That can save your whole comedy" (133).

The finale of the play-within-a-play brings the onstage audience to near pandemonium. When Death appears wearing a horrible mask, the wife of the First Bourgeois swoons. Her husband tells her to calm down, but when she fails to respond, he removes her from the theater amid general confusion. Onstage, meanwhile, Hero addresses Death: "Who are you?" Death replies, "Look me in the face!" Hero retorts: "Be off with you! You fill me with dread!" To which the First Scandalmaker adds from the audience, "Me too!" Laughter can then be heard from other members of the audience. Others try to quiet them down, shouting "Pst!" but, when Death says to Hero, "Do you not summon me?" the Second Scandalmaker yells out, "Who *did* call him?" More shouts of "Pst!" can be heard, followed by the contradictory "He's right!" (138). Any further attempt at a resumption of the dialogue between Hero and Death is rendered impossible by the jibes and whistling of the two scandalmakers and others in the audience.

When the Director and Author fall to arguing between themselves over the disastrous turn of events—surely a projection of Schnitzler's own difficulties with theater directors, hence another dimension of the parody of his play—the marionettes all step forward to absolve themselves of any guilt for what's happened: "Don't blame us poor things, / Show us again your kind grace. / The Author alone must you blame! / The Author alone is at fault!" Declaring this to be some "mad apparition," the Author orders the marionettes from the stage, echoing a complaint heard elsewhere in the drama built around the puppet or marionette theme, that the created figures have taken on a life of their own and are rejecting the authority of their creator, namely the Author:

> The play is over! What mad specter this!
> Who protects me from my own dummies?
> Away with you! Enough's enough!
> Don't dare do things your own way here!
> And when I've filled you up with so much soul
> That you can lead your own lives now,
> Is this absurd and saucy ranting
> The thanks my creativity gave birth?
>
>   (141)

The marionettes, however, have absolutely no intention of obeying their creator and rejoice in their newfound freedom:

> Hey, let's do whatever we like!
> Gab, sing, dance, just fool around!
> The devil with the audience,
> It's what we want that matters most!
> Since the author's off his rocker,
> Let's begin our own play now!
>
>   (141)

The theme of the autonomy of manmade beings, which appears elsewhere in the dramatic literature on the puppet and marionette, has wide ramifications for turn-of-the-century art; Schnitzler will explore it in terms of human behavior in his two other *Marionettes*. But the independence of the marionettes here is soon cut short, literally. No sooner do they begin to rejoice than the figure of the Unknown One, who will bring the entire play to an end, makes an appearance. With a long, pallid face and black curly hair, wrapped in a blue cloak and carrying a long sword, the mysterious stranger cuts all the wires of the marionettes, sending them tumbling down in a heap. Perhaps we can see in the Unknown One yet another parodic allusion on Schnitzler's part to some aspect of the *fin de siècle*, this time its propensity toward the occult and supernatural. That the Unknown One was conceived parodically seems evident in the dialogue between him and the Author. Asked by the Author who he is, the mysterious stranger replies that he himself doesn't know what he is supposed to mean. For some time he has been damned, he says, to wander the face of the earth wherever the winds blow him. His sword, however, makes it evident who was just a puppet or a man. To many a proud puppeteer's grief, he goes on, his sword's edge severs the invisible wire as well. Having said this, he cuts across the entire stage with his sword causing all the lights to go out and everyone onstage but himself to fall down in a heap like the marionettes. When the Author remains standing, the mysterious stranger takes a swipe at him and the Author also sinks to the ground. Thereafter, the Unknown One expresses fear at his own might and wonders aloud if he brings truth or night, if he obeys the call of heaven or hell, if he was created according to some law or by chance, if he is a god or a fool, or just like the people in the audience, if he is a real person or just a sign. His last words are addressed directly to the real audience. Advancing to the front of the stage, he declares:

> Yes, when my sword hangs loosely on the arm
> I know how many are they who in sorrow and joy
> Boast of highly questionable reality.
> (*Turning to the orchestra*)
> How goes it, for example, with you there below?
> (141)

At this, the Unknown One quits the stage and everyone immediately gets up, including the marionettes. Life begins to return to normal. Military music is struck up again, the Author runs excitedly back and forth, and the Director returns to the podium to announce a new show: "Ladies and Gentlemen, you are about to see . . . and so on" (141).

The Great Prater Puppet Theater is clearly one of Schnitzler's most clever plays, its brevity notwithstanding. Drawing on the contemporary interest in the puppet and marionette, and especially under the stimulus of the contemporary cabaret's embrace of puppet and marionette theater, he used a marionette play-within-a-play to ridicule through parody the whole complex of naïve, ignorant, and morally hypocritical responses to his own plays among the bourgeois Viennese theater-going public. But the parody cuts in more than one direction, like the Unknown One's sword. Through the figures of the Author and the Director, Schnitzler creates an uproariously satirical sketch of his own relations with the Viennese theatrical bureaucracy. And last but not least, the play-within-a-play presented in the great new marionette theater is nothing more than a burlesque of the puppet shows in which the Wurstelprater abounded in the late nineteenth and early twentieth centuries, here rendered all the more comic because of the use of Viennese dialect.

In his two other *Marionetten*, Schnitzler used the puppet motif ironically rather than parodically. The puppet master is the writer Georg Merklin, who one day accidentally comes across his old friend and admirer, the oboe player Eduard Jagisch. The two friends have not seen each other in eleven years. In reply to Georg's question, Eduard informs him that he is married, and happily so, and that he has an eight-year-old son whom he has named after his friend. Eduard's wife is an attractive blonde named Anna, whom he met at a farewell party arranged by Georg eleven years earlier, shortly before Eduard's departure for the United States to perform in Boston. Georg now tells Eduard that the meeting with Anna was not by chance, that it had been arranged by Georg, who delighted in the role of a puppet master: "The little one who was so sweet to you was just doing what I wanted. You were the puppets in my hands. I controlled the wires. It was arranged for her to act as if she were in love with you" (93). Georg's purpose, he explains, was to prepare Eduard for real happiness by awakening in him the illusion of it. But altruism was not what really motivated him. Being able to exert control over other people's lives, being able to manipulate them like puppets, has come to mean more to Georg than his literary efforts. "I made you into another person. And I really have to say that it is a keener pleasure playing with real people than spinning empty forms in poetic dance" (93).

Georg has not only all but abandoned his writing for the sake of his new passion, he has also given up the far-flung travel he once enjoyed and now never leaves Vienna. Eduard in turn asks Georg about his own girlfriend, Irene, who was also at the farewell party. Disinclined to pursue the subject, Georg just informs him that he and Irene stopped seeing each other and that he has no idea where she is. Eduard jolts Georg further when he reveals to him that his wife, Anna, was once interested in Georg himself and that she went along with the farewell party ruse primarily for the sake of making Georg jealous! Not only that, but she and Eduard had hoped to save Georg from Irene, whom they regarded as a bad influence on his life and career. However, the plan failed and Anna later joined Eduard in Boston. When Anna arrives home, both she and Eduard urge Georg to stay for dinner, but, obviously uncomfortable now, he begs off, saying, "Let me just continue my strolling about and playing with people" (101). Before he leaves, Georg also confesses that he and Irene had in fact been married and that they had had a son. But she left him, and the boy later died. Schnitzler's irony in the play is now apparent. Georg has found greater satisfaction, and obviously a greater sense of power, in playing with real people as if they were puppets than in creating figures and situations out of his own imagination. This power, however, has been proven illusory. Instead of Georg controlling the lives of Eduard and Anna, it was they who attempted to control his. Moreover, fate has dealt the puppet master a cruel blow by turning the tables on him. Seeking to bring happiness to his friend by manipulating his life, he destroyed his own happiness. But as he takes leave of Eduard and Anna at the end, Georg tries to rationalize his failures by saying: "Fate doesn't want me pushed to the ground by everyday anxieties. People like me have to be free if they they are to find fulfilment" (102).

Schnitzler's point in *The Puppet Master* is that men are not puppets and cannot be manipulated by other men as if they were, that life is unpredictable, and that believing that one can control another human being like a puppet or marionette is self-delusion. The point is made again in *The Gallant Cassian*, but in a style that brings that play actually closer to the puppet theater tradition.

Set in a small German city, in a garret furnished in late-seventeenth-century style, Martin is preparing to go on a long journey—for how long, he has no idea. He is restless and yearns for new sights and experiences. His girlfriend, Sophie, a young woman of modest background who lives nearby, is in tears, fearing that he plans to enlist in the army. Martin has told her a great deal about his cousin Cassian, a soldier who has had an adventurous life. Almost immediately thereafter, Cassian himself shows up attired in a fantastic uniform. He was passing through town and decided to visit his cousin, whom he has not seen in a long time. The chance encounter recalls the meeting between Georg and Eduard in *The Puppet Master*. In private conversation with Cassian, Martin divulges that he is leaving town because of his infatuation with a dancer named Eleonora Lambriani, who happens to be the mistress of the duke of Altenburg. A fanatic gambler, Martin further reveals that he is going to Homburg, where Eleonora is dancing and where festivities are being held in conjunction with a meeting of monarchs there. Lured by the probability that gamblers from all over Europe will also assemble in Homburg, his intention is to win a fortune and then lay it at Eleonora's feet. Cassian teases him, saying that he will win her away from him. But Martin is as sure of himself as Georg was in *The Puppet Master*. He boasts that he cannot lose, that the dice always fall his way, and that, where women are concerned, he knows how to make them do what he wants. As for Sophie, about whom Cassian asks, he says that their relationship was just a learning experience for him.

During a farewell meal prepared by Sophie, Cassian upsets his cousin by lavishing praise on Sophie and stealing his thunder by describing his extraordinary adventures. When Cassian declares his intention of rejoining his regiment as soon as a wound he has suffered heals, Sophie expresses the desire to go along with him. Already jealous of his cousin, Martin opposes this. To pass the time until Martin's servant returns from an errand, Cassian proposes they play dice. Martin loses badly but insists on continuing and, as a last wager, decides to gamble Sophie. The young woman has by this time become infatuated with Cassian and now sits on his lap and embraces him. His loss at dice and Sophie's transfer of her affections to Cassian become more than Martin can bear, and he insults Cassian and challenges him to a duel. Cassian stabs him in the heart and, as Martin lies dying, Cassian taunts him about Eleonora Lambriani. Upset that Cassian now seems intent on pursuing Eleonora, Sophie jumps out of a window, but Cassian follows her, catches her, and both land safely. At the end of the play, Martin, who has instructed his servant to have his corpse fetched at midnight, plays the flute as he dies and bemoans his fate, which did a complete about-face in just a quarter of an hour.

Despite the obvious similarities with *The Puppet Master*, *The Gallant Cassian* seems written as if intended for puppet theater performance. In this respect it is closer in spirit to *The Great Prater Puppet Theater*—without, of course, any of that play's complex parodic design. The fairy tale aspect of *The Gallant Cassian*, together with its playfulness, leaves no doubt as to Schnitzler's purpose. Cassian's account of his fanciful adventures is right out of the Baron Münchhausen tradition. Martin's boasts about his gambling prowess and success with women, as well as his duel with Cassian and his flute-playing accompaniment to his own death, recreate the theatrics of puppet performance. So too does the play's tongue-in-cheek humor. The "wound" Cassian tells Sophie he is recovering from is nothing but a broken nail on one of his small fingers. When Cassian follows Sophie out of the window in an effort to save her, Martin is too weak to move in order to see what has happened and asks his servant to do so. The servant reports, in the appropriate make-believe idiom of the puppet theater: "The most extraordinary thing has just happened. The leaping gentleman caught the leaping young lady in the air and both reached ground safe and sound." The translation doesn't do the original justice. The passage in German reads: "Höchst Wundersames hat sich ereignet. Der springende Herr hat das springende Fräulein in der Luft aufgefangen und beide sind wohlbehalten unten angelangt" (118).

Martin's dying words close the play in the spirit of the work as a whole: "It is painful to die alone, when just a quarter of an hour ago one was loved, prosperous, and full of the most wonderful hopes. This is truly a bad joke, and I am not at all in the mood to play the flute" (118).

Within just a few years of Schnitzler's marionette plays, in 1907, the outstanding Expressionist poet and painter Oskar Kokoschka became actively involved in Vienna's Cabaret Fledermaus.[3] As a painter, it was natural for Kokoschka to contribute to the cabaret's decorations and programs. But a few of Kokoschka's literary efforts, notably as a dramatist, made their first public appearance as program numbers. One of them was his long poem *Die träumenden Knaben* (*The Dreaming Lads*), which was read at the Fledermaus toward the end of 1907. Two others were dramatic works: the shadow play *Das getupfte Ei* (*The Spotted Egg*), which was previously discussed; and one of the best known of his early dramatic works, *Sphinx und Strohmann* (*Sphinx and Strawman*), which exists in different versions. The original (consisting of just a single scene) had first been performed improvisationally in 1907 by Kokoschka's fellow students at the Vienna School of Arts and Crafts. It was subsequently revised and performed, under the same title, at the Fledermaus cabaret on 12

March 1909. It was staged a second time that year, on 4 July—together
with Kokoschka's most famous early Expressionist play, *Mörder, Hoff-
nung der Frauen* (*Murderer, Hope of Women*)—at the same outdoor theater near the Kunstschau, an exhibition of contemporary Viennese art in
which Kokoschka also participated. A slightly expanded version dates
from 1913 and was published that year in an edition of Kokoschka's *Dramen und Bilder* (*Plays and Paintings*). This served as the basis for the production mounted by the founders of the Dada movement, Hugo Ball and
Tristan Tzara, at the opening of the Cabaret Voltaire in Zurich on 14 April
1917. A final version of the play was given an entirely new title, *Hiob*
(Job).[4]

   Like *Murderer, Hope of Women*, *Sphinx and Strawman* relates to the
broad current of turn-of-the-century literature devoted to the dynamics of
sexual conflict. In the background of the cuckolded Herr Firdusi,[5] his
erotic antagonist, Herr Kautschukmann (Rubberman), and Firdusi's sexually ravenous wife, Lilly, stands the theater of Strindberg and Wedekind
and the new study of human sexual behavior initiated by Sigmund Freud
and by Otto Weininger, whose *Geschlecht und Charakter* (*Sex and Character*, 1903) was one of the most controversial books of its time.

   Exemplifications of Weininger's ideas on sexual degeneration, Lilly (the
"Sphinx" of the play) and Kautschukmann (also the "snakeman" with
"lobster-red face") act out an erotic play of lust and passion which inevitably brings about Firdusi's ruin. The thin plot pivots on a visual metaphor.
Herr Firdusi's outstanding physical characteristic is an enormous head of
straw connoting his weakness in relation to his wife's strength; as a
sphinx, she is part woman, part animal. Firdusi's head also revolves and
thus becomes the means by which Lilly, symbolizing woman's power over
man, "turns his head" both literally and figuratively. At the beginning
of the play, Lilly has already deserted Firdusi for her "muscleman"
(Kautschukmann). When she reappears during a conversation between
Firdusi and Kautschukmann, Firdusi turns his head around slowly, without moving his body, to follow her with his eyes. But she stays out of his
line of vision until his head is turned around completely and he is unable
to return it to its normal position. Thus Firdusi never sees Lilly to the end
of the play. Apart from suggesting Firdusi's blindness with respect to
women, the device enables him to propose marriage to his wife without
realizing who she is. As if anticipating *The Bald Soprano*, Ionesco's later
absurdist satire on modern marriage as the foundation of bourgeois soci-

ety, *Sphinx and Strawman* dramatizes the complete estrangement between Firdusi and Lilly by means of a new marriage between them in
which Firdusi is unaware that he is marrying his own wife. At the end of
the play, finally perceiving what he has done, Firdusi suffers a shock and
falls dying. Hardly have the wedding rings been exchanged than Lilly, true
to her nature, gives herself to Kautschukmann and, implacable and unrepentant to the end, steps over the now dead body of her husband like a
"parade horse." [6]

The impossibility of resolving the sexual conflict, of achieving unity of
spirit and flesh, of man and woman, is conveyed by the play's final curtain.
Nine black suits and nine top hats are painted on it, representing nine gentlemen who have been invited as wedding guests. When the curtain closes
on Firdusi's death, the men poke their heads through the holes in it from
behind, one after the other. Snarling and hissing, the heads—embodied
now as pasteboard, one-dimensional figures—symbolize the eternal conflict between the sexes, which, in Firdusi's death, has merely claimed another victim.

In its original version, and as staged at the Cabaret Fledermaus, *Sphinx
and Strawman* was subtitled a *Comedy for Automatons* (*Eine Komödie
für Automaten*). Although capable of being performed by puppets or
marionettes, it was not. But its conception as a play for "automatons" reflects both Kokoschka's enthusiasm for puppet theater going back to his
childhood and his awareness of the "rediscovery" of puppets and marionettes by modernist artists, in particular those involved in the new cabaret
culture. Kokoschka recalled the impact of marionette theater on him in his
memoirs: "When I was a child, a marionette theater given me by my father
represented the whole beauty of existence as far as I was concerned; it was
surely responsible for my passion for the theater." [7]

The puppet and marionette motif in *Sphinx and Strawman* functions
both theatrically and metaphorically. On the purely theatrical level, the
puppetlike aspect of the characters is intended to introduce the element of
the grotesque. This is nowhere more evident than in the case of Firdusi's
gigantic revolving straw head. The same character's incapacity for physical love, transformed grotesquely into an advocacy of sexual abstinence,
is also represented symbolically by a puppet figure. Notwithstanding his
attitude toward sex, Firdusi yearns to have a son, who as wish fulfilment
is represented in the play by a small rubber figure Firdusi carries around
with him and names Adam. Leaving no doubt that Adam is a puppet, Ko-

koschka describes him in the stage directions as a *"figure made of rubber which one sticks on one's thumb and moves by flexing the digit, as if operating a hand puppet."* In a study on Kokoschka, Gerhard Lischka draws a parallel between *Sphinx and Strawman* and the Italian Futurist Marinetti's 1910 novel, *Mafarka le futuriste*.[8] In Marinetti's work, the automaton Gazurmah, the son born without a woman, is awakened to life by a kiss from his father. When Kautschukmann, to whom he shows his little rubber "son," points out to Firdusi that Adam also requires a father if he is to come to life, Firdusi, in the proto-absurdist style of *Sphinx and Strawman* as a whole, acknowledges that his "son" also needed a mother.

It is on the metaphoric level that the puppet/marionette motif of Kokoschka's play resonates most. Embodying a common theme of turn-of-the-century literature, all the characters are marionettes manipulated by the invisible strings of the erotic drive, or by their fear of it. Lilly is the spirit of pure lust—Kokoschka's image of woman at the time—and can act only in conformity with her own nature. In her hands, Kautschukmann, for all his physical strength, is but a helpless marionette controlled by Lilly's all-dominant sensuality. Firdusi also, though fundamentally lacking the erotic drive, cannot resist the lure of Lilly's sexuality. This is symbolized, as we have seen, by his confusion over her identity and his gigantic head, which she turns, figuratively in his submission to the impulse to follow after her with his eyes and literally in the complete revolving of the head to the point where he cannot turn it back. Firdusi's incompleteness as a human being, as a man, is also rendered in puppet terms by means of the little rubber figure of the son he can never have yet yearns for.

In the early version in which *Sphinx and Strawman* was performed at the Cabaret Fledermaus, the play appeared to be, at least on the surface, a farcical treatment of the theme of sexual conflict, which Kokoschka had dramatized in grimmer, more macabre terms in *Murderer, Hope of Women*. Besides the comic aspect of its puppet and marionette elements, *Sphinx and Strawman* incorporated a variety of clown routines and sight and verbal gags, some of which exhibited traces of the old Jewish burlesque theater as well as of the Viennese folk comedy of the leading nineteenth-century Austrian dramatists, Johann Nestroy and Ferdinand Raimund, with its strong parodic tradition. The play came alive onstage with acrobatic stunts and the physical dynamics of pantomime; like Craig, Marinetti, Meyerhold, and other revolutionaries of the late nineteenth- and early twentieth-century stage, Kokoschka too had come to believe that in the theater movement could surpass spoken language in expressiveness.

Although different as dramatic writers, Schnitzler and Kokoschka shared the turn-of-the-century obsession with sexuality and the view of man as a marionette animated by the strings of his passions. Both were attracted to the new performance environment of the cabaret and wrote short plays capable of presentation in its restrictive confines. In both instances, these plays reflected the emergence of the cabaret as a venue for a new type of puppet and marionette theater and the broad contemporary appeal of the puppet and marionette figure as a metaphor for the human condition.

SIX

Poland and Prussia as Puppet Shows

Stanisław Wyspiański and Gerhart Hauptmann

The ease with which the puppet figure could be adapted to political satire is handsomely exemplified in two of the most provocative plays from the early twentieth century by the foremost contemporary dramatists of Poland and Germany, Stanisław Wyspiański and Gerhart Hauptmann respectively. Although the plays are very different in nature, they have a common purpose and theatrical strategy: to expose what the dramatists considered the greatest flaw in the national psyche—complacency and excessive attachment to the myths of the past among the Poles and chauvinism and the spirit of Prussian militarism among the Germans.

STANISŁAW WYSPIAŃSKI AND THE FIDDLING STRAW MAN

The evening of 16 March 1901 was memorable in the history of the modern Polish stage. It was then, at the Cracow Theater, that the premiere took place of one of the most haunting plays in the Polish language. The play was *Wesele* (*The Wedding Celebration*), by Stanisław Wyspiański, the most gifted dramatist of turn-of-the-century Poland. A poet as well as a dramatist, a watercolorist of impressive talent, Wyspiański grew up in Cracow and delighted in its history, architecture, and legends. The city figures prominently in his art. So too does his concern for Polish history. In a series of striking dramatic works, Wyspiański commemorated above all the events of the November Uprising of 1830, a romantic rebellion against Russian rule inspired by the hope of regaining some measure of Polish independence after the partitions of the late eighteenth century divided the hapless country among Russia, Prussia, and Austria. The uprising was crushed within a year, but its impact on the Polish consciousness was so profound that it inspired literature and lore long after the event itself had become history.

Wyspiański's strong interest in that calamitous period extending from the partitions of 1772–95 to the collapse of Poland's nominal ally, Napoleon, and the defeat of the November Uprising of 1830 was stimulated by the one hundredth anniversaries of several of the key events. The past is always a powerful presence in the Polish consciousness, and it is not difficult to imagine the chronological imperative to revisit the defeats of the late eighteenth and early ninteenth centuries at the turn of the twentieth. Coming to grips with the national past, attempting to understand the passage from greatness to ignominy, seeking to draw hope from disaster—these had long constituted the deeper commitment of Polish artistic creativity. And so it was with Stanisław Wyspiański.

Surveying the debris of Polish national pride and aspirations from the vantage point of the turn of the century, Wyspiański set himself the task in some of his boldest dramatic writing of interpretively recreating the events especially of the November Uprising, which he, like many Poles, regarded as a pivotal moment in Polish history. Plays such as *Warszawianka* (*The Varsovienne*, 1898), *Lelewel* (*Lelewel*, 1899), *Legion* (*The Legion*, 1900), *Wyzwolenie* (*Deliverance*, 1903), and *Noc listopadowa* (*November Night*, 1904) addressed such issues as the roles of the poet and poetry in Romantic society and rebellion, the nature of Romanticism itself, the Polish martyrological complex, and the intervention of fate in human affairs. Mythology and symbolism invested the political events with an element of timelessness.

A product of a post- and anti-Romantic ideology, which laid the blame for the failure of the November Uprising at the doorstep of Romanticism itself, Wyspiański's recreation of historical events was no mere excercise in national self-pity. But his awareness of the flaws and limitations in the Romantic outlook was tempered by a willingness to acknowledge the essential nobility of its strivings and sacrifices. By distinguishing between gesture and deed, true nobility of spirit and narcissistic myopia, Wyspiański hoped to retrieve from the calamities of the past that which could still nurture belief in the inevitablitity of national regeneration.

Wyspiański's most imaginative and complex plays were written between 1901 and 1904; their different subjects notwithstanding, all pivot on the issue of the regeneration of the Polish nation and the resurrection of the Polish state. These include *The Wedding Celebration*, acknowledged as his greatest play, *Deliverance*, *November Night*, and *Akropolis* (*Acropolis*, 1904). *Deliverance* and *November Night* deal directly, though uniquely, with the events of the November Uprising. *The Wedding Celebration* can be perceived as an ironic commentary on the Polish society of Wyspiański's time. *Acropolis* is an extraordinary rumination on the Polish past and future in which classical Greek heroes, mythological deities, Polish figures from the past, and Jesus Christ intermingle.

Employing compositional techniques ultimately reconcilable with the aesthetics and metaphysics of eary modernism, Wyspiański created stage works of considerable symbolic resonance and plasticity. Besides the sense of theater so evident in his electrifying production in 1901 of Adam Mickiewicz's previously unstaged monumental Romantic drama *Dziady* (*Forefathers*, 1823–33) and his intriguing adaptation of Shakespeare's *Hamlet* in 1905, Wyspiański brought to his dramatic writing his broad experience as one of the better watercolor painters of his day. This underlay his feeling for color and form and the vividness of his images; it is also reflected in his set and costume designs.

A striking common denominator in Wyspiański's four greatest plays is his animation of inanimate forms. In *Deliverance*, for example, the play's central figure remains behind onstage after a performance to wage an extraordinary symbolic battle with a series of Masks, representing his own inner contradictions, and with a stone monument to a Genius generally interpreted as alluding to Mickiewicz and the legacy of nineteenth-century Polish mystico-messianic Romanticism. Statues of Greek deities leave their pedestals in Warsaw's parks and interact with historical personages of the November Uprising in *November Night*. Time and geography collapse and merge in *Acropolis* as figures step out of old tapestries on the walls of the royal castle on the Wawel Hill in Cracow and various statues come to life; the Vistula River, above which the Wawel stands, miraculously becomes the Skamander of ancient Troy as classical and mythological Greece and modern Poland converge in a parable-play about death and resurrection.

The Wedding Celebration is Wyspiański's boldest play, and not solely on the basis of the animation of inanimate figures. The work is based on an actual and seemingly modest event, the marriage of a well-known poet and friend of Wyspiański's, Lucjan Rydel, to a young peasant woman named Jadwiga Mikołajczykówna. She was the younger sister of the wife of the painter Włodzimierz Tetmajer, who ten years earlier had married Anna Mikołajczykówna. Although the actual marriage took place in November 1900 in the medieval Church of Mary in the Main Market Square in the heart of Cracow, the wedding reception was celebrated in the nearby village of Bronowice, in the home of the Tetmajers. What attracted special attention to the marriage of Lucjan Rydel and Jadwiga Mikołajczykówna, as it had previously to that of Włodzimierz Tetmajer and Anna, was its symbolic social significance. Rydel, like Tetmajer, belonged to the landed gentry (*szlachta*); they were, in other words, members of the nobility, and marriages between noblemen and peasants were still an unusual occurrence in late-nineteenth-century Poland. Social barriers were slow to crumble, and those between members of the gentry and the peasantry were the most formidable. Significantly, Tetmajer and Rydel were both artists, and the boldness of their taking peasant wives was looked upon as a step—undertaken by members of society less bound by convention—in the direction of social change at the beginning of a new century. As a friend of both Rydel's and Tetmajer's, and as a member of the wedding party, Wyspiański was well aware of the symbolism of the event and used it as the basis of an extraordinary play about contemporary Polish attitudes and the prospects for national regeneration.

Before considering the all-important matter of the play's structure and its relationship to the subject of this book, let us first familiarize ourselves with its main characters and events. *The Wedding Celebration* is set in the home of the Tetmajers who appear as the Host and Hostess. When the curtain rises, the festivities are in full swing. Just as the marriage of Rydel and his peasant wife symbolizes a reconciliation of the classes, the participants in the celebration represent a broad spectrum of village and town society. Peasants rub shoulders with members of the nobility as well as with representatives of the Cracow intelligentsia, and a local parish priest and Jewish tavern keeper round out the picture. There is a great variety of dress, enhancing the visual aspect of the play's setting—the rooms and furnishings of the cottage where the celebration is held. The set is basically a split stage. The wedding celebration, a noisy, boisterous affair, takes place in a side room; this is where couples dance. The rest of the stage is taken up with a kind of reception or drawing room with a banquet table in disarray, surrounded by simple chairs of white wood, and a rear wall with doors leading primarily to the larger part of the cottage containing the bedrooms. Although the festivities are held on a dark, gloomy November evening, a garden can be seen through a window on a side wall, and in the garden a flower bush wrapped up in a straw man (*chochoł* or *chachoł*) for protection against the winter cold and snow. The interior of the cottage is a grayish sky-blue color, which envelopes furnishings and people alike. Historical pictures and portraits as well as various arms adorn the walls.

The conversation between guests dancing, or taking a respite from the noisy dancing in the drawing room, is mostly the inane banter common to such occasions. The characters appear two at a time and the dialogue between them is in a short rhymed verse conveying both a folkish style and that of puppet theater. Peasants also speak partly in dialect, which adds to the folkish aspect. Speech, in general, is colloquial and appropriate to the individual character. As the peasants exchange banalities, the bride and groom talk about their feelings for each other, a poet attired in the modish idiom of the day flirts with a female guest, young girls voice their romantic fantasies, and the Jewish innkeeper and the parish priest settle business matters (the priest owns the land on which the tavern is located and is due rent). The atmosphere is one of complacency and unconcern. The village of Bronowice seems snugly insulated from worldly strife; even the "Polish question" is not uppermost in people's minds.

The mood, however, begins to change with the arrival of Rachel, the poetically inclined and worldly daughter of the innkeeper. From her first appearance (act 1, scene 18), the wedding celebration and the Tetmajers' cottage become enveloped in the aura of something magical:

> A little cloud lured me here,
> a fog, the vapors of night;
> this cottage, illuminated
> from afar, like an ark in a flood,
> mud all around, heavy rains,
> drunken peasants carrying on;
> this hut, illuminated,
> playing music in the dark night,
> seemed so very pleasant to me,
> like an ark in the shape of a boat of charms,
> and so I came.[1]

And, a little later, in conversation with the Host:

> My thought suspended on wings,
> I came, through mud up to my knees,
> from the tavern to the courtyard.
> Oh, this cottage throbbing with song,
> this throng alive with dance,
> you'll see, I tell you,
> will be fit for poetry.
>   (45)

The mood of poetic anticipation, of the approaching magicality of a wedding celebration in a peasant village, is also underscored by the Poet's words to the Host a few scenes later:

> We are as if cursed,
> that phantoms and marvels allure us,
> the product of melancholic imagination
> seizes the heart, provokes the senses;
> that mists have covered our eyes;
> we coddle ourselves just with dreams,
> while our genius transforms
> everything around us:
> in our eyes the peasant grows
> to the power of King Piast![2]
>   (58)

Against this background of Rachel's poeticizing vision and the Poet's observation of the Polish propensity for self-delusion, the stage is set for the meeting of the two and the subsequent magical transformation of the wedding celebration. As both imaginations interact, the Poet exhorts poetry to roam

> from larder to larder,
> from rose garden
> to the garden of those sleeping bushes
> you can see them from the window.
> And when the young lady here approaches,
> some bush brushes against her shawl,
> thus imparting to ordinary straw
> her melancholy and sadness,

and from the bush sorrow and shade
unconsciously flow into the young lady.
>   (83)

Carried along by the Poet's word picture, Rachel imagines herself walking through the garden while he stands and observes her from the window
of the cottage. He tells her that he will be happy to watch her wandering
about the dark garden, "as if in love and errant, / half maiden and half angel, / inclined over the straw man as if in a painting by Burne-Jones" (84).[3]
As Rachel and the Poet fix their attention on the straw man, Rachel ironically proposes inviting it in to the wedding celebration. Entering her realm
of fantasy, the Poet announces to the Bridegroom his own intenion of inviting in the straw man. The Bridegroom and the Bride mockingly repeat
the invitation:

> *Bridegroom.*
>   Ha, ha, ha—ha, ha, ha,
>   Come, straw man,
>   to the wedding party.
>   I invite you, I, the Bridegroom,
>   to the banquet
>   into the inn!
> *Bride.*
>   There's so much to eat and drink,
>   you can enjoy yourself at our expense!
>   (89)

But the straw man comes to life—by the power of poetry?—in the next
act. When he first appears, at midnight, he is ridiculed by the peasant
woman he first encounters; but such is the aura of enchantment with
which the village and cottage are now enveloped that the peasant reacts
with amusement rather than incredulity that a straw man who can walk
and talk has come into the cottage. Ordered to leave by the peasant, he
shuffles away, to return only at the end of the play in its haunting finale.

The enchantment heralded by the arrival of the animated straw man at
the beginning of the second act extends throughout the act and becomes
the basis of the play's irony and social satire. As night deepens, phantoms
and apparitions appear to several of the guests. The young woman
Marysia is visited by the ghost of a dead lover; the journalist is sought out

by Stańczyk, the sharp-witted court jester of Renaissance Poland, later regarded as a sage concerned about the fate of Poland; an uncomprehending Poet is exhorted to action by Zawisza the Black (Zawisza Czarny), a famous Polish knight who fought against the Knights of the Teutonic Order at the Battle of Grunwald in 1410; the Bridegroom is terrified by the appearance of Great Royal Hetman (Commander) Franciszek Ksawery Branicki or Branecki, a co-instigator of the Targowica Confederacy, which led to Russian involvement in Polish internal affairs and resulted in the first partition of Poland in 1772; the ghost of Jakub Szela, the leader of a bloody peasant massacre of the Polish landowning nobility in the Austrian-dominated province of Galicia in 1846, appears to an old peasant; the Host is taken by surprise by the appearance on horseback, a lyre at his side, of Wernyhora, a legendary eighteenth-century Cossack bard whose prophetic powers forecast the resurrection of Poland and a union of the Polish and Ukrainian nations. Wernyhora was a popular figure among the Polish Romantics and became the subject of a work by the outstanding nineteenth-century painter of historical canvases Jan Matejko (a reproduction of the painting was believed to have hung in the real cottage of the Tetmajers). The magic of the night is now near its point of culmination.

The nocturnal visitations primarily by apparitions of well-known figures in Polish history and legend are meant to rouse the participants in the wedding celebration from the torpor of their daily lives. Their appearance—each appropriate in some way to the person visited—carries profound associations with turbulent events in the Polish past. These towering figures of bygone days, including even the despised Hetman Branicki and the peasant leader Szela, also function contrastively by pointing up the strength of will and character of which Poles were once capable. All this suggests that *The Wedding Celebration* carries an indictment of the Poles of Wyspiański's time as a people preoccupied with petty concerns, too easily given to poetic fantasies, and lacking in a strong sense of national purpose. Wernyhora's arrival, in particular, sets in motion a chain of events intended to level this indictment in unequivocal terms.

Before his visit is over, Wernyhora commands the Host to send out riders to call the peasants to arms. They are to assemble at dawn before the local church, there to await the sound of hoofbeats thundering along the road from Cracow. They will then unite in a march on Warsaw and begin the liberation of Poland. As he departs, Wernyhora hands the Host a golden horn with which to announce the launching of the campaign. The Host barely comprehends what is happening, and his wife is yet more incredulous, ascribing her husband's rantings and ravings to too much drink:

> *Host.*
>> We've got to get things together, belts, bags,
>> my musket, pistols,
>> and I'll take both the swords!
> *Hostess.*
>> Oh Jesus, some nighttime brawls,
>> where, what's going on?
> *Host.*
>> I've got to be ready.
> *Hostess.*
>> Heaven help us!
>> You can barely stand, you're sick.
> *Host.*
>> I've got to mount my horse at once.
>
> (167)

The Host instead entrusts the golden horn to the peasant Jasiek and orders him to ride out and signal the great march when all the peasants have been roused. After everyone has retired for the night, the Host is awakened by the peasant Czepiec, scythe in hand, who tells him that the peasants have assembled and are awaiting further orders and that everything is in readiness in Cracow. The Host, however, has no idea what he means. With the approach of dawn, the enchantment of the night has worn off, the apparitions and phantoms are barely a memory. In contrast to the gentry, who listen to him in disbelief, only Czepiec recalls what he and the other peasants were to do. But none bestirs himself until the Hostess reports seeing what appears to be an army assembled in a field on the road to Cracow. Fragments of recollection begin to trouble the Host—an old man, with a gray beard, dressed in a large red sheepskin coat. Others help him along with additional details—a white horse, a lyre on his saddle. At last the Host remembers the nighttime visitation of Wernyhora and his command to take up arms. As they all strain to catch the sound of the trumpet blast signaling the beginning of the march on Warsaw, hoofbeats become audible. Their excitement is almost palpable. But when the rider appears, it is not Wernyhora with the archangel in the lead, but Jasiek, who wonders why everyone is standing around as if stupified. Then he remembers:

> Aha, right, by God in heaven,
> I was supposed to blow a horn.
> Must 'ave gotten lost, though.
> Maybe got unraveled.
> Lost the golden horn somewhere,
> Nothin' but the cord left now.
>
> (252)

What Jasiek does not remember is that, just after he started out on his ride, he returned to retrieve his cap with peacock feathers which had fallen off; when he bent over to pick it up, the golden horn slipped off its cord. Before anyone can react to Jasiek's words, the straw man enters with a swaying action and completes Jasiek's thought: "When the cap with feathers fell from you." As Jasiek runs out, as if in a daze, to see where people have gathered, the straw man follows him, swaying as usual, his straw rustling against those he bumps into. When Jasiek reenters the cottage, the straw man is right behind him. Jasiek describes the fear and dread on the faces of the assembled peasants, who no longer know what to do with themselves. The straw man tells him to collect their scythes and unsheath their swords and then to fetch him a fiddle. Taking up the fiddle in his ungainly limbs, the straw man begins playing a haunting melody, which Wyspiański describes as follows:

> (There can be heard, as if coming from the azure sky, wedding music, soft but lively, unique but captivating the heart and lulling the soul to sleep, slow, swooning, but alive like a source of blood, uneven in measure, bloody like a fresh wound—a melodious sound coaxed out of the Polish depths with pain and ecstasy.) (256)

As he continues playing, the straw man intones a kind of indictment of Jasiek's lapse:

> You boor, you had a golden horn,
> You boor, you had a hat of feathers.
> The wind carries the cap away,
> the horn sounds through the woods.
> The cord is all that's left you now,
> The cord is all that's left you now.

The crowing of a cock reminds Jasiek of his mission; he feverishly calls his fellow peasants to mount their horses and grab their arms, for the Wawel courtyard is awaiting them. But the only answer he gets is the straw man's refrain:

All that's left is just the cord.
-- -- -- -- -- -- -- -- -- -- -- --
You boor, you had a golden horn.
     (257)

Growing hoarse, Jasiek keeps on yelling for the peasants to take up their arms and mount their horses. But as if enchanted by the straw man's music, a large number of couples now assembled onstage form pairs and begin dancing in a circle, slowly, barely speaking, their trousers and skirts hardly rustling, their boots and shoes inaudible against the floor. The dance is trancelike, somnambulistic. In despair, overcome with fear and grief, unable to speak further, Jasiek falls to the ground, knocked down by the circle of dancers he tries in vain to separate. With the cock crowing and the straw man fiddling continously while repeating over and over "You boor, you had a golden horn," the dancing couples form a festive wreath, slowly, serenely—a closed wedding circle. On this note the play ends.

The implications and symbolism of *The Wedding Celebration* are unmistakable. Just as the straw man indicts Jasiek for his loss of the golden horn, so does Wyspiański indict the Poland of his own time as too mired in the petty and banal, too enslaved by gesture and image, to carry out Poland's liberation effectively. This will have to wait for another time, another generation. The couples dancing around somnambulistically at the end of the play emblematize a Poland lulled to sleep by complacency, a Poland incapable of greatness. The image of the straw man come to life in the play is electrifying. Used to protect rose bushes in a garden against the winter cold and snow, the straw man acquires the symbolism of a Poland destined to flower again some spring, the season of rebirth, but stripped prematurely of its protective covering through the magic of beguiling poetry. As an inanimate thing brought to life by the poetic game playing of Rachel and the Poet, the straw man contrasts vividly with the dancers at the end of the play. It is they who appear like puppets, marionettes, inanimate beings, manipulated now by the haunting melody played by the straw man. Roles are reversed. The dancers, collectively representing contemporary Poland, are inert matter animated in their dance by the animated straw man. The irony of the role reversal is grim.

Metaphorically, Wyspiański's entire play, not just its finale, conjures the image of a puppet Poland, a nation of inanimate beings, frozen somewhere between sleep and waking, set in motion by the music of a straw man—puppeteer itself brought to life by the poetry that hangs over the Polish will like a curse. The puppet dimension of *The Wedding Celebration* resides not only in metaphor. The dialogue, with only two speakers present at a time, is taken from the puppet theater. The verse, with its short, rhymed, eight-syllable lines and frequent repetitions, hints at the same source yet actually owes more to the Polish folk tradition. Far more important, however, than any of the individual features linking *The Wedding Celebration* with puppet theater is the model on which the play's architectonics is based—the Polish *szopka*, which was discussed previously in the context of the Cracow cabaret.

The word *szopka* means "small hut," or "booth." But as a type of theater, *szopka* refers, as I noted earlier, to the Nativity puppet show, which over time became associated with the city of Cracow. Whatever its origins, possibly in France, *szopka* came to be regarded as an indigenous Polish puppet theater. From about the early eighteenth century, the custom of using puppets or marionettes to depict primarily scenes of the Nativity on fixed, immobile crèches spread from Warsaw throughout Poland.[4] In other words, a small puppet theater was built around the traditional *jasiełka*, or crèche. Perhaps in the early nineteenth century, and first of all in Cracow—the chronology is imprecise—the idea originated of replacing the crèche with a miniature theater and making the *szopka* movable. Such a mobile *szopka*, which could be carried from one location to another for multiple performances, came to be designated as a *szopka krakowska* (Cracovian *szopka*). Further contributing to the transformation of the *szopka* into a full-fledged puppet theater was the exclusive use of rod puppets and the design of its architecture to resemble either of Cracow's two major monuments, the medieval Church of Mary in the Main Market Square, and the Renaissance royal castle on the Wawel.

In its earlier stages of development, the *szopka* was used for dramatic presentations of traditional biblical scenes related to Christmas. The performers were usually schoolboys and parish church sextons. Secular scenes gradually came to be introduced in order to depict the various non-biblical figures who come to pay homage to the newborn Christ. Eventually, these secular scenes began taking on a life of their own and operated independently of the religious text. That is to say, the secular scenes came to feature primarily local types—peasants, landlords, clerics, Jewish tavern keepers, soldiers, Russian Orthodox priests, Cossacks, Ukrainians, and so on—in everyday situations not necessarily related to the Nativity. In a certain sense they recalled the medieval and later *intermedia* or *interludia*, comic scenes with ordinary characters speaking the vernacular language interpolated between the acts of school mystery or morality plays in Latin.

In the traditional Cracovian *szopka* modeled on the Church of Mary or the royal castle, the miniature stage had two levels, or tiers. Biblical scenes depicting the Nativity were played out on the lower level, while the upper level was reserved for the nonbiblical secular scenes. Much of the humor of the *szopka* performance derived from the interaction of the two groups and from the contrast between the folkish but biblical Polish of the Nativity scenes and the everyday colloquial speech of the secular characters.

Wyspiański clearly adapted this basic pattern in the design of *The Wedding Celebration*. Stage space is divided into two planes, in two different ways. In the first instance, the stage is split between the room containing the dancers and merrymakers, as in act 1, and the drawing room to which the revelers retire for relief from the music and noise in the side room. The transition from one act to another also signals a shift from a realistic plane, or level, to a fantastic one, as in act 2 when the various phantoms and apparitions appear. Adding to the complexity of the play's design, this movement from one plane to another, from one sphere of experience to another, blurs the lines between real and fantastic. This is particularly true of the third and last act, where the interaction between the two spheres is more subtle as the author depicts the vacillation between memory and forgetfulness, action and inaction. There is also a third plane on which the drama of *The Wedding Celebration* is played, and that is the social. Two milieux are contrasted, that of rural, peasant Bronowice, where the wedding celebration takes place, and that of urbane Cracow, from which the members of the gentry and intelligentsia derive. The symbiosis of nobility and peasantry which the wedding is meant to symbolize occurs only on an exceptionally limited and individual level. No broad-based coming together of the classes has yet taken place; fundamental social division is still the reality.

Wyspiański's indebtedness to, and highly original treatment of, the

Typical Polish szopka *construction, early twentieth century.*
(Courtesy Jagiellonian University Library, Cracow)

szopka form stands as one of the most artistically noteworthy uses of an indigenous puppet tradition in all European modernist drama. Where other dramatists, as in Spain, for example—the Catalan Rusiñol and later Federico García Lorca—borrowed individual figures or techniques from a native puppet or marionette theater, the purpose generally was to infuse new life into a moribund or ultraconservative traditionalist drama by reaching down into the roots of folk culture. As we shall see in the case of the Russian Aleksandr Blok's play *Balaganchik* (*The Fairground Show*, 1906), the old Russian fairground show booth tradition was borrowed for the frame of a dramatic work that deals primarily with the transformation of the poet's own outlook and values. Little of the Russian fairground puppet theater survives in Blok's play, and the lead figures are drawn from the commedia dell'arte, as in the manner of Benavente, Martínez Sierra, Čapek (in *The Fateful Game of Love*, 1921), and others. What Wyspiański did, however, in *The Wedding Celebration* was to adapt the domestic Polish *szopka* not for the purpose of breathing new life into the contemporary Polish stage or of revitalizing an indigenous puppet theater, as with Lorca, but in order to convey the image of Poland itself—the Polish nation, since no Polish state existed at the time—as a kind of puppet show, with real people behaving like puppets or marionettes, going through the motions of being alive but not actually living. Wyspiański shared with his counterparts elsewhere in early-twentieth-century Europe an interest in folk culture shaped by the new creative impulses of the turn of the century. But that interest, which led to the discovery of the potential of the *szopka* for a serious play about the Polish nation in his own time, was translated into an extraordinary, even unique, achievement of dramatic art.

PUPPETIZING PRUSSIAN HISTORY:
THE CASE OF GERHART HAUPTMANN

It was entirely natural that the town fathers of Breslau would turn to Gerhart Hauptmann, as the foremost German dramatist of his time, with a request that he write an appropriate theatrical work to commemorate the one hundredth anniversary of the German "wars of liberation" against Napoleon of 1813, 1814, and 1815.[5] Breslau had legitimate reasons for civic pride. On retreat from the French, the Prussian king, Friedrich Wilhelm III, halted at Breslau, where he determined to forge an alliance with Russia and declare open war against Napoleon. It was, therefore, from that city, on 19 March 1813, that Friedrich issued his patriotic appeal to all Germans to join him in the great campaign to liberate the nation from the French yoke.

Although it was not so formally presented to Hauptmann, it was clearly the expectation of the Breslau town fathers that the "greatest son of Silesia" would compose a rousing work of deep patriotic sentiment which would highlight Breslau's role in the wars of liberation and would be eminently appropriate both to the occasion and to the new Centennial Hall. While cordial in his response to the invitation, Hauptmann had some doubts about technical aspects of such a production and seemed rather reluctant initially to go ahead with the project. However, he finally decided to accept the invitation, which circumstances anyway might have made it difficult for him to decline. But what he created for the great event not only aroused considerable controversy in its time but was regarded as downright scandalous.

The form alone of the work raised eyebrows. Bearing the weighty title *Festspiel in deutschen Reimen zur Erinnerung an den Geist der Freiheitskriege der Jahre achtzehnhundertunddreizehn, -vierzehn und -fünfzehn aufgeführt bei der Jahrhundertfeier in Breslau 1913* (*Festival Play in German Verse in Commemoration of the Spirit of the Wars of Liberation of*

Cover of original edition of Gerhart Hauptmann's Festspiel.

the Years 1813, 1814, and 1815, Presented on the Centenary Celebration in Breslau in 1913), it was conceived as a puppet performance on the grand scale.[6] What the audience beheld when it entered the Centennial Hall consisted of a flight of three stages rising from behind an orchestra. At the back of each stage was a curtain, which, when opened, revealed a curtained stage behind it, until the third and topmost stage was reached. Although there is no specific indication that this was indeed the case, Hauptmann may well have intended the series of stages to suggest, if not precisely represent, the boxlike performance areas of a puppet theater.

The shattering of audience expectation occurs with the entry of the first character, the Director, garbed in a long robe and wearing the tall cap of a magician, both covered with heavenly symbols. He excuses his appearance on the grounds that the mime who was supposed to speak the prologue to the play has left the company, his contract broken. He then attempts to explain the different nature of the production the audience is about to behold:

> How would you call the piece? That's hard to say.
> The type's no longer common in our land.
> Perhaps a "mimus," mimic supposition,
> Such as invented by Philistion,

Who scorned the world and died of laughter?
Yet when I read it over in my thoughts,
I do indeed find mimic irony,
But truly a more modern fantasy.
Well, it's all the same; whatever name it bears,
The work acclaims its author's head and hand.
And in its motley mix of shifting scenes,
It shows a continent's most fateful hour.[7]
  (947–48)

Shortly thereafter, Philistiades, a slender, scantily clad youth, appears from behind the curtain and tells the Director that at a nod from him he will open his sack and let all the Director's puppets out to dance. Heeding the Director's order that he instead display the puppets to the waiting audience, Philistiades begins removing them from his sack. As he does so, he counters the audience's presumed laughter with the following words:

You laugh! With mirth you'll soon have done,
As soon as you behold the things they do.
Though stiff they seem, they move quite well indeed,
And are unspeakably cantankerous a lot.
At first you'll think your eyes are playing tricks,
The way they shoot and stab and bash each other's heads,
Choke, massacre, and murder one another
  . . .
Puppets, carved entirely true to life,
And each will bleed at just the slightest cut.
  (949–50)

At this point, the Director intervenes for fear that Philistiades may be moving too fast. He has the young man hand him the puppets one at a time so that he can introduce them to the audience with appropriate commentary. Symptomatic of Hauptmann's orientation in the work, the puppet introduced at greatest length represents Napoleon. If the enormous Breslau audience had at first been taken aback by the now obvious conceptualization of the *Festspiel* as a grandiose puppet show—with the obvious associations with fairground and children's entertainment—it could only have been further jolted by the author's emphasis on and preoccupation with the figure of Napoleon. Any expectation that the play was going to be a rousing exercise in heroic dramatics was dissipated first by the unexpected introduction of the puppet motif and then by the brusque dismissal of the crowned heads of state as the leading players in the piece. As the Director declares:

Now comes an article that's truly rare:
A Prussian king, a kaiser, and a czar.
But these are puppets hardest to control,
We'd better drop them from the play right now.
If one of them should ever break a limb,
My position would be grave, to say the least.
 (951)

With little further ado, the Director signals the action to commence. First dramatized are scenes of the French Revolution culminating in the crowning of Napoleon as emperor. These are followed by a carnival procession in which buffoons draw a float containing a huge, ridiculously attired dummy meant to represent the Holy Roman Emperor. Full of boisterousness and buffoonery, the scene conveys the helplessness of the emperor before the humiliation of the eagle symbolizing the German nation. He is spared further indignities by the appearance of a Frenchified King Frederick, "der alte Fritz," who boasts of his leading his country to self-esteem and pride. Napoleon, his marshals, and Talleyrand appear next to bring the carnival to a close by heaping disdain on the Germans and ordering the dummy of the Holy Roman Emperor to be stoned and torn to pieces.

Hauptmann's mocking treatment of the German crowned heads of state carries over into his presentation of the philosopher Hegel as an enthusiast of Napoleon, whom he credits with turning his philosophy of history into prophecy. The dramatist's outlook is by now apparent. Thwarting all expectations concerning the work in light of the events it was intended to celebrate and its place of production, Hauptmann deliberately refused to turn his play into a cheap glorification of the leadership of the Prussian royal house in the German liberation struggle against Napoleon. The conventional reading of history assigned just such a place to Friedrich Wilhelm III, whose appeal to Germans from Breslau to rise up and follow his lead in casting off the French yoke was regarded as the turning point in the campaign. The *Festspiel* all but totally ignores this aspect of the history. This very deliberate subversion of audience expectation—this snub, if it can be so regarded—was much less a caprice on Hauptmann's part than the reflection of a conscious populist interpretation of the events. To Hauptmann—and the *Festpsiel* conveys this unequivocally—the real heroes of the German wars of liberation were not the crowned heads, sovereigns of one sort or another, or princes, but real patriots such as Turnvater (Gymnast) Jahn, who first appears to make light of Hegel's praise of Napoleon as so much empty verbiage, Freiherr (Baron) von Stein, an ardent champion of German unity, Scharnhorst, who pleads eloquently for German patriotism and national self-pride, and the poet and dramatist Heinrich von Kleist, who yearns to pass from word to deed. It is especially in Stein's mouth that Hauptmann puts words embodying the ideological core of the play, the idea that love of fatherland supersedes class and is the true measure of a man's nobility:

> But why should not the monarchies
> Pull with us on the self-same track?
> Why should they not for Germany burn?
> For who is it who holds so high a rank,
> But higher yet his fatherland does stand?
> If he loves it no better than his life,
> He's not the equal in nobility
> To him prepared to sacrifice his life,
> To spill his blood for his united land.
> The humblest toiler who has done this thing
> Is then in truth the princely man.
>
> (974)

But the exhortations of true patriots fall on the deaf ears of German Francomaniacs and ordinary citizens, whose innate conservatism and suspicion bar the way to unity. Following an account of the Prussian defeats at Jena and Auerstädt, Philistiades appears to introduce the philosopher Johann Gottlieb Fichte, in academic gown. His lengthy monologue on the need for the Germans to throw off the yoke of alien culture and at last realize their potential as a people provokes heated argument between patriotic students who take his words to heart and ordinary citizens who mock them and are unflatteringly portrayed as small-minded, servile, and defeatist. When the argument threatens to get out of hand, the crowd is temporarily restrained by the appearance of one of the greatest Prussian heroes of the wars of liberation, Marshal Gebhart Leberecht Blücher. Now seventy years old, the white-haired Blücher delivers a rousing call to arms as the only sure means of defeating Napoleon. But hardly are these words spoken than a detachment of French soldiers appears to drive Fichte from one stage while the second stage opens to reveal the bodies of eleven officers of Prussian hussars slain by the French. When the drum of Drummer Death ceases to beat, the third stage opens and Napoleon and his marshals again appear. Derision of the Germans and bombastic talk of world domination serve as prelude to the account of the campaign against Russia. Again, as in the case of the Prussian defeats at Jena and Auerstädt, the narration is delivered by the Fury (Die Furie), symbolizing the spirit of war, who races about the now empty stage brandishing a torch and heralding the greatness of Napoleon's victories. When the Fury leaves the stage, Napoleon, enthroned as Zeus, appears on a higher level. Lightning flashes in his hand and an earsplitting clap of thunder is heard.

The picture of Napoleon at the zenith of his power fades out at this point in growing darkness and is accompanied by an advancing snowstorm representing the retreat of the Grande Armée from Russia. When the stage brightens, it is dominated by mothers lamenting the loss of their sons, French and German, to Napoleon's ambition and war machine. As a grenadier appears to take the First Mother into captivity for her seditious talk, a group of students and teachers intervenes to liberate her. One student, resembling Karl Theodor Körner, the patriotic poet who died in battle against the French, steps forward to attribute the French defeat in Russia to Mother Russia's giving birth to

> A child both wild and fierce of countenance,
> A son all-powerful and lion-natured,
> Stronger than kings, than all armed forces!
> Its name: the honor of a nation!
> (997)

The student then draws the allegorical parallel between Mother Russia and the German mother whose arrest has just been blocked. He hails her as

> dear Mother Germany.
> Do you know her, degenerate son?
> 'Twas she who bore Dürer, Luther, Melanchthon;
> 'Twas she who bore our heavenly tongue.
> Now she shall bear the god of vengeance!
> (997)

The stage is now set for the final movement of Hauptmann's *Festspiel*, which confronts the audience with yet another jarring surprise. Napoleon's defeat in Russia thus interpreted allegorically as Mother Russia's birth of an avenging son, the students turn to the German mother as the embodiment of a parallel national spirit and ask her blessing to take to the field of combat and conquer for her. The mother is led up to the next stage, but as she ascends, she undergoes a transformation. Her figure appears to grow; a mass of auburn hair is loosened and rolls down her back to the earth. She now appears "*an apparition of almost superhuman kind.*" In altered voice, she calls on the Germans "to forget envy and fraternal strife / Be as one and show the world who you are!" (999). Baron von Stein appears to lead the mother to an altar surrounded by priestesses in Greek garb; there, as a German Pallas Athene, she will be German unity's eternal defender. Hailed by the crowd below, she exhorts them to heed her three commands: to free Germany from alien rule, to unite the land, and to be free themselves. As she seizes two young men by their long blond hair and bends their heads over the altar as for sacrifice amid the clamor of the throng and the singing of martial songs, the vast scene grows dark and still and Philistiades appears. Apologizing for spoiling the solemn consecration, he says that the Director has ordered him to intervene at this point. In an obvious allusion to the expectations of the Breslau Centennial Hall audience, Hauptmann has Philistiades express his personal preference for

> Plutonic and Olympian fire.
> I also would have liked to bring before you
> The destructive path of molten lava.
>   (1001)

But the Director forbade this on the grounds that "art is abbreviation." So constrained, Philistiades rapidly recounts the rest of the story: the defeats of the Germans at Lützen and Bautzen, the reversal of Napoleon's fortunes at Leipzig and Waterloo, and his exile. When Philistiades at last takes notice of Athene Deutschland (Athene Germania), the façade of a Gothic cathedral gradually becomes visible on the topmost stage above her. Her helmet, shield, and spear shedding a steadily growing radiance, she appears bathed in mystic illumination. Beholding the meaning of her life and shining arms, she now exhorts her listeners to pursue the path of love and peace, to forge unity between one people and another, and to turn swords into plowshares. Hardly an appeal calculated to win favor for

Hauptmann's play among an audience assembled to commemorate the centenary of the hard-fought wars and for whom the well-savored victory of the Franco-Prussian War of 1870–71 was still a living memory.

Athene Germania's plea for peace and brotherly love then comes to life, as it were, in a procession celebrating universal peace and goodwill that must surely have taxed the resources even of Breslau's great new Centennial Hall:

> (*In the orchestra appears the head of a well-proportioned procession embracing all the activities and blessings that peace contains. With banners, flags, and festooned tools, the craftsman marches alongside the farmer, the noble alongside the commoner, the miner alongside the sailor and fisherman. Beautiful women of all classes, but especially country girls, are among them carrying baskets of fruit, sheaves of grain, and so on. The procession is crowned, as it were, by great men of all ages. Portraitlike representations of artists, poets, scientists, philosophers, composers, and inventors are visible. Also included are some rulers who were truly committed to the wellbeing of their people. Boys bedecked in wreaths carry garlanded nameplates behind the distinguished figures.*) (1003–4)

Athene Germania's final words, intended as a celebration of the unity symbolized by the procession, admonish the audience that it is blind hate that alone can loose ignorance into the world, not "the divine that dwells in men" (Nicht, was Göttliches im Menschen wohnt). This can only be so, she exults,

> For this divine impulse is Eros! Eros is
> the forming one, creator! All that lives
> Is Eros, comes from Eros, grows in him, and him
> Begets anew. And he begets the world anew!
> What is the sense of sight without him? He
> Alone reveals the beautiful to ear, to eye,
> To sense of smell, to feeling—last but not least,
> To lightning-swift thought, which in a flash
> Infinity traverses. No better servants
> Serve the gods. And so let us praise Eros now!
>   (1004–5)

This paean to Eros, the audience's reaction to which one can only imagine in light especially of the play's other "novelties," effectively brings the

Festspiel to an end. The great procession slowly disappears into the interior of the cathedral and the curtains close. The Director steps out in front of the first one in order to say a few concluding words, much as he had opened the play, functioning like prologue and epilogue combined. But he is interrupted by Marshal Blücher, who comes running up the steps with rattling sabre and insists on being heard even when reminded that he is, after all, a puppet, the shadow of a dead general. Doubtless intended by Hauptmann as a way, at least partially, of appeasing the audience's thus far badly battered expectations, Blücher bellows and blusters about all the sounds of peace he hears, declaring himself to be for infantry and cavalry. It would not be excessive to imagine a resounding roar of approval from the Breslau audience at this point. A familiar, beloved military hero, the barked commands of the leader ("Buglers! Forward! Play the assembly!"), martial fervor, the ultimate victory a cause for communal rejoicing in the triumph of German arms—just the sort of the thing the audience filled Centennial Hall to hear. The last moments of the play even have a comic aspect as the Director orders Blücher back to his box and the old soldier refuses and draws his sword menacingly. The Director, in the *Festspiel*'s final words, calms him by promising him that "his word shall live. / I make a gift of it to Germany and burn it in her heart—/ not your joy in battle, but your—Forward!" (1006). And so, at the play's conclusion, when it appears for a moment that Hauptmann is on the verge of offering the audience a sop in the form of the antics of the puppet representing Marshal Blücher, he again subverts anticipation. Rejecting the old soldier's joy in combat, he subscribes only to his command "Forward!" whose meaning is wholly unambiguous in the context of the play's repudiation of war, martial clamor, and jingoism and its celebration of peace and universal brotherhood. If, understandably, never staged again, Hauptmann's *Festival Play in German Verse* remains one of the true oddities of modern German theater and one of the most exceptional uses of the puppet motif in twentieth-century European drama.

SEVEN

When Mr. Sleeman Comes

Hjalmar Bergman's Marionettes and Shadows

Highly respected and popular in Sweden, Hjalmar Bergman has never acquired the international fame of his better-known countryman August
Strindberg, yet he is generally regarded as his country's foremost novelist
and its second greatest dramatist. His best-known plays, which have become part of the Swedish national repertory, include *Hans nåds testa-
mente* (*The Baron's Will*, 1910), a dramatization of his novel of the same
name and a folk comedy verging on farce; *Ett experiment* (*An Experiment*, 1918); *Markurells i Wadköping* (*Markurells of Wadköping*), a
1929 dramatization of the novel of the same name which was originally
published a decade earlier, and a comedy with serious undertones; *Swedenhielms* (1925), an extraordinarily popular work regarded as the Swedish national comedy; *Patrasket* (*The Rifraff*, 1928); *Sagan* (*The Legend*,
written in 1919–20 but first published only in 1942); and the trilogy *Marionettspel* (*Marionette Plays*, 1917), consisting of the two-act *Dödens
Arlekin* (*Death's Harlequin*) and the one-act plays *En skugga* (*A Shadow*)
and *Herr Sleeman kommer* (*Mr. Sleeman Is Coming*).[1]

Mr. Sleeman Is Coming is not only the most dramatically effective of the
group but also an acknowledged Bergman masterpiece. Before looking at
it more closely, let us first consider the trilogy as a whole. All three plays
were published in 1917 in a single volume. In an interview with the lead-

ing Stockholm daily, *Dagens Nyheter*, on 2 March 1917, in conjunction with the premieres of the first two plays, Bergman was asked to explain why they were collectively titled *Marionette Plays*. He replied:

> I have called my plays *Marionette Plays* because they belong to a group of plays that I wrote based on a common basic idea. In them I regard my people as marionettes because they are directed by a power behind them about which they themselves are unconscious. In one case it is their own past that determines their fate; in another the force of circumstances, or, as in *Death's Harlequin*, one of the plays now being produced, it is a strong person who arranges his environment onstage according to his own will; and finally the greatest authority of all, Death, makes his appearance.[2]

Fixated on death, like Maeterlinck—an obvious influence—Bergman builds each of the plays around the death of a central figure, with the distinction that in the last, *Mr. Sleeman Is Coming*, death is symbolic rather than actual. *Death's Harlequin*, the first play (written in 1915), and the point of departure for the trilogy, appears to have been inspired by Bergman's memories of the death of his father. The father figure in the two-act play is the autocratic, respected, but feared Consul Alexander Broman, the owner of the Tofta Shipyards. Echoes of Ibsen commingle with those of Maeterlinck. The play pivots on the behavior of Broman's three children and others close to him when he is on his deathbed. Never brought into view, isolated in a sickroom just off his offices at the shipyards which other characters enter and leave without its interior ever being revealed, Broman is a powerful offstage presence. Ill and close to death—which comes finally at the very end of the play—he is still a force to be reckoned with. Everything that happens onstage is as if controlled from Broman's room offstage.

The play is the more effective for never permitting Broman to be seen. It is also in this way that the marionette theme is insinuated with greater dramatic intensity. Broman is in effect the play's puppet master, manipulating the strings of all the other characters but never showing himself. The manipulation need not always be conscious. It emanates from the force of Consul Broman's authority (*auktoritet*), to which reference is made throughout. Neither Broman's children nor his immediate subordinates at the shipyards can function effectively without him. It is as if the sheer strength of his powerful personality paralyzes the will of others.

Broman's three children—his son, Bertil, and his two daughters,

Magda and Tyra—are, like everyone else in the play, defined by their attitudes toward Consul Broman, which are now forced into the open by his approaching death. Bertil, a paranoid thirty-five-year-old engineer, is a self-acknowledged weakling who is acutely aware of his inability to sit in his father's chair at the head of the Tofta Shipyards, despite his desire to take over. His insecurity is further fueled by his belief that his father hates him. Bertil is urged to assume leadership by the dean of the Tofta church, whose principal interest is in meeting debt obligations on the new church building to which he is dedicated. Consul Broman had pledged his support to the project before he fell ill, but now that he is incapacitated and no longer in need of a church (as his words are reported to the dean), he withdraws his pledges. Although a group of Tofta engineers, representing an advisory committee headed by the dean, is more skeptical of Bertil's ability to replace his father, they too urge him to take on the leadership for the sake of the company and the church project. But Bertil is so intimidated by his father's presence, even in his grave illness, that his anguish over his own weakness cripples his resolve.

The authority of Consul Broman is the agency through which he exerts his will over others, the way the puppeteer pulls the strings of his figures. So powerful is this authority that no one can imagine the Tofta Shipyards running the same without it. Reflecting perhaps Bergman's own feelings about his deceased father, the play makes it clear that Broman's authority is also rooted in his autocratic treatment of all around him. His is the driving will to which everything else must be subordinated. It is he, and he alone, who controls the strings, and in their inability to act independently of his authority, all others become marionettes, figures outwardly resembling human beings but bereft of will. This is true as well of the only woman Broman seems to have ever truly loved and for whom he sacrificed his marriage—the mysterious lady (Damen) who appears in the second act, garbed entirely in black like an angel of death, to pay her final respects to the lover she has not seen for twenty years. Powerless to resist the force of the consul's will, she had eloped with him while still married to another man.

Broman's daughters are contrasting characters. Like Bertil, who complains that his father crushed his spirit, Magda nurses grievances against her father, convinced that he never loved her or any of his children. Even at the end of the play, when Consul Broman is at death's door, she cannot bring herself to go into his room and pay her last respects. She relents only when the "mystery lady" advises her of her father's longing to see her, and she at last perceives that her father's love, for which she has long been hungering, is real:

> *The Lady.* Magda . . . before it's too late.
> *Magda.* I'm afraid to . . . afraid to . . .
> *The Lady.* Magda, your father is longing to see you.
> (*Magda slowly raises her arms, takes herself around the head, and walks, tottering slightly, toward the rear of the stage.*)
> *Magda (with mixed triumph and pain, childishly).* Father is longing to see me. He loved me . . . loved me . . . loved me. (427)

Consul Broman's other daughter, Tyra, is presented as kind and friendly, lacking Magda's hypersensitivity and sense of hurt. She berates Magda for hating their father and even wanting him dead. Tyra's preoccupation is less with her father's condition than with a sleigh party, complete with bells and torches and culminating in a dance in the big workers' hall, which she and head engineer Morsing are organizing in her father's honor. Tyra's party, and the sounds and lights associated with it, directly relate to the play's marionette theme. In the lengthy conversation early in the play with Gabriel Lerche, Tyra's husband and a sardonic observer of the Broman family, Dr. Brising, the Tofta physician, bares his own feelings about Consul Broman. It was the consul who had paid for his medical studies and brought him to Tofta as its resident physician. But Brising harbors his own grievances. Anxious at the outset of his stay in Tofta to impose his own authority in matters of medicine and hygiene, Brising was thwarted by Broman's higher authority. Although the specific reasons for Brising's disenchantment remain largely unspecified, his painful recollection of the subversion of his own authority by Consul Broman's prompts his discovery of the parallel between his own situation and that of a marionette. Elucidating, Brising actualizes the play's central metaphor. "He is born authority," Dr. Brising says, referring to the consul. "God has placed the strings in his hands and we marionettes dance" (372). With the exception of just a few people in the Tofta community, all the rest are just marionettes, according to Brising. "We marionettes," he continues, "who once were men still have a little bit of conscience remaining. And so we have a prejudice we never quite get rid of" (372). The doctor then likens himself, as a marionette, to Death's Harlequin, who precedes the Grim Reaper, jingling bells. This is the role he is now about to play in the life of Consul Broman. When Gabriel Lerche asks him to explain what he means, Dr. Brising recalls a marionette theater he once saw in Paris which made an unforgettable impression on him because of its spoof of "us poor death doctors":

> It was familiar to me from my own marionette theater. I have seen it so often, so often. I—a death doctor. Mouths opened for prayers are twisted to scorn. Devout eyes sparkle at evilness or an obscene joke. Harlequin, I believed, is now ringing his bells and performing conjuring tricks at our expense. I have seen hands that began to sustain a dying person slipping on devious paths. (386)

Just as Brising's recollections realize the play's metaphoric substratum, the specific image of Death's Harlequin acquires further resonance in the bells related to Tyra's sleigh party, a resonance that has an ironic dimension. Refusing to yield to melancholy, and harboring no rancor toward her father, as do Magda and Bertil, Tyra has planned the sleigh party as a celebration honoring Consul Broman; the party coincides with his dying. The sound of the bells, at first in the distance and then drawing closer and louder, is audible throughout the play's final moments. After Magda has finally gone in to see her father, who is virtually at death's door, Dr. Brising appears after being absent for a while and is asked by Gabriel Lerche if there is any hope for the patient. When he is told there is none, Lerche asks him if he has come too late. Brising replies that he has, and that he neglected his duty. His explanation is that the "sleigh bells lured him" ("bjällrorna lockade"), "Harlequin's bells" ("Arlekins bjällror," 428). Just at this moment hundreds of bells ring and the light of flickering torches plays against a window of the room. Now they are too insistent a reminder of his role as Death's Harlequin; Brising shrieks, "The bells! The bells! The bells!" and slams an open window shut. When a voice cries out, "Long live the master of Tofta, long live Alexander Broman," Brising roars back, "Shut up! Shut up! Shut up!" (428). Almost immediately thereafter, Tyra's voice, filled with dread, is heard as if in questioning reply, "Father? Father?" Her question goes unanswered. As the sound of the bells recedes, a mute scene follows in which all of Consul Broman's colleagues and the church dean tiptoe into the room one by one and line up alongside a wall to one side. The "mystery lady" then enters from the rear carrying a lamp, which provides the only light for the final scene, and a portrait of Broman as a young cadet which she had earlier requested of Magda as a memento.

Unmindful of the men's presence, she stares intently at the portrait, then bows her head and presses her face against it. The dean approaches her and asks with tear-filled voice: "Alexander? Our dear Alexander?" (429). The Lady has the final word. A smile on her face, but without irony, she tells him that they can now speak aloud, an allusion to her earlier admonishment that the men lower their voices because of the patient in the next room. Consul Broman is at last dead. Tyra's party of celebration has taken on the semblance of a grand funeral procession.

A Shadow is closer in subject and style to Mr. Sleeman Is Coming than it is to Death's Harlequin. It consists of a single act and has a small number of characters. As in Mr. Sleeman Is Coming, a young girl is being given in marriage to a much older man whose sole virtue is wealth and whom she does not love. Like Anne-Marie in Mr. Sleeman Is Coming, she too is romantically drawn to a young man who would like to rescue her from the impending marriage. Since the purpose of Bergman's "marionette plays" is to demonstrate the lack of control individuals have over their own destinies, neither the bride (Vera) in A Shadow nor Anne-Marie in Mr. Sleeman Is Coming can alter fate's course. Anne-Marie comes closer to escape than Vera. When Walter, Anne-Marie's young hunter, persuades her to flee with him to the forest, she does so, knowing full well that she will return home in time for Mr. Sleeman's arrival the next morning. Anne-Marie has a brief taste of love before she yields to the inevitabilty of her return and marriage to Mr. Sleeman. Intuiting that Sleeman is her destiny, that she is powerless to oppose her two maiden aunts whose ward she is, she understands that she cannot outrun the mora-wood clock, whose ticking away of time is the play's most relentless sound. Vera's love for Erik in A Shadow is undone by forces neither really has any control over; even Anne-Marie's brief flight with her lover into the forest is denied her.

A Shadow is more melodramatic than Mr. Sleeman Is Coming. Erik, like Walter, is an unacceptable mate for his beloved because of his poverty. And, like Walter, he sneaks into her home in order to take her away in flight with him. But Erik's arrival coincides with Vera's marriage to the older man identified only generically in the play as Bridegroom (Brudgummen). Vaguely anticipating the Spaniard Valle-Inclán's "mystery plays for silhouettes," in which the interplay of light and dark is an integral part of the dramatic structure, A Shadow, as its title suggests, uses the actual shadows in the work as a metaphor for insubstantiality. This is both social and ironic. Erik is perceived, and seen, as a mere shadow, insubstantial because of his impecuniousness, nobody to be taken seriously, an adventurer. He does not exist, therefore, as a serious alternative to the Bridegroom as a husband for Vera. Insecure because of his age and unattractiveness, the Bridegroom becomes anxious when he inadvertently overhears Vera mention Erik's name in her sleep. He tells Vera's mother, who has engineered the marriage, but the woman dismisses Erik as a likable but penniless scamp and advises her soon-to-be son-in-law not to go looking for shadows ("Inte forska efter skuggor!" 440). But "shadow" has a more than figurative meaning to the Bridegroom; he believes that he has seen a shadow entering the house:

> Yes, of course! A shadow—downright stupid, it is. A shadow! But how often does a shadow glide over the steps to a house? A stranger goes by, his shadow stretches up to the door, which seems then to open. What more? There isn't even a spot to wipe away. Who can say it was there? Does a shadow leave footprints? Does it have fingers to knock with? A key with which to open? Hands that clasp? No. All right, there was nothing there. But wait a second. Just a second (*changing his tone*), one damned eternal second. (*Changing his tone*) Gone, gone without a trace. And she asleep in there had no idea at all that a shadow slid past her door, as silent as a dreamed caress. (441)

Despite the mother's reassurance that "no shadow will fall on my daughter" (444), the Bridegroom, of course, has good cause for suspicion since Erik has indeed stolen into the house like a shadow. He is accompanied by his accomplice, who is identified simply as Drängen ("farm hand" or "manservant"), a childhood friend who, as Erik explains to Vera at one point, "went astray" (447). The appearance of the two men is dramatically conceived as the entrance of shadows; that is, in the provocative play of light and dark in the part of the house in which they first appear, they are perceived as moving shadows.

In a time-honored romantic tradition, Erik plans to abduct Vera to save her from the repugnant marriage. The accomplice's task is to wait for the young couple with a coach in an hour's time. The melodramatic element in the play, to which its tragic finale is related, develops from the tension that arises between Erik and his accomplice over the latter's greed. In order to entice Vera into marrying him, the Bridegroom has laid out an impressive array of jewelry on a table in the anteroom to her bedchamber. This catches the eye of Erik's accomplice, who wants to steal it. Erik strictly forbids him. But when Vera goes to pack and Erik's attention is diverted, the accomplice grabs as much of the jewelry as he can. When Erik orders him to put it back, his accomplice tries vainly to convince him that the jewelry was given to the girl and so no longer belongs to the Bridegroom. Vera also refuses to take any of it, saying that the only jewelry she has and wants is the cheap ring that Erik once gave her. As the tension mounts between Erik and his accomplice, Erik orders him to be on his way, but he refuses unless he is given the jewelry: he has, as he says, nothing to lose. Erik eventually placates him by promising to pay him his due as best he can, and the two men appear reconciled. As they shake hands and are about to part, however, the accomplice pulls out a knife and stabs Erik to death. He conceals the body in the drapery of the antechamber, fills his bag with jewelry, and is about to leave when he has to hide because of the arrival of members of the wedding party coming to escort Vera to the ceremony. However, expecting Erik to come and take her away, Vera holds back, puzzled as to his whereabouts and intent on putting off her escorts as long as possible. Adding to her confusion is the carriage waiting below—the one she was to flee in with Erik—which is unattended by a coachman.

The Bridegroom soon shows up but, before proceeding with Vera to the wedding ceremony, insists on talking to her about something that has been bothering him the whole night, namely that the evening before, as he was standing at his window, he saw a shadow gliding up to her door. Moreover, in the light of the moon, he saw a white arm extending from the opened door and then the shadow disappearing. Visibly shaken, Vera hurls aside the bouquet of flowers he has just given her. Anxious to calm her, the Bridegroom begins to talk to her about shadows, alluding of course to Erik. He dismisses shadows as nothing more than darkness that for a while assumes forms, a game of light and dark, a caprice, a "fancy of nature with which to banish a dreary day in one's early years when a cloud silently glided over still water" (468). In a more pointed reference to Erik, the Bridegroom asks: "Can a shadow build a house? No. Run a home? Can a shadow light a fire when you're cold? Give you something to drink when you're thirsty, a chair when you're tired? No" (468). The more the Bridegroom defines a shadow for Vera's edification, the more obvious the allusions to Erik. At last understanding his meaning, Vera challenges him, at the same time reinforcing the play's shadow/puppet equation:

You think a shadow, like the water sprite in a fairy tale, is just fleeting spume, just a whim, a game of longing, which for a moment assumes a human figure? A restless illusion that tires our senses and leaves us unsuspecting?

But tell me, do you believe that a shadow has honor, pride, a conscience? You don't believe it? (*Ironically*) Well then, you must conclude, therefore, that a person who has honor and a conscience isn't just some shadow. (469)

With her mother present as well, Vera speaks directly and boldly of her feelings for Erik:

Indeed, my friend is an adventurer—I never denied it—a vagabond. Many times he went past my door without knocking. I guess he didn't know that I was waiting for him day and night. Oh, how many nights I stayed up waiting for his shadow to fall over my door. And I wanted to ask him: Shadow, don't you have a tongue?

And he came. And I asked him. And he answered. (*Exploding*) Yes, mother, he did have a tongue. He didn't rove about senselessly. He had a tongue. Oh yes! (*Quietly*) He was here the whole night. He's still here. (469–70)

Then, to prove to her mother especially that Erik is a man of honor, Vera pulls aside the curtain concealing the table with the Bridegroom's jewelry to show that it is all still there and that Erik, though he had the chance, took none of it. But the jewelry is not on the table, and instead the figure of the accomplice is revealed. When he tries to run away, claiming that he was just doing his master's bidding, Vera cries out that he is the thief. Groomsmen rush in at the shouting and try to grab him, but he brandishes his knife at them, tosses the bag with the jewelry to the floor, and makes his getaway. Dazed, not knowing what to believe, Vera begs for a few hours' rest and begins to open the door to her bedroom when one of the bridesmaids notices something wet on the doorhandle. Vera, nonetheless, proceeds into the bedroom, while outside her mother and the Bridegroom also notice a stain on the new drapery over the door to Vera's bedroom. A moment later, they hear Vera's screams from inside her room; she has found Erik's body lying on her bed. As the play ends, Vera coldly repulses the sneer on the Bridegroom's face as he observes the dead body of her lover:

What are you smiling at? Sneering, are you? (*Calmly, proudly, without irascibility or adopting a pose*) He has eyes, lips, a chest, arms, hands. And you call him a shadow? He gave his life for his honor. Imagine, you didn't believe it?

    And he was more generous than you. He gave me everything I desired. (*Collapsing and supporting herself heavily on her mother with gentle sobbing*) But I didn't desire everything . . . I opened the door . . . I desired nothing . . . (*Raising her head, looking at the* Bridegroom) Why are you smiling? Yes, yes, you were right.

    He glided by. (473)

The suspense at the beginning of *Mr. Sleeman Is Coming* is different from that of *A Shadow*. Unlike Vera, Anne-Marie is unaware that the old gentleman coming to call that evening—her mother's former guardian and only support—is the man the two maiden aunts (Bina and Mina) she lives with have selected as her husband-to-be. As the very young Anne-Marie recalls Mr. Sleeman, the portrait is that of a man who is not only along in years but also infirm. In a stiff, formal letter Aunt Bina reads aloud, Sleeman informs the aunts that the only way he can see to help them financially is by marrying their niece and "assuming all expenditures necessary to her person" ("åtar jag mig all de utgifter, som äro för hennes person nödvändiga," 483). Mr. Sleeman is in fact due to arrive by train the following morning at eight o'clock. From the time the hour is mentioned, Anne-Marie becomes obsessed with time, knowing that each passing minute advances the inevitability of her marriage to a sick old man for whom she has no love.

While tidying up the apartment alone that night, Anne-Marie is visited by a young hunter named Walter, who wants to take her walking in the forest they both love. Although he has to leave because they have been overheard by her aunts, Walter later returns through a window and is drawn, at Anne-Marie's insistence, into a tender, romantic scene. Realizing that there is no practical way out of her impending marriage to Mr. Sleeman, Anne-Marie wants to stop time, stop the clock ticking incessantly, and enjoy a night of freedom and romance before the grim reality of Sleeman materializes the next morning. Alone with Walter in her room, Anne-Marie at first wants to draw him into a dance, but she changes her mind and dances alone. Instead of dancing with him, she now wants to dance for him, for the man she loves. But she has never learned to dance and her steps are at first halting. Soon, though, she submits to the ecstasy of the moment and, panting breathlessly, whirls about the room. There are echoes here of Nora's dance in Ibsen's *Doll House*. Both dances are improvised and represent a release, momentary in the case of Bergman's Anne-Marie, permanent in Nora's. But Anne-Marie's enraptured yet awkward steps lack the degree of latent eroticism of Nora's uninhibited tarantella. Moreover, Anne-Marie's rapture lasts for only a few brief moments. Unable to keep thoughts of Sleeman from entering her mind, she imagines herself becoming older and dancing like a respectable wife. At that moment, her dance becomes stiff and uncertain. When she begins measuring steps, she immediately makes the involuntary association with the approaching footsteps of Mr. Sleeman:

> No—no—now age claims its due—now I'm a respectable wife—trip along so neatly—one step forward—one step to the side—then I circle about so lightly—so lightly—in a pirouette—and then a step this way—a step—(*The dance becomes increasingly heavier, her tone changing.*) step—I hear—his step—step—(*Stops dancing and stares straight ahead.*) he's walking—a little slowly—(*Supports herself on the chair*). (495)

When Walter urges her to come with him into the forest, she at first demurs but then gives in to the spirit of the moment and allows herself to be carried off. Her aunts discover her absence but react differently. Bina is irate, but Mina is almost glad, and when Bina's back is turned, she throws a kiss at the feather from his hunter's cap that Walter left behind. She is happy that her niece will have a taste of the romance that she herself never had yet certain that Anne-Marie will be back in time to greet Mr. Sleeman.

As a gloomy dawn breaks the next day, Anne-Marie does indeed return home. She is pale, stiff, and expressionless. Her movements are those of a puppet. So too seem those of her aunts as they bustle about their apartment arranging everything for Mr. Sleeman's arrival. Until his footsteps are heard and Anne-Marie invites him in, the scene is entirely mimed, the only sound being that of the mora-wood clock striking. When Mr. Sleeman finally arrives, his movements reinforce the puppetlike character of the scene as a whole. In the stage directions, Bergman describes Sleeman's entrance this way:

> (*He walks the way Anne-Marie described, bent backward, slowly and mechanically raising his legs; even the movements of his arms seem automatic, rather much like the movements of a tabetic though lacking the true characteristics of one.*) (499)

When Anne-Marie goes over to greet him, her gestures are cast in the same style but not for parodic effect, as Bergman notes in the stage direction:

> *(She walks toward him with measured step, raising her right hand slowly as she does so. This gesture must not create the impression of something strange or parodic, which is in fact prevented by* Sleeman's *coming forward somewhat to meet her in order to kiss her hand.)* (500)

The puppet aspect of the scene now yields briefly to grotesque irony as Sleeman declares his romantic feelings for her in precisely the same words used earlier by Walter. As soon as Anne-Marie mechanically expresses her happiness, barely able to hold back the tears, the side doors open and her two aunts sweep into the room, each bearing a large bouquet and wearing an artificial smile. When Aunt Bina notices that her niece is indeed crying, Mr. Sleeman closes the play by assuring the aunts that "happiness, too, has its tears" ("Glädjen har också tårar," 501).

The Maeterlinckian aura of *Mr. Sleeman Is Coming*—with reference, that is, to the so-called marionette plays of 1894—is unmistakable. The dialogue, while lacking the repetitive, incantatory quality of Maeterlinck's, is spare and simple. The stiff, mechanical, puppetlike movements of the characters, above all in the mime scenes, is vintage Maeterlinck. So too is the sense of impending doom conveyed by the approaching footsteps of Sleeman and by Anne-Marie's fixation on footsteps as she attempts to dispel a sense of encroaching dread through the improvised dance she performs for Walter. When Sleeman finally puts in an appearance, it is difficult not to think of the arrival of Death in Maeterlinck's plays, save that Death in Maeterlinck is always a presence, felt but never seen. Bergman wanted it understood that Sleeman does not represent Death; but in his dreadful appearance and manner—almost a corpse himself—he is like the symbolic figure of Death, now male instead of female, in a medieval *Todentanz* ("dance of death"), come to take into his deadly embrace the embodiment of youth and beauty.

Despite its brevity, *Mr. Sleeman Is Coming* justifiably enjoys the reputation of being Bergman's finest play. Indeed, it is a small masterpiece. The dialogue, where nothing seems out of place or superfluous, is splendidly apt. Within a very limited space, Bergman has succeeded in informing his characters with individuating features. While outwardly resembling each other, the maiden aunts are not wholly alike—as witness the different reaction on the part of Bina to Anne-Marie's obvious romantic interlude with her young hunter. That Bina is experiencing vicariously the youthful romance she herself never had, yet longed for, is patently obvious. Anne-Marie runs a relatively wide gamut of experiences, from her naïve innocence at the beginning of the play, to the hinted eroticism of the dance scene, to the fatalistic acceptance of her marriage to Mr. Sleeman and the barely concealed strong emotions lying just beneath the surface when she formally "accepts" him. The short play has humor and romance and irony and a grimness that becomes all the more terrifying in the irony of Sleeman's final words. And Sleeman himself is a marvelous theatrical creation, grotesque, courtly, at once human and mechanical.

EIGHT

Petrushka to Revolution

Russian Variations

The old Russian carnival puppet theater tradition of Petrushka seemed poised to take on new life and vigor at the turn of the century when "high" art sought inspiration from within the fairground.[1] It was, after all, to the puppet tradition—to which such outstanding Russian dramatists of the nineteenth century as Nikolai Gogol and Aleksandr Sukhovo-Kobylin were hardly indifferent—that theater people and others now turned in their efforts to find a way of resolving the "crisis of the stage" about which so many hands were being wrung from one end of Europe to the other. Perhaps because of the relative youth of theater in Russia, the anguish seemed greater there than elsewhere.

However, as Catriona Kelley argues in the introduction to her book on Petrushka and the Russian carnival puppet theater, the Russian Symbolists of the late nineteenth and early twentieth centuries, despite their professed desire to reach the masses through drama, generally ignored the popular theater (3). The director Vsevolod Meyerhold is also faulted for ignoring the Russian fairground in his oft-cited essay "Balagan" ("The Fairground Booth," 1908) and for discussing popular theatrical forms only in terms of French and Italian medieval and Renaissance fairgrounds. Even Mikhail Bakhtin, the author of the critically acclaimed *François Rabelais and His World*, is taken to task for asserting that Russia had never had carnivals in the Western sense.

In view of the interest in popular culture and puppet and marionette theater elsewhere in Europe in the modernist period, it would be difficult to imagine that Russia would loom large as the sole glaring exception. Indeed, it was not. Kelley's criticism of the Russian Symbolists and enthusiasts of popular culture such as Meyerhold and Bakhtin is justified to the extent that they appear to have been indifferent or even hostile to *Russian* popular culture. Since her book deals with the Petrushka tradition, she was obviously struck by the apparent indifference to it among the self-proclaimed advocates of popular culture in Russia in the late nineteenth and early twentieth centuries. But given the abyss separating the world of high culture from that of the masses in pre-Soviet Russia, the disregard for a popular theatrical tradition such as Petrushka should not come as too great a surprise. Russian Symbolism developed strongly under the aegis of the French, and whatever its unique features, it owed a great deal to Western theory and practice. The prominence of medieval settings and motifs among Western Symbolists—for example, the fashionable neo-medievalism of the turn of the century—could not easily have yielded a distinctly Russian equivalent in light of the paucity of monuments of Russian medieval culture. Tatar domination in the Middle Ages denied Russia the conditions in which to develop a flourishing medieval culture in any way comparable to that of the West. Therefore, if Russian artists wanted to incorporate that dimension of Western Symbolism into their own practice, it was undertsandable that they would assimilate Western medieval culture, particularly the French and Italian. This is clearly exemplified in the case of one of the outstanding poets and dramatists of the period, Aleksandr Blok, of whom more shortly.

The apparent indifference to the indigenous Petrushka tradition was certainly unaccompanied by any similar inattention to, or disdain for, the new interest in the puppet and marionette endemic to European modernism. If Meyerhold slighted domestic Russian culture in his "Fairground Booth," his enthusiasm for the fairground booth itself—and by this we understand both popular theater and puppetry—was undiminished, as the following excerpts from his essay demonstrate:

At the present time, when the cinematograph is in the ascendant, the absence of the fairground booth is only apparent. The fairground booth is eternal. Its heroes do not die; they simply change their aspects and assume new forms. The heroes of the ancient Atellanae, the foolish Maccus and the simple Pappus, were resurrected almost twenty centuries later in the figures of Arlecchino and Pantalone, the principal characters of the *commedia dell'arte*, the traveling theater of the late Renaissance. Their audience came not so much to listen to dialogue as to watch the wealth of movement, club blows, dizzy leaps, and all the whole range of tricks native to the theater.

The fairground booth is eternal. Even though its principles have been banished temporarily from within the walls of the theater, we know that they remain firmly embedded in the lines of all true theatrical writers.[2]

Meyerhold also pointed to the connection between the new cabarets of the turn of the century and the fairground booth:

Banished from the contemporary theater, the principles of the fairground booth found a temporary refuge in the French cabarets, the German Über-brettl, the English music halls and the ubiquitous "variétes." If you read Ernst von Wolzogen's Überbrettl manifesto, you will find that in essence it is an apologia for the principles of the fairground booth. (136)

Meyerhold's enthusiasm for the fairground booth cannot easily be separated from his experience directing Aleksandr Blok's play *Balaganchik* (*The Fairground Booth*, sometimes translated as *The Fairground Show* or *The Show Booth*) at Vera Komissarzhevskaya's theater in Saint Petersburg in 1906. One of the more unusual Russian dramatic works of the early twentieth century, by a writer whose literary career began under the aegis of Symbolism, *The Fairground Booth* also enjoys the distinction of being one of the few Russian Symbolist plays to reach the stage. It was Blok's most successful theatrical work and the most exciting production of Meyerhold's early career.

Reflecting the widespread turn-of-the-century interest in the Italian commedia dell'arte—which was to become one of the major influences on Meyerhold's early stage work—*The Fairground Booth* was conceived as a puppet show featuring the traditonal figures of the commedia: Pierrot, Columbine, and Harlequin. In his brief account of it in *A History of Russian Literature*, Victor Terras first characterizes it as "an allegory of multiple ambiguities," then later finds its symbolism less elusive: "In retrospect, the symbolic meaning of the play is fairly obvious."[3] Catriona Kelley speaks of the play's "dense symbolic structure."[4] Let us now consider its symbolism, dense or otherwise, through a close look at the text.

Written in a combination of prose and often stunning verse, *The Fairground Booth* opens with a group of Mystics of both sexes sitting around a lighted table in deep concentration. A little to one side, by a window, sits Pierrot *"in a loose white overall, dreamy, distraught, pale, without whiskers and eyebrows, like all Pierrots."*[5] The Mystics express fear of something mysterious which they expect to happen any moment. Although Terras, among others, makes no point of it, there is every reason to believe that in the characters of the Mystics, Blok is parodying Maeterlinck and, moreover, the archetypical Maeterlinck Symbolist play. The slow, heavy cadence of the Mystics' dialogue, the portentousness, the sense of dread about something soon to occur, the allusion to darkness—all recall the style of Maeterlinck's early plays such as *The Intruder*, *The Blind*, *On the Inside*, and *The Death of Tintagiles*. Blok's parody of Maeterlinck can also be understood, in large measure, as a form of autoparody. Blok is parodying the Maeterlinckian otherworldliness of his own earlier Symbolist writing from which he is now taking his leave in the aftermath of the revolution of 1905. The event had a profound imact on the poet-dramatist's social consciousness and resulted in a reevaluation of his art. Also, it would not be unreasonable to imagine that the very conception of *The Fairground Booth* as a puppet show was also parodic. Blok was certainly aware that Maeterlinck's early plays were designated as having been written "for marionettes." By casting his own anti-Maeterlinck playlet as a puppet show inspired at least in its external form by the puppet booths of the Russian fairground tradition, Blok was parodying both the spirit and the form of Maeterlinck's early plays. The down-to-earth realism of the indigenous Russian *balagan* is contrasted, in other words, with the spiritualized symbolism of the marionette figure in Maeterlinck.

When the Mystics are through expressing their fear, Pierrot plaintively sings of his longing for his unfaithful Columbine. But as soon as his song ends, the Author—as a character in the play—interrupts the proceedings and, of course, dissipates the spell by directly addressing the members of the audience to complain that what they are seeing is not the play he wrote. "I didn't write my play for a fairground show," he insists, and then he hides behind the curtain again as if embarrassed by his appearance onstage. But when the Mystics begin speaking about a mysterious maiden who will be coming from a distant land, all white and bearing a scythe on her shoulder, the Author reappears for an instant without saying anything and then disappears, as if yanked from behind. In the best theatricalist style of the early twentieth century, Blok uses the appearances of the Author as a way of distancing the audience from the surface eeriness and Romanticism of the play and of reminding them that the whole thing is no more or less than a spoof.

When Columbine at last arrives, beautiful, clad all in white, a scythe on her shoulder, the Mytics proclaim her as Death. The allusion to the approach and arrival of Death in the early Maeterlinck plays is unmistakable here. Although Pierrot tries to assure the Mystics that the newcomer is his beloved Columbine, they insist that she is Death and that she has come to them as their divine savior. Distraught, Pierrot declares that he is either an unhappy madman or a lonely, misunderstood dreamer and moves toward the exit. But as Columbine goes after him, telling him she won't leave him, a handsome youth dressed as Harlequin appears to take her away with him. In a clever bit of stage business attributable to the puppet theater, Blok has the Mystics, dejected at Columbine's departure, fold up into themselves in such a way that their hands and heads are no longer visible. The stage direction reads:

> (All hang lifelessly on their chairs. The sleeves of their frock coats have stretched out and covered their hands, as if they had no hands. Their heads have sunk down into their collars. Empty frock coats seem to be hanging on the chairs.) (13)

It is at this point that the Author reappears, again to beg the audience's forgiveness that the actors are not performing the play he wrote but instead are willfully acting out "some old legend." But again he is yanked back behind the curtain, this time by a hand visibly protruding from it. Whether Blok was aware of it or not, his theatricalist business involving the Author touches on a recurrent motif in the drama and fiction incorporating puppet and marionette figures, the rebellion by the inanimate creatures against their creator. Pinocchio rebels against his master by behaving contrary to his wishes, while in Karel Čapek's R.U.R. (1920) and Jacinto Grau's Mr. Pygmalion (1921) the rebellion of puppets or marionettes against their makers assumes more serious proportions. In both Čapek's play and Grau's, the animated figures go so far as to kill their creators.

When the curtain goes up again after the disappearance of the Author, the scene is a masked ball with dancers whirling about to the soft rhythms of dance music. Sad Pierrot sits in the middle of the stage recalling how Harlequin and he both came to realize that the Columbine both of them loved was nothing more than a cardboard fiancée, in the metaphoric sense. Just as Blok had earlier settled scores, in a sense, with his own "Maeterlinckianism," so too in the Pierrot-Columbine-Harlequin romantic triangle does he lay to rest his previous obsession with the Beautiful Lady, the eternal feminine, who inspired much of his Symbolist lyric poetry and is represented here by the figure of Columbine. In the aftermath of the revolution of 1905, Blok bids farewell to the make-believe world of his Symbolist poetry, dominant themes of which he reviews not only through the figure of Columbine but also through the three couples who appear consecutively at the masked ball. The first couple—he dressed in blue, she in pink—imagine themselves in a church, gaze up into the cupola, and encapsulate the religio-mystic Symbolist concept of romantic love. The next couple—she in black mask and red cape, he in red mask and black cape—symbolize the fashionable turn-of-the-century obsession with the demonic woman. The third couple represent the lifeless landscape of Maeterlinckian medievalism symbolized here by the cardboard helmet and large wooden sword worn by the male, a stern figure of "severe, straight lines, big and pensive." The dialogue can only be regarded as an outright parody of the style of Maeterlinck's early plays:

> *He.* Do you understand the play in which we are playing a not
>   unimportant role?
> *She* (*like a quiet and audible echo*). Role.
> *He.* Do you know that the maskers made our meeting today marvelous?
> *She.* Marvelous.
> *He.* You believe me then? Oh, today you are lovelier than ever!
> *She.* Ever.
> *He.* You know everything that was and will be. You understood the
>   meaning of the circle drawn here.
> *She.* Circle.
> *He.* Oh, how captivating your words! Diviner of my soul! How much
>   your words speak unto my heart!
> *She.* Heart.
> *He.* Oh, eternal happiness! Eternal happiness!
> *She.* Happiness.
> *He* (*with a sigh of relief and triumph*). Nearly dawn. It's ending—this
>   sinister night!
> *She.* Night. (17)

At this point, Blok sets aside parody and autoparody for stage slapstick in the spirit of the puppet theater. One of the clowns present at the masked ball runs up to the lover of the third couple and sticks out his tongue at him. The lover takes a swipe at his head with his wooden sword. The clown folds up over the footlights and hangs there, a stream of cranberry juice spurting from his head. From now until the end of the play, mime action, again in the spirit and style of the puppet theater, outweighs dialogue in importance. When the clown gets up and leaves, noise and confusion erupt onstage. Harlequin emerges from a torchlight procession of maskers to deliver the monologue that underscores the play's essential meaning:

> I dragged a fool behind me
> Through sleep and snowy streets!
> The world opened to rebellious eyes,
> The snowy wind sang above me!
> Oh, how my young breast wished
> To sigh deeply and go out into the world!
> To finish in a deserted place
> My happy springtime feast!
> Here no one dares to understand
> That spring flows high above!
> Here no one knows how to love;
> here they live a mournful dream!
> Greetings, world! You're with me again!
> Your soul has long been close to me!
> I go to breathe the spring
> Through your golden window!
>   (18)

The lengthy stage direction that follows calls entirely for mimed action. Harlequin dives through the window into a distance that turns out to have been painted on paper. As the feminine figure of Death appears against the background of dawn, everyone else onstage rushes in different directions in terror. As Pierrot approaches Death, she turns out to be Columbine. Just when Pierrot is about to touch her hand with his, the Author appears to gloat that the play seems, after all, to be ending as the conventional boy-loves-girl-loses-girl-wins-girl romantic comedy he had originally written. But as he starts to join their hands, all the stage scenery rolls up and flies upward. The maskers flee, and the Author is seen bent over Pierrot, who is lying helplessly on an empty stage in his white costume with its red buttons. His plaintive song about his fiancée turning out to be made literally just of cardboard and his hard lot in life closes the play.

Commenting on *The Fairground Booth* (whose title she translates as *The Little Balagan*), Catriona Kelley acknowledges that it is "almost the only important Symbolist dramatic action which is based on the performances given at the Russian fairground."[6] She then goes on to discuss those important facets of the play that have nothing to do with the fairground tradition. Pierrot and Harlequin, for example, speak in the language of Blok's lyric poetry. On language in *The Fairground Booth*, in general, Kelley comments:

> The weight of the language in the play is very different from the weight of the language in the *balagan* pantomimes, where language was always subordinated to action. In fact, Blok has taken a fairground genre in which the text was of little importance, and adapted it as a play in which the text is of primary importance. The visual effects of *balagan* pantomime, with its transformations achieved by lighting, stage mechanics and explosions of powder, its *lazzi*, or comic gestures and nimble acrobatics, are of no significance to this text. (151)

Blok, of course, has taken a fairground genre and adapted it to his own purposes which have to be seen, I believe, as essentially parodic. The very choice of the fairground show booth as the play's frame alludes mockingly to Maeterlinck's plays "for marionettes" which embody archetypical Symbolist qualities of Blok's own lyric poetry repudiated in *The Fairground Booth*. As we have seen elsewhere, the traditional puppet and marionette theater is usually adapted to serve a writer's particular outlook and artistic goals, so Blok is anything but unique in this respect. But in fairness to *The Fairground Booth*, it is important to recognize the extent of its visual effects, its pantomime, its slapstick, its comic gestures, and its acrobatics. These may not conform entirely to the patterns of the Russian fairground genre, as Kelley indicates, but it would seem possible to argue that Blok has tried to preserve aspects of the *balagan* for contrastive purposes. By situating his rejection of Maeterlinckianism and his own previous Symbolist lyric poetry within the frame of a popular fairground entertainment—whatever liberties he has taken with the original form—Blok is using that form itself to make a statement about the redirection of his outlook and writing. The fairground show booth frame of *The Fairground Booth*, with its origins in popular culture, is one of the ways by which Blok conveys his "rediscovery" of the real world around him.

In his production of *The Fairground Booth* in 1906, Meyerhold accentuated the play's puppet theater dimension. Blok's text calls just for an ordinary room onstage with three walls, a window, and a door. When the curtain goes up, the Mystics are seen sitting around a lighted table. The title of the play in the original, *Balaganchik* (a little *balagan*, or small fairground booth), conveys the image of a fairground puppet theater. Meyerhold, however, delineated a separate, smaller interior booth on the stage so that there would be no confusion as to the puppet nature of the performance. He achieved this by hanging blue drapes at the sides and rear of the entire stage, the expanse of blue serving as a background as well as reflecting the color of the little booth erected on the stage. This booth then had its own stage, curtain, prompter's box, and proscenium opening.[7]

PÉTROUCHKA

Apart from Blok's *Fairground Booth*, which draws on the Russian fairground puppet theater in a limited way and for purposes that have nothing inherently to do with the puppet figure, literally or metaphorically, the most successful and influential adaptation of the Petrushka tradition in the Symbolist period was the world-famous ballet *Pétrouchka*, for which Igor Stravinsky composed the music, Michel Fokine devised the choreography, and Aleksandr Benois designed the sets and costumes. The premiere performance of the ballet took place at the Théâtre du Châtelet in Paris on 13 June 1911, with Benois as artistic director. It was also Benois who invented the ballet's central action, which in certain important respects departs from the original Petrushka. In the ballet, during the traditional Russian Shrovetide festivities, the old Magician, of Oriental appearance, exhibits before an astonished crowd the animated puppets Petrushka, the Ballerina, and the Moor, who perform a wild dance. Thanks to the Magician's magic, the puppets are endowed with human feelings, especially Petrushka, who keenly feels the Magician's power over him as well as his own ugliness and ridiculous appearance. It is because of his appearance and odd behavior that the Ballerina, whom Petrushka loves, shuns him. She turns her attention instead to the splendid-looking Moor who, despite his evil nature, fascinates her and leads her to seduce him. Just at the moment of the love scene, Petrushka appears in a jealous rage, but he is thrown out by the Moor. Amid the general revelry of the Shrovetide merrymakers, the rivalry between Petrushka and the Moor becomes violent. A blow with the Moor's saber fells Petrushka, and he dies in the snow, surrounded by the holiday crowd. But the Magician brings

Petrushka back to life again as a puppet, and he invites the public to verify that the head is wooden and the body filled with bran. When the crowd disperses, the Magician is horrified to see Petrushka's ghost above the little theater, menacing him and making mocking gestures of everyone the Magician has fooled. As Catriona Kelley points out in her study of *Petrushka*, Benois reversed the roles of Petrushka and the Moor as found in some traditional variants of the original. Rather than Petrushka tormenting the Moor and mocking him when he begins to sing at Petrushka's encouragement, it is the Moor who humiliates Petrushka in the ballet. It is also the Moor who ends up killing Petrushka rather than the other way around, as in some *Petrushka* texts. In the latter, Petrushka's fiancée is hideously ugly, while in the ballet she is the attractive Ballerina, who spurns him in favor of the Moor. What Benois did, in effect, was to transform the original Russian puppet play from a comedy into a tragedy of bitter love rivalry, degradation, and death.

Benois's adaptation of the Petrushka story for the Stravinsky-Fokine ballet was wholly consonant with the Symbolist outlook and aesthetics. The choice of setting—the fairground and Shrovetide revelry—reflected the Symbolists' attraction to folk and popular culture as new sources of artistic inspiration. Their interest in puppets and marionettes was similary motivated. Moreover, the puppet figure became the perfect embodiment of the turn-of-the-century metaphysical outlook that saw humans as tragically helpless playthings of Fate, of occult, supernatural powers that they had no more ability to control than a marionette the strings or wires animating it. This supernatural orientation of the Symbolists manifests itself in the *Pétrouchka* ballet in the Benois-invented figure of the Magician-Showman and in the reappearance at the end of Petrushka as a ghost to revenge himself on the Magician. The latter idea could also have been suggested to Benois by Gogol's famous story "Shinel" ("The Overcoat," 1842), in which the central figure, the downtrodden petty clerk, Akaki Akakievich, reappears as a ghost to haunt Saint Petersburg after the theft of his most precious possession in life, his fine new overcoat.

Benois's voluminous memoirs are also informative on his early enthusiasm for Petrushka:

> The first theatrical presentations I had been entertained by were the Petrushka shows. But I cannot recall when I saw the very first one; there were so many of them even in my earliest childhood, and I was delighted by them in so many different places. In any case, I remember Petrushka in the sum-

mer house, when we still lived in cavalry officers' quarters. I could hear in the distance the penetrating squeal, the laughter, and some words or other—all that produced by the puppeteer by means of a special device that he inserted into his cheek (you can reproduce the same sound by pressing both nostrils together with your fingers). After receiving our parents' permission, my brothers summoned Petrushka to our house. The colored print screens quickly go up, the "musician" places his barrel organ on a folding sawhorse, his nasal, plaintive notes create a particular mood and stimulate your curiosity. Then suddenly, above the screens, appears a tiny, hideous little person. He has a huge nose, and on his head is a pointed hat with a red peak. He is astonishingly nimble and quick in his movements, with tiny hands with which he gesticulates very expressively, and thin little legs which he has thrown over the top of the screen. Petrushka immediately assails the organ player with silly, impudent questions, to which the latter replies with complete indifference and even gloom. That is the prologue, after which the drama itself unfolds. Petrushka is in love with the terribly ugly Akulina, he asks her to marry him, she agrees, and they perform a sort of wedding stroll, tightly holding each other by the hand. Then in comes Petrushka's rival—a sturdy, moustachioed policeman, whom Akulina obviously prefers. In a fury, Petrushka strikes the guardian of law and order, for which he is conscripted into the army. But military training and discipline do not suit him, he continues to cause havoc, and—oh, heavens!—he winds up killing his noncommissioned officer.[8]

Benois further recalls other Petrushka shows, some of a quite democratic character, others more aristocratic such as those presented at all Christmas parties and children's dances. The affection for Petrushka crossed social boundaries:

> I saw such shows dozens of times, but I never lost my interest in them. In elegant, lordly apartments, the Petrushka show was usually set up in the doorway of the drawing room which was almost always hung with luxurious drapery, and this added a festive and theatrical character to the performance. And it was no simple, dirty puppeteer from the street who was invited to put on the show, but a "gentleman of the salon" all but decked out in evening dress. (286)

Besides Petrushka shows, Benois also delighted in marionettes and fondly recalls in his memoirs

> the marionettes grandmother Cavos brought me from Venice. These were "absolutely lifelike" little cavaliers in felt hats and caftans with gold tinsel,

a gendarme in a tricorn hat with a sabre in his hand, Harlequin with his *batte* [wooden sword], Pulchinello with a tiny little lantern, and Columbine with a fan. They had tiny wooden or tin hands and feet that dangled lightly at every movement. Some of these "Venetians" lived with me for many years, and several of them were even used by my children. (287)

As with many other artists whose fascination with puppets and marionettes began in childhood, Benois mentions that the strongest theatrical impressions of his childhood were the marionette shows of Thomas Olden, an American who brought his marionette theater to Petersburg for the 1882–83 season. Benois recalls seeing Olden's marionettes for the first time at the Shrovetide fair in 1877 or 1878, but his memory may be faulty here. Olden first performed in Petersburg at the Renaissance Theater on 5 December 1882.[9] Benois's further experiences at Russian Shrovetide fairs and their typical entertainments, including harlequinades, are also affectionately recalled in his memoirs. These experiences, together with his extensive command of puppet and marionette theater, were complemented additionally by his interest in the "human doll" theme, which he relates to his discovery of the world of E. T. A. Hoffmann. "Indeed, the human doll played a significant role in my thinking, and this has been reflected in my art. It suffices for me to recall that the subject of *Pétrouchka* is a distant echo of all the thoughts and moods induced by 'automatons' " (330). Not just the fascination with the "human doll" motif, but all the impressions and recollections of years of contact with fairground entertainments and puppet and marionette theater stood Benois in good stead when the opportunity presented itself much later for him to collaborate with Stravinsky and Fokine on the ballet *Pétrouchka*.

ANDREEV: *THE LIFE OF MAN*

Equally indebted to the turn-of-the-century fascination with the puppet and marionette, if not to any specific Russian popular entertainment such as *Petrushka*, was Meyerhold's next production (and the last of the season) after *The Fairground Booth* at Vera Komissarzhevskaya's theater, on 22 February 1907. The play was *Zhizn cheloveka* (*The Life of Man*, 1906) by a writer of extraordinary international renown in his lifetime, Leonid Andreev. Although later denigrated as pretentious and philosophically shallow and ignored for a long time, especially in the Soviet Union, Andreev's reputation has been considerably rehabilitated both in his own country and abroad in the second half of the twentieth century. In his own

time, however, he and Gorky were the most widely regarded Russan literary figures, their fame by far eclipsing Chekhov's. A prolific dramatist as well as prose fiction writer, Andreev became best known for his
play about circus life, *Tot, kto poluchaet poshchechiny* (*He Who Gets
Slapped*, 1915).

A theatrical event when it premiered in 1907, as well as a source of controversy and ridicule, *The Life of Man* was usually dismissed as a feeble
imitation of Maeterlinck and a pseudo-Symbolist allegory about the universal human condition. Its somberness, bleak view of humankind, and
austere, sometimes incantatory dialogue do recall Maeterlinck. The Belgian dramatist was much the rage throughout Europe in the late nineteenth and early twentieth centuries, and his influence would have been
difficult to resist. But Andreev wrote very different plays from Maeterlinck's, and the resemblances, such as exist, are superficial.

The Life of Man, which brings to mind the medieval morality play *Everyman*, as much as Maeterlinck, dramatizes Andreev's view of the
bourgeoisie rather than of the human condition in general. The play is divided into five acts without scenes. Each act corresponds to a period in the
life cycle: birth; marriage and the privations involved in establishing a career; fame and fortune; adversity and decline; and death. Andreev was a
typical turn-of-the-century writer in this respect, and his view of the
bourgeoisie was shaped by a contempt for the materialism and question-
able values attributed to bourgeois society. The picture of the bourgeois
everyman's life cycle which emerges from *The Life of Man* is appropriately
bleak and depressing. Any pleasure that Andreev's Man, an architect,
achieves is accompanied and offset by suffering or loss. The joy of birth is
tempered by the terrible pains of the mother in labor; the happiness of love
and marriage is qualified by the misery of poverty; along with achievement and reward come envy and insincerity; decline and loss—in this
case, the dissipation of wealth and the death of Man's son—are the inevitable harvest of success; in the end there is nothing but death, and when it
comes to claim Man, it is in loneliness and despair; and beyond death?—
Andreev remains silent; his Man is denied even the solace of eternal life.

Accompanying Man on his bittersweet journey through life is a shadowy figure identified just as Someone-in-Gray called He. Possibly representing fate, expressionless, He appears with a candle in his hand, its
length and the brightness of its flame symbolizing the period of life and the
length of the road yet to be traveled. An appropriate chiaroscuro, extend-

ing from the prologue to the end of the play, sets the mood. Figures move from darkness or grayness into a dim, hazy light, or into the flickering light of a candle, or conversely, from bright warm light into an ever encroaching darkness.

Andreev's conception of his characters is typical of the modernist metaphoric use of the puppet and marionette. They are helpless figures controlled by the strings of the bourgeois way of life and by destiny. Andreev conveys this puppet dimension of Man and his world by their stiff and jerky movements, which are paralleled in the stylized, artificial rhythms of the dialogue. The sole exception to the pattern occurs in the second act when Man and his wife escape from their poverty in a game- and flower-filled private world of dreams and illusions. The puppetlike artificiality of the society into which Man is born comes through clearly, for example, in the behavior of his relatives immediately after his birth:

Elderly Lady. Let me congratulate you on the birth of your son, dear brother. (*Kisses him.*)

Elderly Man. My dear brother-in-law, I heartily congratulate you on the birth of your son, which we have so long been waiting for.(*Kisses him.*)

The Rest. We congratulate you, dear uncle, on the birth of your son. (*They kiss him. The* Doctor *leaves.*)

Man's Father (greatly moved). Thank you! Thank you! You are all very good, very nice, dear people, and I love you very much. I had my doubts before, and thought that you, dear sister, were a little too preoccupied with yourself and your own importance; and that you, my dear brother-in-law, were somewhat too pedantic. The rest of you I thought were too cold to me, and that you come here only for the sake of the dinners. Now I see I was mistaken. I'm very happy. A son is born to me who resembles me, and then all at once I see myself surrounded by so many good people who love me.
(*They kiss.*)

Young Girl. Uncle dear, what are you going to call your son? I hope you'll give him a lovely, poetic name. So much depends on a person's name.

Elderly Lady. I should like him to have a simple, solid name. People with pretty names are always frivolous and rarely succeed in life.

Elderly Man. It seems to me, dear brother-in-law, that you should name your son after some older relative. That way, you preserve and strengthen the line.[10]

In the stage direction preceding this dialogue, Andreev describes his characters as if they were caricatures, or puppets. Each appears grotesque in appearance and gesture, and their characteristics are "*exaggerated in the extreme*" (184). This puppetization is handsomely displayed in the third act, titled "A Ball at Man's House." Man is now at the pinnacle of his career and lives in a sumptuous mansion, his wealth reflected in the tasteless abundance of gildings. The ball is given to celebrate his success. The guests are divided into two camps: those who admire Man's prominence and wealth and fawn on him and his family, and those who envy him and slander him behind his back. Act 3 is meant to contrast with act 2, in which Man and his wife, at an earlier period in their life, live in terrible poverty but take heart in their love for each other and their hope for the future. The third act, however, is a puppet play-within-a-play of artificiality and insincerity. Andreev uses the common associations suggested by the puppet and marionette figure at the turn of the century to paint bourgeois society in the most grotesque and repulsive satirical terms. The mood of the act is established in the description in the stage directions of the disharmonious aspect of the drawing room where the ball takes place:

> *(There is a certain irregularity about the room in the correlation of its parts and their different sizes. Thus, the doors are very small in proportion to the windows, producing a strange, rather irritating impression, as of something disharmonious, something lacking, something superfluous and as if from without. Everything is pervaded by a chilly whiteness, the monotony of which is broken only by a row of windows along the rear wall. They are very high, reaching almost to the ceiling, very close to one another, and dense with the blackness of night. Not one gleam, not a bright spot appears in the empty spaces between the window frames.)* (203)

The grotesque, caricature-like description of the relatives in the scene following the birth of Man is paralleled in the description of the three musicians playing at the ball. They resemble their instruments, the flute player, for example, "*very tall, very thin, with an elongated face, and firm, thin legs.*" Their playing is labored, stiff; they are a band of puppets or marionettes:

> *(They beat time, swing their heads, and shake their bodies. The tune is the same throughout the ball, a short polka in two musical phrases, producing a merry, hopping, extremely insipid effect. All three instruments play a bit out of tune, giving rise to a certain peculiar detachment, vacant spaces, as it were, between them and the individual sounds.)* (203)

Andreev also contrasts the young people dancing at the ball and the Guests. The young men and women, all of whom are handsome and well formed, dance dreamily and smoothly; there is a slight mannerism in their dancing. But in their very handsomeness and smoothness, they are like programmed automatons; no individuating features appear, they are all pretty mannequins. The Guests, on the other hand, symbolize adult bourgeois society. Seated along the walls, on gilded chairs, they are

> (. . . constrained in stiff poses. They barely move their heads. Their conversation is similarly stiff. They neither whisper to one another, nor laugh, nor scarcely look at one another. They speak abruptly, as if chopping out only those words inscribed in a text. Their hands look as if they had been broken at the wrists and hang vacantly and arrogantly. In the extreme, sharply etched monotony of their faces, they all wear the same expression: self-satisfaction, haughtiness, and inane respect for the wealth of Man.) (204)

When Man and his wife appear, they are followed by his Friends and, at a slight distance behind them, by his Enemies. The two groups are contrasted in appearance and movement; both groups are puppets, animated, on the one hand, by self-esteem, and, on the other, by envy. The first group, the Friends, are described this way:

> (They all resemble one another greatly—noble faces, high, open foreheads, honest eyes. They stride proudly, throwing out their chests, stepping firmly and confidently, and looking, now to one side, now to the other, with condescension and slight disdain. They wear white roses in their buttonholes.)

The Enemies also closely resemble one another:

> (Mean, cunning faces; low, heavy foreheads; long, apelike arms. They walk uneasily, pushing, bending, and hiding behind one another, and casting sharp, mean, envious, sidelong glances from beneath lowered lids. Their buttonholes have yellow roses.) (207–8)

Russian artistic interest in puppets and marionettes, unrelated to the Petrushka theme, quickened in the decade after Blok's *Fairground Booth* and Andreev's *Life of Man*. In a lengthy, historical article on marionettes and puppets ("Marionetka") published in the Symbolist journal *Apollon* in 1916, the well-known Petersburg theater and literary critic Yuliya Slonimskaya (Sazonova) extolled marionette theater as the purest form of theater because of its embodiment of the basic element of theater, namely

movement. Finding parallels between the theatrical function of the marionette and algebra, she declared: "The marionette gives the theatrical formula without corporeal expression. Just as algebraic signs replace specific
numerals of quantity, so does the convention of the marionette's flesh replace the real flesh of the human being. The role of the marionette in the
theater is similar to the role of infinitesimals in mathematics; it seems to
integrate complicated theatrical phenomena, indicating their basic initial
forms."[11] Slonimskaya also stressed the familiar link between the marionette and the human condition. "It was not the marionette that became
like man, but the contrary; man likened himself to the marionette, which
became a symbol of man in the world. Philosophers and poets of all ages
compare man to a marionette that fulfils in the theater of life some author's will; man appears a tragic marionette directed by Fate" (1). In one
of her more incisive comments, Slonimskaya also noted the distinction between the genuine illusion created by marionette theater and the false one
for which the contemporary theater was then striving:

> The illusion created by the theater of marionettes is entirely different from
> the one toward which the contemporary theater erroneously strives.
>   The law of artistic necessity reigns in the theater of marionettes. This law
> so dominates the spectator that he forgets about the laws of real life. It
> seems to him that the only absolute is that which is taking place before him.
> . . . The marionette does not imitate life. It creates its own fabled life, which
> bends creator and spectator alike to its own laws. Such an illusion is the
> only necessary theatrical illusion, when everything is organically fused,
> everything is suggested by the law of artistic necessity. . . .
>   The law of existenial necessity penetrated the theater of living people
> through the living flesh of the actor and substituted itself for the law of the-
> atrical creativity. Subordinate to the law of art alone, the marionette could
> serve as the way of salvation for the theater, which has gone astray in the
> region of existential phenomena alien to it. (41)

Slonimskaya's interest in puppets and marionettes extended beyond
the theoretical. In 1916 the tradition of professional puppet theater took
on new life in Russia with the debut of the gifted puppeteer Nina
Simonovich-Efimova at an evening of the Moscow Association of Artists.
Simonovich-Efimova had begun her career as a painter, but as if guided
by Slonimskaya's views on puppet and marionette theater as expressed in
her article in *Apollon*, she found herself increasingly attracted to the
miniature stage because of its primacy of movement and play. Slonim-

skaya's direct involvement in puppet theater that same year (1916) may in fact have been stimulated in turn by the rediscovery of puppet theater by such painters as Simonovich-Efimova, Alexandra Exter, and Nechama Szmuszkowicz. When the opportunity presented itself for her to participate in the puppet theater (Kukolny teatr) organized by the Mir Isskustva (World of Art) group in Petrograd (as Saint Petersburg was then known), Slonimskaya organized performances of puppet plays. The first, and possibly the best known, was a seventeenth-century French comedy of uncertain authorship, *Les Forces de l'amour et de la magie* (*The Forces of Love and Magic*). The puppets were beautifully carved in the manner of French or Italian marionettes by the painter and decorator Nikolai Kalmakov and are shown in Slonimskaya's article in *Apollon*.[12] Another prominent artist affiliated with the World of Art group, Konstantin Somov, also created pieces for the theater.

Further attesting to this great enthusiasm for puppets and marionettes among Russian modernists in the first two decades of the twentieth century was the career of Alexandra Exter, a celebrated marionette artist of exceptional talent. A true cosmopolite who was closely associated with the European Cubists and Futurists in the period 1908–14, Exter exhibited her own art work in Paris and Rome as well as in Moscow, Saint Petersburg, and her native Kiev. In 1915 and 1916 she turned her attention to theater design and did the sets and costumes for Aleksandr Tairov's Kamerny Theater production of *Famira Kifared* (*Thamyris Kitharodos*) by the Symbolist poet Innokenty Annensky. In 1917, the year of the Russian Revolution, she designed the sets and costumes for the Kamerny production of Oscar Wilde's *Salome*. Between 1918 and 1926, the year in which she created the marionettes for which she is most remembered, she was extraordinarily active on a broad artistic front. She established her own studio in Kiev; undertook decorations for agitprop steamers on the Dnieper River; executed set and costume designs for a variety of productions by the Kamerny Theater and the Moscow Art Theater; began designing textiles; collaborated with the Moscow Children's Theater; participated in the first exhibition of Russian art in the Galerie Van Diemen in Berlin; and began work on costumes for the well-known film *Aelita* by Yakov Protazanov (produced 1924). In 1924 she and her second husband, Georgi Nekrasov, emigrated to Paris, where Exter was engaged principally as a teacher of theatrical design and painting at Fernand Léger's Académie d'art moderne. Although she continued to exhibit her theater, cos-

Alexandra Exter, Pierrot, *1926.*
Photograph by Lee Stalsworth.
(Courtesy Hirshhorn Museum and
Sculpture Garden, Smithsonian
Institution, The Joseph H.
Hirshhorn Bequest, 1981)

Alexandra Exter, Columbine, *1926.*
Photograph by Lee Stalsworth.
(Courtesy Hirshhorn Museum and
Sculpture Garden, Smithsonian
Institution, The Joseph H.
Hirshhorn Bequest, 1981)

tume, and other designs from New York to Prague at least until 1937,
Exter became known in her émigré period above all for the superb marionettes she designed in 1926. Many of them were exhibited in major European cities in the late 1920s and 1930s. Her work is also by now well
known in the United States. An exhibition of her marionettes was held at
the Leonard Hutton Galleries in New York in 1975 and at the Hirshhorn
Museum and Sculpture Garden of the Smithsonian Institution in Washington, D.C., in 1980.

Exter's marionettes were created in Paris in 1926. Although there may
have been forty in the original collection, twenty were on display at the

Alexandra Exter, Arlequin Gris,
1926. Photograph by Lee Stalsworth.
(Courtesy Hirshhorn Museum and
Sculpture Garden, Smithsonian
Institution, Gift of Joseph H.
Hirshhorn, 1977)

Alexandra Exter, Arlequin Blanc,
1926. Photograph by Lee Stalsworth.
(Courtesy Hirshhorn Museum and
Sculpture Garden, Smithsonian
Institution, The Joseph H.
Hirshhorn Bequest, 1981)

Leonard Hutton Galleries; this seems the largest number ever exhibited publicly. The marionettes are believed to have originally been designed for a film proposed but never realized by the Danish filmmaker Peter Urban Gad. Exter may have met Gad through the Russian director Yakov Prota-zanov, with whom she collaborated on costumes for *Aelita,* or perhaps even earlier, in 1910–14, when her work with the Union of Youth in Saint Petersburg brought her into contact with Scandinavian artists. Although Gad's film never reached fruition—if indeed that had been the original stimulus for her marionettes—Exter completed her designs and then en-trusted their fabrication to a fellow Russian émigré in Paris, Nechama

Alexandra Exter, Arlequin Noir, *1926.*
(Courtesy Leonard Hutton Galleries)

Alexandra Exter, Djudi, *1926. Photograph by Lee Stalsworth. (Courtesy Hirshhorn Museum and Sculpture Garden, Smithsonian Institution, The Joseph H. Hirshhorn Bequest, 1981)*

Alexandra Exter, Gendarme Americain, *1926. Photograph by Lee Stalsworth. (Courtesy Hirshhorn Museum and Sculpture Garden, Smithsonian Institution, Gift of Leonard Hutton Galleries, 1977)*

Szmuszkowicz, who had also worked with Léger at his Académie d'art moderne. The inspiration of Léger himself in the Exter-Szmuszkowicz project should be taken into account. For his 1924 film *Ballet Méchanique,* he had made a marionette of Charlie Chaplin with which he introduced the film.

Some two feet tall, Exter's marionettes command attention for their basically simple but imaginative forms, costumes, colors, and materials. Intended wholly for adult viewers, notwithstanding her work with children's theater, the most impressive of the figures (Djudi, Arlequin Noir,

Alexandra Exter, Dame en Rouge, *1926. Photograph by Lee Stalsworth.*
(Courtesy Hirshhorn Museum and Sculpture Garden, Smithsonian Institution,
Gift of Joseph H. Hirshhorn, 1977)

Arlequin Blanc, Arlequin Gris, Pierrot, Colombine, Polichinelle, Longhi I, Longhi II, Longhi III, Robot, L'Homme Réclame, L'Homme Sandwich, and Danseur Espagnol) are geometric in shape and appear most like constructions of boldly colored cubes and cylinders. Angular and essentially spare, the marionettes are particularly striking for their movement in space, their kineticism, which Exter, like Slonimskaya and Simonovich-Efimova, appreciated as the essence of puppet and marionette theater. In this respect they wholly accorded with Exter's Constructivist conception of the stage as a dynamic three-dimensional space. The marionettes became, in effect, moving sculptures, and while obviously related to her earlier set and costume designs in their geometric stylization and bold patterns of colors and shapes, they stand apart from her theater work as arguably her most durable artistic achievement.

The idea, articulated by Yuliya Slonimskaya in her article "Marionette," that marionette theater could lead the theater of living actors out of the morass of inauthenticity into which it had fallen was suggested by other writers identified with the Symbolist movement. Somewhat similar sentiments had been expressed eight years earlier in the well-known essay "Teatr odnoy voli" ("The Theater of One Will") by the gifted but idiosyncratic Symbolist prose writer and dramatist Fyodor Sologub (real name: Fyodor Teternikov). The piece was published in a collection of Symbolist essays on theater in 1908. In it, Sologub, like Slonimskaya, takes contemporary Russian drama to task for its banal realism. His goal, of course, is a Symbolist theater, in which eternal mysteries are performed as if in a temple. Posing the question, What remains of the actor's art in the theater of realism and naturalism? Sologub answers it himself by saying that the actor becomes a talking marionette. He then continues:

> But this cannot be pleasing to the actor, who loves winning roles and the attention of the stalls directed at him, the cries of the simpleminded gallery, and the clamor of the press surrounding his name. Such a theater is unacceptable to the contemporary actor. He will say contemptuously: "This will not be a theatrical performance but simply a literary recital conducted in conversations and movements. Better then openly to establish a theater of marionettes, an entertainment for children. Let painted puppets move about; let someone with seven voices speak behind the curtains; let him speak, and pull the cord."

But when you come right down to it, why shouldn't the actor be like a marionette? It's not an insult for a human being. Such is the immutable law of universal play that a human being should be like a marvelously constructed marionette. He cannot escape this, nor is he even allowed to forget it.

A specified time will arise for each of us when each of us, visible to all, will turn into an immobile and lifeless puppet no longer able to play a role. . . .

An actor, even the most talented, is no longer a human being. His role, even the most successful, is less than life, and easier than it. And, of course, better for him to be a talking marionette and move about, obeying the intelligible and passionless voice of the reciter, than despairingly muddling his role beneath the wheezy murmuring of a prompter hidden in a box.[13]

Toward the end of his essay, Sologub, in his unique visionary-ecstatic style, alludes to the relevance of the marionette and puppet figure to his new Symbolist theater of mystery:

Such is the projected form of the theatrical spectacle. And the content interpolated into this form—the tragic game of Fate with its marionettes—a spectacle of the fateful of all earthly masks—the mystery of complete self-assertion.

Playing, I play with puppets and masks, and in full view of the world, the masks and veils fall away and mysteriously just my visage opens up, and, rejoicing, my will alone triumphs.

. . . The whole world is just window-dressing concealing the creative spirit. My spirit. Every earthly countenance and every earthly body is just a mask, just a marionette, each for a single performance, for the earthly tragicomedy, a marionette introduced for the word, gesture, laughter, and tears. (158)

GUMILYOV: *A CHILD OF ALLAH*

Sharing the critic Slonimskaya's interest in puppets in the practical sense, but the author as well of a charming play for puppets, was the poet and dramatist Nikolay Gumilyov. A Symbolist who eventually became a leading representative of the Acmeist movement in Russian literary modernism which spurned mysticism and metaphysicality in favor of concreteness and precision in imagery and language, Gumilyov was also a writer of the exotic and adventurous. He traveled extensively in black and Islamic Africa in the teens of the twentieth century and drew on these experiences in several of his works. His delight in physical bravery and adventure owed most to his military service in World War I.

Gumilyov's interest in the Islamic world and his knowledge of its culture lend his play *Ditya Allakha* (*A Child of Allah*) an appealing exotic flavor. The work was first published in the journal *Apollon* in 1917, a year after Slonimskaya's article on the marionette, then issued as a separate publication in Petrograd in 1918. Subtitled *An Arabian Tale in Three Scenes*, it was written by Gumilyov for the puppet theater he and N. I. Butkovskaya organized in Petrograd. When exactly Gumilyov wrote the play is uncertain, but it was most likely in 1916 and early 1917. Neither is there any information as to whether it was ever staged in his puppet theater. The outbreak of the Revolution in 1917 might well have interfered with plans for such a production. Gumilyov himself ran afoul of the Bolsheviks and was executed in 1921 for alleged counterrevolutionary activities.

Written in melodious rhymed iambic pentameters, *A Child of Allah* recounts the true love on earth a *peri* finds with the Persian poet Hafiz. In Islamic lore *peris* are maidens living in Paradise for the purpose of giving pleasure to its inhabitants. In this play, as well as in his longer *Otravlennaya tunika* (*The Poisoned Tunic*, 1918), Gumilyov displayed his knowledge of Middle and Near Eastern culture by assigning prominent roles to classical poets of the region, the Persian Hafiz in the puppet play, and the pre-Mohammedan Bedouin poet Imr-ul-Qais in *The Poisoned Tunic*.

After she finds a horseshoe belonging to Mohammed's mare, Peri (as she is called in *A Child of Allah*) is offered a reward and chooses to be sent to earth "among the sons of Adam" where she hopes to become the beloved "of the best of them." The Dervish, a holy man, is assigned to look after her and guide her. He gives her a white unicorn, which will kill the impure, and Solomon's ring, with which she will test the strength or weakness of the man on whose finger she puts it. In rapid succession, Peri encounters three suitors, each of whom represents distinct male vanity. To each she poses the question, Are you the best of Adam's sons? The first is a young man in a camel caravan returning from Baghdad. He is at once attracted to her and wants to bed her without delay. Although attracted to him as well, Peri is unsure what to do and consults the unicorn, which promptly kills the young man. The next potential soulmate is a Bedouin on horseback who boasts of his physical and martial exploits and wants to claim her as his prize. But he is slain by a visitor from the other world, the shade of Alexander the Great (or Iskander, as he is known in the Islamic world). The last "pretender" is the Caliph, who represents worldly power. He first appears on a hunt attended by his faithful astrologist. When Peri, to test him, gives him Solomon's ring, he falls dead.

Upon entering Baghdad the crestfallen Peri and the Dervish encounter relatives of the three dead men. The scene is laced with irony and humor. The mother of the young man slain by the unicorn is more concerned about the fate of her camels. The sheik, the Bedouin's brother, professes a desire for revenge on Peri but is only too happy to sell her to a pirate. The haggling between the two men over price is one of the play's funnier moments. The son of the Caliph, with whom the Dervish pleads for Peri's life, intends to shower her with jewels in gratitude for being the cause of his becoming caliph and master of his country; but he will then have her thrown into the sea as punishment for the death of his father.

However, all plans for revenge on Peri evaporate as soon as word spreads that the magnificent Sindbad has arrived in Baghdad. In the third and final scene, Peri and the Dervish come to the gardens of the poet Hafiz. When he hears of Peri's adventures, he summons the spirits of the three men for whose death she was responsible. The first two tell her they are happy in heaven and forgive her; the Caliph is enjoying the afterlife to such an extent that he won't even hear of a return to earth and sends an Angel of Death as his spokesman. Her conscience thus set at ease, Peri can now devote herself to the pleasure of Hafiz's poetry. The two fall in love, and to her delight she learns that the unicorn and Solomon's ring originally belonged to Hafiz but that he lost them. At the end, Peri tells Hafiz that she is his slave and urges him to take her beneath his tent. Happy that everything has worked out in accordance with Allah's grand design, the Dervish takes his leave and the play ends.

A short summary of Gumilyov's *Child of Allah* does little justice to its charm. Its Oriental coloration, which recalls Oskar Kokoschka's shadow play *The Spotted Egg*, is not limited to setting and characters. The work abounds in images drawn from the literaure and mythology of the Islamic East. Like *The Spotted Egg*, Gumilyov's work has the quality of a fairy tale, but a fairy tale for adults rather than children. Its verse pattern—rhymed imabic pentameter—is light and melodious and creates the aura of children's literature. Rhyme becomes more complex in those passages where Hafiz and the birds in his garden alternately sing couplets, but the change in verse blends comfortably with the overall pattern of the play. Gumilyov's decision to write the play for puppet theater might well have been motivated by his desire to enhance its naïve, fairy tale–like aspect.

By conceiving *A Child of Allah* as a puppet play for adults, Gumilyov remained faithful to the romantic-escapist orientation of his dramatic writing in general. Yet none of his other plays, whatever their interest, approaches *A Child of Allah* in charm and ironic humor. It remains arguably the best play written originally for puppets by a major twentieth-century Russian poet and dramatist.

JASIEŃSKI: *THE MANNEQUINS' BALL*

Only a decade separates Gumilyov's execution in 1921 from Bruno Jasieński's *Bal manekinov* (*The Mannequins' Ball*, 1931), but politically the two writers were light years apart despite the similar circumstances of their deaths. Gumilyov barely took pains to conceal his disdain for the Bolsheviks and his monarchist sympathies. His cavalier attitude cost him his life. Bruno Jasieński, on the other hand, was an ardent communist whose political and literary credentials still failed to keep him out of the net of the 1936 purges. He was arrested that year and died near Vladivostok in 1939 on his way to a concentration camp in Kolyma.[14]

Jasieński, a native Pole, began his literary career under the aegis of Futurism with a volume of poetry in Polish, published in 1921 under the title *But w butonierce* (*A Boot in a Buttonhole*). Within a year he became a champion of the Russian Revolution and a writer who hoisted high the banner of social protest. His next three important poetic works (also in Polish) were all conceived in the spirit of his new political outlook: *Pieśń o głodzie* (*Song on Hunger*, 1922), *Ziemia na lewo* (*Earth to the Left*, 1924), and *Słowo o Jakubie Szeli* (*Song about Jakub Szela*, 1926), a dramatic poem about the leader of a peasant rebellion in 1846 (the same character who appears as an apparition in Wyspiański's *Wedding Celebration*). It was while he was in Paris, where he worked as a journalist after leaving Poland, that Jasieński completed his second novel, *Je brûle Paris* (*I Burn Paris*). It was published in 1928 by the communist daily *L'Humanité*. The novel was the straw that broke the camel's back. Already suspect because of his leftist agitation, Jasieński's *I Burn Paris*, with its antibourgeois sentiment and prediction of the city's downfall, was too much for the French authorities. Jasieński was expelled from France as an undesirable alien and sought refuge in the Soviet Union, where he began a new literary career in Russian as an exponent of Socialist Realism. His satirical-political play about mannequins and French industrialists, *The Mannequins' Ball*—which has little in common with Socialist Realism—came out in 1931. The following year, Jasieński published the work for which he is best known, the novel *Chelovek menyaet kozhu* (*Man Changes His Skin*), which is regarded as one of the best Soviet industrial novels of the 1930s. Jasieńksi went on to become a member of the executive committee of the Soviet Writers' Union, but even this did not spare him from becoming another victim of Stalin's infamous purges of 1936–38.

The Mannequins' Ball, Jasieński's best dramatic work, was written originally in Russian and was subsequently translated into Polish by Anatol Stern, one of the leading poets of Polish Futurism.[15] The play is a satire on capitalist industrialists, in this case French, and their corrupt labor politics. Although thoroughly antibourgeois, like Jasieński's novel *I Burn Paris*, and procommunist, *The Mannequins' Ball* is an entertaining fantasy-satire built around the interplay of mannequins and real people. Set in Paris in the 1930s, it opens on the annual ball of animated mannequins. On this one occasion in the year when they are free to leave their fixed positions, tailors' mannequins from all over Paris come together in a leading fashion house, where an annual ball in the salon provides them the music for their own dance elsewhere in the building. The mannequins are typical headless tailors' dummies. Their bitter remarks about the cruelty of humans, which denies them the liberty to move about freely, recalls the theme of puppets, marionettes, and other inanimate figures that eventually rebel against their creators and masters. Needless to say, the mannequins' complaints about their lot in life, the success or failure of their strikes, and that more and more they are being replaced by mannequins with heads, reflect Jasieński's views on capitalist exploitation of workers.

The mannequins' ball is interrupted by the hurried arrival of a female mannequin who appears almost human because of the scarf she wears around the rod in which each mannequin's neck ends. Hardly has she explained to the others that she is eluding a man who has been pursuing her than the man himself appears. He assumes that the mannequins' ball is a masked ball, a masquerade of sorts. Since the mannequins can't afford to have the secret of their annual ball revealed, they refuse to let the man go. Their captive, it appears, is Paul Ribandel, a member of parliament and the head of a socialist workers' syndicate. He is on his way to a ball being held at the mansion of Arnaux, an automobile manufacturer. A strike has been called at Arnaux's plant the following day, and Ribandel and Arnaux are supposed to head it off. After a rump trial presided over by judges representing the largest sizes among them,[16] the mannequins kill Ribandel by cutting off his head with a huge pair of scissors. In the surreal fantasy world devised by Jasieński in *The Mannequins' Ball*, everything is possible, so no sooner does Ribandel lose his head than he tries to retrieve it and, failing to do so, runs away. The mannequins make no move to stop him; since he is headless, no one will believe his story. They hold a lottery among themselves to determine the winner of Ribandel's head as a trophy. The mannequin who wins it attaches it to his own body and takes off for Arnaux's ball in place of Ribandel.

The scenes set in Arnaux's mansion are intended to portray the pillars of capitalist industry as cynical, corrupt, and manipulative. If Arnaux is unable to deliver on a large order on schedule because of the impending strike, his competitor, Levasin, is prepared to create a panic in the financial world by dumping large quantities of Arnaux's stock. Moreover, Devignard, of the Banque de France, on which Arnaux relies for loans, will withhold further support in the event of a strike. Both Arnaux and Levasin are counting on Ribandel, whom they expect to appear at the ball any moment, to support their respective positions. The support of his workers' party, for or against the strike, is sufficient to decide the outcome of the matter. Both Arnaux and Levasin are prepared to give Ribandel huge bribes, and they are equally prepared to use female members of their families to sway him, knowing his weakness where women are concerned (the mannequins who rifle his billfold after his execution find photographs of nude women). The family life of capitalists, as represented by Jasieński, is as morally bankrupt as their industrial policies. Arnaux will use his willing daughter, Angelica, to lure Ribandel to his side, while Levasin will exploit his virtually estranged wife, Solange, for the same purpose. Adding spice to the mix is that Arnaux and Solange are having an affair at the same time that Levasin has designs on Angelica.

When the mannequin wearing Ribandel's head shows up at Arnaux's mansion, he is taken for the real Ribandel, and the campaign for his support gets under way in earnest. The humor of the situation rests on the utter innocence and literalness of the mannequin. He takes bribes from both Arnaux and Levasin and allows himself to be flirted with by both Angelica and Solange. When members of the workers' party come to ask for instructions on the strike, he tells them to support the first appeal they read him, which is in favor of the strike and happens to have the backing

of the communists. He also orders them to support strikes in both Arnaux's and Levasin's plants and to double their demands. Further bewil-
dering the two delegates from Ribandel's syndicate, he hands over to them
the two checks for 250,000 francs given him as bribe money by Arnaux
and Levasin, as well as 10,000 francs in banknotes taken from Ribandel's
billfold, this last to go directly to the strike committee. Unable to fathom
their "leader's" instructions, the two delegates decide that he is up to a
very shrewd game of politics that only he can handle because he has a
"head" on his shoulders. (There is a lot of similar punning about "heads,"
or the lack of them, in the play.) Not long after the delegates leave, the real
Ribandel shows up demanding the return of his head. But he is unceremo-
niously tossed out by Arnaux's servants, who refuse to take him seriously.
In the meantime, the mannequin-Ribandel is being challenged to duels by
Arnaux and Levasin after being discovered in compromising situations
first with Angelica and then with Solange. Knowing nothing about dueling, the mannequin is terrified and wants to flee Arnaux's; but because of
demonstrations outside the mansion related to the impending strike, the
police bar everyone from leaving. The situation further deteriorates when
Arnaux and Levasin at last learn how the mannequin-Ribandel "betrayed" them by supporting both sides, encouraging the workers to double their demands, and then turning their bribe money over to his workers'
syndicate. Levasin demands the duel take place. The mannequin shoots
and misses, as planned, but before Levasin can fire, the room goes dark.
The interruption of service is attributed to a general strike, for which the
communists are blamed. Just as the duel is about to resume by candlelight,
in comes the real Ribandel. The mannequin acknowledges the true identity of Ribandel, puts the dueling pistol in his hand, moves him into his
place on the firing line, returns his head, and tells those assembled that the
duel can continue. He then jumps out of a window and the play ends.

Overt propaganda in *The Mannequins' Ball* is outweighed by the play's
satire and humor. As the mannequin moves to return Ribandel's head to
its proper place in the final scene, he expresses his disenchantment with
human heads in terms whose meaning is self-evident:

> When I won your head, it seemed to me that I found a treasure. But to hell
> with your heads! Now I understand why you need them! Ours was a fair
> decision to cut off this pineapple's head (*pointing to the Leader* [Ribandel]).
> But can all of yours be cut off? There aren't enough scissors. Anyway, it's

not our affair. Some will come who will do it a lot better than we can. We thought that it was just us you wouldn't let live! But as it turns out, there are those who want to settle scores with you. (208–9)

Jasieński's interest in mannequins—in inanimate creatures that, in this instance, function as living beings—relates to the broad current of experimentation with puppets, marionettes, and similar wooden or mechanical figures by modernist and avant-garde artists in the early twentieth century. There is a clear reflection here, I believe, of Jasieński's literary origins in the Futurist movement. Hence it comes as no surprise that he would think of casting his anticapitalist satire in the form of a fantasy in which tailors' dummies would play the key role. One can also fairly assume that he may have felt encouraged along these lines by the freewheeling experimentation in the arts in Russia during the so-called NEP (New Economic Policy) of 1921–28. At the same time, he could not have been unaware when writing *The Mannequins' Ball* of the storm clouds of Stalinist repression gathering over such avant-garde flights of fancy. Hence the political obviousness of the play's closing lines, as well as the satirical treatment of the capitalist industrialists in the work as a whole. But it is doubtful that the finale would have had as strong an impact on audiences as the hilarious scenes involving the mannequin impersonating Ribandel and the two women who try to seduce him. It is these compromising scenes that result in the mannequin being challenged to a duel. Since the mannequin is a tailor's dummy, hence more knowledgeable about styles and sizes than romance, his literal responses to the women's flirtation produce probably the play's funniest moments. When Angelica asks him, for example, if he goes for the Solange type, the mannequin replies: "Hm . . . She's relatively well-shaped, but for a size 40 a little too flat in the hips." The dialogue continues:

> *Angelica.* How you analyze women in detail! You just undress them with a gaze. As for her, you're wrong. Her legs are too short. You can't tell it when she's dressed since she makes her waist high. But if you see her undressed, and I am sure you will soon enough, you'll see for yourself . . . Besides, that woman has no interest in sport, except love. And that doesn't necessarily make for a good figure. . . .
> *Mannequin (authoritatively).* Every woman has flaws. They all lack something. . . .
> *Angelica.* What flaws have you observed in me?

Mannequin (*scrutinizing her very carefully*). You have almost no bosom
at all. That's why dresses don't fit you very well.
Angelica (*insulted*). Wha-a-a-t? That's just impertinence, you know.
(*Impetuously undoes her shoulder straps and bares her breasts, her
back turned to the audience.*) Well, do you still stick to that opinion?
Mannequin (*very calmly casting the glance of a connoisseur over her, then
turning her slightly with his right hand and touching her shoulders
with his fingers*). Shoulder blades stick out a bit. (176)

Scenes like this, and the fantasy aspect of the play as a whole, were a
virtual guarantee that *The Mannequins' Ball* would raise serious objections in some Soviet quarters. There seems no doubt that Anatoli Lunacharsky, the Soviet Union's first commissar of national enlightenment and
a formidable writer and intellectual in his own right, had these in mind
when he wrote the preface to the original edition of Jasieński's play in
1931. He begins by stating that "Bruno Jasieński is unafraid of setting
himself on the track of the most contemporary artistic effects. Bold construction, fantasy unrestrained by improbability, overt satirical tenden-
tiousness, the pathos of indignation —these are the things that attracted
us in such previous works of his as *I Burn Paris* and *The Common Matter.*" Lunacharsky then goes on to speak about the recent debate in Soviet
literature and literary scholarship as to whether "the proletarian style of
literature consists of psychological realism or whether closer to the proletarian is free stylization, hyperbole, caricature, creating posterlike means
of expression in contrast to the naturalistic image"(119). Admitting that
he did not know what position Jasieński took in the debate, Lunacharsky declares that "in any case, in his splendid comedy, *The Mannequins'
Ball*, Jasieński for all practical purposes stood on the side of artistic-
tendentious fantasy." Lunacharsky then raises the question posed by
some critics as to whether such fantasy was necessary; would it not have
been possible to present the same events and types in their natural conditions in a realistic comedy? Of course, answers Commissar Lunacharsky,
but he then points out that "the relatively small amount of material presented by Jasieński on this occasion for the concrete characterization of
his bourgeois and socialists gains considerably by virtue of its being
shown to us in an unexpected mirror that distorts proportions unreally
but because of that superbly underlines the features of the phenomena presented which the author wished to show us in as plastic a way as possible"(120). By supporting Jasieński's right to fantasy in a political satire,

Lunacharsky threw the weight of his prestige behind the artistic experimentation that made the 1920s the most artistically extraordinary period in the Soviet Union's seveny-four-year history. But the automatons of party right-think could not be held at bay indefinitely. When the long night of Stalinist terror descended on Soviet culture, Jasieński was among its first victims.

NINE

Italian Futurism, *Teatro Grottesco*, and the World of Artificial Man

THE FUTURISTS AND THE PUPPET

A causal relationship need not be established between experiments with puppets, marionettes, and mechanical figures among the Italian Futurists and the subsequent prominence of the puppet motif in works of the *teatro grottesco* ("theater of the grotesque"), that eminently characteristic form of Italian drama that arose during World War I. Nevertheless, the Futurist rejection of traditional theatrics, which led to the attempt to find substitutes for the living actor, and the very short span of time separating the birth of Futurism from the *teatro grottesco*, suggest, at the very least, a common denominator.

Filippo Tommaso Marinetti, the founder of Italian Futurism, had in fact made a name for himself as a playwright on the basis of two early works both written originally in French. The first was *Le Roi Bombance* (*Bombance the King*), which was published in the *Mercure de France* in 1905 and caused a sensation when it was staged for the first time by Aurélien Lugné-Poe in 1909 at the Théâtre de l'Oeuvre, which had already established a reputation for sensation-provoking plays with its production of Alfred Jarry's *Ubu roi*. The second was *Poupées Electriques* (*Electric Puppets*), which was published by Sansot in Paris in 1909—the year in which Marinetti published his "Foundation and Manifesto of Futurism"—and was produced, in Italian translation, under the title *La donna è mobile* (*Woman Is Fickle*) on 15 January that same year by the Teatro Regio [Alfieri] of Turin.[1]

Electric Puppets is the more interesting of the two plays for present purposes because of its curious attempt to relate puppets and women to the Futurist adoration of electricity as the hallmark of sociotechnical transformation.[2] In its original version—that is, as Marinetti wrote it in French—the three-act play had an essentially traditional character, though it was rich in irony. In a health resort (*Kursaal*) on the Côte d'Azure, Mary, the Egyptian-born Levantine wife of the American engineer John Wilson, tries to console her friend Juliette Duverny, who is convinced that her fiancé, the naval officer Paul de Rozières, does not love her and is attracted to other women. To make matters worse, Juliette believes that Paul has fallen in love with Mary. Possibly suspecting the same, John Wilson expresses his dislike of Paul and orders his wife not to talk about him. At the end of the first act, Juliette, high-strung and distraught, commits suicide by throwing herself into the sea from a cliff as soon as Paul boards a ship for the Far East.

Although the first act supplies the information that John Wilson is an engineer in charge of several electric works and is well known as the inventor of electric puppets, Marinetti makes no use of the puppet motif until the second act, where it becomes dominant. The two puppets onstage are the life-size Monsieur Prudent, identified as a magistrate, and his female counterpart known as La Mère Prunelle because of her resemblance to Juliette's mother, Madame Rose Duverny, nicknamed Mère Prunelle. John Wilson's interest in puppets becomes clear during the act. Basically misanthropic, he prefers their company to that of humans. Moreover, their presence adds spice to his romantic life. Pretending that they are real people, he enjoys making "furtive" love to his wife behind their backs. For John, this is a way of keeping his marriage from growing stale. Mary is less enthusiastic about the family game and quarrels with John about the puppets. But convinced now that his wife's beauty obviates the need for any extraneous, artificial props to their marriage, and himself irritated by their frequent coughing and snoring, John decides to dump the puppets into the sea. The fishermen who see him do this believe that the puppets are real people and that John has committed some crime; they insist on calling the authorities. However, John has one of his servants retrieve the puppets and so prove to the fishermen that they are not human beings.

They still regard John as mad. In the third act, after the puppets have been stored again in the attic in which John keeps the others he invented, the romantic conflict returns to the forefront. Paul de Rozières returns from the Far East, ostensibly interested in visiting Juliette's grave and sharing memories of her with Mary. But it soon becomes obvious that uppermost on his mind is making love to Mary. Just as Paul sweeps Mary into a passionate embrace, John bursts in, revolver in hand. However, instead of firing at them, he hands the gun to his wife and tells her, with no small irony, that it will be her most useful and faithful companion during his absences. Hardly does Mary take the gun than she turns it on herself, expressing the wish as she falls dead to the ground that maybe now John will love her the way he does Juliette.

Although the puppets add greater interest to *Poupées Electriques*, their presence is limited to one act, and they are in general not well integrated into the action. They help define John's eccentricity and misanthropy but serve no larger purpose. The play on the whole is a rather trivial attempt to create drama out of the tangled relations of insubstantial characters. Apart from John himself, Mary is perhaps the most interesting figure, a typical Marinettian high-strung female. She is compared in the play to John's puppets in that both are animated by electricity, which may be the only other purpose the puppets serve in the work. In Mary's case (as in Juliette's) the current comes from the atmosphere as much as from the hypersensitive female nervous system to which Marinetti, as a Futurist, always felt a strong attraction.

When *Electric Puppets* was staged in Turin on 15 January 1909 as *La donna è mobile*, with appropriate but minor Italianization of locale and characters, it caused an uproar and was continuously interrupted by hisses and bursts of laughter. Reviews describe the evening as more pandemonium than performance. Only the pleas of the actors alone and then the actors and Marinetti together made it possible for the first act to continue. When further outbursts occurred, Marinetti took the stage again and addressed the following words to the audience: "I thank the organizers of this hooting, which profoundly honors me." It was like waving the red flag in front of the bull. The audience needed no further encouragement to reduce the rest of the evening to a shambles.[3]

When his ideas on Futurist theater and especially the highly compressed *sintesi* ("syntheses," short theatrical works) had crystallized, Marinetti did an abbreviated Italian version of his *La donna è mobile* under the title *Elettricità* (*Electricity*) or *Elettricità sessuale* (*Sexual Electricity*). This was in fact just the second act of the original play. It was first performed under the first title in Palermo on 14 September 1913; but the most important of the early productions was the one staged at the Teatro Dal Verne in Milan by the company of Gualtiero Tumiati on 16 January 1914. Marinetti himself appeared onstage at a certain point for the purpose of giving a political speech. However, the reaction of the audience was again so hostile that when the Futurist painter Umberto Boccioni followed Marinetti, he was not permitted to speak. The first Italian edition of *Sexual Electricity* appeared in Milan in 1920; it bore the subtitle *Sintesi futurista* (*Futurist Synthesis*), which now left no doubt as to Marinetti's intentions regarding the work. When the play was produced by Anton Giulio Bragaglia's famous Teatro degli Indipendenti on 28 May 1925, its title had undergone yet another change; it was now *Fantocci elettrici* (*Electric Puppets*), a translation into Italian of its original French title.[4]

Electricity or *Sexual Electricity* or *Electric Puppets*, although an abbreviated version of his *Poupées Electriques*, became a more important work in Marinetti's canon from the standpoint of the Italian theatrical tradition. Its eventual translation into Italian notwithstanding, *Roi Bombance* (*Re Baldoria*, in Italian) is generally related to early-twentieth-century French Symbolism and treated apart from Marinetti's Futurist theatrical works in Italian. By reducing *Poupées Electriques* to a single act divided into three short scenes, and by concentrating primarily on the interaction of humans and mechanical beings, Marinetti determined that the work would henceforth have to be situated within the context of the development of Futurist theater. It has been so treated since the first productions of *Electricity* in 1913 and 1914.

Marinetti's intention to highlight the puppet aspect of *Sexual Electricity* (as it will henceforth be referred to) is obvious the moment the curtain goes up. Dominating the set, before any actors appear, are the two puppets, Italianized now as Professor Matrimonio and Signora Famiglia. The completely bald Professor Matrimonio is attired in a green dressing gown, which exaggerates his paunch and clashes violently with his ruddy coloring and red sideburns. His lower lip is large and somewhat drooping; his large, myopic eyes become visible from time to time when he removes his pince-nez. His feet ensconced in huge slippers, he is seated in a rocking chair alongside a table piled high with old books. Seated nearby at a linen-covered table, Signora Famiglia holds in her hands some lace and a crochet needle. Her appearance is described in greater detail. Her hair is speckled gray, her face is tired but has a nasty expression around the mouth, her brow is wrinkled, and six greasy-looking curls hang down over it. She is wrapped in a chestnut-colored shawl.

When the first human characters make their appearance, the centrality of the puppets is underscored by the attention paid them. The place of John and Mary Wilson in the shortened Italian version is taken by Riccardo Marinetti and his wife, Maria. The scene is set in their villa (Monbonheur), which is located some two hundred meters from the *Kursaal*. The first speaking characters onstage are the servants Giovanni, Pietro, and Rosina. Rosina is an elegant young chambermaid who has recently entered the employ of the Marinettis and is now being shown by Giovanni how the puppets are operated. By inserting a lever of some sort into a small aperture in the puppet and then pressing a button, Giovanni makes Professor Matrimonio remove his pince-nez, wipe them with a handkerchief, and put them back on his nose. He will then pick up a newspaper or book placed on the edge of the table. By pressing a button concealed in one of Signora Famiglia's sleeves, Giovanni can make this puppet cough. Both puppets, in fact, are capable of coughing and snoring.

When Rosina expresses delight in her master's genius at being able to construct such puppets, Giovanni agrees, but he tells her that she still doesn't know what purpose they serve. Pietro is quick to enlighten her. It is, he says, a question of nerves. Referring to Riccardo and Maria Marinetti, he explains that there are people who are afraid of silence and solitude. The Marinettis spend entire evenings observing the puppets in action. So it would seem that the puppets were originally created for the sake of companionship, the permanent presence in their private quarters of someone other than the Marinettis themselves. But Rosina knows there is more to the story. The day before, she overheard the Marinettis talking, and she believes she understands the real reason for the puppets. The Marinettis enliven their romantic life by pretending to deceive the puppets by kissing and embracing behind their backs! As Rosina observes knowingly, "Stolen apples are tastier than bought ones . . . In love, it's the same thing."[5] This is an almost nightly ritual for which the Marinettis have an ample supply of puppets in the attic of their residence, although the only two who appear onstage are Professor Matrimonio and Signora Famiglia.

When Riccardo and Maria first enter in the second scene, Riccardo touches Professor Matrimonio's shoulder, which sets the puppet to coughing. Maria obviously doesn't share her husband's fascination with the puppets and confesses her exasperation at what she refers to as the "joke." Riccardo attributes her irritation to her high-strung, sensual nature, which masochistically derives pleasure from suffering. Maria also cannot get the recollection of Giulietta's suicide over Paolo out of her mind. This is, of course, a reference to the characters Juliette and Paul in the original *Poupées Electriques*. Riccardo suggests, hinting at her feelings for Paolo, that Maria's unhappiness was not caused only by the suicide of her friend Giulietta. When they begin to make love, a strong gust of wind from the open balcony doors extinguishes the two oil lamps on the tables at which the puppets are seated. Maria's discomfort at suddenly being plunged into darkness is intensified by the sound of one of the puppets snoring. Before his servants come to turn on the lights again, Riccardo plays a cruel joke on Maria by pretending to be Paolo who has come to kiss her before departing on his journey to the Far East. He also tells her that it is only she whom he loves.

When Maria complains bitterly about the poor taste of his actions, Riccardo tells her that it was just a little joke because she was never able to get used to living with his puppets and that she regards as bizarre and absurd the idea of his mixing his puppets into their love life. Although she confesses that the presence of the puppets sometimes does get on her nerves, she tells her husband, for the sake of placating him, that she doesn't really mind them that much. She then asks him: "Have you forgotten the first evening we spent in this villa? How we laughed when Professor Matrimonio coughed three times at the sound of our kissing!" (443). Puppetry and electricity come together at this point. Maria's sensuality is manifest in the delicacy of her nerves. When she complains that the puppets sometimes get on her nerves, Riccardo is quick to add that that happens "when there is much electricity in the air." Her simple "yes" in agreement excites him and he exclaims: "Oh! My little dynamo! All it takes is a bit of a storm to get you all worked up!" She takes this as proof of his contempt for women and tells him that he regards her as one of his puppets. Riccardo agrees, adding that she is the prettiest of all of them. He then declares that their mechanisms are identical: "Electricity causes our nerves to vibrate like well-conducting wires of delight." That is precisely why he likes to have the two puppets with them on "tempestuous nights like this . . . Their presence, in my view, is a splendid stimulant for the heart! It's like alcohol for my love . . . It keeps it awake and inebriates it." "I know," says Maria, "it excites you to kiss me behind the back of these good people" (444).

As Maria and Riccardo continue to argue over their respective feelings toward the puppets, another dimension of Riccardo's fondness for them emerges, one distinct from their role as an erotic stimulus. They represent, he tells Maria, symbols of everything that exists outside of their love, symbols, therefore, of the whole horrible reality ("simboli di tutta l'orribile realtà"): propriety, money, virtue, the old ways, monotony, boredom of the heart, weariness of the flesh, stupidity of lineage, social laws, and so on (446). Marinetti's puppet concoctions in *Sexual Electricity* are now clearly revealed as Futurist in inspiration. They are created by Riccardo as representations of the bourgeois world so detested by the Futurists. Their constant presence reaffirms his contempt for bourgeois society and validates his misanthropy. Animated by electricity, like the passionate woman Marinetti venerated and emblematizes in Maria in the play, they reflect the obsession with electricity as the great transformer of society on the part of Marinetti and the other Futurists. In 1910, in his manifesto *Contro Venezia passatista* (*Against Past-Loving Venice*), Marinetti, for example, called for "the reign of Holy Electricity" finally to come and "liberate Venice from its venal moonshine of furnished rooms."[6] His manifesto *Guerra solo igiene del mondo* (*War, the World's Only Hygiene*, 1911–15) contains a paean to "electrical war." The famous treatise on the variety theater of 1913 similarly hails the common origin of man and variety theater in electricity: "The Variety Theater, born as we are from electricity" ("Il Teatro di Varietà, nato con noi dall'Elettricità").[7]

Another Futurist-inspired interpretation of the puppet figure appears in the *sintesi Ombre + Fantocci + Uomini* (Shadows + Puppets + Humans), which was first published in the third number of the Futurist review *Teatro* in 1927, by Luciano Folgore (real name Omero Vecchi). Like Giacomo Balla, Umberto Boccioni, Francesco Cangiullo, Carlo Carrà, Paolo Buzzi, Luigi Russolo, Gino Severini, and others, Folgore appears in several of Marinetti's writings as one of the founders of Futurism.[8] Known especially for his many parodic poems, as well as for the poems he composed for the Futurist aerial theater, Folgore was one of the Italian and other European avant-garde dramatists whose works were presented in the Teatro

Sperimentale degli Indipendenti founded in Rome in 1923 by Anton Giulio Bragaglia, an assiduous promoter of Futurist art.[9]

A typical Futurist *sintesi*, or very short play reflective of the Futurists' celebration of rapid change and velocity as signposts of the new century, Folgore's *Shadows + Puppets + Humans* is especially interesting for its interplay of humans and puppets. In this respect, it foreshadows one of Massimo Bontempelli's best-known plays, *Siepe a nordovest* (*Hedge to the Northwest*, 1927). The plus signs in the title of Folgore's plays merit a word of explanation. Marinetti writes about mathematical signs in *Lo splendore geometrico e meccanico e la sensibilità numerica* (*Geometric and Mechanical Splendor and the Numerical Sensibility*, 1914). They are used, he declares, to achieve "marvelous syntheses and share, with their abstract simplicity of anonymous gears, in rendering the geometric and mechanical splendor."[10] Obviously related to the Futurist assault on syntax, the plus sign in particular conveys, or is meant to convey, synthesis, acceleration, and the clustering of equivalent sensations. Simultaneity, which the plus sign also connotes, was one of the principal tenets of Futurist artistic theory. Probably the earliest manifestation of its importance to the Futurists was the publication of Marinetti's play titled simply *Simultaneità* (*Simultaneity*) in 1915. The concept was developed even further by Marinetti in another play, *I vasi communicanti* (*The Communicating Vases*), which followed *Simultaneity* by a year.[11]

What simultaneity meant in Futurist practice was the occurrence of different events at the same time, action onstage, for example, taking place simultaneously in different locations. Although this was in part an attempt by the Futurists to parallel the cinematographer's ability to move instantaneously from one locale to another, it was also reflective of their sense of the rapidity with which change was occurring in their own time. Certainly one way of rendering the fast pace of modern times was to move back and forth between several unrelated, or apparently unrelated, events, collapsing in the process both space and time. Hence in Folgore's *Shadows + Puppets + Humans*, the plus signs indicate that the actions of the three components of the play occur at the same time.

The humans of Folgore's play are Job, Maxim, and Blu', who is the only female. When we first meet them, it is midnight and they have just entered some room in an indeterminate country. Contrasting with the ordinary parlor furniture of the room is a large "*opaline window with a transparent door in a rear wall. Everything sumptuously illuminated.*"[12] Exhausted from a three-year rush around the world without ever stopping and resting, the three humans are delighted to be in what Maxim calls a "dream province" far away from everything. Here, at last, will they be able to enjoy peace and quiet. Job announces his intention to marry Blu' and set up a "hut of leaves," far from all the streets. As if in mockery of the Futurist obsession with speed, Folgore's characters express only disillusionment with the pace and technology of urban life. They have been crammed into an American elevator and a tiny Japanese house with its transparent walls. After so much "laughing and jumping on the trampoline of pleasure," Job, like the others, yearns just for rest and the simple life. After a while they stop conversing, and darkness follows silence in the room. While they apparently sleep, apparitions appear in the form of three marionettes who are so insignificant that they resemble three ordinary puppets. One is dressed in red, one in green, and one in yellow. They are joined by three shadows of different size which appear against the rear window. As the three humans talk in their sleep with voices "*as if changed*," and with slow gestures, the shadows and the marionettes execute different movements. Maxim is the first to speak, and he sets the pattern for the other two humans. Unlike their professed longing for rest and solitude while awake, the characters utter diametrically opposite sentiments in their sleep. Maxim, who previously described himself as a "little old man" ("piccolo vecchio"), confesses to "dangerous desires," a lust to grab "young flesh," and to enjoy "a little fresh love." Making fun of having been referred to as a "young girl," Blu' confesses to a desire to appear "entirely nude before a crowd" and thrills at the thought of beholding two men fighting to the death over her. Job denounces the "calm and serene happiness" he had previously praised; "I am," he declares, "a very stupid and very overbearing cynic. I don't give a hoot in hell for education" (77). As the shadows and marionettes coordinate their various movements with the humans' speech and actions, Folgore's intention seems clearer. While awake, the humans mouth insincere platitudes like manipulated marionettes. Their true natures reveal themselves in sleep and emerge as both shadows and marionettes to mock their alter egos. The apparitions that mimic their actions in sleep in fact mock their marionette-like behavior in the wakeful state.

Some knocks at the door awaken the humans and the stage is again illuminated. As they look at one another, the humans no longer seem to recognize themselves and indeed ask who they are. Although the shadows have obviously disappeared, the marionettes are still visible; but each falls to the floor as the characters in turn express ignorance of one another. They discover that what they have in common is that each disembarked that morning from the same steamship after sailing around the world for three years. The curious fact that they sailed aboard the same ship without ever having met they now ascribe to "perhaps life in velocity" ("forse la vita in velocità," 78). When Job finally opens the door to see who has been knocking, a bourgois family enters and immediately expresses outrage at finding strangers in their lodgings. As Job, Maxim, and Blu' are about to exit the room, Job remarks that when a person comes to a halt after three years of traveling all around, it's easy to lose one's way when looking for something. "It's the force of inertia," he says, "that causes the unexpected to happen" (79). Just then, the bourgeois mother notices the three marionettes lying on the floor and asks what they are. Picking one up, Blu' exclaims "Marionettes!" The bourgeois father orders the intruders to take their toys (*giuocattoli*) with them. Shouting "Our toys!" in unison, Job, Blu', and Maxim bring the *sintesi* to an end indignantly rejecting the notion that they would still be dragging anything as useless as marionettes around with them. Maxim actually has the last word, the better to convey the irony of the play. In sleep he revealed the hypocrisy of his life which, while he wears the mask of a philanthropist, has never lost the opportunity to crush the joy of others. Now he declares, with reference to the marionettes, "A philanthropist like me is interested only in human beings" (79).

Surpassing Futurist efforts in the drama were the experiments by Futurist visual and scenic artists to create a new "plastic theater" of objects built around mechanistic and geometrized puppets and marionettes intended to replace the living actor and ballet dancer. The most noteworthy of these was the marionette spectacle *Balli plastici* (*Plastic Dances*), which was staged for the first time in April 1918 at the Teatro dei Piccoli puppet theater, founded by Vittorio Podrecca in Rome in 1914 on the premises of the Palazzo Odescalchi. Consisting of four short performances—"Pagliacci" ("Clowns"), "L'uomo dai baffi" ("The Man with the Moustache"), "L'orso azzurro" ("The Blue Bear"), and "I selvaggi" ("The Savages")— the spectacle featured brightly colored marionettes in a Cubistic land-

Fortunato Depero, "I miei Balli Plastici," Balli Plastici.
(Courtesy Museo di Arte Moderna e Contemporanea di Trento e Rovereto)

scape especially striking for the fairy tale–like and tropical flora and fauna
of the first and fourth segments, respectively. The work was the brainchild
of the now all but forgotten Swiss writer and amateur Egyptologist Gilbert Clavel and his close friend, the Futurist painter and sculptor Fortunato Depero.[13] Depero designed and built the marionettes for *Plastic
Dances*, Clavel and Depero collaborated on the choreography, and Al-
fredo Casella (the editor of the Rome review *Ars Nova*) took charge of the
musical direction. Also assisting in the production were Gerald Tyrwhitt
(Lord Berners), an English composer, painter, and writer who had studied
music with Casella and Stravinsky, the musicians Francesco Malipiero
and Chemenow (which some believe was a pseudonym for Béla Bartók),
and the well-known puppeteer Gorno Dell'Acqua, who asumed responsi-

Fortunato Depero, "Selvaggi rossi i neri," Balli Plastici.
(Courtesy Museo di Arte Moderna e Contemporanea di Trento e Rovereto)

bility for the movement of the figures, a particularly demanding task in view of the "extreme robotization"—as Maurizio Scudiero terms it[14]—of the marionettes. It was, in fact, as a result of the problems posed by the rigidity of the wooden figures in *Plastic Dances* that Depero began giving serious consideration to the design of a more flexible marionette-robot made of rubber or tin and one that might even be transparent.[15]

These new ideas came to be realized in his subsequent theatrical work, especially the synthetic mechanical "drama" *Anihccam del 3000* (first staged in Milan on 10 January 1924), in which the principal protagonists are two locomotives in love with the central railroad station, and in the Cabaret del Diavolo, which Depero created in the basement of the Hôtel Elite et des Etrangers on Rome's via Basilicata in late 1921 and early

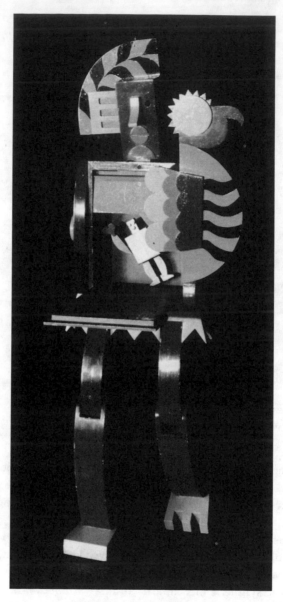

Fortunato Depero,
"La Grande Selvaggia," Balli Plastici.
(Courtesy Museo di Arte Moderna
e Contemporanea di Trento e Rovereto)

1922.[16] The inauguration of the cabaret took place on 19 April 1922 before an elite audience of prominent Futurists—Marinetti, Folgore, and Casella—and other artists on the fringe of the Futurist movement, such as the dramatist Massimo Bontempelli. Enrico Prampolini, like Depero a leading Futurist painter and scenographer, was the author of the manifesto *Scenografia e coreografia futurista* (*Futurist Scenography and Choreography*, 1915). Going beyond Meyerhold, to whom (as well as to Stanislavsky) he attributed a "nauseating classicism," and Gordon Craig, whom he credited at least with making "some limited innovations," Prampolini advocated two principal means for the renovation of the theater.[17] The first, obviously inspired by the Futurist obsession with electricity as the principal source of light in modern technological society, was an "illuminating stage," to consist of

> electrochemical colors, fluorescent mixtures that have the chemical properties of being susceptible to electric currents and diffusing luminous colorations of all tonalities according to the combinations of fluorine and other mixtures of gases. The desired effects of exciting luminosity will be obtained with electric neon (ultraviolet) tubes, systematically arranging these mixtures according to an agreed-upon design in this immense scenodynamic architecture.

The second—and here Prampolini went beyond not only Craig but also Marinetti himself—called for the abolition of the living actor from the stage:

> In the final synthesis, human actors will no longer be tolerated, like children's marionettes or today's supermarionettes recommended by recent reformers; neither one nor the other can sufficiently express the multiple aspects conceived by the playwright. . . .
>
> Vibrations, luminous forms (produced by electric currents and colored gases) will wriggle and writhe dynamically, and these authentic actor-gases of an unknown theater will have to replace living actors.

Prampolini sought to realize the supercharged ideas advanced in his manifesto by means of the marionette figures he designed for productions of the Russian Leonid Andreev's quasi-Maeterlinckian play *The Life of Man* and the Frenchman Pierre Albert-Birot's Symbolist drama *Matoum et Tévibar*, which he mounted in Rome in 1917 and 1919, respectively. Prampolini's inclination toward greater abstraction is especially evident in his subsequent work at Ricciardi's Teatro del Colore (Theater of Color) in 1920, as well as in his pantomime *Il mercante di cuori* (The Peddler of Hearts, 1927), in which inanimate abstracted human shapes suspended from cords appeared alongside live actors. Other Futurist artists also contributed to the creation of a mechanical theater. Ivo Pannaggi, who together with Vinicio Paladini issued the first *Manifesto dell'Arte meccanica* (*Manifesto of Mechanical Art*) in 1922, also staged his own *Ballo meccanico* (Mechanical Ballet) on 2 June that same year at the Circolo delle Cronache d'Attualità of Bragaglia's Casa d'Arte before it officially became the Teatro Sperimentale degli Indipendenti di Roma. In April 1927, Bragaglia mounted another example of Futurist "mechanical art," *L'Angoscia delle macchine* (*The Anguish of the Machines*, first published in German in *Der Sturm* in 1925) by Ruggero Vasari. By the time Futurist scenography, with its emphasis on an abstracted, geometrized, and mechanistic theater of objects and colors, had run its course by the early 1930s, Marinetti's pre–World War I manifestoes on the variety theater and the Futurist synthetic theater had come to seem relatively tame.

THE *TEATRO GROTTESCO*: LUIGI CHIARELLI, ROSSO DI SAN SECONDO, AND ENRICO CAVACCHIOLI

While Futurist painters and scenographers such as Depero, Prampolini, Pannaggi, and Vasari were devoting their energies to a mechanical theater of robotized marionettes, the dramatists associated with the *teatro grottesco* were exploring the metaphoric potential of the puppet figure. Although often identified with Pirandello, who was spiritually akin to it, the *teatro grottesco* was in fact inaugurated by the play *La maschera e il volto* (*The Mask and the Face*, 1916) by Luigi Chiarelli. Not only did *The Mask and the Face* launch the grotesque movement in Italian drama in the early twentieth century, but it also became Chiarelli's best-known, most celebrated play and the basis of his reputation as a dramatist.

Although *The Mask and the Face* features no puppet figures as such, its exploration of illusion and reality in contemporary bourgeois society, of the masks social conventions impose on the individual, sets the stage for the related use of the puppet motif in subsequent Italian grotesque drama. Subtitled *A Grotesque Comedy*, Chiarelli's play has a Lake Como setting and pivots on the theme of marital infidelity. When he discovers that his wife, Savina, has been unfaithful to him, Count Paolo forces her into exile and pretends that he has killed her and dumped her body into the lake. The lawyer who agrees to handle Paolo's defense is, in fact, Savina's lover, and he accepts the case as the best way of avoiding suspicion concerning his own possible guilt. Paolo is sentenced to prison but acquitted some ten months later on the grounds that he committed his "crime" in order to protect his honor. Although he returns to his hometown in triumph, Paolo becomes dismayed at the fallout from his deception. The reputation of his wife had to be further destroyed by his lawyer in order to win his acquittal, and in a characteristically grotesque turn of events, the lawyer's wife, caught up in the joyous welcome of Paolo back from prison, gives herself to him. Shortly after a corpse is fished from the lake and identified as Savina, Savina herself returns to offer Paolo, as she says, the pardon of his victim. Discovering that he still loves his wife, Paolo hides her. Her former lover, Paolo's lawyer, suffering pangs of conscience, comes in the meantime to confess that it was he who was Savina's lover. Paolo orders him out of his house in disgust. On the afternoon of Savina's "funeral," Paolo understands at last that despite what transpired between them, he still loves his wife and must somehow reestablish a life with her. When Savina's return becomes known, Paolo is threatened with prosecution for perjury and chooses to flee abroad with Savina rather than attempt to rationalize his behavior to the town. As he and Savina take flight at the end of the play, a funeral march is heard in the background, closing the work on a note appropriate to the grotesque character of the comedy as a whole.

The basic theme addressed by Chiarelli in *The Mask and the Face* was taken up by other Italian dramatists identified with the grotesque movement for whom the puppet or marionette figure seemed of equal metaphoric value to that of the mask. The best examples occur in plays by Rosso di San Secondo (Pier [Luigi] Maria) and Massimo Bontempelli.

Of a Sicilian noble family and educated in Rome, Rosso di San Secondo's most notable play, *Marionette che passione!* (*Marionettes, What Passion!* 1918), also happens to be one inspired by the metaphoric implications of the marionette. As soon as the work was finished, toward the end of 1917, Rosso sent a copy to Pirandello, with whom he enjoyed a friendship going back to the time he first came to Rome, to study law at the university. Convinced of its potential, Pirandello proposed it to the director Virgilio Talli, who, while initially confused by the play, eventually decided to stage it. It was a smashing success and became the foundation of Rosso's international reputation as a dramatist.

In a note to the actors ("Avvertenza per gli attori"), Rosso makes clear his intention that the main characters in *Marionettes, What Passion!* be understood as marionettes controlled by the wires of passion. He insists, however, that the actors play the parts not comically but in such a way as to convey a "sense of tragic humor" ("un sentimento di tragico umorismo") since the sufferings of his three leading figures are in fact profoundly human.[18] The sufferings Rosso refers to are those of passion, and it is passion that reduces his humans to marionettes, hence his characterization of them in his note to the actors as "uomini, ridotti marionette" ("humans who have become marionettes"). Although by no means consistent in this respect, the world of twentieth-century Italian grotesque drama is primarily that of urban bourgeois society. The distortions and exaggerations of the grotesque style become the means by which the alienation and estrangement, the fundamental isolation, of urban man are exposed. As we shall see later, the Franco-German writer Yvan Goll shared with his counterparts in Italy and elsewhere the belief that only an art of the grotesque was appropriate for demasking the spiritual emptiness of bourgeois society.

Rosso di San Secondo's three human characters-become-marionettes are urban everymen identified only as the Lady in Blue Fox (La Signora dalla Volpe Azzurra), the Gentleman in Gray (Il Signore in Grigio), and the Gentleman in Mourning (Il Signore a Lutto). They all meet by chance in certainly one of the most forlorn of European urban settings, the darkish main telegraph office in Milan on a drab, drizzly Sunday afternoon. Rosso was at such pains to establish the gloominess and monotonousness of the setting that he preceded his play text with an extended word picture of it in the form of a four-page *preludio* (prelude). Echoes of Marinetti are also audible here. Rosso speaks of the "somnolent boredom" of the big city on an inclement Sunday afternoon as being conducive to unusual encounters among the flotsam and jetsam of humanity precisely in such refuges for the lonely as the portico of a theater, a corner of the stock exchange, or the entrance hall of the main post and telegraph office. Such people, to whom he refers, in the manner of Marinetti and the Futurists, as "organisms of electric sensibility," feel, react, and judge in an instant:

> And if their anguish is stronger than the contempt that each has for the miseries of the other similar to his own, all that's needed is the rub of an elbow, the movement of a hand, the poke of an umbrella, a glove let fall, a sigh, a word that gurgles or murmurs in the throat before being uttered, because once the mask of reserve is shattered, they will abandon themselves viscer-

ally to an all-consuming orgy of confessions, in order suddenly to start knitting, barely following the hasty *mea culpa*, the first strand of a more complicated sin which in an hour will thrust them among the meanders of the most grotesque tragedy. (70 71)

And so the Lady in Blue Fox, the Man in Gray, and the Man in Mourning are just such "organisms of electric sensibility" whom chance throws together at a writing table. They have all come to send telegrams to those responsible for their present emotional misery. The Lady in Blue Fox has run away from the lover she believes has cheated on her; the Man in Gray has obviously suffered much at the hands of a woman; and the Man in Mourning mourns the wife who has betrayed him and thus no longer exists in his eyes. The first to appear are the Lady in Blue Fox and the Man in Mourning. The man initiates a conversation when he observes that the woman is having as difficult a time as he is in drafting a telegram, which in the end neither will be able to send. Further conversation triggers the exchange of confessions Rosso mentions in the above quotation; the sense of betrayal and wretchedness of the characters comes to the surface, and before long the Man in Mourning suggests that for the sake of their mutual emotional consolation, they take an apartment and live together. At this point, the Man in Gray, who has seated himself at the same writing table, overhears the conversation between them, gets up, and in a lengthy monologue addressed primarily to the Lady in Blue Fox, argues persuasively against the arrangement. So convinced is he of the wrongness of such a course, on the basis obviously of his own experience, that he foresees a calamitous end to their relationship if they move in together: "If tomorrow you don't become ashamed of yourselves like a couple of thieves and can continue the fiction of helping one another, of being able to overcome your passion for one, two, or maybe three months, later on it's going to be worse. You'll wind up hating each other, and in the end one of you will kill the other" (88).

In the stage direction preceding this monologue, Rosso di San Secondo establishes the apparent lucidity and rationality of the speaker. But however the actor playing the part is to achieve the effect, the eyes of the Man in Gray possess a "*vitreous sparkle*" that reveals the "*abnormality of his state*" (87). Thus, all three principal characters are distinguished by their electrically charged, highly emotional condition, which produces their grotesque behavior throughout the play and in turn transforms them into marionettes pulled now this way, now that, by the wires of passion.

Convinced that the Man in Gray is right after all, the Lady in Blue Fox takes her leave of both men and heads for the apartment—rooming house she is temporarily sharing with her friend, a singer, and two young ballerinas. Shortly afterward the Man in Gray appears there, ostensibly to return a glove left behind in the telegraph office by the woman. The watchman who had retrieved the glove originally had also found a crumpled note with the singer's address. Since the Lady in Blue Fox has not yet returned, the Man in Gray takes advantage of her absence to warn the singer of her friend's great vulnerability and the danger posed, he believes, by the Man in Mourning. Soon the Lady in Blue Fox appears, followed immediately by the Man in Mourning, who, upon seeing the other man, is convinced the latter warned the woman off just so as to pursue her himself. A wild emotional scene ensues with the Lady in Blue Fox dissolving into spasms of hysterical laughter and uncontrollable weeping. Intensifying the grotesqueness of the situation are the efforts of the singer to restore calm and the presence of the two young ballerinas, with whom the Man in Gray suggests he and the Man in Mourning dance to change the mood. The scene (and the second act) ends with the singer getting the Lady in Blue Fox and the two men to agree to join her for supper at a *trattoria* that evening after she leaves the theater.

The grotesque comes full circle in the last act. When the three principals arrive at the *trattoria*, the Man in Gray has a waiter set a separate table for three additional guests, who most likely will not appear. He has in mind the one man and two women responsible for all their misery. The Man in Mourning and the Lady in Blue Fox oppose the idea, but the Man in Gray, who now dominates the action, insists. As they await the arrival of the singer, they drink, their mood lightens, and the Man in Gray ecstatically proposes that they become a threesome and travel the world over with the money he still has. But the mood evaporates with the surprise appearance of the lover of the Lady in Blue Fox, identified just as the One Who Was Not Supposed to Arrive. The others try hurriedly to hide the woman, but her lover catches the scent of familiar perfume, spots her fur, and demands her presence. When she emerges from hiding, she is deathly pale and weak on her legs. Without saying a word, she lets him virtually drag her away. The despair of the two men left behind is palpable. Just before he bids a hasty farewell to the Man in Mourning, the Man in Gray empties the powdery contents of a small paper envelope in a glass of champagne and drinks it. It is obviously poison. A few moments after he leaves, the singer finally arrives from the theater. When the Man in Mourning informs her of what happened to her friend and then indicates the empty envelope left behind on the table by the Man in Gray, she wants to run and look for him. But the Man in Mourning tells her that it is useless and then breaks down, sobbing and begging her to stay and help him live. The play ends on the poignant yet ironic exclamation by the singer, the Man in Gray on her mind: "A pity! Maybe I could have loved him!" (117).

Consciously opposing the turn-of-the-century neoromantic celebration of the power of the will as embodied in the Nietzschean (and D'Annunzian) "superman," Rosso di San Secondo dramatizes in *Marionettes, What Passion!* the insufficiency of the will when confronted with the omnipotence of passion. The gross exaggerations and ironies of the grotesque vividly convey the utter helplessness of his main characters in the grip of passion, the futility of their attempts to overcome passion, and their ultimate reduction to the level of marionettes. The profound despair felt, for example, by the most important of the characters, the Man in Gray, proceeds as much from the awareness of the impotence of his own will as from the final blow to his fragile mental stability. Suicide becomes the only way out. The social relevance of a play such as *Marionettes, What Passion!* resides in its implied indictment of urban bourgeois life as the root cause of the impotence represented by the characters. It is the spiritual emptiness of bourgeois society, the sense of alienation and isolation it gives rise to, that creates conditions conducive to the emotional debilities dramatized in the play. To read Rosso di San Secondo's most striking dramatic work only, or primarily, as a response to the superman syndrome of the turn of the century is to miss that other important level on which it operates, its use of the grotesque to paint a grim picture of a society in which humans become impotent in the hands of their own emotions, merely puppets of passion.

Another dramatist of the *teatro grottesco* who probed the ramifications of the puppet or marionette figure was Enrico Cavacchioli. Although he began his career as a Futurist poet, Cavacchioli turned to playwriting while in his twenties and scored his first big success with *L'uccello del paradiso* (*The Bird of Paradise*, 1918). Gigi Livio, an authority on the *teatro grottesco*, calls the play "the work most harmonic in its structure and the clearest in its poetics of the Italian grotesque theater of the early twentieth century." [19] In *The Bird of Paradise*, as well as in his more problematic but well-received play *Quella che t'assomiglia* (*She Who Resembles Herself*,

1920), Cavacchioli uses the puppet motif both to convey the outlook of the grotesque on contemporary society and to demolish what remained of bourgeois drama.

The trite, conventional plot material Cavacchioli draws on in *The Bird of Paradise* for the purpose of theatrical subversion is that of marital infidelity. The unfaithful partner in this instance is Anna, the wife of a professor of ornithology named Giovanni Ardeo. After a year of marriage, Anna has left her husband to travel around the world with a succession of lovers. Their daughter, Donatella, remains behind to be raised by her father. When Donatella turns eighteen, Anna persuades her to join her, in effect inviting her into her own way of life with its travels, lovers, and seductions. But the arrangement turns sour when Anna's most recent lover, an unscrupulous young adventurer named Mimotte, falls in love with Donatella. However, before the relationship takes its natural course, Anna succeeds in ending it by making Donatella privy to all her secrets, including the nature of her own relationship with Mimotte. Donatella returns to live with her father, while a distraught Anna can now contemplate living out the remainder of her life in loneliness. So much for the basic plot of *The Bird of Paradise*.

The play's most intriguing character, indeed the one about whom "the play pivots," as Cavacchioli himself advises in a note, is none of the abovementioned principals. It is instead the figure identified just as He (Lui). Cavacchioli's description of him alludes to the enigmatic and surreal: "A personage-abstraction, unreal, philosophical. An old centenarian. His body survives. His spirit is from the other world. He has a cadaverous head. But his bearing is still youthful, faultless, most elegant. His ironic, sharp, ingratiating intonation consists of vocal contrasts: a slow and deep voice, empty and thin falsettos. Bragging, sneering, demonic."[20]

First appearing as an acquaintance of Anna's, He's function in the play is that of an ironic observer of the frailties of the ordinary mortals into whose midst he has been set. But in his uncanny, almost prophetic ability to see where events are heading, he assumes the aspect of a puppeteer who controls the wires of his puppetlike humans and delights in beholding the working out of actions he himself has set in motion. There is an echo here of the character of Georg Merklin in Schnitzler's *Puppet Master*. When asked his profession in act 2, He replies: "I cross life like threads of skein, until the skein becomes inextricable. . . . I have no impulses, because I have no ideals to defend. I have no remorse, because I have no virtue to

follow. I take no oaths, because I have no beliefs. I just fabricate life"
(211).

Later, alluding to his otherworldliness, He tells Mimotte that he is not
a man, not even a dream, just a shadow, and that he represents the "four
stages of putrefaction of sentiment" (224). Toward the end of the play, he
speaks unequivocally of his role as a puppeteer:

> The romance is over. It's time to change the subject because the catastrophe
> is near and the knot has come undone. I have done my best to give all these
> puppets a soul, but I squeezed out nothing but words. A false love, false ma-
> ternal piety, masculine egoism, a few small, violent quarrels. But nothing
> that rose higher than two centimeters off the ground, and logic according
> to others instead of according to me. (244–45)

He closes his final address with the caustic remark that he is now going in
search of "living people."

Enigmatic and emblematic at the same time, Cavacchioli's He in *The
Bird of Paradise* is characterized by Franco Angelini, an authority on
twentieth-century Italian drama, as a contemporary version of the superman, now attired in such a way, as befitted the times, to suggest a mechanical and marionette-like figure. Moreover, He unites in himself the epic
personage and the new concept of the stage character as marionette, that
is, in Angelini's words, "the scenic figure deprived of any naturalistic distinguishing features (such as name, profession, attributes, and so on) and
the simple bearer of an existential petition resolved in terms of a theatrical
function."[21] To Silvio D'Amico, whose *Il teatro dei fantocci* (1920) enjoys
the reputation of a seminal study of twentieth-century Italian avant-garde
drama, a figure such as He originated in the "marionettistic tendency [of
post-Naturalist Italian comedy] toward the concentration in a few and
very marked grimaces of a dreamt quintessence of human comedy and
tragedy."[22]

Cavacchioli continued his subversion of bourgeois drama in *She Who
Resembles Herself*, but with a few different twists and without achieving
the clarity of conception of *The Bird of Paradise*. The subject is again marital infidelity. This time the errant wife is a young woman named Gabriella
who seeks comfort in the arms of another man to whom she turns in despair when it appears that her husband, Gabriele, will never return from
the World War. He has been gone four years and has apparently disappeared without a trace. In descriptions of the main characters appended

to the *dramatis personae*, Cavacchioli introduces elements of the surreal and grotesque, in keeping with the play's designation as a "vision." Gabriella, for example, has "green hair." She is also "fickle, carnal, and rancid in sentiment ["rancida di sentimento," *rancido* being one of Cavacchioli's favorite adjectives], finding her humanity only in sentiment."[23] Her lover, Leonardo, who runs a fortunetelling parlor, is "in his forties, bald, moustached, and with a large paunch. He represents the static, showy, frightful sense of life" (580). The play's principal character, derivative of He in *The Bird of Paradise*, is the Mechanic. His description is somewhat similar to that of He: "He is the inexorable, mechanical practicality of existence. He has two wheels where his eyes should be. He resembles in all a contraption of levers and small gears rather than a man" (580). Like He, the Mechanic also stresses his own un-humanness. Hardly is he ushered into Leonardo's fortunetelling parlor early in the play than he declares that it isn't easy for him to introduce himself because he doesn't belong "to humanity, or at least to your [Leonardo's] humanity" (596). When Leonardo makes light of this—"Ah, you've come from the other world. I understand. It's the fashion nowadays" (596)—the Mechanic replies with a reference to the theater, and to the character of He himself, which makes greatest sense only if viewed in the context of Cavacchioli's assault on the traditions of bourgeois drama initiated above all in *The Bird of Paradise*:

> That may be. I went one evening to a theater, to take in a bad comedy. The same old plots. The same old artifices of bourgeois romanticism.... Among others, a character—he's called He—made the improbable claim of being a little terrestrial and a little metaphysical, of representing a little the conscience, a little the remorse of people, and he moved his ideological strings in such a way as to give his living puppets a soul instead of words. An error! (596)

Unlike He, the Mechanic has a more terrestrial presence—he is in reality Gabriele's uncle, whose real name is Giampiero Morèno. It is he who comes to Leonardo's parlor to tell him, and Gabriella, that Gabriele has returned from the war alive, but blind and badly wounded. He demands that Leonardo allow Gabriella to return to her husband to pick up the threads of their war-shattered life. Leonardo adamantly refuses and implores Gabriella to remain with him. The contest over the young woman's will between Leonardo and the Mechanic, between two antagonists—two forces, really—representing different attitudes toward man and life, becomes the focus of much of the play's interest. For her part, Gabriella, full of remorse and despair, in the end returns to her husband as the only honorable course open to her.

In attempting to define his own essence in *The Bird of Paradise*, He declares that he is not human, not even a dream, but a shadow. Although he speaks of himself this way, He is seen only corporeally. Gabriele, however, appears most of the time just as a shadow who speaks but who can be seen and heard only by the audience. Physically, he is, in a sense, little more than a shadow of his former self. But in his description of him, Cavacchioli seems to have given him some of He's attributes or, to put it another way, to have distributed some of He's attributes to both the Mechanic and Gabriele: "Tall, lean, spectral, mournful, he is the ideal that is always trampled" (580).

It is, nevertheless, the Mechanic who remains the most riveting, if problematic, character in *She Who Resembles Herself*. Whereas in *The Bird of Paradise*, He only speaks of manipulating ordinary people like puppets, the Mechanic actually creates puppets who resemble real people, in a clear reminiscence of Marinetti's *Electric Puppets*. He is, in fact, called the Mechanic because, as he says, he makes "wheels and contraptions." However, his principal mechanical activity consists in assembling puppets who not only resemble real people but, when activated by a lever, can speak. It is by means of his puppets, of which we see only those of Gabriella and Gabriele in the play, that his darker vision of life is conveyed.

Critical of He in his introductory dialogue with Leonardo because of He's original desire to create puppets with souls, the Mechanic goes on to explain what he means, thereby divulging his own outlook:

> An error, I said. I have created mechanical puppets to whom I have chosen to give words instead of souls. The mechanism! I have discovered the mechanism! And my puppets, to be sure, speak like humans. Do you understand me? They behave like humans. All I have to do is move a little lever for the mechanism to repeat regularly, phonographically, that which humans are accustomed to repeating. One, ten, a hundred, thousands of times. (596)

Leonardo continues to insist that none of this interests him and that he would like the Mechanic to leave his establishment; but the latter has no intention of doing so and goes on discussing his pet project:

> I wanted to add that my creations lack the power to reason and possess the sole logic of the artifice that I have constructed. Thus, when I return to my

quarters, and the irritated little pseudo-human fanfare takes hold of me, I am completely happy. I have constructed my poor wife, my mother-in-law, your landlord, the confessor, the porter. And you. Even you! I direct scenes that are real masterpieces. Irresistible. Overwhelming. Whoever happens to hear himself grasps the comic side of his tragedy, measures the intensity and capacity of his own wickedness, justifies and exalts his own coward-ice. (597)

Reacting to the Mechanic's order that he not stand in the way of Gabriella's return to Gabriele, Leonardo asks, continuing the puppet theme, "Am I myself a puppet in the hands of destiny?" The Mechanic replies: "Oh, lying god! God of illusion! Peddler of toy trumpets! What are my puppets worth, what are your words worth, compared to this man, returned so terribly alive, so desperately alive, that though his eyes are closed he can see, through an inner convulsion, and twist his own soul like a snake around the prey that is about to suffocate!" (598).

The puppet motif moves from the abstract to the concrete in the second act of the play. When she learns at last that Gabriele is alive, Gabriella, already remorseful over her relationship with Leonardo, is beside herself with grief. She also expresses regret over her loss of contact with Gabriele's family, who are soon to appear. The Mechanic tries to comfort her by telling her that he created a puppet in her likeness as a consolation of sorts for Gabriele's family, who never stopped asking about her:

They came to see it with tear-filled eyes. To touch it with a curiosity born of anxiety and fear. Then I pulled a lever. Your voice could be heard rising from the mechanical tangle and freeing itself from the steel needle on the groove of the recording I made. Oh, you can't imagine: the convulsive joy, the farce of hearing your voice. The joy of seeing you a ridiculous mario-nette, without a soul, without life! The eyes remained ecstatic behind the glass of tears. And the grimace of the mouth stretched itself into a mad laugh! (601)

The puppet figures of Gabriella and Leonardo are now brought before the audience and activated. No sooner does the Mechanic tell Gabriella that his puppets can serve as an example to many people than he shows her two niches containing the figures. He then pulls the levers, setting them in motion, and they begin a dialogue in the only instance in which any of the Mechanic's constructions are actually seen and heard in the play. In its coarse humor, the dialogue between the puppets of Gabriella and Leonardo recall the style of the popular puppet theater. Gabriella ridicules Leonardo's physical appearance, and when he tells her that she might have been the mother of his child, she says that she "destroyed" it ("l'ho distrutto") because it didn't look like him (605). As the insults fly back and forth, Leonardo's insistence on his love for Gabriella only annoys her all the more.

If the puppet show was intended in some way to illuminate the truth of Gabriella's relationship with Leonardo, she can't bear watching it and threatens to destroy "the ridiculous, cruel puppets" (606). Her outburst provides the Mechanic with the pretext to launch his most meaningful utterance in the play. Rhetorically asking Gabriella if she wants to destroy herself by destroying her puppet likeness, he urges her to continue to watch the puppets in order to hear in their words the "infinitely tragic":

> If all those who engage in any action were afraid to see themselves reproduced this way, in order to relive an hour of their past, they would be just like you at this moment. They would see their tragedy reduced—beyond the stage, beyond time, beyond space—to a ridiculous farce of no importance or tone, and they would abandon themselves only to instinct, to words, to gesture, renouncing ever having had any soul. (606)

Notwithstanding the literariness of much of Cavacchioli's dialogue, the figure of the Mechanic embodies an avant-gardist demystification of language, or language in a conventional bourgeois sense, common to both the Italian Futurists and the dramatists of the *teatro grottesco*. The representation and presentation of humans in puppet form, as in Marinetti and Cavacchioli, is, of course, intentionally reductive with respect to bourgeois society. But Cavacchioli surpasses Marinetti by endowing his puppets with speech and suggesting thereby that spoken language operates on the level of instinct and gesture. In the absence of the soul, which the Mechanic rejects, speech is hollow, little more than a series of reflex actions. This outlook is established even before the initiation of the play's action by the introductory statement to the thumbnail descriptions of the main characters: "The personages of this vision are the harshest antithesis of their verbal expression" (580).

Cavacchioli wants us to understand that Gabriella's seduction results as much from Leonardo's skill with words as from her frustration over the apparent loss of Gabriele in the war. The fortuneteller's verbal prowess is abundantly displayed in the first scene in his meetings with clients in his studio. That is why the play begins with this scene, since it is important to later character relationships that the audience understand the true nature of Leonardo's power. As a fortuneteller-magician, a magician of words, Leonardo is able to carry off his seduction of Gabriella not only by exploiting her unhappiness but by casting a spell over her. Gabriella herself is painfully aware of this when she tells her lover at one point that their entire relationship arose out of, was built on, words ("Tutto è cresciuto sulle parole," 591). And, in the same vein, shortly thereafter: "And you began to speak. You intoxicated me on words. And it seemed to me that a strange drowsiness put me to sleep. That a silent and destructive venom had entered me" (591).

Words, speech, are the principal instrument of human deception in bourgeois society as well as the malady from which the traditional stage suffers, in Cavacchioli's view. By creating puppets without souls but able to speak, the Mechanic has gone He of *The Bird of Paradise* one better by holding before the audience concrete—or, better said, concretized—metaphors of the human condition. Revealingly, because of what he suffered during the war, Gabriele often prefers solitude or the company of the village children, who have become his friends and who adore him for the improbable stories he tells them. With adults, toward whom the war has instilled in him "a type of terror of people" (615), he prefers silence.

FROM PUPPETS TO ARTIFICIAL MEN: THE DARKENING VISION OF MASSIMO BONTEMPELLI

A native of Lake Como, Massimo Bontempelli had an exceptionally productive literary career—in a wide variety of genres—and on 23 October 1930 was elected a member of the Italian Academy in recognition of his achievements.[24] An erstwhile collaborator with the Futurists, Bontempelli had also joined the Fascist party in 1924 (the same year as Pirandello) and in 1928 became national secretary of the Fascist Syndicate of Authors and Writers (Sindacato Fascista Autori i Scrittori). He began distancing himself from Fascist politics from about 1936, and in 1938 his party card was revoked. Although he published a tragedy in verse (*Costanza* [*Constancy*]) as early as 1905, Bontempelli's serious playwriting began in 1919 with *Siepe a nordovest* (*Hedge to the Northwest*), in which puppets observe a curious interplay of humans and marionettes. Two other dramatic works in which the human being–puppet analogy is explored followed within a few years: *Nostra Dea* (*Our Dea*, 1925) and the play widely regarded as Bontempelli's best, *Minnie, la candida* (*Minnie the Candid*, 1927).[25]

Hedge to the Northwest, a "farce in prose and music," has distinct Pirandellian undertones that come as no surprise in light of Pirandello's influence on Bontempelli.[26] Yet despite the obvious Pirandellian echoes in several of his works, Bontempelli was an original dramatist who followed his own creative path. We can see this, for example, in *Hedge to the Northwest*, which was first staged on 18 January 1923 in Rome at Bragaglia's Teatro degli Indipendenti. To a certain extent the play brings to mind Pirandello's *Six Characters in Search of an Author*. However, the original formula of Pirandello is reversed here. It is now actors representing people performing before puppets and alongside marionettes. There are, therefore, three distinct sets of characters, and three points of view. The puppets, consisting just of Colombina (Columbine), from the commedia dell'arte tradition, and Napoleon, appear at the beginning of the play and before each act in a miniature puppet theater set up in a corner of the stage. Colombina introduces the play proper—*Hedge to the Northwest*—and invites a grumbling, skeptical, and humorless Napoleon to watch it with her. By assuming, moreover, the roles, or functions, of the author's spokesman as well as a metaphor for the audience viewing the play, the Colombina and Napoleon puppets embody an accurate realization of the mechanism of estrangement.

Hedge to the Northwest unfolds along two parallel tracks, one consisting of the drama of real people, the other, of marionettes. These two "inner" plays are of quite different character and converge only toward the end. Moreover, both sets of characters, while often inhabiting the same space, are presumed not to be able to see or hear one another. Touch is a different matter. Movements of the marionettes can be felt by the people. Conversely, the marionettes respond to objects, or constructs, introduced by the people. But the interaction between the two groups of characters, human and marionette, is greater than would appear at first glance. This shows up primarily in the different natures of the two parallel dramas.

The drama of the humans, as perhaps it ought to be called here, has a banal plot—marital infidelity, once again. Laura is married to Mario but becomes involved in an affair with their mutual friend Carletto. The marionette play has a fairy-tale–epic character. It is set in a city kingdom atop a hillock, which appears onstage as part of the landscape in which the humans move. The marionette kingdom is a perfect realm except for one thing. Winds blowing from the northwest glide through the little forest surrounding the hillock, pass over the latter, and strike with extreme force against the principal districts of the city. The first minister of the realm informs the king that the problem has been studied and recommends that a commission be formed, representing all political parties. The antics of the royal ministers, above all their bureaucratic passion for commissions, is an obvious jibe on Bontempelli's part at the gridlock complexities of Italian politics. But the king is an activist who tolerates no delays and wants work begun at once on a construction project to blunt the force of the winds. Epic and fairy tale meet in the relationship between the king's daughter, the princess, and his foremost knight, identified simply as Hero. Hero is in love with the princess and would like to marry her, but she is drawn to God and cannot think of earthly marriage. When benches seem to move about mysteriously and a huge screen appears out of nowhere— the result, of course, of actions by the humans Laura and Carletto, which are intended to conceal their romanic trysts from Mario's suspicious eyes—the marionette workers engaged in the construction project interpret these as supernatural events and are terrified. The king asks Hero to investigate the matter. If he reports what he finds as a miracle, Hero fears the princess will take it as a heavenly sign confirming the correctness of her wish to become a nun. When the time comes for him to explain what he has discovered, he interprets the supernatural events in a way favorable to himself and succeeds in winning the princess's hand in marriage and the king's blessings.

In its heroic and noble aspect, the fairy tale romance between the knight and the princess of the marionette kingdom is developed by Bontempelli as a contrast to the trite infidelity of Laura and Carletto. The wooden dolls thus expose the shallowness as well as banality in the lives of the human beings. Irony also informs the implicit inversion in the roles of humans and marionettes. In their weakness of will and inability to control their own destinies, the human beings resemble marionettes manipulated by forces they cannot gain control over and inhabit a realm utterly devoid of real communication. Bontempelli's marionettes are thus intended, through ironic contrast, to expose the marionette-like behavior of human beings in a bourgeois society.

The essential contrast between the marionettes and the human beings is also established within each inner drama by allusions to freedom of will and mechanical and metaphorical wires depriving the individual of self-control. When Hero tries to win over the princess romantically and reminds her of her obligations to her father and her people, she replies that she feels irresistibly drawn toward God, "as if a heavenly wire were bearing her to Him, were guiding all her steps." Hero counters with these words: "No, princess, we shouldn't talk that way. There is nothing irresistible when one is endowed with conscience and will, the way we are. We are not paltry tools in some worker's hands. We are divine sparks, we are the masters or rulers of our will and of our reflexes."[27] Shortly thereafter, in a scene between Laura and Carletto, Laura confesses that she feels a strong force drawing her toward him and that she suffers trying to struggle against it. Carletto urges her to abandon further struggle, arguing that only the gods have control over their own actions. "Don't think about it any more. Let yourself go. We are not gods; we are just humble creatures, nothing more than marionettes pulled by wires, Laura" (54).

In the second play, *Our Dea*, the titular heroine is a woman whose outlook, behavior, and speech are shaped by the clothes she wears.[28] Dea, in other words, is again puppet as human being, but, in a novel twist, manipulated this time by clothing rather than passion. And the clothing in turn can be viewed as an allegorical representation of an environment in which the alienation of the individual is carried so far that clothes literally make the man. From the moment she first appears onstage, it is apparent that Dea is mannequin-like. Her face is expressionless, her gestures those of a puppet, mechanical, abrupt, her speech slow and syllabized. She has no opinion about anything. All this changes, however, as soon as she is dressed. She is very sensitive to color, a point made by her older maid, Anna, to Dea's male friend Vulcano. If the colors are bright and vivacious—red, let's say—then Dea is similarly bright and vivacious. If the colors are muted, Dea is subdued.

The sinister dimension of Dea's clothes-dictated mood changes is revealed in the course of a thin plot that functions merely as a platform for the display of Dea's shifts. Countess Orsa is in love with a naval officer named Dorante, whom she hasn't seen in two years. She learns, however, that he will attend a great ball being given that evening, but that he will leave the very next day. She is desperate to see him, but her jealous husband, Count Orso, who cannot attend the ball because of other obligations, forbids her to go alone. The only way the countess can hope to go is by getting a letter from Dea inviting her to attend with her. Since Count

Orso trusts nobody as much as Dea, the ruse is guaranteed to work. When first approached by the countess, Dea had agreed to write the letter. But the clothes she had on at the time had put her in a compliant and accommodating mood. On the day of the ball, wearing different clothing, Dea stubbornly refuses to write the letter and barely has any recollection of ever having promised to do so. Aware of the effect that clothes have on Dea, Vulcano, who is also Countess Orsa's friend, maneuvers to have Dea dressed in a conservative turtledove-colored outfit, which puts her in a sweet, agreeable mood. Her behavior again transformed by a change of costume, Dea happily writes the letter to the countess.

The ball is a magnificent affair that enables Bontempelli to arrange a scene rich in color and sound. Men and women attired mostly in costumes and masks execute a series of turns about the stage, four abreast, before marching in a procession toward the dining hall, where dinner is served. The entire procession takes on the aspect of something mechanized, reminiscent of the mannequin-like ball scene in the Russian playwright Leonid Andreev's *Life of Man* (1910). As it marches to dinner, the procession, preceded by trumpeters, shouts in chorus, "in excited rhythm, at once puerile and neurotic—'To dinner, to dinner!'"[29]

When Dea makes her entrance, she is encased in a tight-fitting, sparkling green, serpentine outfit. Her behavior at the ball accords with her snakelike appearance. Manipulating everyone around her as surely as she herself is manipulated by the outfit she has on, Dea launches into a game of deceit and treachery. Desperate to meet again with Dorante but unsure where and when he will appear at the ball, Countess Orsa begins a frantic search for him with the help of Vulcano and his friend Marcolfo. On her own, however, Dea discovers the whereabouts of Dorante and sends a servant to fetch him. When they meet, she creates the impression that Orsa is no longer interested in him and has another lover. To Orsa and the others, Dea pretends that she has seen Dorante at the ball, but in the company of some beautiful woman. After much maneuvering, which lends a certain frantic pace to the ball scene, Orsa and Dorante are at last brought together. After initial mutual recrimination and confusion, they realize that Dea's troublemaking has been behind it all. When confronted, Dea pretends that she was just playing a game. But hardly are their backs turned than she resumes her mischief-making by having a letter taken to Count Orso in which she apprises him of what is taking place.

Shortly thereafter, Vulcano brings Dea a change of costume for a dance in which people will be garbed either as monks or devils. He has chosen for her a monk's habit. Once in it, Dea's behavior again undergoes the appropriate transformation. Humble and contrite, she now confesses to Vulcano that she tried to separate Orsa and Dorante and that she has also summoned Count Orso to the ball to save his adulterous wife. Vulcano orders Marcolfo to block Count Orso's entry at all costs. While the men are distracted, Dea's seamstress (Donna Fiora) returns and dresses her again in the serpentine outfit, but this time with her hair loose and disheveled. As soon as he returns and sees Dea so attired, Vulcano realizes the danger and struggles with her and Donna Fiora to remove the outfit. In the course of the struggle, the outfit is torn to shreds, once again transforming Dea's personality, this time into that of a pitiful beggar. Marcolfo escorts her home and Vulcano remains to deal with the count.

At home, still garbed in tatters and with a crown of vine leaves on her head, Dea dances around as if inebriated. Anna brings in an elegant dressing gown for her to change into, and she is again transformed. She is now a grande dame formally thanking all for accompanying her to the ball and for the splendid evening she had. As the play draws to a close, Anna prepares Dea for bed by stripping her of the different costumes she has on, moving in rapid succession from the dressing gown to the torn beggar's outfit to the serpentine costume. As she does so, Dea's speech passes through a series of disjointed changes corresponding to the different articles of clothing being stripped away. At the end, she appears in the same "combination" or motley outfit she had on at the beginning of the play, and in the same puppet posture: "she turns toward the public. Her arms remain a bit raised. Her movements are mechanical. She is apathetic and pronounces words by syllables in an empty voice with a slight falsetto." The dialogue reinforces the puppet-like regression:

> *Anna.* There we are, I've prepared the bed for you. (*She goes to the sofabed.*)
> *Dea.* I un-der-stand.
> *Anna* (*drawing back the bed covering a little and inviting* Dea *from a distance with a gesture*). If you'd care to get in . . .
> *Dea* (*turning around*). I think—that—I—am—sleepy. (689)

Bontempelli again situates a woman at the center of the action in *Minnie the Candid*. The play addresses the same basic theme of alienation and dehumanization through mechanization as *Our Dea*, but with far more sinister undertones.[30] It also has a greater strangeness of character and ambiance. Minnie herself is an odd creature whose first appearance easily brings Dea to mind. The scene is a café in a big city in summer. In conversation with her intended, Skagerrak, Minnie seems almost a simpleton. She asks the meaning of such terms as *definition* and *university* and has no idea even of which city she is in. As the dialogue progresses between Minnie, Skagerrak, and his friend Tirreno, who soon joins them, it appears that Minnie's background is every bit as strange as her apparent simplemindedness. She was born in Siberia, of an Indian father and a Norwegian mother who had spent most of her life in Italy and with whom she traveled a great deal until her death. The only language she speaks well is Italian, and she met her boyfriend, Skagerrak, in Constantinople.

The generally aimless conversation in the café provides the information that Minnie and Skagerrak intend to leave soon for America, where they will be married; Tirreno, after marrying his girlfriend, Adelaide, will settle in Germany. Again, as in *Our Dea*, *Minnie the Candid* barely has a plot in any conventional sense. It is set in motion by the appearance of a man transporting a huge fishbowl, which will be set up in a new park nearby. The man pauses for a while at the café, which gives Minnie and the others a chance to examine the fishbowl. In response to Minnie's delight at the beauty of the fish, Tirreno tells her that they are actually man-made, manufactured, yet so lifelike they are indistinguishable from the genuine article. When Minnie wants to touch them, Tirreno tells her that she can't because the fish are electrified, which is what makes them move, and that she would get a bad shock if she did. Obviously teasing the naïve and gullible Minnie, Tirreno also tells her that the same people who made the fish made other artificial animals, birds, for example, which can fly and sing. When Minnie asks the logical question, for her, why more is not made known about the artificial birds, Tirreno tells her it is because they would no longer represent something rare. Swearing her to secrecy, he tells her, moreover, that artificial people were also manufactured, six men and six women. Nobody knows where they are now because a few days after their manufacture, two or three years ago, they escaped from the laboratory and have been abroad in the land ever since. All subsequent efforts to find them have failed. Worse still, the artificial people themselves do not know that they are artificial and believe themselves real.

From the moment she learns of the "existence" of the artificial people, Minnie becomes obsessed, and no effort on the part of either Tirreno or

Skaggerak to convince her that it's all a joke does any good. Her fears seem fulfilled at the end of the first act when, on leaving the café, she hears a noise behind her, turns around, and catches sight of six men and six women dressed as globe-trotters as they enter the stage on one side, cross it, and then exit on the other.

During the preparations for the characters' various departures in the next act, Minnie gets nowhere trying to convince Tirreno and Skaggerak that she actually saw the artificial people. They reassure her that the whole thing was a joke, a bad joke at that, but they cannot talk her out of what is now a terrifying obsession. In the hope at least that Adelaide, as a woman, will believe her, Minnie tells her about seeing "them" in the street just a little while ago on the way to Skaggerak's house. She continues:

> They are terrible. I still don't know all the signs, but I'm thinking. They are all manufactured, all parts of them, and even their souls and the way they speak. And they don't know it, and that's why it's hard to understand. But one can feel it a bit. We've got to be careful since they're afraid, you understand. They (*indicating* Tirreno *and* Skaggerak) say that it doesn't make any difference to them, but you're a woman and understand what it is to see someone who seems real and was made by a machine.[31]

Skaggerak and Tirreno await the arrival of Skaggerak's uncle, who has also been invited to the farewell meal. In the meantime, the family to whom Skaggerak has rented his house appears. Minnie by now is so overwhelmed with fear that she pleads with Skaggerak not to leave her alone for a single moment. As the others continue packing, Minnie expands at length—to everyone's confusion or consternation—on what she perceives to be the difference between the fabricated being and the real one. The fabricated being, she declares, is "absolutely perfect" ("tutto molto molto perfetto") while the real one has flaws, defects, something funny about him that can make one laugh. She then goes on to describe what it is about each of her friends—Adelaide, Skaggerak, Tirreno, Astolfo (the waiter from the café), and Arabella—that makes them real people in her eyes. Just as they are about to leave finally, Skaggerak's uncle appears and insists that they stay awhile with him as long as they have time.

Uncle (Zio, the only name he goes by in the play) prides himself on being in perfect equilibrium between modesty and vanity, an ideal situation, he declares, that has helped him enormously in following the road that he has chosen in life. The more he talks, the more Minnie suspects that he really is one of "them." When Skaggerak at one point tells his uncle that he is funny, Minnie hastens to disagree, saying that there is nothing funny about him. She then asks Uncle if on the road of life he ever took a wrong turn. Her meaning is obvious. Believing, however, that Minnie is trying to find something in him to criticize, Uncle takes umbrage and tells her that it would be indeed difficult to criticize him: "First of all, because of God's grace, and then, above all, because of my strong will I am able to mold myself in a way that, yes, I would dare call perfect" (215). With her usual naïveté, Minnie asks him what "mold myself" ("foggiarmi") means. His answer is all she needs to confirm her suspicions:

> *Uncle.* Mold myself, yes, make myself, that's it; I can say of being myself made by me.
> *Minnie* (*screaming*). Oh God, can one even make himself by himself? No no, Skager, let's be careful, take me, Skager, carry me way from here immediately, I still don't understand. (215)

As they all begin exiting the apartment, Uncle springs the surprise that he intends accompanying Minnie and Skaggerak all the way to America. This is enough to send Minnie into a panic. When he approaches Skaggerak to embrace him, she throws herself on Skaggerak's chest to protect him, crying out: "No, Skager, protect yourself. Get far way from here, immediately. He's manufactured, completely perfect, made by machine, artificial. Away, I don't want you to touch him, Skager, I don't want you to go with him. . . . Order him to go away. Don't you understand what he is? I know the signs, believe me" (217). Deeply offended, understanding nothing of what is going on, Uncle all but storms out. Adelaide, now also angry, joins him. Minnie, engulfed in madness, refuses to leave the apartment and begs Skaggerak and Tirreno to stay with her. Now that Uncle and Adelaide have left, she says that "others" have come, "from all over, from everywhere, the whole city is full of them, the whole world" (219).

In the last act, Minnie, Skaggerak, and Tirreno have secluded themselves in the apartment for four days, in obvious disarray. Adelaide rejoins them for the sake of her relationship with Tirreno. Minnie spends much of the time in bed and refuses food. Even a doctor the others have consulted says there is nothing he can do for her. In the meantime, the new tenant, who was supposed to have already moved into the apartment, threatens to have them all evicted and in any case will move in with his entire family on the following day. When Minnie finally puts in an appearance, dressed in a nightgown, her paranoia is indescribable. She cannot even bear the thought that Tirreno might leave the apartment for an hour for fear that he will run into the "artificial people." When Minnie falls asleep again, Skaggerak opens a window and beholds the view outside. The scene could easily have been inspired by such Futurist paintings of urban landscapes and artificial illumination as *The Riot*, of 1911, by Umberto Boccioni and Giacomo Balla's *Arc Lamp*, of 1911–12. It is night and the city appears all illuminated.

(Bright fragments of advertisements are visible, some of them animated; in different languages; some consisting of syllables without meaning. During the dialogue that follows, new ones are added to them. It is all a pulsating of lights against a dark background.) (228)

Looking out at the scene, too, Tirreno is struck by its artificiality. "It's all artificial," he declares. "There's no sky any more. Look, high up, it's a reddish fog that falls from the sky over the entire city" (228). But Skaggerak is struck by the quantity of signs he sees, signs for everything, all made of light, like so many stars or, as Tirreno puts it, new planets that at one time did not exist. "There used to be others," says Skaggerak, "but these new ones displaced them from the heavens. They are artificial constellations; maybe they're prettier?" (229).

The greatest fear of Skaggerak and Tirreno at this point is that Minnie will think that one of them, or both, perhaps, are also artificial people. But when she again awakens, she asks for as much light as possible, studies herself in a mirror, and decides that it is she herself who is not real: "It's certain. Yes, now, yes, I see clearly, it is I, I. I am not real, no, no . . . I am one of them, of those poor . . . manufactured ones. Stay far away from me, far . . . be afraid, be afaid of me (231)." Convinced that "the others" have come for her, that she can hear them below, she sends Skaggerak and Tirreno down to receive them, and as soon as they leave the room she locks it. She then extinguishes all the lights. The only illumination is from the neon signs outside. Opening a window, she mounts the sill, turns skyward, and then plunges to her death. The play ends.

The effectiveness of *Minnie the Candid* as a commentary on the alienation of modern man in a world of changing values depends on the character of Minnie. Bontempelli may have gone too far with the matter of her exotic background and naïveté; she is scarcely believable. But this is a secondary consideration. In order to make his point about the artificiality of society and the alienation to which urban life gives rise, he needs the innocence, simple-mindedness, and gullibility of a figure such as Minnie. Because of her strange background, she herself is rootless. The language she knows best, Italian, is not only spoken imperfectly but also in so curious a way as to suggest something artificial. Minnie's lack of culture, her lack of sophistication, her childlike nature, rationalize the gullibility that transforms Tirreno's innocent little joke into a terrifying vision of a world in which authenticity no longer exists. The inevitable fear that she herself may be inauthentic leaves Minnie no way out but suicide.

TEN

From Puppet to Robot

The Brothers Čapek

Although they collaborated on several works, especially in their younger days when they lived together and functioned as a team, Karel Čapek became far better known as a writer than his brother Josef. Karel's literary output was huge and encompassed a broad variety of genres from the essay to the drama. Productive also in his own right as a literary figure, Josef, however, was an important painter whose extensive writings on art tended to eclipse his efforts in fiction and his occasional excursions into philosophy. Unlike his older brother, Karel had a strong interest in theater and wrote several plays, a few of which went on to achieve great fame. These became the basis of his international reputation; without them, despite the high regard in which his novels, short stories, and essays are held, it is doubtful if Karel Čapek's literary renown would have been substantially different from that of his brother Josef's.

The play that made Karel Čapek a celebrity worldwide was *R.U.R.* (*Rossum's Universal Robots*, published 1920, first performed 1921). The original English title of the play was meant to suggest the multinational nature of the robot-manufacturing corporation. But the Czech elements in it should not be overlooked. *Rossum* probably relates to the Czech word *rozum* ("mind, reason"), while *robot* is a Czech coinage based on the word *robota*, meaning "strenuous work." Reflecting both the widespread interest in science fiction literature in the 1920s and Karel Čapek's own reservations about modern technology and industrialism, *R.U.R.* was the first of several works dealing with scientific and utopian themes. The play *Ze života hmyzů* (*From the Life of the Insects*; also known as *The Insect Play*, *The World We Live In*, and *And So Ad Infinitum*), which Karel and Josef wrote jointly, was published in 1921 and first staged in 1922. The same year as that play's premiere, Karel Čapek's novel *Továrna na absolutno* (*Factory of the Absolute*; also known as *The Absolute at Large*) was published, and another play on an anti-utopian theme, *Věc Makropulos* (*The Macropoulos Secret*; also known as *The Makropolous Affair*), had its premiere as well. A second science fiction novel, *Krakatit*, which deals with the invention of an atomic bomb, appeared in 1924. A third novel, *Válka s mloky* (*War with the Newts*), which masks political and economic satire beneath the guise of science fiction, was published in 1934.

Karel Čapek's science fiction writings were rooted in serious reflection, extending over most of his adult life, on the roles of science, technology, and modern industrialism in society and their impact on human beings. He proffered no ready answers. He appreciated the contributions of science and technology, but he felt that if they were permitted to develop out of control, if their progress was not rationally controlled, man would ultimately end up enslaved and dehumanized. Karel Čapek's concerns were widespread in the 1920s and gave rise to a significant body of anti-utopian literature. The Russian writer Evgeni Zamyatin's novel *My* (*We*, corrupt text 1927, complete text 1952), which anticipated Aldous Huxley's *Brave New World* and is believed to have been the inspiration for George Orwell's *1984*, is widely acknowledged as a classic of the genre.

Behind the anxieties concerning the dangers posed by advances in science and technology lay the horrible memories of the use of machines for mass destruction during World War I. If the Futurists celebrated the triumph of technology and machine culture before the war, the postwar Expressionists voiced their horror at the cost in human suffering brought about by the machine. But Karel Čapek as a writer was never attracted to extremes. If he was well aware of the dangers inherent in the unrestrained cultivation of science, technology, and industrialism, he could also find things to be optimistic about. It was, if you will, his Czech nature. That is why his plays on science fiction themes, above all *R.U.R.*, are essentially comedies. With its subject of robots who rebel against their creator and become humanlike in their ability to love and reproduce, *R.U.R.* reiterates familiar motifs of the literature dealing with puppets, marionettes, automatons, and other inanimate creatures who come to life in one way or another. Robots who rebel against their master in this play relate directly to those works we have already looked at in which puppets or marionettes similarly rebel and move to take control of their own lives. Also, the inspiration of *Pinocchio* should not be overlooked; like the wooden puppet who wants to and finally does become a real live boy, the robots here eventually yearn to live as full human beings.

Long before Karel Čapek wrote *R.U.R.*, both brothers gave ample evidence of a literary interest in puppets and the possible ramifications of the puppet figure. As early as 1908 and 1910 they wrote two related stories about puppets, "Povídka poučná" ("An Edifying Tale," 1908) and "L'Eventail" ("The Fan," 1910). Both deal with a figure we met earlier in this book, the French inventor Henri-Louis Jacquet-Droz, who together with his father, Pierre Droz, created a series of automatons that could, for example, dance, play musical instruments, and exchange kisses, and which acquired international renown.

"An Edifying Tale," which is divided into three small sections, deals mainly with Henri Droz's death, posthumous reputation, and the view of some (represented by the character Rodbury) that his talent for creating androids, as they were called, would have been better used in more practical, socially beneficial ways. The Čapeks lay the matter to rest by suggesting that with Droz dead and buried, it was too late for such moralizing.[1]

"L'Eventail" is the more interesting of the two stories.[2] Reminiscent of an Italian Renaissance novella, the work is set in the year 1789. At a garden party given by the Neapolitan prince Bondini, a widower, the host is chagrined to discover his mistress, Countess Reccò, called Terrine, shamelessly flirting with a poet named Fosco. Unable to control his anger and jealousy, Bondini takes vengeance in an unusual way. One of the guests at the ball is none other than the inventor Henri Droz. Bondini approaches him and asks him to exhibit his androids. The most intriguing is a life-size female puppet dubbed L'Eventail because of the fan with which she covers her face. Besides being able to operate a fan, the puppet can also speak the words *yes* and *no* in regular alternation. Later that evening the last entertainment at the ball is presented: a puppet show featuring two characters, the female puppet with the fan and a red mask, and a man. The man is attired in a black mask and a black coat, with a sword at his side. It is, in fact, Bondini. Concealed behind his mask, the prince enters into a dialogue with the puppet, addressing her as if she were his mistress, Terrine, and alluding to their relations and, obliquely, the fidelity of women. But the seemingly contradictory answers of the puppet, who can say only *yes* or *no*, anger the prince. At one point, for example, he asks her: "Before I become your slave, tell me, must a man become a slave in order to be worthy of a woman's love?" (129). Her answer this time is *yes*, to the prince's dismay. It is *yes* again, a little later on, when he he accuses her, as a woman, of lying, with words, looks, actions, of being capable of lying with her whole body. After voicing the threat of vengeance, the enraged prince dashes from the stage into his garden. A storm is raging, but the prince finds the poet in the midst of it and kills him. "And so ended the garden fame of Prince Bondini," concludes the tale. In yet another extension of the symbolism of the puppet, the figure in "L'Eventail" is used to represent the eternal enigma of the female. Woman, in essence, is beyond man's comprehension, and the *yes* or *no* of Droz's life-sized puppet conveys the Čapeks' belief in the relativity of all truth.

The image of woman as puppet, and love itself as a comedy fit for puppets, recurs in the story "Ex centro," which was published a year after "L'Eventail," in 1911. Two fashionable gentlemen, Adolf Berti and Julius Argyl, exchange thoughts on women and love during a variety theater performance. Their image of the female of the species is shaped more by dread than attraction. "The [variety theater] performer is like a woman," declares Berti, "because he loves his body and lives from it."[3] Berti further pontificates: "God created man as a likeness of Himself, and woman as a likeness of life. The incident of our progenitors in paradise is the victory of woman over man, hence the victory of life over God. Man is God in miniature; therefore, he creates. Woman is nature in miniature; therefore, she bears" (230). After enumerating the dangers posed by woman, Berti smilingly suggests that perhaps the ideal woman would actually be a female puppet. In agreeing with him, however, Argyl is deadly serious, and during the next part of the variety theater program expatiates at some length on the virtues of the female puppet from his point of view:

Just imagine . . . a puppet very much like a real woman, with color and softness very similar to a woman's complexion, with a completely fluid movement of the limbs, in short a puppet as suggestive as possible. Seat her beside yourself on the couch, look at her, tell her sweet and intelligent things, charming improvisations as well as confessions illumined with the light of your mind. See, here you have the illusion of an intimate tête-à-tête, the delights of delicate togetherness when a woman listens, and the man, nearly leaving his body, inspired by the tender silence of the woman, becomes a speaker and a herald of the human heart. And, please note, such a mistress at least will never interrupt the compositions of our dreams, will never interrupt your magniloquence with her coarse, vulgar, and realistic voice. . . .

And afterward . . . if you take this mistress into your arms, kiss her, embrace her, arouse her with your closeness, you will have a harmless and calming being who beneath this enchanting exterior will do nothing unfriendly to you. (233)

When Argyl is finished, his and Berti's attention is drawn to a brother-and-sister team performing on a trapeze in the high-wire act. But a tragic accident occurs and the sister falls to her death. When her distraught brother reaches the ground, he picks up her lifeless body and cries out "P—pup—pe!" ("doll," "puppet"). Almost immediately, an even more terrible cry is shouted from the box containing Berti and Argyl. After the performance, both the acrobat and Argyl are taken off to an insane asylum in separate cars. But they are content there, especially the former man about town, Argyl, who has been allowed to have a large female puppet all dressed in pink which he introduces to new arrivals as his wife but to his most intimate friends as his mistress. For the Čapeks, life, and especially relations between man and woman, cannot exist without contradictions, which the female puppet figures in "L'Eventail" and "Ex centro" are meant to represent. But as discomforting as these contradictions may often be, they are fundamental to human nature and cannot be eliminated wihout depriving man of his individuality, or worse. The puppet is thus a negative figure in these works, a symbol of the artificiality against which man must rebel.

The most important literary work by the Čapeks on the puppet theme before Karel wrote *R.U.R.* was the one-act play in nineteen scenes entitled *Lásky hra osudná* (*The Fateful Game of Love*). It was written in 1910, the year in which "L'Eventail" was published and a year before "Ex centro." The play appeared first in the journal *Lumír* in 1911, and as a separate publication in 1922; it had its premiere at the National Theater in Prague on 15 May 1930. More complex than it may appear at first glance, *The Fateful Game of Love* operates on more than a single level.

On one it is clearly a parody of contemporary theatrical tastes and the disdain for the lyrical and poetic in favor of realism and naturalism. The parody assumes the form of a spoof of the Italian commedia dell'arte, the widespread revival of which in the early twentieth century could also have been a target of the Čapeks' satire. In a contemporary setting, and in almost exaggeratedly contemporary dress, such familiar stock figures as the Dottore (here Baloardo), Scaramouche (the Harlequin counterpart), and Brighella (called Fichetto, Finochetto, or Zane) are joined by a Pierrot-like Gilles, a decadent poet, Trivalin, an aggressive hulk of a shopkeeper, Isabella, a Columbine knockdown who is the object of their affection, and Isabella's aunt, Zerbine. The prologue, which is introduced by a character identified simply as Prologue (Prolog), makes it quite clear from the outset that the play is neither traditional commedia dell'arte nor merely an updated version of the old Italian improvised comedy. Prologue's thumbnail sketches of the characters in his introduction barely conceal their mockery, and when the other characters join Prologue, they reveal themselves as a quarrelsome, unappealing bunch. Unhappy over Prologue's description of Brighella, for example, Gilles insists on setting the record straight, before the public, by declaring that Brighella writes pornography, which he sells on the side, and that he also accepts tips for bringing peasant men to Zerbine, who in turn introduces them to Isabella. Mutual recrimination then deteriorates into an argument over Isabella's virginity, or lack of it.

With the tenor of *The Fateful Game of Love* already established by the Prologue, the play proper begins with the Dottore, as the oldest member of the company, rhetorically inquiring as to why the audience has come to the theater. If it is for the catharsis about which Aristotle speaks, he declares, then they will see good and bad in the play about to unfold and will rejoice in the triumph of good. The intrigue is advanced soon enough appropriately by Brighella who has already been characterized as a schemer. The wily part-time pornographer tells Gilles and Trivalin, in turn, that the young and fair Isabella is desperately anxious to give herself completely to a man, and that he is her choice. After Brighella confides in Gilles that Zerbine allows men to see Isabella only upon payment of fees that she then turns around and lends at interest, Gilles rushes out to the aunt to get her to change her ways. Zerbine, it seems, has no admirers among the other members of the company who would like to expel her from it. But since even Prologue owes her money, as do some of the others, expulsion is out of the question.

Not much time elapses before the audience is thrust onto the other important level on which *The Fateful Game of Love* operates. The motor of much of the action is money. Brighella writes pornography for the sake of earning extra money and for the same reason conspires with both Gilles and Trivalin in their pursuit of Isabella's affections. When Brighella tells Trivalin that he cannot hope to make progress with Isabella unless he plies Zerbine with presents, the shopkeeper says that he has no money to spare. But Brighella has already foreseen that eventuality; he will lend Trivalin money at a substantial rate of interest. Gilles is also impecunious and, moreover, owes Zerbine money, which he now wants to pay off with a loan from Brighella. Brighella and Zerbine are the play's principal financial schemers, but the web of financial intrigue ensnares all the characters.

The Čapeks' motive in their revisionary spoof of the commedia dell'arte becomes still clearer. Besides using the conventions of the old Italian comedy to comment on the theatrical tastes of their own time, the Čapeks also make them a vehicle for the deep misgivings, of Karel Čapek in particular, concerning capitalist commercialism. He was anything but a revolutionary when it came to social issues. He was a liberal, a democrat, characteristically Czech in his middle-class, middle-of-the-road attitudes and his avoidance of extremes. But for all his apparent passivity with respect to political and social issues, for which he was occasionally taken to task, he had a deep and abiding sense of morality, a caring nature that expressed itself in a sincere concern for his fellow human beings. The dehumanization threatened by machine culture was paralleled, in Karel Čapek's view, by the demoralization attributable to the false values and artificiality for which capitalism and commercialism were responsible. Thus, there are no absolute moral values in *The Fateful Game of Love*. The relativity addressed by the Čapeks in their earlier works on puppet themes is present here as well. Only a Pierrot-like decadent poet like Gilles, who lives just in and for literature, has any sense of beauty and honor. Yet Gilles is a ludicrous, parodic figure and he too is entangled in the play's money web. The other characters view personal relationships only in cynical financial terms, with the prize—Isabella—in effect going to the highest bidder. Traditional values associated with love and romance no longer exist in *The Fateful Game of Love*, their place taken by scheming and bidding. The "game" of the play's title is *hra* in Czech, which can mean both "game" and "play," in the theatrical sense. The Čapeks themselves play with the term, since *The Fateful Game of Love* is a play about love as a game, in this case a game of chance.

In order to improve his relations with Zerbine, Gilles, who owes her money, asks Brighella to lend him the money to pay off his debt. Brighella further incites him on the issue of money by telling him that Trivalin has money and intends to use it to "buy" Isabella as his wife. Gilles's plaintive comment that a woman loves poetry and can be won over only by spirit strikes a note of quixotic irrelevance. When Gilles pleads his case to Isabella in poetic imagery laden with flowers and dreams, Brighella taunts him with his theatrical obsolescence, telling him that the public now wants pathos, heroism, tragic figures, action, and the like. The schemer then tells Trivalin the same thing about women, that they are weak and love heroism and that he can win her over by a show of manly strength. When Trivalin declares his love to Isabella he boasts that he will challenge any man to a fight over her. Brighella eggs him on toward a confrontation with Gilles by telling him that the poet is planning to carry Isabella away. Gilles further antagonizes Trivalin by declaring that he doesn't have to buy what he can have with love. In an angry scene, one echoing the Čapeks' own views, Gilles berates Trivalin for his mercantile idea of possession:

> To possess, to be owner, neither understanding nor honoring, not calling as goods something greater than myself, no, just to possess, merely to possess, possess, be the owner of and touch with your hands and declare, "That's mine," and tear everything down to the level of your ownership, and to possess a woman the same way, the way I possess this glass, this splinter of mirror, how awful! (*Smashes his little mirror on the floor.*) Such terrible stupidity: to possess a woman; to shout "That's mine," and reckon all her charms and call them "mine." What's yours, you fool?[4]

The expected happens: Trivalin challenges Gilles to a duel. While the others try to talk Gilles out of it, the poet declares his willingness because of his love for Isabella. But the persistent image is that of the decadent poet stylizing his own demise. In the event of his death, he instructs the Dottore: "Open this mother-of-pearl box that I carry around with me. It contains several manuscripts. Publish them in pink satin covers, on smooth vellum paper, and affix my portrait, an etching in the style of Watteau.

Don't forget the etching"(42). When Zerbine protests the duel on the grounds that she can't afford for Gilles to be killed since he owes her money, Brighella sarcastically remarks that Gilles can leave her the publishing rights to his manuscripts, his poetry. Zerbine replies, incredulously: "You think I can make anything on them?" Brighella's practical suggestion is that she "print them in small print on cheap paper, without binding, the way stuff is published for the folk. Nowadays that's the only kind of publishing that pays off. Besides, Gilles can bequeath you his personal estate" (44).

When the duel at last takes place, Gilles is shot in the back because he has forgotten to turn around to face his opponent on the count of three. As he lies dying, poet to the end, and delirious, he takes the kerchief of Isabella which he wears on his chest, notices blood on it, and imagines it to be now a garden full of red and white roses, now a woman all in white, now many women, and finally an ever increasing number of angels. As the play ends, it is the wily, unscrupulous, scheming Brighella who triumphs. When Trivalin, justifying his duel with Gilles, demands Isabella as now rightly his, Zerbine informs him that Brighella made over to her the promissory note that he, Trivalin, had signed earlier with the Dottore and Scaramouche as guarantors. Trivalin complains that Brighella didn't give him even a cent for it, but Zerbine declares that he can't prove a thing and, besides, Brighella has already left, taking with him not only Trivalin's suitcase and clothing but also Isabella. Except for the satisfaction of seeing the boorish, grasping Trivalin defeated at the end, *The Fateful Game of Love* affords an audience little pleasure despite its patent parodic aspect. At its core, the play is a bleak commentary on the impact of capitalism on human relations and the perversion of the concept of ownership. The meaning of Brighella's ultimate triumph is unequivocal.

R.U.R., Karel Čapek's most stunning work on the puppet theme, concludes on a happier note despite its overall apocalyptic character. It also marks, in a sense, the logical fulfilment of the playwright's previous interest in puppets and automatons. By the time he came to write *R.U.R.*, Čapek's anxieties about the dangers to society of mechanization and materialism had deepened to the point where his surrogate human being has been transformed from an ingenious mechanical doll or a puppet figure into a full-scale robot manufactured purely for commercial purposes. Refining a process by which his father, the old philospher-scientist Rossum, had hoped to create a human being, Rossum's son has made it possible

to produce instead living and intelligent labor machines—robots, in other
words. More mechanically perfect than people, with an astounding intellectual capacity, the robots lack only a soul, which of course they do not
need for the tasks assigned them and which, moreover, would only com-
plicate their lives. The robots last on average twenty years, when their
mechanisms wear out and they "die." Here is Harry Domin, the central
director of the Rossum's Universal Robots corporation, explaining the robot manufacturing process to Miss Helena Glory, the daughter of President Glory:

> *Domin.* The Robots don't know when to stop working. At two o'clock
>   I'll show you the kneading troughs.
> *Helena.* What kneading troughs?
> *Domin* (*drily*). The mixing vats for the batter. In each one we mix enough
>   batter for a thousand Robots at a time. Next come the vats for livers,
>   brains, etcetera. Then you'll see the bone factory, and after that I'll
>   show you the spinning mill.
> *Helena.* What spinning mill?
> *Domin.* The spinning mill for nerves. The spinning mill for veins. The
>   spinning mill where miles and miles of digestive tract are made at once.
>   Then there's the assembly plant where all of this is put together, you
>   know, like automobiles. Each worker is responsible for affixing one
>   part, and then it automatically moves on to a second worker, then to a
>   third, and so on. It's a most fascinating spectacle. Next comes the
>   drying kiln and the stock room where the brand new products are put
>   to work.
> *Helena.* Good heavens, they have to work immediately?
> *Domin.* Sorry. They work the same way new furniture works. They get
>   broken in. Somehow they heal up internally or something. Even a lot
>   that's new grows up inside them. You understand, we must leave a bit
>   of room for natural development. And in the meantime, the products
>   are refined.
> *Helena.* How do you mean?
> *Domin.* Well, it's the same as "school" for people. They learn to speak,
>   write, and do arithmetic. They have a phenomenal memory. If one read
>   them the *Encyclopedia Britannica* they could repeat everything back in
>   order, but they never think up anything original. They'd make fine
>   university professors. Next they are sorted by grade and distributed.
>   Fifty-thousand head a day, not counting the inevitable percentage of
>   defective ones that are thrown into the stamping-mill . . . etcetera,
>   etcetera.[5]

The noble idea behind the mass production of robots is to speed the manufacturing process, reduce costs by substituting as many robots as possible for human workers, and thus be able to bring finished goods to the consumer at a cheaper price. In time, there will be a superabundance of everything, want will be wiped from the face of the earth, and people, freed from the necessity to work, will live only to perfect themselves. As Domin explains to Miss Glory: "But then the subjugation of man by man and the slavery of man to matter will cease. Never again will anyone pay for his bread with hatred and his life. There'll be no more laborers, no more secretaries. No one will have to mine coal or slave over someone else's machines. No longer will man need to destroy his soul doing work that he hates" (52).

But not everything works out as planned in the paradise-in-the-making. In the play's second act, which takes place ten years later (with Helena Glory now a permanent member of the R.U.R. "family"), clashes have erupted between robots and human workers angered over being supplanted by robots. Led by a new, more unpredictable and aggressive strain created by Dr. Gall, the head of the physiological and research divisions of R.U.R., the robots are clearly gaining the upper hand. Not only are they armed by manufacturers who are well aware of the advantages they represent, but they have also been taken over by governments and trained as soldiers. They have already accounted for seven hundred thousand civilian deaths in the Balkans alone. There are other ominous developments. The robots are uniting to destroy mankind and take over the world since they regard themselves as superior to men and have no need of them. This robot rebellion against their creators and masters echoes, as we have seen, the rebellion of puppets and marionettes elsewhere in literature and the drama. In this regard it may be useful to recall that Karel Čapek's *R.U.R.* was published a year before the Spaniard Jacinto Grau's *El Señor de Pigmalión*.

Striking a universal dystopian note in the play, Čapek also predicts the end of humanity even before the completion of the robots' conquest. It is reported that women are no longer having babies, threatening the extinction of the species. Alquist, the chief of construction of R.U.R., who has turned against the production of robots, explains why:

Why have women stopped giving birth? Because the whole world has become Domin's Sodom! . . . It has! It has! The whole world, all the lands, everything's become one big beastly orgy! People don't even stretch out

their hands for food anymore; it's stuffed right in their mouths for them so
they don't even have to get up—Haha, yes indeed. Domin's Robots see to
everything! And we people, we, the crown of creation do not grow old with
labor, we do not grow old with the cares of rearing children, we do not grow
old from poverty! Hurry, hurry, step right up and indulge your carnal passions! And you expect women to have children by such men? Helena, to
men who are superfluous women will not bear children! (64–65)

In order to counter the rebellion of the robots and reestablish the authority of human beings, Domin and Gall intend creating robot factories
throughout the world whose purpose will be to produce national robots.
By creating robots of different color, nationality, and tongue, and with humans fostering their prejudices and nurturing their mutual lack of understanding, they scheme to turn different communities of robots against one
another and so preclude the possibility of further unified revolts. Before
this happens, the R.U.R. officials hope to end the present revolt—which
has apparently left only themselves alive—by threatening the robots with
their own extinction by witholding from them Rossum's formula for their
creation. But this becomes impossible when Helena reveals that she
burned the mansucript in order to prevent further manufacture of the robots she has come to fear and hate. Not long afterward, robots invade the
quarters where Helena and the R.U.R. officials have taken refuge and kill
everyone except Alquist, who is permitted to live because he is a builder,
hence similar to a robot, and will be put to use serving them.

In the finale, the robots fear that they will die out if they cannot reproduce. Alquist is unable to reconstruct Rossum's formula, and there are no
other people left on earth to help the robots, whose numbers are dwin-
dling. When all else fails, the ruler of the robots, Damon, asks Alquist to
experiment on his body in the dissecting room. However, once the operation begins, and blood appears, Alquist loses his nerve. The robot, too,
now with a keener human awareness of life, prefers to live. After Alquist
falls asleep, two other robots, Primus and Helena (named for Helena
Glory), enter the laboratory and begin poking around. Primus becomes
interested in Alquist's scientific paraphernalia, but Helena quickly diverts
his attention to the sun rising and birds singing. The Adam and Eve of the
new civilization have appeared. Helena and Primus begin experiencing
human emotions—a sensitivity to nature and a new awareness of each
other as male and female. Helena tells Primus that she has found an amaz-

ing place where people used to live but which is now uninhabited and overgrown. Primus asks her to describe it, and Helena's description represents the dream come true of the average bourgeois of Čapek's time:

> Just a little house and a garden. And two dogs. If you could see how they licked my hands, and their puppies—oh, Primus, there's probably nothing more beautiful! You take them on your lap and cuddle them, and just sit there until sundown not thinking about anything and not worrying about anything. Then when you get up you feel as though you've done a hundred times more than a lot of work. (105)

The conversation between the two robots then turns personal and hints at vague feelings of affection they are unable to understand or fully verbalize. When an awakened Alquist observes their behavior he insists on dissecting one or the other to determine if Gall's new series of robots might contain the key to their future reproduction. Helena offers herself for the experiment in place of Primus, but the latter staunchly refuses. When Alquist asks him why, he blurts out: "We—we—belong to each other?" Alquist immediately understands that the dawn of the new age is at hand. Where robots previously had been sexually differentiated, it was solely for commercial reasons (female robots as maids and seamstresses, for example; they had no knowledge of, or need for, human procreation). But now, Alquist perceives that these robots represent a new species, capable of love and procreation. He tells them to go out into the world wherever they wish and hails them as Adam and Eve: "Go, Adam. Go, Eve—be a wife to him. Be a husband to her, Primus." As the pair of humanizing robots leave, Alquist, alone onstage, empties out the remains of his test tubes, picks up the Bible, and begins reciting from Genesis. His last words before the curtain descends are a joyous celebration of love as the basis of life:

> Only we have perished. Our houses and machines will be in ruins, our systems will collapse, and the names of our great will fall away like dry leaves. Only you, love, will blossom on this rubbish heap and commit the seed of life to the winds. Now let Thy servant depart in peace, O Lord, for my eyes have beheld—beheld Thy deliverance through love, and life shall not perish! (*He rises.*) It shall not perish! (*He stretches out his hands.*) Not perish! (109)

For Karel Čapek, the robot, the culmination of machine culture, represented the Apocalypse. The ultimate anti-utopian nightmare would be fulfilled. Humankind would destroy its own species through the invention of a humanlike machine that would make humans obsolete. The potential of the puppet, marionette, and automaton would at last be realized; humans would have succeeded in creating their own perfect surrogates. But Čapek's native Czech sense of optimism could not permit him to leave his audiences with this ghastly image of the future. Hence the banality, if you will, of *R.U.R.*'s ending: love will conquer all; the robots will become human, discover the joys of home and hearth, fall in love, marry, and have children. Life will go on, after all, and the future will be bright. Humans may destroy their own world, yet they will plant the seed of a new civilization and a new society issuing from a new Adam and Eve. Thirteen years after the publication of *R.U.R.*, in 1933—five years before his death and at a time when he was writing fairy tales and children's literature—Karel Čapek wrote his last puppet-inspired work, the slight play called *Jak pejsek s kočičkou slavili 28. říjen* (*How Puppy and Kitty Celebrated the 28th of October*), about Czech independence day. After *R.U.R.*, the anticlimax was almost palpable.

ELEVEN

Man as Machine

Methusalem to Bauhaus

The love-hate dichotomy at the heart of the twentieth-century avant-garde's attitude toward the machine is well known. The Futurists extolled the machine as the foundation of a postbourgeois Europe. The Expressionists viewed the new technological era with profound anxiety, fearing the domination of humans by machines. Whatever the differences between them in outlook, aims, and methods, both camps freely employed machine imagery to strike back at the perceived common enemy—the bourgeoisie. Karel Čapek's *R.U.R.* embraces the common Expressionist vision of humans so overwhelmed by machine culture that they become subservient to and are ultimately swept away by the very robots they have created to lighten their own burden. But just when things look bleakest, Čapek saves the day for humankind by transforming his robots into a new species of man hankering for the old bourgeois ideal of home and hearth. No such facile solution compromises the Expressionist vision of the underrated Franco-German writer Yvan (or Iwan) Goll.

Of mixed Alsatian-Lotharingian background, Goll had native proficiency in both French and German. Following his graduation from the University of Strasbourg, he became active in Expressionist circles in Berlin, where he published his first poetry. When World War I erupted, he joined the impressive community of émigré artists who chose to sit out the conflict in neutral Switzerland. Most of his time was spent in Zurich, where he moved in the company of such fellow émigrés as James Joyce, Hans Arp, Hugo Ball, Jules Romain, Franz Werfel, and Stefan Zweig. This Swiss period was productive for Goll. He published his first French poetry in 1916, and that same year, during a stay in Geneva, he met Claire Studer, the woman who became his wife and lifelong literary companion. A visit to Ascona in 1917 brought him into fruitful contact with the avant-garde filmmaker Viking Eggeling, whose film *Symphonie Diagonale* created a stir when first shown in Berlin in 1919. By the time he and Claire resettled in Paris in 1919, Goll had a fair literary reputation based on his German and French poetry. A great admirer of Apollinaire, he drew close to the Surrealists and collaborated with the short-lived review *Surréalisme*. He also became director of the Rhein-Verlag, under whose auspices he published the first German translation of Joyce's *Ulysses*. Goll pursued an active literary career in Paris, writing mostly poetry in both French and German, some of the French poetry jointly with his wife. His best-known prewar collections were *Poèmes d'amour* (*Poems of Love*, first published in 1925 in an edition with engravings by Marc Chagall); *Poèmes de jalousie* (*Poems of Jealousy*, 1926); *Poèmes de la vie et de la mort* (*Poems of Life and Death*, 1927, which appeared with x-rays of both the Golls' brains); and *La Chanson de Jean sans terre* (*The Song of Landless John*, 1936). Goll also wrote several novels (in French) about contemporary society, an opera entitled *Royal Palace*, with music by Kurt Weil, and a few plays in German, the best known of which was *Methusalem oder Der ewige Bürger* (*Methusalem, or The Eternal Bourgeois*, 1922).

Iwan and Claire Goll remained in Paris until the outbreak of World War II, when they emigrated to the United States. They settled in Columbia Heights, Brooklyn, spending summers in the artists' colonies of Yaddo in Saratoga Springs and MacDowell in Peterborough, New Hampshire. Besides editing the Anglo-French bilingual poetry review *Hémisphères* (June 1943–August 1945), Goll learned English well enough to do a bilingual edition of his *Landless John* poems and to publish a collection of original English poems under the title *Fruit from Saturn* (1946). Following his return to Paris in May 1947, Goll busied himself with the preparation for publication of works written during his stay in the United States. Two of his most interesting works from the late '40s reflect his North American experiences: *Le Mythe de la roche percée* (*The Myth of the Pierced Rock*, 1947), based on a trip to the Gaspé Peninsula in Canada, and the two-cycle *Elégie d'Ihpétonga, Suivie de Masques de cendre* (*Elegy of Ihpetonga, Followed by Masks of Ash*, 1949), notable for their poetic interpretation of New York's skyscrapers, and originally illustrated with four lithographs by Picasso. Goll also continued writing poetry, in French and German, his last major collection being the German *Traumkraut* (*Dream Herb*), which was published posthumously in 1951. While he was still in the United States, Goll was discovered to have incurable leukemia. His condition worsened some time after his return to France, and he had to be hospitalized in Strasbourg from September 1948 to January 1949. Ater a three-month trip to Italy in late autumn 1949, he entered the American Hospital in Paris, where he died on 27 February 1950.

While he is still well regarded as a poet in French—the language in which most of his poetry was written—Goll's reputation today would seem to rest primarily on his dramatic writings in German.[1] *Methusalem*, in particular, is generally acknowledged as a major Expressionist play text, especially in the English-speaking world. Goll's very short piece on "superdrama" (*Das Überdrama*, 1919) is similarly regarded as a representative programmatic statement on the "new drama" as necessarily grotesque in style.

A logical introduction to his own dramatic writing, *The Superdrama* echoes the militant despisal of the bourgeois by the early-twentieth-century avant-garde and forcefully states the case for the appropriateness of the grotesque:

> The purpose of art is not to make the fat bourgeois so comfortable that he'll shake his head and say, "Yes, that's the way it is all right! Now we're headed for the refreshment room!" Insofar as art seeks to educate, better, or in some way be effective, it has to knock the ordinary person flat on his back, terrify him, the way a mask does the child, the way Euripedes did the Athenians, who emerged reeling. Art should turn adults back into children again. The simplest means is the grotesque, but without provoking laughter. The monotony and stupidity of people are so enormous that one can get the best of them only with enormities. The new drama will be enormous. And also abnormal.[2]

An embodiment of Goll's ideas on the new drama of the grotesque, *Methusalem*, subtitled *A Satirical Drama*, was performed for the first time in Berlin on 13 October 1924. The production, which was critically well received, was directed by William Dieterle with décor by George

Grosz. In keeping with Goll's outlook, *Methusalem* was a fierce attack on the bourgeoisie, on its banality, commercialism, lack of morality, and debasement of language. In his preface to the play, Goll defended its alogicality and reiterated his purpose—previously stated in *The Superdrama*—of remaking adults as children. Consonant with the outlook of other avant-garde writers of the early twentieth century, his aim was to recover the spontaneity, freshness, and fantasy of the child:

> In order to avoid being a groaner, a pacifist, and a Salvation Army type, the author has to turn a few somersaults so that you can all become children again. For this is what he is after: to give you dolls, teach you how to play with them, and then toss the sawdust of the broken dolls back into the wind again.[3]

Through a series of images involving automatons and other animated inanimate entities, Goll conjures up a grotesque vision of the debasement of humans as machines in bourgeois society. The central figure is the shoe manufacturer Methusalem himself, the archetypical bourgeois, whom Goll describes in these terms:

> (Methusalem, *the original bourgeois, is seated in a large plush armchair, smoking a fat cigar, and buried beneath a pile of unnaturally large newspapers. He suffers from gout and his right leg is wrapped up in woolen bandages. His face is dark red, fat bald head, tiny eyes, no beard. He wears a finger-thick solid copper watch chain across his belly, with a miniature safe as a charm on it. As a tiepin, a golden shoe the size of a pocket watch: the trademark of his shoe factory.)* (175)

Before he is shot dead near the end of the play by the revolutionary Student in the vanguard of a communist uprising, Methusalem is a grotesque study in bourgeois venality, greed, and hypocrisy. His world is one of money and profits. The only humor in his life is dispensed from a robotlike figure identified in the text as a *Blechautomat*, which means literally an "automaton made out of sheet metal." The size of a normal candy-dispensing machine (a "chocolate-machine," in German), the automaton has the shape of a man and is attired in tails, white tie, top hat, and so on. When he wants it to speak, Methusalem winds it up and inserts a coin between its lips, whereupon the automaton moves with little steps and arm movements and tells jokes in a blaring voice. So banal are the jokes that they are hardly worth repeating; that is indeed the point of Goll's figure. So debased has humor become in bourgeois society that Goll can suggest it only by means of the grotesque image of the automated joke teller. In a sense, it is the automaton that has the last laugh. After Methusalem falls to the floor from the Student's bullet, the revolutionary mob begins to withdraw. As it does so, somebody puts a coin in the joke machine's mouth. This sets the automaton in motion; it clatters forward with little steps, takes up a position before Methusalem's corpse, and begins reciting its inane jokes. The image effectively demonstrates Goll's concept of the grotesque. Here, by way of example, is the first joke the auomaton recites over Methusalem's corpse: "Mikosch wants to go riding! 'Janosch,' Mikosch called to his servant one morning, 'I want to go riding; go see if the barometer has fallen.' Janosch goes and comes back quickly: 'It ain't fallen, sir; the barometer's still hangin' tight on its nail' " (209).

The grotesqueness of the scene is compounded when Methusalem's son, Felix, who is the *reductio ad absurdum* of his father's obsession with business, comes in, delivering, automaton-like, his usual business quotations: "Allo, allo. Order for Bucharest. Seventy-five pairs Toreador. Three thousand pairs new Liebknecht brand!" Not receiving an answer, he notices his father's corpse at his feet and addresses him as usual: "Allo, allo, Papa! Business is great. Come, get up!" Just then his mother, Amalie Methusalem, comes in, a grotesque image of the bourgeois wife, interested chiefly in food and public opinion. The following dialogue over Methusalem's body typifies, and underscores, Goll's utter contempt for the bourgeoisie and his sense of the appropriateness of the grotesque for his satire:

> Amalie (*coming in with a steaming bowl*). Here's the goulash, the good old goulash. Don't let it get cold. (*Shouting.*) Heavens, you're always letting everything get cold. It takes all the pleasure out of things.
> Felix (*who has bowed his head, solemnly*). I believe we're about to come into an inheritance!
> Amalie (*bowing her head similarly*). Now listen to me, hubby. Are you trying to get me upset again? The goulash! (*Weeps.*) You just can't die on me at this moment! What will the Darmkatas say? They've invited us for tomorrow.
> Felix. I've got to buy a black necktie.
> Amalie. Have you wept already?
> Felix. Allo, allo. Only hope the lawyer's at home.
> Amalie. And what kind of a funeral? What do you think? Third class? Just see to it you don't cause me any unnecessary expenses, understand? Children are always spendthrifts. (210)

Other bourgeois types are depicted in much the same machinelike terms. The sixth scene, in which three bourgeois couples are guests at the Methusalems', more than faintly recalls the treatment of the guests at the ball given by the architect and his wife in Andreev's *Life of Man*. In view of Goll's political sympathies and his interest in Russian culture, both pre- and postrevolutionary, Andreev's influence here is plausible. Immediately on entering the Methusalem home, the guests begin examining all the objects in the room, handling them, and so on. From time to time they also inspect things through opera glasses. If they are not in uniform ball dress, as in the Andreev play, they are still similarly attired and in part defined by dress. The men all wear identical ready-made suits. They are further dehumanized by masks expressing greed, envy, and curiosity. The women are decked out in absurd hats, in the shape of pots of geraniums, stuffed birds, or cardboard miniature replicas of state buildings. They also carry zebra and buffalo hides and wear dresses either with very long trains or reaching just above the knee. Their conversation is as banal and mechanical as that of Andreev's human marionettes in the ball scene in *The Life of Man*:

> *Frau Himmelreich*. Reading newspapers is very unhealthy. The "extras" disturb your sleep.
> *Frau Bäuchlein*. Did you happen to hear about the latest little murder? About a son who stuck a genuine silver fork into his grandmother's heart in order to kill her? It's more fantastic than Shakespeare. Just imagine, a fork with four sharp points. How the blood must have spurted out!
> *Frau Darmkata*. And cauliflower has gone up a lot.
> *Methusalem (coming in)*. My dear friends! How hard life is! (*Sits down.*)
> *Frau Himmelreich*. The end of the world.
> *Herr Bäuchlein*. Yes, nowadays!
> *Herr Himmelreich*. In the meantime I think . . .
> *Methusalem*. Well, what do you think?
> *Frau Bäuchlein*. Listen, Bäuchlein, Herr Himmelreich thinks something!
> (193)

Besides the joke-telling automaton, there is another animation of the in-animate in *Methusalem*. When Methusalem falls asleep at the end of the first scene, various artificial or stuffed animals lying about the room come to life and speak. The scene recalls Orwell's *Animal Farm*, though in a less

ominous and sinister way. Under the leadership of the bear, the animals
rant and rave against humans and spout revolutionary slogans; the few
voices of moderation are drowned out in the militant clamor of the overwhelming majority. What Goll has done here is to satirize contemporary
extremist political sentiment in his characteristically grotesque style:

> *Monkey.*
> But the spirit! The spirit! The ideal!
> A new time-reckoning begins!
> It's not a matter of gobbling up all humans,
> But of our sacred rights as animals.
> The right to sniff at all trees, bushes, lampposts,
> And walls, without consideration of phony morality.
> The right to mate in the middle of streets and avenues
> Without fear of scolding old maids,
> The right to piss on monuments, kiosks, and fountains,
> Even during ceremonial occasions,
> The right . . .
> *Bear.*
> Silence! Nonsense! Rubbish!
> I am the bear! Attention!
> Revolution has nothing at all to do with idealism!
> Mankind must die out,
> Lock, stock, and barrel!
> Attention! Chest out!
> Parade of the military organizations!
> Jews not admitted.
> A toast to the Fatherland.
> (180–81)

The most stunning use of machine imagery in *Methusalem* relates to
Methusalem's son, Felix, whom we have already met. As Goll notes in his
prefatory direction to the fourth scene, in which Felix first appears, Methusalem's son is "modern mathematical man" ("der moderne Zahlen-
mensch"). His speech consists almost entirely of stock quotations and
business communiqués. A chip off the old block, he is the bourgeois carried to the logical extreme. In place of a mouth, he wears a copper megaphone; in place of a nose, he has a telephone receiver; in place of eyes, he
has two five-mark coins; in place of a forehead and hat, he has a typewriter
with antennae on top of it which light up whenever he speaks. Almost

every sentence he utters is accompanied by a continuous "Allo! Allo!" His first appearance at once establishes his origin in the distorted vision of grotesque art:

> *Felix.* Allo, allo! Mornin', Pappy. Market's flat.
> *Methusalem.* Damn.
> *Felix (Pulls out a notebook and reads off everything. Sometimes he notes something down in it. Businesslike.).* Russian leather, 3 3/4.
> *Methusalem.* Damn.
> *Felix.* Toreador brand competitive. Sixty-two marks.
> *Methualem.* Damn.
> *Felix.* Revolution in the Hawaiian Islands, allo, allo.
> *Methusalem.* Damn.
> *Felix.* Lady cashier in the Hamburg branch pregnant. Leave. Allo.
> *Methusalem.* Swine. (184)

Goll's avant-gardist antibourgeois exercise in the grotesque in *Methusalem* carries the social implications of the modernist obsession with the puppet, marionette, and automaton to an extreme. In an age in which the development of machine culture evoked contrary responses, especially in the wake of World War I, human beings, in the bourgeois social context, were seen as reduced to the level of machines, capable only of pro-grammed responses, living a bleak life of petty materialist concerns and reliant on a grotesque piece of machinery for humor.

About the time that Goll was writing *Methusalem*, an outwardly parallel approach to the machine was occurring elsewhere in the German art world. The experimental theater of the renowned Bauhaus gradually be-gan to take shape after Oskar Schlemmer joined its staff in 1921.[4] To-gether with Laszlo Moholy-Nagy and Farkas Molnár, Schlemmer created an unusual laboratory essentially of the actor and devoted principally to the translation into spatial terms of the "emblems" of contemporary soci-ety. These emblems were determined to be abstraction, mechanization—which Schlemmer describes as "the inexorable process which now lays claim to every sphere of life and art" (17)—and the new potentials of tech-nology and invention. In line with other early-twentieth-century avant-garde theorists of the stage, Schlemmer emphasized the detachment of the actor as a corporeal entity from the literary text: "Today's actor bases his existence as player on the writer's word. Yet when the word is silent, when the body alone is articulate and its play is on exhibition—as a dancer's is—then it is free and its own lawgiver"(20). Like Kleist before him, Schlemmer acknowledged the primary limitation of the human form—"the law of gravity, to which it is subject"—and he recalled previous considerations of ways by which the limitation might be overcome:

> Acrobatics make it possible to partially overcome physical limitations, though only in the realm of the organic: the contortionist with his double joints, the living geometry of the aerialist, the pyramid of human bodies.
>
> The endeavor to free man from his physical bondage and to heighten his freedom of movement beyond his native potential resulted in substituting for the organism the mechanical human figure [Kunstfigur]: the *automaton and the marionette*. E. T. A. Hoffmann extolled the first of these, Heinrich Kleist the second.
>
> The English stage reformer Gordon Craig demands: "The actor must go, and in his place comes the inanimate figure—the Übermarionette we may call him." And the Russian [Valeri] Bryusov demands that we "replace actors with mechanized dolls, into each of which a phonograph shall be built." (28)

Again, Schlemmer extols the new possibilities opened up by contemporary technological advancements and the ideal represented by the artificial or mechanical human figure both in and of itself and as model:

> The artificial human figure [*Kunstfigur*] permits any kind of movement and any kind of position for as long a time as desired. It also permits—an artistic device from the periods of greatest art—a variable relative scale for figures: important ones can be large, unimportant ones small.
>
> An equally significant aspect of this is the possibility of relating the figure of natural "naked" Man to the abstract figure, both of which experience, through this confrontation, an intensification of their peculiar natures. (29)

Schlemmer's views were echoed in his colleague Laszlo Moholy-Nagy's contribution to *The Theater of the Bauhaus*, "Theater, Circus, Variety." In one section of his essay Moholy-Nagy speaks of the need for what he called the "mechanized eccentric" ("die mechanische Exzentrik"):

> Man, who no longer should be permitted to represent himself as a phenomenon of spirit and mind through his intellectual and spiritual capacities, no longer has any place in this concentration of action. For, no matter how cultured he may be, his organism permits him at best only a certain range of action, dependent entirely on his natural body mechanism. . . . The inade-

quacy of "human" *Exzentrik* led to the demand for a precise and fully controlled organization of form and motion, intended to be a synthesis of dy-
namically contrasting phenomena (space, form, motion, sound, and light).
This is the Mechanized Eccentric. (53–54)

While accepting the potential of the machine for the transformation of
existing forms of theater, Schlemmer cautions against mechanization for
its own sake, fearing the theatrical analogue of the spiritless mechanization of bourgeois man depicted by Goll: "This materialistic and practical
age has in fact lost the genuine feeling for play and for the miraculous.
Utilitarianism has gone a long way in killing it. Amazed at the flood of
technological advance, we accept these wonders of utility as being already
pefected art form, while actually they are only prerequisites for its creation" (31). Moholy-Nagy also tempered his enthusiasm for the mechanical and technical by never excluding man from the new theater: "Man, as
the most active phenomenon of life, is indisputably one of the most effective elements of a dynamic stage production (*Bühnengestaltung*), and
therefore he justifies on functional grounds the utilization of his totality
of action, speech, and thought" (57).

Viewed in terms of concrete theatrical events, the theater of the Bauhaus
took the form essentially of a nonverbal, dance-inspired theater of objects—living actors stylized as geometric, often Cubistic shapes, resembling modernistic marionettes and automatons, Aleksandra Exter's marionettes come to life, if you will, and organized in a variety of spatial
patterns. These included the dance trilogy *Das triadische Ballet* (*The Tri-
adic Ballet*), which was organized as early as 1912 in Stuttgart but the first
complete performance of which took place at the Stuttgart Landestheater
in September 1922 (it was also performed in 1923 at the Nationaltheater
in Weimar during the Bauhaus Week and subsequently in other German
cities); a production of Kokoschka's *Murderer, Hope of Woman* at the
Stuttgart Landestheater in 1921 featuring moveable architectural props
and metallic colors; *Das Figurale Kabinett I* (*The Figural Cabinet I*), described as "half shooting gallery, half *metaphysicum abstractum*," which
was first performed in 1922; *Das mechanische Ballet* (*The Mechanical
Ballet*), with actors as mechanical figures, also performed at the Jena
Stadttheater during the Bauhaus Week of August 1923; *Meta oder die
Pantomime der Orten* (*Meta or the Pantomime of Places*), a Bauhaus stage
improvisation produced in Weimar in 1924; and *Mann am Schaltbrett*

(*Man at the Switchboard*), first performed in 1924 at the Bauhaus. Most of the Bauhaus theatrical experiments were conducted as small-scale space and form "dances," dramatic gesturing, and pantomime. Sets seldom consisted of more than simple flats of wood and white canvas which could be slid back and forth on a series of parallel tracks and could do double duty as screens for light projection. Stage lighting was similarly extremely simple, and colors were "pure" in the sense that they were stripped of all other associations. Although the Bauhaus theater people were logically interested in marionette theater, very little is actually known of what work was undertaken in this sphere. Only one marionette play, *Die Abenteuer des kleinen Buckligen* (*The Adventures of the Little Hunchback*), is mentioned in *The Theater of the Bauhaus*. It was designed by Kurt Schmidt and executed by T. Hergt, with the figures conforming to the same mechanistic style of other Bauhaus performances.

The experiments of the Bauhaus theater, if quantitatively and qualitatively less significant than those of the Italian Futurists, are interesting primarily when situated within the context of the avant-garde preoccupation with the machine in the teens and twenties of the twentieth century. Oriented toward the elegant simplicity, the "purity," of abstraction, the Bauhaus assimilation of machine culture avoided the emotional involvement, hence the extremes, of Futurism and Expressionism. It offered further testimony of the grasp on artistic consciousness of modern technology and the complex pattern of responses to the new age in which man's genius for invention contained the seeds of his own destruction.

Epilogue

Our concentration in this book on the impact on modernism and the avant-garde of that most ancient and, in some respects, most basic art, that of puppetry, was motivated by the extraordinary range of affinities expressed by artists of the period with puppets, marionettes, automatons, and related forms of human likenesses. The impact of the puppet and similar figures on the literary and theatrical imagination stretches far back in time, as we had occasion to observe in our exploration of works of fiction and the drama from *Don Quixote* to the Symbolists. But it was with the new sensibility of modernism that the serious artistic interest in puppets, marionettes, and the like acquired a depth, and breadth, never previously realized. It may be overly dramatic to speak of a crescendo of such interest being reached in the teens and twenties of the twentieth century; but the emergence of Futurism and Expressionism in those years carried the preoccupation with inanimate human likenesses to their logical extremes. From the exploration of the various ramifications of the human-as-puppet metaphor to the celebration of the puppet or marionette as model of animated perfection, the avant-garde grafted the culture of the machine age onto the inanimate figure and then animated it with all its anxieties, exhilarations, and disillusionments. Once art had worked its way through the reduction of human to machine or, as in the case of Karel Čapek's *R.U.R.*, from human being to robot and robot back to human being, the modernist and avant-garde obsession with puppetry had run much of its course.

The literary and theatrical interest in the puppet and marionette continued to bear fruit well into the 1930s, as we saw especially in the career of the Belgian Michel de Ghelderode, though here the dramatist's personal commitment to a rich indigenous puppet theater tradition needed little or no external creative stimuli. As late as 1949 even George Bernard Shaw was persuaded to write a puppet play and to express his feelings about the eternal allure and mystery of the puppet figure. But if puppet theater itself is alive and well in the waning years of the twentieth century, the evidence of a literary and theatrical fascination with the puppet figure approximating the intensity of that of the first half of the century is unconvincing. This is not to minimize the importance of puppet and similar figures in post–World War II European and also American drama. In *Motel*, the third part of his trilogy *America Hurrah* (1965), the American dramatist Jean-Claude Van Itallie makes chillingly effective use of larger-than-life dolls (actually actors within doll figures) in a scathing satire of the tastelessness and violence of contemporary life in the United States. As the proprietress of a run-of-the-mill motel—herself one of the dolls—describes her establishment, addressing no one in particular, Man and Woman, representing Mr. and Mrs. American Everyman, enter, make love, scribble obscene graffiti on the walls, and finally smash the place to smithereens. As the theater fills with the deafening sound of blaring rock and roll music and a civil defense siren, Man and Woman bring the terrifying play to an end by dismembering the proprietress. *Motel* had its premiere at the Café La Mama in New York City in spring 1965 and became a huge success both in the United States and abroad.

The formerly East German dramatist Heiner Müller, widely acknowledged as Brecht's successor, similarly employed puppets, dolls, and robots for satirical purposes in his play *Leben Gundlings Friedrich von Preussen Lessings Schlaf Traum Schrei* (*Gundling's Life. Frederick of Prussia. Lessing's Sleep. Dream Scream*, 1977).[1] A grotesque indictment of Prussian history for its tradition of repression, Müller's play is, in this instance, ideologically compatible with the outlook of the former East German communist state. Distancing itself as far as possible from the Hitler regime, the German Democratic Republic never lost an opportunity to discredit its West German rival by charging it with harboring former Nazis and keeping alive the spirit of Prussian repression. Its ideological dimension notwithstanding, Müller's *Gundling's Life* is of particular interest to us here for its basic similarities to Gerhart Hauptmann's *Festival Play in German Verse*. Since Prusso-German history was a favorite whipping boy of East German ideologues, Müller could well have conceived his satire without any assistance from Hauptmann. But Hauptmann's towering reputation in German drama and his bold repudiation of Prussian militarism in the *Festival Play*, particularly in light of the circumstances in which the play was written and first staged, would doubtless have attracted Müller to the work.

Constructed of a series of disparate scenes from Prussian history in the time of Frederick William I, Müller's mixed prose and verse play dramatizes the repressive, militaristic nature of Frederick and his legacy. This is seen primarily in the elder Frederick's attitude toward the training of his son and in his disdain for intellectuals of the stamp of Jacob Paul Baron von Gundling, whom he makes his court fool at the same time as he appoints him president of the new Royal Academy. The deflationary function of puppets in Hauptmann's *Festival Play* recurs in Müller's *Gundling's Life*, but with the important structural distinction that, whereas Hauptmann's work is cast as a grandiose puppet show, scenes with puppets and related figures are only intermittent and brief in Müller. A make-believe military campaign of Frederick II, for example, is interrupted for a "patriotic puppet play" ("ein patriotisches Puppenspiel") under the title *The School of the Nation* (*Die Schule der Nation*). It depicts, in a single short scene, puppet Prussian soldiers in World War II German Wehrmacht uniforms goose-stepping into a wall of fire and being graded on their performance by Frederick, the highest grades going to those who fall dead or suffer the gravest wounds. Thus, in a single stroke, Müller makes the proper ideological link between the Prussia of Frederick II and the Nazi era. The younger Frederick's contempt for his father is expressed shortly thereafter when he takes a doll wearing the mask of Frederick William, slaps it, throws it on the floor, and then dances on it. Dolls figure again prominently in a brief mimed scene entitled "Heinrich von Kleist Plays Michael Kohlhass," in which the writer Heinrich Kleist executes a macabre reenactment of the obsession with vengeance of the eponymous hero of his best-known novella. Of an old Prussian military family but unattracted to military life, Kleist appears in uniform and savagely mutilates and hacks to pieces the dolls of a horse, a woman, and finally himself. The scene is followed by the appearance of an actor playing the part of the distinguished writer Ephraim Lessing; he delivers a somber monologue of a man of letters who, because of all he has seen, feels only a growing disgust with literature and the academies.

Since the Western powers, and above all the United States, were another favorite target of East German propaganda, Müller doesn't miss the opportunity to weave elements of political satire against them into his play. Again, his method relies primarily on inanimate figures. While Frederick II plays at war with his soldier-dolls in *The School of the Nation*, enormous representations of John Bull and Marianne divide the world among them by throwing at a globe the knives they pull from the corpses of dead Indians and blacks. Very near the end of the play, in the "Dream Scream," Lessing leaves Prussia for the United States and, together with Nathan and Emilia Galotti—the protagonists in his two most famous plays—encounters the "last president of the U.S.A." in an automobile junkyard in Montana. He is a faceless robot seated in an electric chair, surrounded by car wrecks and images of death. The play ends with a bizarre symbolization of the spiritual entombment of the artist and intellectual in the Prusso-German tradition: stagehands dressed as members of the audience pour sand on a torso while waiters simultaneously fill the stage with busts of poets and philosphers. Despite the different style of his play, with its grotesque, bizarre, and macabre elements, its calculated offensiveness, Heiner Müller shared with his illustrious predecessor Gerhart Hauptmann a loathing for Prussian militarism and repression. And as in Hauptmann's work, or perhaps because of Hauptmann, the grotesqueness of Müller's vision owed much to his use of puppets and other inanimate figures.

Arguably the most outstanding interpretation of the puppet in postmodern drama can be found in works by the internationally celebrated Polish visual artist and theatrical director, Tadeusz Kantor. Primarily through his Cricot 2 company, which he cofounded with Maria Jarema in 1955, Kantor became a world-famous theatrical practitioner and theorist, his contributions to the visual arts and the stage discussed—and honored—at an international symposium hosted by the French Ministry of Culture at the Georges Pompidou Center in Paris in June 1989. Known outside Poland on the basis of such productions as *The Dead Class* (1975), *Wielopole/Wielopole* (1980), *Let the Artists Die* (1985), *I Shall Never Return* (1988), *Silent Night* (1990), and *Today Is My Birthday* (1990), Kantor was a total man of the theater, engaged in virtually every aspect of the stage and indeed appearing onstage, in one form or another, in nearly every one of his productions. Reexamining and in the process often redefining both traditional and nontraditional stage forms, Kantor fashioned a unique theatrical idiom that charted a new course and defies conventional classification.

Kantor's interest in puppetry can be traced at least as far back as 1938, when he founded a puppet theater, the Ephemeric (Mechanic) Theater, at the Academy of Fine Arts in Cracow, which he attended from 1933 to 1939 and where, in 1948, he became a professor.[2] (The professorship was revoked a year later when Kantor refused to abide by the principles of Socialist Realism.) His major puppet theater production was a Bauhaus-influenced version of Maurice Maeterlinck's *Death of Tintagiles* in an experiment aimed at reconciling Symbolism and the avant-garde. Kantor never abandoned this early enthusiasm for puppets, although his interest shifted from the puppet theater as such to experimentation with puppet figures—or mannequins, as he preferred to call them—in productions of plays by other dramatists and eventually in his own works. The Polish dramatists toward whom he felt the strongest affinities were Stanisław Wyspiański—whose *Powrót Odysa* (*The Return of Odysseus*) he staged in 1944 and 1945—and especially Stanisław Ignacy Witkiewicz, the leading avant-garde dramatist of interwar Poland. Kantor began staging Witkiewicz in 1956, when the end of the Stalinist period facilitated that extraordinary dramatist's "rediscovery"; most of Kantor's subsequent productions were based on Witkiewicz's plays.

By the time Kantor brought to the stage his first original production—*Umarła klasa* (*The Dead Class*)—in 1975, his ideas on puppets, marionettes, and mannequins had crystallized and were incorporated into his essay "The Theater of Death." Taking as its point of departure Gordon Craig's views regarding the marionette and supermarionette, the essay surveys nineteenth- and twentieth-century attitudes toward the artificial creations of man and finally disputes Craig's belief that the human actor could ultimately be displaced in the theater by the marionette. Kantor first considers the traditional attitude of disdain for such figures and yet their ineluctable theatrical "magic":

> Mannequins and Wax figures have always existed on the peripheries of sanctioned Culture. They were not admitted further; they occupied places in FAIR BOOTHS, suspicious MAGICIANS' CHAMBERS, far from the splendid shrines of art, treated condescendingly as CURIOSITIES intended for

the tastes of the masses. For precisely this reason, it was they, and not academic, museum creations, which caused the curtain to move at the blink of an eye.[3]

From here, Kantor develops his novel idea of the connection between the mannequin figure and death:

MANNEQUINS also have their own version of TRANSGRESSION. The existence of these creatures, shaped in man's image, almost "godlessly," in an illegal fashion, is the result of heretical dealings, a manifestaion of the Dark, Nocturnal, Rebellious side of human activity. Of Crimes and Traces of Death as sources of recognition. The vague and inexplicable feeling that through this entity so similar to a living human being but deprived of consciousness and purpose there is transmitted to us a terrifying message of Death and Nothingness—precisely this feeling becomes the cause of—simultaneously—that transgression, repudiation, and attraction. Of accusation and fascination. The very mechanism of action called their attention to itself, that mechanism which, if taken as the purpose, could easily be relegated to the lower forms of creativity! IMITATION AND DECEPTIVE SIMILARITY, which serve the conjurer in setting his TRAPS and fooling the viewer, the use of "unsophisticated" means, evading the concepts of aesthetics, the abuse and fraudulent deception of appearances, practices from the realm of charlatans.

Definitively rejecting Kleist's and Craig's preference for the marionette over the live actor, Kantor discovers the relevance of the mannequin for his own theater:

I do not share the belief that the MANNEQUIN (or WAX FIGURE) could replace the LIVE ACTOR, as Kleist and Craig wanted. This would be too simple and naive. I am trying to delineate the motives and intent of this unusual creature which has suddenly appeared in my thoughts and ideas. Its appearance complies with my ever-deepening conviction that it is possible to express *life* in art only through the absence of life, through an apeal to DEATH, through APPEARANCES, through EMPTINESS and the lack of a MESSAGE.

The MANNEQUIN in my theater must become a MODEL through which pass a strong sense of DEATH and the conditions of the DEAD.

A model for the LIVE ACTOR.

Death and memory intertwine in Kantor, and the mannequin functions as the mediator. In *The Dead Class*, for example, the class referred to is that of Kantor's own school days restored fragmentarily to the present by memory. The Old People who appear in the work, all garbed in dark clothes, funereally, are both past and present, recalled from the past yet participants in a collective act of recollection to revisit scenes of childhood before becoming dead themselves like the past. At a certain point in the performance, they disappear from the scene and reenter with the wax figures of children, "looking like dead bodies or TUMORS of their CHILD-HOOD," on their backs. These are the doubles of their childhood, manne-quins, images of death, and at the same time the "weight" of memory hu-mans carry with them through life. Through the interaction of the live actors and the wax figures, Kantor examines the processes of memory and the obsession with pastness and death.

More personal than *The Dead Class*, and without the interpolation this time of characters and episodes from Kantor's modernist predecessors— the plays of Stanisław Ignacy Witkiewicz, the absurdist novel *Ferdydurke* by Witold Gombrowicz, the *Cinnamon Shops* collection of stories by Bruno Schulz—*Wielopole/Wielopole* carries the audience back to the lo-cus of Kantor's youth, the village of Wielopole in Polish Galicia. As Kan-tor himself defines the theatrical space, as he usually does in his produc-tions, seated in the center of the stage in his customary formal black suit and white shirt, the dead members of his family—or, to be precise, actors hired to play the various members of his family—begin appearing, like suddenly animated figures in faded photographs, and set about randomly, repetitively, and contentiously reconstructing past space. Kantor's typical text, splendidly exemplified in *Wielopole/Wielopole*, is in fact a parallel one: dialogue, generally very sparse, on one side, and descriptions of ac-tion, often with Kantor's own commentary, on the other. Since the bulk of the text consists of the latter, a work such as *Wielopole/Wielopole* can be thought of as largely pantomimic. Acknowledging this, however, does not facilitate its description in view of the play's fragmentary and repetitive nature and the always exceptionally important visual and auditory ele-ments in Kantor's productions. It is easier to speak of certain scenes and scenic images than to attempt to convey a nonexistent sense of a unified whole.

As in *The Dead Class* and in the other works of his "Theater of Death," Kantor retrieves fragments of the past as an inevitable confrontation with death. And the dead in turn are usually represented by means of manne-quins, dummies, wax figures, the doubles of their living selves. A platoon of soldiers in Austro-Hungarian World War I garb tramps through the play at certain intervals spreading death and destruction as they go. The figure representing Kantor's mother, Mother Helka, becomes a dummy tossed about by the soldiers, raped, and then left dead. But as in Witkiewicz's plays, the dead reappear live and return to participate in the action. The Priest who marries Kantor's father and mother dies in the early moments of the play, comes back to life, is bayoneted by the soldiers, returns again, only to die in a grotesque reenactment of the crucifixion of Christ on Golgotha. During the crucifixion, a Little Rabbi, described as a *"marionette-like figure in synagogue garment,"* intrudes on the scene, sings a music hall "funeral" song, and is then gunned down by the soldiers. But the dead Priest following the Coffin-Cross lifts him up, the Little Rabbi takes up his song again, is shot once more, and "so it goes on," Kantor declares in the parallel text, "a number of times, repeated as things are in my theater. Then the Rabbi leaves forever."[4] In an insinuation of the ultimate fate of the soldiers, a cattle wagon appears teeming with conscripts being transported to war, their uniformed bodies jumbled in a swarming mass together with the naked wax figures of conscripted convicts. The scene evokes the image of cattle being carted to the slaughterhouse.

By far, the strongest use of the puppet/mannequin motif clusters about the figure of the Priest. By virtue of his profession a mediator between life and death, the Priest generates several of the play's most compelling images. Early, he expires in a huge bed likened to a piece of machinery. It is in fact a revolving machine of death: "The top, made of unplaned boards, can rotate around a shaft, which ends in cog-wheels and a crank. As the top is made to rotate, each of its sides becomes alternately the upper or the under side. For the time being we can see the Priest lying on top, a barefoot wax figure in a mortuary gown" (28). With the Priest now dead, the rotation of the bed displays either the wax figure—that is, the dummy of the dead Priest—or the Priest alive, appropriately attired, and prepared to enter into various activities with members of the family. On one such "return," for the purpose of conducting a second wedding ceremony between Kantor's mother and father, both of whom appear in the play more puppetlike than real, dead and alive at the same time, the Priest is reconciled with his double. Kantor's grandmother seats him, as a motionless, still unburied corpse, in a chair near a table. She then turns to the Double of the Priest on the floor, leaning against the bed, picks him up, and seats him next to the first. The two will be sitting thus, elbow-to-elbow, "menacingly alike, with an air of anticipation of something conclusive to take place about them. Their stillness broods over this room which *exists not*" (54). Later, in act 5 ("The Last Supper"), the deathbed machinery containing the Dummy of the Priest on one side, and the Actor playing the Priest on the other, is actually rotated as members of Kantor's family, split into two groups, try to talk now to the Dummy, now to the Actor, uncertain as to which is live. When they tire of the rotation, they all drag the Priest down from the bed, pull him this way and that, then drop him on the floor and swiftly exit. As Kantor notes at this point, "All this is inexplicable and absurd" (83). Alone, the Priest soon rises again, battered and exhausted, and starts to make his way out of the room. But he is prevented by the reenactment—one of several in the work—of his earlier crucifixion by child soldiers, who nail him to a huge cross they drag in with them. Here is Kantor's description in act 5, scene 3:

> We are to witness another imperfect repetition—imperfect, for nothing can be retrieved from the past with absolute exactness. The Dummy-Doubles have their own, not quite reputable, part in the incident. After all, art is always a counterfeit. Which gives it its measure of profundity and of tragic fascination. Storming into the room are the Family together with the Child-Soldiers wearing priests' birettas and carrying rifles with fixed bayonets. They pull a huge cross along, and the Dummy of the Priest. The Child-Comedians' game has gone a bit too far. There is no stopping it. We may as well let things come to a head, in this way, through the welter of events and confusion of facts, towards an irrevocable outcome. (84)

The "irrevocable outcome"—before all the actors make their final exit from the stage, followed by Kantor himself, the last to leave—takes the form of the anarchic, destructive intrusion of naked corpses of soldiers (dummies) into the Last Supper. The stage becomes a living hell of the dead at the end, the reality of the war insinuating its terrible presence, shattering family life, turning the recollected fragments of childhood into the chaos of battlefield.

The examples drawn from the major texts of Kantor's "Theater of Death"—*The Dead Class* and *Wielopole/Wielopole*—suffice to demonstrate how one of the most original of post–World War II theater artists succeeded in bringing a fresh perspective to bear on the puppet figure. There is no need for further supporting evidence from Kantor's subsequent productions—*Niech sczezną artyści* (*Let the Artists Die*, 1985) and *Nigdy tu już nie powrócę* (*I Shall Never Return*, 1988)—essentially variations on themes already engaged in *The Dead Class* and *Wielopole/*

Wielopole, with similar uses of mannequins. Although Kantor's work ex-emplifies the potential for relevance of wooden and other imitations of man in the postmodern period, it does not signal a new wave of enthusi-asm for puppets, marionettes, and related forms among dramatists and theatrical practitioners. For all the universal reach of Kantor's stage work, his art cannot be separated from his experiences as a Pole, and as a Pole of Jewish origin, of the massive destruction and severe dislocations visited on his country by two world wars. Kantor's obsession with death and pastness, with the urgencies and fragilities of memory, are rooted in his Polishness. Extrapolating, therefore, from his own unique use of manne-quins and dummies in his "theater of death" to any broader postmodern literary or theatrical interest in the puppet cannot be justified. Perhaps, like other cultural phenomena, the obsession with puppets, marionettes, and their kin in the period 1890–1935 was a product of the times them-selves, a condition of modernism and the avant-garde.

Notes

CHAPTER 1. PUPPETS AND THEIR KIN IN FICTION AND DRAMA

1. Bernard Shaw, *Complete Plays with Prefaces* (New York: Dodd, Mead & Co., 1962), 5:19–20.

2. For an interesting consideration of more abstract aspects of puppetry, see Steve Tillis, *Toward an Aesthetics of the Puppet: Puppetry as Theatrical Art* (New York: Greenwood Press, 1992).

3. Miguel de Cervantes Saavedra, *Don Quixote de La Mancha*, trans. Walter Starkie (New York: New American Library, 1964), 703–20.

4. Miguel de Cervantes, *Entremeses* (Mexico City: Editorial Porrua, 1968), 76–77.

5. Robert E. Knoll, *Ben Jonson's Plays: An Introduction* (Lincoln: University of Nebraska Press, 1964), 160. See also Jonas A. Barish, " 'Bartholomew Fair' and Its Puppets," *Modern Language Quarterly* 20 (1959): 3–17.

6. Ben Jonson, *Bartholomew Fair*, ed. Eugene M. Waith (New Haven: Yale University Press, 1963), 164.

7. Knoll, *Ben Jonson's Plays*, 151.

8. Jonathan Swift, *The Selected Poems*, ed. A. Norman Jeffares (London: Kyle Cathie, 1992), 124–25.

9. *The Works of the Right Honourable Joseph Addison*, ed. Richard

Hurd, trans. George Sewell (London: Henry G. Bohn, 1856), 6:580. The Latin text appears in ibid., 1:249–51.

10. On Goethe's early interest in puppetry, see Eleonore Rapp, *Die Marionette im romantischen Weltgefühl: Ein Beitrag zur deutschen Geistesgeschichte* (Bochum: Deutsches Institut für Puppenspiel, 1964), 23–38.

11. For the German text of the play, see Johann Wolfgang Goethe, *Sämtliche Werke*, vol. 2, pt. 1, *Erstes Weimarer Jahrzehnt 1775–1786*, ed. Harmut Reinhardt (Munich: Carl Hanser Verlag, 1987), 213–34. The translation appears in Paul McPharlin, ed., *A Repertory of Marionette Plays* (New York: Viking Press, 1929), 243–73.

12. McPharlin, *Marionette Plays*, 249.

13. Very few of Goethe's biographers discuss his interest in puppet theater while in Weimar. There are some comments in Curt Hohoff, *Johann Wolfgang von Goethe: Dichtung und Leben* (Munich: Langen Müller, 1989), 29, 258ff. My translations from *Wilhelm Meisters Lehrjahre* are based on the text as it appears in Johann Wolfgang Goethe, *Wilhelm Meisters Lehrjahre*, 2d ed. (Zurich: Artemis Verlag, 1962).

14. For a good biography of Kleist in English, see Joachim Maass, *Kleist: A Biography*, trans. Ralph Mannheim (New York: Farrar, Straus & Giroux, 1983).

15. My translations are from Heinrich von Kleist, *Über das Marionettentheater: Zur Poetik* (Reinbek bei Hamburg: Rowohlt, 1964), 5–12. There is a good English translation in *An Abyss Deep Enough: Letters of Heinrich Kleist with a Selection of Essays and Anecdotes*, ed. and trans. Philip B. Miller (New York: E. P. Dutton, 1982), 211–16.

16. Gaetan Vestris, the most celebrated dancer of the Paris Opéra at the time, and probably the most famous in Europe in the eighteenth and nineteenth centuries.

17. Kleist, *Marionettentheater*, 8.

18. *Der Automaten-Mensch: E. T. A. Hoffmanns Erzählung vom "Sandmann,"* ed. Lienhard Wawrzyn (Berlin: Verlag Klaus Wagenbach, 1976), 39.

19. The text of the essay is included in *The Complete Tales and Poems of Edgar Allan Poe*, intro. Hervey Allen (New York: Modern Library, 1938), 421–39.

20. Georg Büchner, *The Complete Collected Works: "Woyzeck,"*

"Danton's Death," "The Hessian Messenger," "Lenz," and "Leonce and Lena," trans. and ed. Henry J. Schmidt (New York: Avon Books, 1977).

21. There is a considerable literature on Büchner in different languages. For three good introductions in English to his life and work, see A. H. J. Knight, *Georg Büchner* (London: Methuen, 1974), first published by Basil Blackwell, 1953; Ronald Hauser, *Georg Büchner* (New York: Twayne, 1974); David G. Richards, *Georg Büchner and the Birth of Modern Drama* (Albany: State University of New York Press, 1977).

22. Büchner, *Complete Collected Works*, 138. For another English translation of *Leonce and Lena*, see Georg Büchner, *"Leonce and Lena," "Lenz," "Woyzeck,"* trans. Michael Hamburger (Chicago: University of Chicago Press, 1972). Rudolf Drux, in his German study *Marionette Mensch: Ein Metaphernkomplex und sein Kontext von E. T. A. Hoffmann bis Georg Büchner* (Munich: Wilhelm Fink Verlag, 1986), 109–46, discusses the polyvalence and transformation of function of a metaphoric motif in Büchner.

23. Büchner, *Complete Collected Works*, 168–69.

24. Victor Erlich, *Gogol* (New Haven: Yale University Press, 1969), 103.

25. N. V. Gogol, *Sobranie sochineniy*, vol. 4, *Dramaticheskie proizvedeniya* (Moscow: Khudozhestvennaya literatura, 1985), 57–58.

26. *The Trilogy of Alexander Sukhovo-Kobylin*, trans. Harold B. Segel (New York: E. P. Dutton, 1969), 205–6.

27. See, for example, Ruth Jordan, *George Sand: A Biography* (London: Constable, 1976), 267–69; and especially Gay Manifold, *George Sand's Theatre Career* (Ann Arbor, Mich.: UMI Research Press, 1985), 108–44 ("A Theatre of One's Own").

28. Manifold, *George Sand's Theatre Career*, 118. Five of the puppet plays—performed between 1863 and 1879—have been translated into English. See Maurice Sand, *Plays for Marionettes*, trans. Babette and Glenn Hughes (New York: Samuel French, 1931).

29. My account follows the description in McPharlin, *Marionette Plays*, 104–5.

30. On Sand and the commedia dell'arte, see Manifold, *George Sand's Theatre Career*, 118–21.

31. George Sand, *L'Homme de neige*, in *Oeuvres Complètes* (Geneva:

Slatkin Reprints, 1980), 15:156. For a complete English translation see George Sand, *The Snow Man*, 2 vols., trans. G. Burnham Ives (Philadelphia: George Barrie & Son, 1901).

CHAPTER 2. THE PUPPET IN TURN-OF-THE-CENTURY
LITERATURE, DRAMA, AND THEATER

1. The best general study of *Pinocchio* in English, and one of the best in any language—to which I am happy to acknowledge my own indebtedness—is by Nicolas J. Perella. It appears as "An Essay on *Pinocchio*" (1–69) accompanying his fine translation of *Pinocchio*. See Carlo Collodi [Carlo Lorenzini], *The Adventures of Pinocchio: Story of a Puppet*, trans. Nicolas J. Perella (Berkeley and Los Angeles: University of California Press, 1986). This is the complete text in a bilingual edition, and my quotations are based on it.

2. These are discussed in substance in Perella, "Essay on *Pinocchio*."

3. For a very close critical reading of the text, see especially Jacob Steiner, *Rilkes Duineser Elegien*, 2d ed. (Bern-Munich: Francke Verlag, 1969), 73–100. For analyses in English, see Rainer Maria Rilke, *Duinesian Elegies*, trans. Elaine E. Boney (Chapel Hill: University of North Carolina Press, 1975), 85–89, which contains the German text and a commentary; and especially Kathleen L. Komar, *Transcending Angels: Rainer Maria Rilke's "Duino Elegies"* (Lincoln: University of Nebraska Press, 1987), 71–87. The *Duino Elegies* have been translated into English several times. Very readable in English, though probably not translated directly from the German, are the translations by the American poet Gary Miranda. See Rainer Maria Rilke, *Duino Elegies*, trans. Gary Miranda (Portland, Ore.: Breitenbush Books, 1981).

4. My translations of the elegy are based on Rainer Maria Rilke, *Gesammelte Werke*, vol. 3, *Gedichte* (Leipzig: Insel-Verlag, 1930), 274–75. Despite the fact that translation rarely does justice to Rilke's thought and style, I have, for reasons of space, omitted the German originals.

5. Wolfgang Leppman, *Rilke: A Life*, trans. Russell M. Stockman (New York: Fromm International Publishing, 1984), 283.

6. Peter Krumme discusses this in his study of Rilke, *Eines Augenblickes Zeichnung: Zur Temporalität des Bewusstseins in Rilkes "Duineser Elegien"* (Würzburg: Königshausen & Neumann, 1988), 90–93.

7. Rainer Maria Rilke, "Puppen," *Sämtliche Werke*, vol. 6, *Kleine Schriften* (Frankfurt am Main: Insel-Verlag, 1966), 1069–70, 1072.

8. Maurice Maeterlinck, *Théâtre* (Brussels: P. Lacomblez, 1904), 2:188.

9. For a good study of Craig as a director, see Christopher Innes, *Edward Gordon Craig* (Cambridge: Cambridge University Press, 1983).

10. Craig's own marionette plays, written under the name Tom Fool, include *Mr. Fish and Mrs. Bone, The Tune the Old Cow Died Of, The Gordian Knot,* and *The Men of Gotham.* They appeared in Craig's periodical, *The Marionette,* the first number of which was published in Florence, Italy, on 1 April (April Fool's Day) 1918. Another marionette play by Craig, *School or Thou Shalt Not Commit,* originally published in the *English Review* 26 (January 1918), is reprinted in Paul McPharlin, *A Repertory of Marionette Plays* (New York: Viking Press, 1929), 29–37. The marionette play *The Azure Sky,* a "sketch," was also published in the *English Review* 32 (March 1921). *Romeo and Juliette* (1916) was published in only twenty-five copies in the same style and format as *The Marionette.* "The Gods Themselves Battle Stupidity in Vain" still exists only in manuscript. For a superbly edited collection, in Italian, of previously unpublished texts and materials by Craig, see *Il trionfo della marionetta, testi e materiali inediti di Edward Gordon Craig,* ed. and trans. Marina Maymone Siniscalchi (Rome: Officina Edizioni, 1980).

11. Quoted in *Craig on Theatre,* ed. J. Michael Walton (London: Methuen, 1983), 84.

12. For a detailed survey of the turn-of-the-century European cabaret, see Harold B. Segel, *Turn-of-the-Century Cabaret: Paris, Barcelona, Berlin, Munich, Vienna, Cracow, Moscow, St. Petersburg, Zurich* (New York: Columbia University Press, 1987).

13. Quoted in ibid., 106.

14. For a very good, and illustrated, account of puppet theater in Munich, see especially Ludwig Krafft, *München und das Puppenspiel: Kleine Liebe einer grossen Stadt* (Munich: Akademie für das graphische Gewerbe, 1961).

15. For an interesting, well-illustrated book on the Turkish *karagöz,* see Metin And, *Karagöz: Turkish Shadow Theatre* (Istanbul: Dost, 1975; rev. ed., 1979).

16. For a good study of the shadow show, with particular reference to France, see Denis Bordat and Francis Boucrot, *Les Théâtres d'ombres: Histoire et techniques* (Paris: L'Arche, 1956).

17. For a valuable, copiously illustrated collection of French shadow

show texts by Lemercier de Neuville and others, as well as detailed descriptions of constructions, see *Les Pupazzi noirs: Ombres animées* (Paris: Charles Mendel, Editeur, 1897).

18. My account of the shadow shows at the Chat Noir follows the discussion in Segel, *Turn-of-the-Century Cabaret*, 66–80.

19. Quoted in ibid., 71.

20. Jules Lemaître, *Impressions du théâtre.* 2ᵉ série (Paris: Libraire H. Lecène et H. Oudin, 1888), 332.

21. I am following the account in Segel, *Turn-of-the-Century Cabaret*, 79–80.

22. Besides such mystery plays as *Orpheus* and *Sanctus*, both first published in 1909, Wolfskehl also expressed his ideas on the genre in a few essays, among them "Über das Drama" ("On Drama," 1904) and "Vorbemerkung über das Drama" ("Preliminary Remarks on the Drama," 1908–9). For the best edition of Wolfskedhl's works in German, see Karl Wolfskehl, *Gesammelte Werke*, 2 vols. (Hamburg: Claassen Verlag, 1960).

23. Bernus's mystery plays are available in Alexander von Bernus, *Sieben Mysterienspiele* (Büdingen-Gettenbach: Avalun-Verlag, 1957).

24. Franz Anselm Schmitt, *Alexander von Bernus: Dichter und Alchymist* (Nuremberg: Verlag Hans Carl, 1971), 54, 63.

25. For a collection of the seven shadow plays by Bernus performed by the Schwabinger Schattenspiele, see Alexander von Bernus, *Sieben Schattenspiele mit vierzehn Schattenbildern* (Munich: Georg Müller, 1910). This edition also contains illustrations of the original silhouettes.

26. Quoted in Segel, *Turn-of-the-Century Cabaret*, 209.

27. My account of the Russian living doll productions follows that in ibid., 265–68.

CHAPTER 3. APRÈS MAETERLINCK:
FROM BOUCHOR'S MYSTERIES TO GHELDERODE'S

1. There is a brief discussion of the Petit Théâtre in Jacques Chesnais, *Histoire générale des marionettes* (Paris: Bordas, 1947), 216–22.

2. Maurice Bouchor, *Mystères bibliques et chrétiens* (Paris: Ernest Flammarion, n.d.), 4.

3. Anatole France, "Hrotswitha aux Marionettes," *La Vie littéraire*, 3ᵉ série, *Oeuvres Complètes Illustrés d'Anatole France* (Paris: Calmann-

Levy, Editeurs, 1949), 7:23; Anatole France, *On Life and Letters*, 3d ser., trans. D. B. Stewart (London: John Lane, The Bodley Head, 1922), 11.

4. Anatole France, "Les Marionettes de M. Signoret," *La Vie littéraire*, 1ᵉ série, *Oeuvres Complètes Illustrées*, 466–67; France, *On Life and Letters*, 1st ser., 137–38.

5. Anatole France, "M. Maurice Bouchor et l'histoire de Tobie," *La Vie littéraire*, 3ᵉ série, *Oeuvres Complètes Illustrées*, 7:215–16.

6. Quoted in Bouchor, *Mystères bibliques et chrétiens*, 7–8.

7. This abbreviated version of the play was also published separately. See Maurice Bouchor, *Tobie: Légende biblique en 3 actes, en vers* (Paris: E. Flammarion, 1899), which was dedicated to Henri Signoret, "Créateur du 'Petit-Théâtre.'"

8. Bouchor, *Mystères bibliques et chrétiens*, 198, 199.

9. *Farigoule* means "thyme" or a plant of the thyme family. However, "Holly" sounds somewhat better for the character's name in English.

10. For a good comprehensive study of Jarry's life and works, see Keith Beaumont, *Alfred Jarry: A Critical and Biographical Study* (Leicester: Leicester University Press, 1984). A highly recommended study of Jarry as a dramatist is Henri Behar's *Jarry dramaturge* (Paris: Librraie A.-G. Nizet, 1980).

11. For a detailed description of the production and its reception, see Beaumont, *Jarry*, 92–107.

12. Alfred Jarry, *Ubu*, ed. Noël Arnaud and Henri Bordillon (Paris: Gallimard, 1978), 31–32.

13. *Oeuvres Complètes de Guillaume Apollinaire*, ed. Michel Décaudin (Paris: André Balland et Jacques Lecat, 1966), 3:620.

14. For the most thorough account of *Parade* in any language, see Debrah Menaker Rothschild, *Picasso's "Parade": From Street to Stage* (New York: Sotheby's Publications, 1991).

15. On Depero and Exter see the later Italian and Russian sections in this book.

16. See the illustrations in Rothschild, *Picasso's "Parade,"* 134–64.

17. Roland Penrose, *Picasso: His Life and Work* (New York: Harper, 1958), 215.

18. Jean Cocteau, *Théâtre* (Paris: Gallimard, 1948), 1:42.

19. Edmund Rostand, *The Last Night of Don Juan: A Dramatic*

Poem, trans. T. Lawrason Riggs (Yellow Springs, Ohio: Kahoe & Co., 1929), 88.

20. Paul Claudel, "Bounrakou," *Oeuvres en prose*, ed. Jacques Petit and Charles Galpérine (Paris: Editions Gallimard, 1965), 1180–81; Paul Claudel, *Claudel on the Theatre*, ed. Jacques Petit and Jean-Pierre Kempf, trans. Christine Trollope (Coral Gables, Fla.: University of Miami Press, 1972), 50.

21. See, for example, such English-language studies as Joseph Chiari, *The Poetic Drama of Paul Claudel* (New York: Gordian Press, 1969), which makes no mention of it; and Harold A. Waters, *Paul Claudel* (New York: Twayne, 1970), 91, where it is mentioned very briefly in passing. Even Bettina L. Knapp's excellent introduction to Claudel's dramatic writing, *Paul Claudel* (New York: Frederick Ungar, 1982), devotes only a line to the play (28).

22. The performance was sponsored by the Paul Claudel Society, the University of Wisconsin–Green Bay, and the Stephen F. Austin State University of Texas. For the transcript of a taped discussion about the performance, see Harold A. Watson and Louise R. Witherell, "Claudel's *The Bear and the Moon* on an American Stage," *Claudel Studies* 1, no. 5 (1974): 23–40.

23. Paul Claudel, *Deux Farces lyriques*, 12th ed. (Paris: Editions Gallimard, 1927), 142.

24. Watson and Witherell, "*The Bear and the Moon*," 29.

25. For a good critical biography of de Ghelderode, see Roland Beyen, *Michel de Ghelderode ou la hantise du masque: Essai de biographie critique* (Brussels: Palais des Académies, 1971).

26. Michel de Ghelderode, *Les Entretiens d'Ostende*, ed. Roger Iglésias et Alain Trutat (Paris: L'Arche, 1956), 97–98.

27. Michel de Ghelderode, *Théâtre* (Paris: Editions Gallimard, 1952), 2:186.

28. Antonin Artaud, *The Theater and Its Double*, trans. Caroline Richards (New York: Grove Press, 1958), 102.

29. Antonin Artaud, *Selected Writings*, ed. Susan Sontag (New York: Farrar, Straus & Giroux, 1976), 244–45.

30. Roland Beyen, *Ghelderode* (Paris: Seghers, 1974), 111–12.

31. Ghelderode, *Théâtre*, 3:39.

32. Michel de Ghelderode, *Le Siège d'Ostende* (Brussels: Louis Musin Editeur, 1980), 17.

33. Beyen, *Ghelderode*, 66–67.
34. Ghelderode, *Le Siège d'Ostende*, 49.
35. Ghelderode, *Théâtre*, 3:164.

CHAPTER 4. PUPPETS, MARIONETTES,
AND THE DEBUNKING OF TRADITIONALISM
AND NATIONAL MYTHS IN SPANISH MODERNIST DRAMA

1. Jacinto Benavente, *Teatro fantástico* (Madrid: Imprenta de Fortanet, 1905), 57.
2. Jacinto Benavente, *Los intereses creados*, ed. Fernando Lázaro Carreter (Madrid: Ediciones Cátedra, 1974), 51–52. The translations are based on this edition and are my own.
3. It is now generally accepted that many of the plays attributed to Gregorio Martínez Sierra were in fact written either jointly with his wife, María, or only by her but published under his name. Since it is difficult to establish specifically which plays were written by María Martínez Sierra and everything was published under Gregorio's name, I am crediting just him with the authorship of *Hechizo de amor*. There is a good discussion of the literary relationship between the Martínez Sierras in Patricia W. O'Connor, *Gregorio and María Martínez Sierra* (Boston: Twayne, 1977).
4. Gregorio Martínez Sierra, *Hechizo de amor, Comedias escogidas* (Madrid: Biblioteca Renacimiento, V. Prieto y Comp.ª, Editores, 1911), 1:249–50. Translation my own. For an embellished translation, see G. Martínez Sierra, *The Cradle Song and Other Plays*, trans. John Garrett Underhill (New York: E. P. Dutton & Co., 1922), 91–114.
5. Santiago Rusiñol, *El titella pròdig, Obres completes* (Barcelona: Biblioteca Perenne, 1947), 1572. For an English translation of the work, see Santiago Rusiñol, *The Prodigal Doll*, trans. John Garrett Underhill, *Drama* 25 (February 1917): 90–116.
6. Jacinto Grau, *El Señor de Pigmalión*, ed. William Giuliano (New York: Appleton-Century Crofts, 1952), 133–34. All further references to the Spanish original are noted in the text. Translations are my own.
7. There are a few respectable studies of Valle-Inclán's life and work in English. See, for example, Anthony N. Zahareas, ed., *Ramón del Valle-Inclán: An Appraisal of His Life and Works* (New York: Las Americas Publishing Co., 1968); and especially Robert Lima, *Valle-Inclán: The Theatre of His Life* (Columbia: University of Missouri Press, 1968). There is also valuable material in Ramón del Valle-Inclán, *Luces de Bohemia:*

Esperpento, trans. Anthony N. Zahareas and Gerald Gillespie (Austin: University of Texas Press, 1976), which has an introduction and commentary by Anthony N. Zahareas. For good studies of Valle-Inclán's dramatic writing, see Sumner M. Greenfield, *Valle-Inclán: Anatomía de un teatro problemático* (Madrid: Altea, Taurus, Alfaguara, 1990); John Lyon, *The Theatre of Valle-Inclán* (Cambridge: Cambridge University Press, 1983).

8. *Teatro Selecto de Ramón del Valle-Inclán: Romance de lobos. Tablado de marionetas. Divinas palabras* (Madrid: Escelicer, 1969), 280.

9. Ibid., 197.

10. Greenfield points out in *Valle-Inclán* (200–201) that Valle-Inclán has interpolated the episode of the Lady of the Cloak for the purpose of ridiculing another formula of Spanish classical comedy—the deceived woman who comes to the king to seek justice for her dishonor.

11. Don Ramón del Valle-Inclán, *Obras escogidas* (Madrid: Aguilar, 1965), 1124–25. For English translations of the play, see Ramón del Valle-Inclán, *The Horns of Don Friolera*, trans. Bryant Creel, *Modern International Drama* 20, no. 2 (Spring 1987): 31–68; and Ramón María del Valle-Inclán, *The Grotesque Farce of Mr. Punch the Cuckold*, trans. Dominic Keown and Robin Warner (Warminster, England: Aris & Phillips, 1991).

12. Julián Zugasti, *El bandolerismo: estudio social y memorias históricas*. For Valle-Inclán's precise indebtedness to this source, see Lyon, *The Theatre of Valle Inclán*, 177.

13. Valle-Inclán, *Obras escogidas* (1965), 918.

14. Federico García Lorca, *Obras Completas*, ed. Arturo del Hoyo (Madrid: Aguilar, 1986), 2:1203.

15. García Lorca, *Obras Completas* 2:112. All subsequent quotations from this text as well as from the *Retablillo de Don Cristóbal* refer to this edition.

16. García Lorca, *Teatro*, ed. Miguel García-Posada (Madrid: Akal Editor, 1980), 1:178–79.

CHAPTER 5. PUPPETRY AND CABARET IN FIN-DE-SIÈCLE VIENNA: SCHNITZLER AND KOKOSCHKA

1. In 1911, Felix Salten, the author of *Bambi* and a well-known feuilletonist and critic of the time, published a series of delightful reminiscences of the various attractions of the Wurstelprater under the collective title *Wurstelprater*. The edition in the Austriaca series published by Wilhelm

Goldmann Verlag (Vienna-Munich-Zurich-Innsbruck) in 1973 also contains the seventy-five original photographs of the Wurstelprater by Dr. Emil Mayer which accompanied the original edition.

2. Arthur Schnitzler, *Das dramatische Werk*, vol. 4 of *Gesammelte Werke in Einzelausgaben* (Frankfurt am Main: Fischer Taschenbuch Verlag, 1978), 130. All my translations from Schnitzler's *Marionetten* are based on the texts in this edition.

3. My account of Kokoschka's work at the Fledermaus follows in part the discussion in the Vienna chapter of my book *Turn-of-the-Century Cabaret: Paris, Barcelona, Berlin, Munich, Vienna, Cracow, Moscow, St. Petersburg, Zurich* (New York: Columbia University Press, 1987), 208–13.

4. For a good English discussion of the different versions of *Sphinx und Strohmann*, see Henry I. Schvey, *Oskar Kokoschka: The Painter as Playwright* (Detroit: Wayne State University Press, 1982), 67–88; English translations of the 1913 version of the play and *Job* appear as appendixes (141–50).

5. Henry Schvey speculates that the name Firdusi is intended primarily as a play on the German words *Führ(st) du sie!* meaning "Lead her!"—ironically alluding to his helplessness in relation to his promiscuous wife, Lilly (*Kokoschka*, 68).

6. Oskar Kokoschka, "*Sphinx und Strohmann*; Komödie für Automaten," *Wort in der Zeit: Österreichische Literaturzeitschrift* 2 (March 1956): 148.

7. Oskar Kokoschka, *My Life*, trans. David Britt (New York: Macmillan, 1974), 183.

8. Gerhard Johann Lischka, *Oskar Kokoschka: Maler und Dichter* (Bern: Herbert Lang, 1972), 56.

CHAPTER 6. POLAND AND PRUSSIA AS PUPPET SHOWS:
WYSPIAŃSKI AND HAUPTMANN

1. Stanisław Wyspiański, *Wesele*, ed. Jan Nowakowski (Wrocław: Zakład Narodowy im. Ossolińskich–Wydawnictwo, 1973), 43. While I generally prefer to translate verse as prose, I thought it best to preserve at least the line structure of the original in order to convey as much of the flavor of the original dialogue as possible without rhyme.

2. An allusion to a legendary powerful king of peasant origin.

3. Edward Burne-Jones was an English Preraphaelite painter known

for his decorativeness, floral imagery, melancholy, and idealized feminine types.

4. For a good, but old, account of the Polish *szopka*, see Jan Krupski, *Szopka krakowska* (Cracow: Nakładem Tow. Miłosników Historyii Zabytków Krakowa, 1904). The bulk of Krupski's book consists, in fact, of a traditional *szopka* text and is particularly interesting for that reason.

5. On the background to and reception of Hauptmann's *Festspiel*, see also Hans Deiber, *Gerhart Hauptmann oder der letzte Klassiker* (Vienna: Verlag Fritz Molden, 1971), 179–89; and Eberhard Hilscher, *Gerhart Hauptmann: Leben und Werk* (Frankfurt am Main: Athenäum Verlag, 1988), 295–301.

6. For the text of the German original, see Gerhart Hauptmann, *Sämtliche Werke*, vol. 2, *Dramen*, ed. Hans Egon-Hass (Frankfurt am Main: Propyläen Verlag, 1965), 943–1006. Quotations are henceforth given only in translation. The page numbers in the text refer to this edition. Translations are my own.

7. A complete English verse translation of the play can be found in *The Dramatic Works of Gerhart Hauptmann*, ed. Ludwig Lewisohn (New York: B. W. Huebsch, 1917), vol. 7. Although for the most part reliable, the translation is now antiquated.

CHAPTER 7. WHEN MR. SLEEMAN COMES: BERGMAN'S MARIONETTES AND SHADOWS

1. One volume of Bergman's plays is available in English translation: *Four Plays by Hjalmar Bergman*, ed. Walter Johnson (Seattle: University of Washington Press, 1968). It contains *Markurells of Wadköping*, *The Baron's Will*, *Swedenhielms*, and *Mr. Sleeman Is Coming*.

2. Quoted in Hjalmar Bergman, *Snödropparna, Marionettspel och annans dramatik* (Stockholm: Albert Bonniers Förlag, 1953), 9. Translations are my own.

CHAPTER 8. PETRUSHKA TO REVOLUTION: RUSSIAN VARIATIONS

1. For a good study of the Russian carnival puppet theater in English, see Catriona Kelley, *Petrushka: The Russian Carnival Puppet Theatre* (Cambridge: Cambridge University Press, 1990).

2. *Meyerhold on Theatre*, ed. and trans. Edward Braun (New York: Hill & Wang, 1969), 135.

3. Victor Terras, *A History of Russian Literature* (New Haven: Yale University Press, 1991), 497.

4. Kelley, *Petrushka*, 151.

5. Aleksandr Blok, *Sobranie sochinenii*, vol. 6, *Teatr 1906–1919* (Leningrad: Izdatelstvo Pisatelei v Leningrade, 1933), 7. For an English translation of *The Fairground Booth*, under the title *The Puppet Show*, see F. D. Reeve, ed. and trans., *Twentieth-Century Russian Plays: An Anthology* (New York: W. W. Norton & Co., 1963). The play was also translated by several hands into German under the title *Die Schaubude* and is included in Alexander Block, *Ausgewählte Werke*, vol. 2, *Stücke, Essays, Reden*, ed. Fritz Mierau (Munich: Carl Hanser Verlag, 1982). A Polish verse translation by Seweryn Pollak and Jerzy Zagorski appears in Aleksander Blok, *Utwory dramatyczne*, ed. Seweryn Pollak (Cracow: Wydawnictwo Literackie, 1985).

6. Kelley, *Petrushka*, 151.

7. I am following Meyerhold's own description of the setting as it appears in *Meyerhold on Theatre*, 70–71.

8. Aleksandr Benua, *Moi vospominaniya*, bks. 1–3 (Moscow: Izdatelstvo Nauka, 1990), 284. For a not entirely faithful English translation of the two-volume memoirs, see Alexandre Benois, *Memoirs*, trans. Moura Budberg (London: Chatto & Windus, 1960–64).

9. Aleksandr Benua, *Moi vospominaniya*, bks. 4–5 (Moscow: Izdatelstvo Nauka, 1990), 640.

10. Leonid Andreev, *Dramaticheskie proizvedeniya v 2-x tomakh* (Leningrad: Iskusstvo, 1989), 1:185.

11. Yu. Slonimskaya, "Marionetka," *Apollon* 3 (1916): 1.

12. A favorable review of the production, signed M. M., appeared in *Apollon* 3 (1916): 54–56.

13. Fyodor Sologub, "Teatr odnoy voli," *O teatre* (Petersburg: 1908), 145–46.

14. For an English study of Jasieński's life and career, see Nina Kolesnikoff, *Bruno Jasieński: His Evolution from Futurism to Socialist Realism* (Waterloo, Ont.: Wilfrid Laurier University Press, 1982).

15. Stern also wrote a fine biography. See Anatol Stern, *Bruno Jasieński* (Warsaw: Czytelnik, 1969).

16. Since I was unable to obtain an accurate printed edition of the original Russian text, my translations are based on the excellent translation

into Polish by Anatol Stern contained in the best Polish edition of Jasieński's works: Bruno Jasieński, *Nogi Izoldy Morgan i inne utwory* (Warsaw: Czytelnik, 1966), 44–50.

CHAPTER 9. ITALIAN FUTURISM, *TEATRO GROTTESCO*, AND THE WORLD OF ARTIFICIAL MAN

1. On Futurist theater and early-twentieth-century Italian drama in general, see Michael Kirby, *Futurist Performance* (New York: E. P. Dutton, 1971); Gigi Livio, *Il teatro in rivolta: Futurismo, grottesco, Pirandello e pirandellismo* (Milan: Mursia, 1976); Franca Angelini, *Il teatro del Novocento da Pirandello a Fo* (Rome-Bari: Editori Laterza, 1976); Mario Verdone, *Teatro del Novocento* (Brescia: Editrice La Scuola, 1981).

2. On the Futurists and electricity, see, for example, Anne Coffin Hanson, *The Futurist Imagination: Word+ Image in Italian Futurist Painting, Drawing, Collage, and Free-Word Poetry* (New Haven: Yale University Art Gallery, 1983), 30–39. This is the catalogue of an exhibition held at the Yale University Art Gallery from April 13 to June 26, 1983.

3. On the reception of the Turin production, see Giovanni Antonucci, *Cronache del Teatro Futurista* (Rome: Edizioni Abete, 1975), 37–41.

4. On different productions of *Elettricità* in 1913 and 1914, see ibid., 47–62. On the 1925 production, see ibid., 207–8.

5. *Teatro F. T. Marinetti*, ed. Giovanni Calendoli (Rome: Vito Bianco Editore, 1960), 2:427. My translations are based on this edition.

6. F. T. Marinetti, *Teoria e invenzione futurista: Manifesti. Scritti politici. Romanzi. Parole in libertà*, ed. Luciano De Maria (Verona: Arnoldo Mondadori, 1968), 30. For a collection of Marinetti's writings in English translation, see F. T. Marinetti, *Let's Murder the Moonshine: Selected Writings*, ed. R. W. Flint, trans. R. W. Flint and Arthur A. Copotelli (Los Angeles: Sun & Moon Classics, 1991; originally published in a different version in 1972 by Farrar, Straus & Giroux).

7. F. T. Marinetti, *Il Teatro Di Varietà: Manifesto futurista* (1913), in *Teatro F. T. Marinetti*, 2: 257.

8. See, for example, Marinetti, *Lettera aperta al futurista Mac Delmarle*; *Lo splendore geometrico e meccanico e la sensibilità numerica*; *Il teatro della sorpresa*; *Introduzione a 'I nuovi poeti futuristi'*; *Manifesto della aeropittura*; *Guerra sola igiene del mondo*; *Futurismo e Fascismo*; *Alessandria d'Egitto*; *Fondazione e manifesto del Futurismo*; *Prima*

spedizione punitiva artistica; *Battaglia di Roma e secondo manifesto politico*; *Onoranze nazionali a Marinetti e Congresso futurista*; *Il paesaggio e l'estetica futurista della macchina*; *Gli indomabili*; *Il poema non umano dei tecnicismi.* Texts in Marinetti, *Teoria e invenzione futurista.*

9. For the best book on Bragaglia and the Teatro degli Indipendenti, see Alberto Cesare Alberti, Sandra Bevere, and Paolo Di Giulio, *Il Teatro Sperimentale degli Indipendenti (1923–1936)* (Rome: Bulzoni Editore, 1984). It is copiously illustrated.

10. Marinetti, *Teoria e invenzione futurista*, 91.

11. The texts of both plays can be found in *Teatro F. T. Marinetti*, vol. 2.

12. The text I use appears in Mario Verdone, *Teatro Italiano D'Avanguardia: Drammi e sintesi futuriste* (Rome: Officina Edizioni, 1970), 75–79.

13. For further information on the *Balli Plastici*, see especially Antonucci, *Cronache del teatro futurista*, 123–32; Maurizio Scudiero, *Fortunato Depero: Opere* (Gardolo di Trento: Luigi Reverdito Editore, 1987), 7–8.

14. Scudiero, *Depero: Opere*, 7.

15. Illustrations appear in ibid., 80, 82, 84, 86, 88, 114; Maurizio Scudiero, *Depero: Casa d'Arte Futurista* (Florence: Cantini Editore, 1987 [?]), 70–72; Maurizio Fagiolo dell'Arco and Nicoletta Boschiero, eds., *Depero* (Milan: Electa, 1988), 28–29; Kirby, *Futurist Performance*, figs. 33–36. See also Antonucci, "I Balli Plastici di Fortunato Depero," *Cronache del Teatro Futurista*, 123–32; Gilberto (Gilbert) Clavel, "Depero's Plastic Theater," in *Art and the Stage in the Twentieth Century*, ed. Henning Rischbieter (Greenwich, Conn.: Greenwood Press, 1968), 75.

16. On Depero's theatrical activity see especially Bruno Passamani, "La vocazione teatrale di Depero," in *I luoghi del futurismo (1909–1944). Atti di Convegno Nazionale di Studio.* Macerata, 30 ottobre 1982 (Rome: Multigrafica Editrice, 1986), 39–51.

17. The translated excerpts from Prampolini's *Scenografia e coreografia futurista* are from Christiana J. Taylor, *Futurism: Politics, Painting, and Performance* (Ann Arbor, Mich.: UMI Research, 1974), 59.

18. Gigi Livio, *Teatro grottesco del novocento* (Milan: Mursia, 1965), 73. All quotations from Rosso de San Secondo's *Marionette, che passione!* are translated from this edition.

19. Ibid., xx–xxi.

20. Ibid., 189.

21. Angelini, *Il teatro del Novocento*, 103.

22. Silvio D'Amico, *Il teatro dei fantocci* (Florence: Vallecchi, 1920), 81.

23. Enrico Cavacchioli, *Quella che t'assomiglia*, in Eligio Possenti, ed., *Teatro Italiano*, vol. 5, *Il Novocento* (Milan: Nuova Accademia Editrice, 1956), 580.

24. For a detailed chronology of Bontempelli's life, see Massimo Bontempelli, *Opere scelte*, ed. Luigi Baldacci (Milan: Arnoldo Mondadori, 1978), xlvii–lii.

25. On Massimo Bontempelli's literary career in general and as a dramatist in particular, see Luigi Baldacci, *Massimo Bontempelli* (Turin: Borla Editore, 1967); Giovanni Cappello, *Invito alla lettura di Massimo Bontempelli* (Milan: Mursia, 1986); Livio, *Il teatro in rivolta*, 119–35. References to the texts and translations from Bontempelli's plays are based on the edition *Teatro di Massimo Bontempelli: 1916–1935* (Rome: Edizioni Di Novissima, 1936).

26. There is a brief discussion of the play also in Cappello, *Invito alla lettura di Massimo Bontempelli*, 72–75.

27. *Siepe a nordovest: Farsa in prosa e musica*, in *Teatro di Massimo Bontempelli*, 53.

28. For discussions of the play in Italian studies of twentieth-century Italian drama, see Franca Angelini, *Il teatro del Novocento da Pirandello a Fo*, 2d ed. (Rome-Bari: Editori Laterza, 1980), 114–16; Livio, *Il teatro in rivolta*, 127–29. See also Cappello, *Invito alla lettura di Massimo Bontempelli*, 75–77.

29. *Teatro di Massimo Bontempelli*, 652.

30. For Italian discussions of the play, see Livio, *Il teatro in rivolta*, 129–31; Cappello, *Invito alla lettura di Massimo Bontempelli*, 77–79.

31. *Teatro di Massimo Bontempelli*, 207.

CHAPTER 10. FROM PUPPET TO ROBOT: THE BROTHERS ČAPEK

1. For the original text of the story, see Bratři Čapkové, *Krakonošova zahrada. Zářivé hlubiny a jiné prózy. Juvenile* (Prague: Československý spisovatel, 1957), 190–98.

2. The original Czech text can be found in Karel Čapek and Josef Ča-

pek, *Ze společné tvorby* (Prague: Československý spisovatel, 1982), 118–33.

3. Bratři Čapkové, *Krakonošova zahrada*, 230.

4. Bratři Čapkové, *Lásky hra osudná* (Prague: Edice Aventinum, 1922), 34–35.

5. Karel Čapek, *R.U.R. (Rossum's Universal Robots)*, trans. Claudia Novack-Jones, in *Toward the Radical Center: A Karel Čapek Reader*, ed. Peter Kussi (Highland Park, N.J.: Catbird Press, 1990), 44–45. Because of the quality of this translation, I saw no reason to retranslate portions of the Czech original myself. For the original text, see Karel Čapek, *R.U.R. (Rossum's Universal Robots)* (Prague: Fr. Borovy, 1935).

CHAPTER 11. MAN AS MACHINE: METHUSALEM TO BAUHAUS

1. For some typical, mostly French critical pieces on him, see the collection Yvan Goll, *Quatre Etudes par Jules Romaine, de l'Académie française, Marcel Brion, Francis Carmody, Richard Exner* (Paris: Editions Pierre Seghers, 1956). The book also contains a respectable collection of Goll's poetry in French. The best German collection of his works, with a very good biocritical afterword by Klaus Schumann, is Iwan Goll, *Gefangen im Kreise: Dichtungen, Essays, und Briefe* (Leipzig: Verlag Philipp Reclam jun., 1982).

2. Goll, *Gefangen im Kreise*, 218.

3. Ibid., 172. For an English translation of *Methusalem*, see J. M. Ritchie, ed., *German Expressionist Plays: From Kokoschka to Barlach*, trans. J. M. Ritchie and H. F. Garten (London: Calder & Boyars, 1968), 79–112.

4. Oskar Schlemmer, Laszlo Moholy-Nagy, and Farkas Molnár, *The Theater of the Bauhaus*, ed. Walter Gropius, trans. Arthur S. Wensinger (Middletown, Conn.: Wesleyan University Press, 1971), 7.

EPILOGUE

1. Original text in Heiner Müller, *Leben Gundlings, Friedrich von Preussen, Lessings Schlaf, Traum Schrei: Ein Greuelmärchen* (Frankfurt am Main: Verlag der Autoren, 1982). For an English translation of the play, see Heiner Müller, *Hamletmachine and Other Texts for the Stage*, ed. and trans. Carl Weber (New York: PAJ Publications, 1991).

2. For the most extensive treatment in English of Kantor's career, aug-

mented by translations of various of his writings, see *A Journey through Other Spaces: Essays and Manifestoes, 1944–1990, Tadeusz Kantor*, ed. and trans. Michal Kobialka (Berkeley and Los Angeles: University of California Press, 1993), which contains a critical study of Tadeusz Kantor's theater by Michal Kobialka. There is also a good discussion of Kantor in G. M. Hyde's introduction in Tadeusz Kantor, *Wielopole/Wielopole: An Exercise in Theatre*, trans. Mariusz Tchorek and G. M. Hyde (London: Marion Boyars, 1990), 7–13.

3. The excerpts from Kantor's "Theater of Death," preserving the author's original capitalization, are from *Journey through Other Spaces*, 111, 112. The translation, by Voy T. and Margaret Stelmaszynski, originally appeared in *Canadian Theatre Review* 16 (Fall 1977).

4. Kantor, *Wielopole/Wielopole*, 86, 88.

Bibliography

Addison, Joseph. *The Works of the Right Honourable Joseph Addison.* Trans. George Sewell, ed. Richard Hurd. London: Henry G. Bohn, 1856.

Alberti, Alberto Cesare, Sandra Bevere, and Paolo Di Giulio. *Il Teatro Sperimentale degli Indipendenti (1923–1936).* Rome: Bulzone Editore, 1984.

And, Metin. *Karagöz: Turkish Shadow Theatre.* Istanbul: Dost, 1975; rev. ed., 1979.

Andreev, Leonid. *Dramaticheskie proizvedeniya v 2-x tomakh.* Vol. 1. Leningrad: Isskustvo, 1989.

Angelini, Franca. *Il teatro del Novocento da Pirandello a Fo.* Rome-Bari: Editori Laterza, 1976.

Antonucci, Giovanni. *Cronache del Teatro Futurista.* Rome: Edizioni Abete, 1975.

———. *Storia del teatro italiano del Novecento.* Rome: Edizioni Studium, 1986.

Apollinaire, Guillaume. *Oeuvres Complètes de Guillaume Apollinaire.* Vol. 3. Ed. Michel Décaudin. Paris: André Balland et Jacques Lecat, 1966.

Artaud, Antonin. *Selected Writings.* Ed. Susan Sontag. New York: Farrar, Straus & Giroux, 1976.

Baldacci, Luigi. *Massimo Bontempelli*. Turin: Borla Editore, 1967.

Beaumont, Keith. *Alfred Jarry: A Critical and Biographical Study*. Leicester: Leicester University Press, 1984.

Behar, Henri. *Jarry dramaturge*. Paris: Libraire A.-G. Nizet, 1980.

Benavente, Jacinto. *Los intereses creados*. Ed. Fernando Lázaro Carreter. Madrid: Ediciones Cátedra, 1974.

———. *Teatro fantástico*. Madrid: Imprenta de Fortanet, 1905.

Benua, Aleksandr. *Moi vospominaniya*. Moscow: Izdatelstvo Nauka, 1990.

Bergman, Hjalmar. *Four Plays by Hjalmar Bergman*. Ed. Walter Johnson. Seattle: University of Washington Press, 1968.

———. *Snödropparna, Marionettspel och annans dramatik*. Stockholm: Albert Bonniers Förlag, 1953.

Bernus, Alexander von. *Sieben Mysterienspiele*. Büdingen-Gettenbach: Avalun-Verlag, 1957.

———. *Sieben Schattenspiele mit vierzehn Schattenbildern*. Munich: Georg Müller, 1910.

Beyen, Roland. *Ghelderode*. Paris: Seghers, 1974.

———. *Michel de Ghelderode ou la hantise du masque: Essai de biographie critique*. Brussels: Palais des Académies, 1971.

Block, Alexander. *Ausgewählte Werke*. Vol. 2, *Stücke, Essays, Reden*. Ed. Fritz Mierau. Munich: Carl Hanser Verlag, 1982.

Blok, Aleksandr. *Sobranie sochinenii*. Vol. 6, *Teatr 1906–1919*. Leningrad: Izdatelstvo Pisatelei v Leningrade, 1933.

———. *Utwory dramatyczne*. Ed. Seweryn Pollak, trans. Seweryn Pollak and Jerzy Zagórski. Cracow: Wydawnictwo Literackie, 1985.

Bontempelli, Massimo. *Teatro di Massimo Bontempelli: 1916–1935*. Rome: Edizioni Di Novissima, 1936.

———. *Opere scelte*. Ed. Luigi Baldacci. Milan: Arnoldo Mondadori, 1978.

Bordat, Denis, and Francis Boucrot. *Les Théâtres d'ombres: Histoire et techniques*. Paris: L'Arche, 1956.

Bouchor, Maurice. *Mystères bibliques et chrétiens*. Paris: Ernest Flammarion, n.d.

———. *Tobie: Légende biblique en 3 actes, en vers*. Paris: E. Flammarion, 1899.

Bratři Čapkové. *Krakonošova zahrada. Zářivé hlubiny a jiné prózy. Juvenile*. Prague: Československý spisovatel, 1957.

———. *Lásky hra osudná.* Prague: Edice Aventinum, 1922.

Büchner, Georg. *The Complete Collected Works: "Woyzeck," "Danton's Death," "The Hessian Messenger," "Lenz," and "Leonce and Lena."* Trans. and ed. Henry J. Schmidt. New York: Avon Books, 1977

———. *"Leonce and Lena," "Lenz," "Woyzeck."* Trans. Michael Hamburger. Chicago: University of Chicago Press, 1972.

Čapek, Karel. *R.U.R. (Rossum's Universal Robots).* Prague: Fr. Borovy, 1935.

———. *Toward the Radical Center: A Karel Čapek Reader.* Ed. Peter Kussi. Highland Park, N.J.: Catbird Press, 1990. Contains a translation of *R.U.R. (Rossum's Universal Robots)* by Claudia Novack-Jones.

Čapek, Karel, and Josef Čapek. *Ze společné tvorby.* Prague: Československý spisovatel, 1982. *See also* Bratři Čapkové.

Cappello, Giovanni. *Invito alla lettura di Massimo Bontempelli.* Milan: Mursia, 1986.

Cavacchioli, Enrico. *Quella che t'assomiglia.* In *Teatro Italiano,* vol. 5, *Il Novocento,* ed. Eligio Possenti, 573–638. Milan: Nuova Accademia Editrice, 1956.

Cervantes Saavedra, Miguel de. *Don Quixote de la Mancha.* Trans. Walter Starkie. New York: New American Library, 1964.

———. *Entremeses.* Mexico City: Editorial Porrua, 1968.

Chesnais, Jacques. *Histoire générale des marionettes.* Paris: Bordas, 1947.

Chiari, Joseph. *The Poetic Drama of Paul Claudel.* New York: Gordian Press, 1969.

Claudel, Paul. *Claudel on the Theatre.* Trans. Christine Trollope, ed. Jacques Petit and Jean-Pierre Kempf. Coral Gables, Fla.: University of Miami Press.

———. *Deux farces lyriques.* 12th ed. Paris: Editions Gallimard, 1927.

———. *Oeuvres en prose.* Ed. Jacques Petit and Charles Galpérine. Paris: Editions Gallimard, 1965.

Clavel, Gilberto. "Depero's Plastic Theater." In *Art and the Stage in the Twentieth Century,* ed. Henning Rischbieter, 75. Greenwich, Conn.: Greenwood Press, 1968.

Cocteau, Jean. *Théâtre.* Vol. 1. Paris: Gallimard, 1948.

Collodi, Carlo [Carlo Lorenzini]. *The Adventures of Pinocchio: Story of a Puppet.* Trans. Nicolas J. Perella. Berkeley and Los Angeles: University of California Press, 1986.

Craig, Edward Gordon. *Craig on Theatre*. Ed. J. Michael Walton. London: Methuen, 1983.

———. *Il trionfo della marionetta: Testi e materiali inediti di Edward Gordon Craig*. Trans. and ed. Marina Maymone Sinischalchi. Rome: Officina Edizioni, 1980.

Crispolti, Enrico. *Storia e critica del futurismo*. Bari: Editori Laterza, 1981.

D'Amico, Silvio. *Il teatro dei fantocci*. Florence: Vallecchi, 1920.

Deiber, Hans. *Gerhart Hauptmann oder der letzte Klassiker*. Vienna: Verlag Fritz Molden, 1971.

Drux, Rudolf. *Marionette Mensch: Ein Metaphernkomplex und sein Kontext von E. T. A. Hoffmann bis Georg Büchner*. Munich: Wilhelm Fink Verlag, 1986.

Erlich, Victor. *Gogol*. New Haven: Yale University Press, 1969.

Fagiolo dell'Arco, Maurizio, and Nicoletta Boschiero, eds. *Depero*. Milan: Electa, 1988.

Franca, Angelini. *Il teatro del Novocento da Pirandello a Fo*. Rome-Bari: Editori Laterza, 1976.

France, Anatole. *Oeuvres Complètes Illustrées d'Anatole France*. 7 vols. Paris: Calmann-Lévy, Editeurs, 1949.

———. *On Life and Letters*. 3d series. Trans. D. B. Stewart. London: John Lane, The Bodley Head, 1922.

Ghelderode, Michel de. *Les Entretiens d'Ostende*. Ed. Roger Iglésias and Alain Trutat. Paris: L'Arche, 1956.

———. *Le Siège d'Ostende*. Brussels: Louis Musin Editeur, 1980.

———. *Théâtre*. Vols. 1–5. Paris: Editions Gallimard, 1950–57.

Goethe, Johann Wolfgang. *Sämtliche Werke*. Vol. 2, pt. 1, *Erstes Weimarer Jahrzehnt 1775–1786*. Ed. Harmut Reinhardt. Munich: Carl Hanser Verlag, 1987.

———. *Wilhelm Meisters Lehrjahre*. 2d ed. Zurich: Artemis Verlag, 1962.

Goll, Iwan. *Gefangen im Kreise: Dichtungen, Essays und Briefe*. Leipzig: Verlag Philipp Reclam jun., 1982.

Goll, Yvan. *Quatre Etudes par Jules Romaine, de l'Académie française, Marcel Brion, Francis Carmody, Richard Exner*. Paris: Editions Pierre Seghers, 1956.

Grau, Jacinto. *El Señor de Pigmalión*. Ed. William Giuliano. New York: Appleton-Century-Crofts, 1952.

Greenfield, Sumner M. *Valle-Inclán: Anatomía de un teatro problemá-tico*. Madrid: Altea, Taurus, Alfaguara, 1990.

Hanson, Anne Coffin. *The Futurist Imagination: Word + Image in Italian Futurist Painting, Drawing, Collage, and Free Word Poetry*. New Haven: Yale University Art Gallery, 1983.

Hauptmann, Gerhart. *The Dramatic Works of Gerhart Hauptmann*. Ed. Ludwig Lewisohn. New York: B. W. Huebsch, 1917.

————. *Sämtliche Werke*. Vol. 2, *Dramen*. Ed. Hans Egon-Hass. Frankfurt am Main: Propyläen Verlag, 1965.

————. *Das dramatische Werk*. Frankfurt am Main: Ullstein, 1974.

Hauser, Ronald. *Georg Büchner*. New York: Twayne, 1974.

Heuschele, Otto, ed. *In Memoriam Alexander von Bernus*. Heidelberg: Verlag Lambert Schneider, 1966.

Hilscher, Eberhard. *Gerhart Hauptmann: Leben und Werk*. Frankfurt am Main: Athenäum Verlag, 1988.

Hoffmann, E. T. A. *Der Automaten-Mensch: E. T. A. Hoffmanns Er-zählung vom "Sandmann."* Ed. Lienhard Wawrzyn. Berlin: Verlag Klaus Wagenbach, 1976.

————. *Nachtstücke. Klein Zaches. Prinzessin Brambilla. Werke 1816–1820*. Ed. Harmut Steinecke, with Gerhard Allroggen. Frankfurt am Main: Deutscher Klassiker Verlag, 1981.

Hohoff, Curt. *Johann Wolfgang von Goethe: Dichtung und Leben*. Munich: Langen Müller, 1989.

Innes, Christopher. *Edward Gordon Craig*. Cambridge: Cambridge University Press, 1983.

Jarry, Alfred. *Ubu: Ubu roi, Ubu cocu, Ubu enchaîné, Ubu sur la Butte*. Ed. Noël Arnaud and Henri Bordillon. Paris: Gallimard, 1978.

Jasieński, Bruno. *Nogi Izoldy Morgan i inne utwory*. Warsaw: Czytelnik, 1966.

Jonson, Ben. *Bartholomew Fair*. Ed. Eugene M. Waith. New Haven: Yale University Press, 1963.

Jordan, Ruth. *George Sand: A Biography*. London: Constable, 1976.

Kantor, Tadeusz. *A Journey through Other Spaces: Essays and Manifestoes, 1944–1990, Tadeusz Kantor*. Trans. and ed. Michael Kobialka. Berkeley and Los Angeles: University of California Press, 1993.

————. *Wielopole/Wielopole: An Exercise in Theatre*. Trans. Mariusz Tchorek and G. M. Hyde. London: Marion Boyars, 1990.

Kelley, Catriona. *Petrushka: The Russian Carnival Puppet Theatre.* Cambridge: Cambridge University Press, 1990.

Kirby, Michael. *Futurist Performance.* New York: E.P. Dutton, 1971.

Kleist, Heinrich von. *An Abyss Deep Enough: Letters of Heinrich Kleist with a Selection of Essays and Anecdotes.* Trans. and ed. Philip B. Miller. New York: E. P. Dutton, 1982.

———. *Über das Marionettentheater: Zur Poetik.* Reinbek bei Hamburg: Rowohlt, 1984.

Knapp, Bettina. *Maurice Maeterlinck.* Boston: Twayne, 1975.

———. *Paul Claudel.* New York: Frederick Ungar, 1982.

Knight, A. H. J. *Georg Büchner.* London: Methuen, 1974. Originally published by Basil Blackwell in 1953.

Knoll, Robert E. *Ben Jonson's Plays: An Introduction.* Lincoln: University of Nebraska Press, 1964.

Kolesnikoff, Nina. *Bruno Jasieński: His Evolution from Futurism to Socialist Realism.* Waterloo, Ont.: Wilfrid Laurier University Press, 1982.

Komar, Kathleen L. *Transcending Angels: Rainer Maria Rilke's "Duino Elegies."* Lincoln: University of Nebraska Press, 1987.

Krafft, Ludwig. *München und das Puppenspiel: Kleine Liebe einer grossen Stadt.* Munich: Akademie für das graphische Gewerbe, 1961.

Krumme, Peter. *Eines Augenblickes Zeichnung: Zur Temporalität des Bewusstseins in Rilkens "Duineser Elegien."* Würzburg: Königshausen & Neumann, 1988.

Krupski, Jan. *Szopka krakowska.* Cracow: Nakładem Tow. Miłośników Historyii Zabytków Krakowa, 1904.

Lemaître, Jules. *Impressions du théâtre.* 2ᵉ série. Paris: Libraire H. Lecène et H. Oudin, 1888.

Leppman, Wolfgang. *Rilke: A Life.* Trans. Russell M. Stockman. New York: Fromm International Publishing, 1984.

Lewisohn, Ludwig, ed. *The Dramatic Works of Gerhart Hauptmann.* Vol. 8. New York: B. W. Huebsch, 1917.

Lima, Robert. *Valle-Inclán: The Theatre of His Life.* Columbia: University of Missouri Press, 1968.

Lischka, Gerhard Johann. *Oskar Kokoschka: Maler und Dichter.* Bern: Herbert Lang, 1972.

Livio, Gigi. *Il teatro in rivolta: Futurismo, grottesco, Pirandello e pirandellismo.* Milan: Mursia, 1976.

———. *Teatro grottesco del novocento.* Milan: Mursia, 1965.

Lorca, Federico García. *Teatro*. Ed. Miguel García-Posada. Madrid: Akal Editor, 1980.

———. *Obras Completas*. Ed. Arturo del Hoyo. Madrid: Aguilar, 1986.

Lyon, John. *The Theatre of Valle-Inclán*. Cambridge: Cambridge University Press, 1983.

Maass, Joachim. *Kleist: A Biography*. Trans. Ralph Mannheim. New York: Farrar, Straus & Giroux, 1983.

Maeterlinck, Maurice. *Théâtre*. Vol. 2. Brussels: P. Lacomblez, 1904.

Manifold, Gay. *George Sand's Theatre Career*. Ann Arbor, Mich.: UMI Research Press, 1985.

Marinetti, F. T. *Let's Murder the Moonshine: Selected Writings*. Ed. R. W. Flint. Trans. R. W. Flint and Arthur A. Coppotelli. Los Angeles: Sun & Moon Classics, 1991. First ed. entitled *Marinetti: Selected Writings* (New York: Farrar, Straus & Giroux, 1972).

———. *Teatro F. T. Marinetti*. Vol. 2. Ed. Giovanni Calendoli. Rome: Vito Bianco Editore, 1960.

———. *Teoria e invenzione futurista: Manifesti. Scritti politici. Romanzi. Parole in libertà*. Ed. Luciano De Maria. Verona: Arnoldo Mondadori, 1968.

Martínez Sierra, G. *The Cradle Song and Other Plays*. Trans. John Garrett Underhill. New York: E. P. Dutton & Co., 1922.

Martínez Sierra, Gregorio. *Comedias escogidas*. Vol. 1, *La sombra del padre. El ama de la casa. Hechizo de amor*. Madrid: Biblioteca Renacimiento, V. Prieto y Comp.ª, Editores, 1911.

McPharlin, Paul, ed. *A Repertory of Marionette Plays*. New York: Viking Press, 1929.

Meyerhold, Vsevolod. *Meyerhold on Theater*. Trans. and ed. Edward Braun. New York: Hill & Wang, 1969.

Müller, Heiner. *Leben Gundlings, Friedrich von Preussen, Lessings Schlaf, Traum Schrei: Ein Greuelmärchen*. Frankfurt am Main: Verlag der Autoren, 1982.

———. *Hamletmachine and Other Texts for the Stage*. Ed. and trans. Carl Weber. New York: PAJ Publications, 1991.

O'Connor, Patricia W. *Gregorio and María Martínez Sierra*. Boston: Twayne, 1977.

Passamani, Bruno. "La vocazione teatrale di Depero." In *I luoghi del futurismo (1909–1944)*. Atti di Convegno Nazionale di Studio: Macerata, 30 ottobre 1982. Rome: Multigrafica Editrice, 1986.

Penrose, Roland. *Picasso: His Life and Work*. New York: Harper, 1958.

Perella, Nicolas J. "An Essay on Pinocchio." In Carlo Collodi, *The Adventures of Pinocchio: Story of a Puppet*. Trans. Nicolas J. Perella, 1–69. Berkeley and Los Angeles: University of California Press, 1986.

Rapp, Eleonore. *Die Marionette im romantischen Weltgefühl: Ein Beitrag zur deutschen Geistesgeschichte*. Bochum: Deutsches Institut für Puppenspiel, 1964.

Reeve, F. D., trans. and ed. *Twentieth-Century Russian Plays: An Anthology*. New York: W. W. Norton & Co., 1963.

Richards, David G. *Georg Büchner and the Birth of Modern Drama*. Albany: State University of New York Press, 1977.

Rilke, Rainer Maria. *Duinesian Elegies*. Trans. Elaine E. Boney. Chapel Hill: University of North Carolina Press, 1975. Contains German text and a commentary.

———. *Duino Elegies*. Trans. Gary Miranda. Portland, Ore.: Breitenbush Books, 1981.

———. *Gesammelte Werke*. Vol. 3, *Gedichte*. Leipzig: Insel-Verlag, 1930.

———. "Puppen." *Sämtliche Werke*. Vol. 6, *Kleine Schriften*. Frankfurt am Main: Insel-Verlag, 1966.

Ritchie, J. M., ed. *German Expressionist Plays: From Kokoschka to Barlach*. Trans. J. M. Ritchie and H. F. Garten. London: Calder & Boyars, 1968.

Rostand, Edmund. *The Last Night of Don Juan: A Dramatic Poem*. Trans. T. Lawrason Riggs. Yellow Springs, Ohio: Kahoe & Co., 1929.

Rothschild, Deborah Menaker. *Picasso's "Parade" From Street to Stage*. New York: Sotheby's Publications, 1991.

Rusiñol, Santiago. *Obres completes*. Barcelona: Biblioteca Perenne, 1947. Contains *El titella prodig*.

———. *The Prodigal Doll*. Trans. John Garrett Underhill. *Drama* (February 1917), 25.

Salten, Felix. *Wurstelprater*. Vienna-Munich-Zurich-Innsbruck: Wilhelm Goldmann Verlag, 1973. Austriaca Series edition.

Sand, George. *Oeuvres Complètes*. Vol. 15. Geneva: Slatkin Reprints, 1980.

———. *The Snow Man*. 2 vols. Trans. G. Burnham Ives. Philadelphia: George Barrie & Son, 1901.

Sand, Maurice. *Plays for Marionettes*. Trans. Babette and Glen Hughes. New York: Samuel French, 1931.

Schlemmer, Oscar, Laszlo Moholy-Nagy, and Farkas Molnár. *Die Bühne im Bauhaus*. Mainz: Florian Kupferberg Verlag, 1965.

―――. *The Theater of the Bauhaus*. Trans. Arthur S. Wensinger, ed. Walter Gropius. Middletown, Conn.: Wesleyan University Press, 1971.

Schmitt, Franz Anselm. *Alexander von Bernus: Dichter und Alchymist*. Nuremberg: Verlag Hans Carl, 1971.

Schnitzler, Arthur. *Das dramatische Werk*. Vol. 4 of *Gesammelte Werke in Einzelausgaben*. Frankfurt am Main: Fischer Taschenbuch Verlag, 1978.

Schvey, Henry I. *Oskar Kokoschka: The Painter as Playwright*. Detroit: Wayne State University Press, 1982.

Scudiero, Maurizio. *Depero: Casa d'Arte Futurista*. Florence: Cantini Editore, 1987 [?].

―――. *Fortunato Depero: Opere*. Gardolo di Trento: Luigi Reverdito Editore, 1987.

Segel, Harold B. *Turn-of-the-Century Cabaret: Paris, Barcelona, Berlin, Munich, Vienna, Cracow, Moscow, St. Petersburg, Zurich*. New York: Columbia University Press, 1987.

Shaw, Bernard. *Complete Plays with Prefaces*. Vol. 5. New York: Dodd, Mead & Co., 1962.

Steiner, Jacob. *Rilkes "Duineser Elegien."* 2d rev. ed. Bern-Munich: Francke Verlag, 1969.

Stern, Anatol. *Bruno Jasieński*. Warsaw: Czytelnik, 1969.

Sukhovo-Kobylin, Alexander. *The Trilogy of Alexander Sukhovo-Kobylin*. Trans. Harold B. Segel. New York: E. P. Dutton, 1969.

Swift, Jonathan. *The Selected Poems*. Ed. A. Norman Jeffares. London: Kyle Cathie, 1992.

Taylor, Christiana J. *Futurism: Politics, Painting, and Performance*. Ann Arbor, Mich.: UMI Research, 1974.

Terras, Victor. *A History of Russian Literature*. New Haven: Yale University Press, 1991.

Tillis, Steve. *Toward an Aesthetics of the Puppet: Puppetry as a Theatrical Art*. New York: Greenwood Press, 1992.

Valle-Inclán, Ramón María del. *The Grotesque Farce of Mr. Punch the Cuckold*. Trans. Dominic Keown and Robin Warner. Warminster, England: Aris & Phillips, 1991.

———. *The Horns of Don Friolera*. Trans. Bryant Creel. *Modern International Drama* 20, no. 2 (Spring 1987): 31–68.

———. *Luces de Bohemia: Esperpento*. Trans. Anthony N. Zahareas and Gerald Gillespie. Austin: University of Texas Press, 1976.

———. *Obras escogidas*. Madrid: Aguilar, 1965.

———. *Obras escogidas*. Vol. 2. 2d ed. Madrid: Aguilar, 1974.

———. *Teatro selecto de Ramón del Valle-Inclán: Romance de lobos. Tablado de marionetas. Divinas palabras*. Ed. Anthony N. Zahareas. Madrid: Escelicer, 1969.

Verdone, Mario. *Teatro del Novocento*. Brescia: Editrice La Scuola, 1981.

———. *Teatro Italiano D'Avanguardia: Drammi e sintesi futuriste*. Rome: Officina Edizioni, 1970.

Waters, Harold A. *Paul Claudel*. New York: Twayne, 1970.

Wolfskehl, Karl. *Gesammelte Werke*. 2 vols. Hamburg: Claassen Verlag, 1960.

Wyspiański, Stanisław. *Wesele*. Ed. Jan Nowakowski. Wrocław: Zakład Narodowy im. Ossolińskich—Wydawnictwo, 1973.

Zahareas, Anthony N., ed. *Ramón del Valle-Inclán: An Appraisal of His Life and Works*. New York: Las Americas Publishing Co., 1968.

Zugasti, Julián. *El bandolerismo: Estudio social y memorias históricas*. 3 vols. Cordoba: Ediciones Albolaifa, 1983.

Index